THE SYLLABI.

Genesis of the National Reporter System

Preface

Michael H. Hoeflich
John H. & John M. Kane Professor of Law,
University of Kansas School of Law

Introduction

William E. Butler
John Edward Fowler Distinguished Professor of Law,
Pennsylvania State University Dickinson School of Law and
Emeritus Professor of Comparative Law at University College London;
Academician of the National Academy of Sciences of Ukraine

THE LAWBOOK EXCHANGE, LTD.
Clark, New Jersey

ISBN 9781616192334 (hardcover)
ISBN 9781616192341 (paperback)

Lawbook Exchange edition 2011

The Lawbook Exchange, Ltd.
33 Terminal Avenue
Clark, New Jersey 07066-1321

Please see our website for a selection of our other publications and fine facsimile reprints of classic works of legal history:
www.lawbookexchange.com

Library of Congress Cataloging-in-Publication Data

The Syllabi : genesis of the national reporter system / preface, Michael H. Hoeflich ; introduction, William E. Butler.
p. cm.
Includes bibliographical references.
Includes reprint of The Syllabi from Vol. 1, no. 1 (Oct. 21, 1876)-v. 1, no. 26 (Apr. 14, 1877).
ISBN-13: 978-1-61619-233-4 (hardcover : alk. paper)
ISBN-10: 1-61619-233-X (hardcover : alk. paper)
ISBN-13: 978-1-61619-234-1 (pbk. : alk. paper)
ISBN-10: 1-61619-234-8 (pbk. : alk. paper)
1. Law--United States--United States--History--19th century. 2. Law reports, digests, etc.--United States--History--19th century. 3. Legal literature--Publishing--United States--History--19th century. 4. National reporter system--History--19th century. 5. Law reports, digests, etc.--Minnesota--History--19th century. I. Hoeflich, Michael H. II. Butler, William Elliott, 1939- III. Title: Syllabi.
KF366.S995 2011
349.7309'034--dc23 2011041184

Printed in the United States of America on acid-free paper

PREFACE

Michael H. Hoeflich

In 1872 John West, a twenty year old fledgling bookseller established his first bookstore, specializing in general law books and related supplies for the legal profession in St. Paul, Minnesota.[1] He conducted his store with a degree of success for four years at which time he convinced his brother Horatio to join him in his venture and together they decided to expand their business by establishing a weekly legal newspaper designed to provide the Minnesota bar with current, reliable legal information including case decisions. They named this newspaper "The Syllabi."

In the first issue for Saturday, October 21, 1876 they explained that their purpose of the new periodical was to "contain the syllabus…of each decision of the Supreme Court of Minnesota, as soon after the same is filed as may be practicable, accompanied, when desirable to a practical to a proper understanding of the points decided, with an abstract of the case itself, and when the decision is one of general interest and importance, with the full opinion of the court." They also promised to do the same for important decisions of the Federal District Court in Minnesota and, when of great enough significance, of the courts of other states.[2]

When the West brothers began their weekly they were not the first to do so. For more than half a century legal decisions had been reported in a variety of formats, including private reports published in book form, weekly and monthly periodicals which did the same, and "official" reports issued by state approved and licensed reporters. At the time *The Syllabi* began its life, however, the reporting system in most American states was highly unreliable and unbearably slow. Contracts for official reports were often awarded based on political connections and these were slow and rarely well edited or printed. Often they were issued without the involvement of a lawyer at all.[3] The West brothers made it clear that their reports would be issued in a timely fashion. To insure accuracy in reporting they hired a lawyer, Homer C. Eller, to supervise the weekly.[4]

The Syllabi was only published for six months. Its demise was caused not by failure but by success. The weekly was embraced by the bar not only in Minnesota but in neighboring Wisconsin. The ever entrepreneurial John West realized that this local weekly could expand into a regional reporter. And, thus, the *North Western Reporter* was born in 1877.[5] The success of that venture led, within a few decades to the establishment of the West legal publishing empire, an empire that exists to this day.

---

[1] See, William W. Marvin, *West Publishing Company .Origin, Growth, Leadership* (St.Paul, 1969); Robert M. Jarvis, "John B. West: Founder of the West Publishing Company," Nova Southeastern University Legal Studies Paper No. 10-003; Thomas A. Woxland, " 'Forever Associated with the Practice of Law': The Early Years of the West Publishing Company," *Legal Reference Services Quarterly* v.5 (1985), 115–124.

[2] *The Syllabi* v. no. 1, 1.

[3] Woxland, Art. Cit. n.1, at 119; Marvin, Op. Cit. n.1, at 32.

[4] Marvin, Op. Cit. n.1, at 34.

[5] Marvin, Op.Cit. n.1, at 37ff.

Although *The Syllabi* was comprised mostly of case reports, it also had other content. Chief among this were advertisements for local professionals and merchants and lists of law books published by the West Brothers. This early example of convergence was pioneered by one of the West brothers' competitors, John Livingston of New York.

Although the material contained in *The Syllabi* has been superseded by later editions, this brief run of weekly newspapers has great significance for law librarians, legal historians, and anyone interested in the history for legal publishing because it is the publication which gave rise to one of the greatest publishing enterprises of the twentieth century.

INTRODUCTION

JOHN BRIGGS WEST AND THE TRANSFORMATION OF AMERICAN LAW REPORTS

W. E. Butler

"There is good reason to suppose", affirms a modern legal historian, that the practice of law reporting "began in England, spreading to the principal papal court at Rome and thence to the rest of Europe".[1] And, it may have been added, to the United States of America, where the plethora of jurisdictions and courts and concomitant numbers of law reports has added a new dimension to the term "ubiquitous".

English Origins of Law Reporting

Insofar as the evidence permits plausible inferences to be drawn, the practice of composing summary accounts of what English judges were doing from about 1275 onwards began when lawyers attended courts and prepared notes on matters of significance. As this was two centuries or so before the Chinese invention of printing had been rediscovered in Europe, the manuscript notes on individual cases were shared, recopied, occasionally bound up into collections and eventually even sets.

This is all perceived to be a matter of private entrepreneurship by the individuals concerned, who may or may not have circulated copies in the interest of earning revenues. The language of the early reports was French, a tradition that persisted for four centuries. Over time the reports lost some of their literary originality and settled into a style and uniformity of presentation that suggests to some the possibility of an organized effort to generate what came to be called the Year Books.

The arrival of printing transformed the informal practices of law reporting and provided commercial opportunities that were rapidly pursued, albeit haphazardly. By the 1480s the manuscript tradition underlying printed Year Books appears to have disappeared. The printers cobbled together collections of old and modern reports and eventually produced selections of cases from about ca. 1325–50 until 1535. Then, for reasons not fully understood, the Year Books ceased to appear from 1535. Two sets of reports, Plowden's *Commentaries* (1571) and Dyer's *Reports* (1585), completed the sixteenth century — both men being law reporters themselves and Dyer's actually appearing posthumously from his case notes. In the meantime, lawyers of the day

---

[1] D. Ibbetson, "Law Reporting in English Common Law", in S. N. Katz (ed.), *The Oxford International Encyclopedia of Legal History* (2009), IV, p. 43. On the role of papal courts and law reports, see G. Dolezalek, "Reports of the 'Rota' (14th – 19th Centuries)", in J. H. Baker (ed.), *Judicial Records, Law Reports and the Growth of Case Law* (1989), pp. 69-99. Baker observed that the earliest known reports of cases in the Rota were kept by English members of the court who were doctors trained at Cambridge rather than common lawyers, and that their reports differed in language and style of the later yearbooks of the common law. See Baker, "Preface", in ibid., p. 8.

prepared their own case notes in the old manuscript tradition and exchanged them, or not, as they preferred.

Why English publishers backed off from the production of modern law reports still seeks an explanation. It has been suggested that Richard Tottell (d. 1593 or 1594), granted a patent monopolizing the printing of books on the Common Law in 1553 that in 1559 was renewed for life, made precisely the opposite commercial decision which confronted John B. West in the Upper Midwest during the 1870s: Tottel may have believed profits lay in the reprinting of earlier case reports rather than in the production of new texts. Whatever the reasons, upon Tottel's death after lengthy court battles the patent was dissolved and the publication of law books in England was open to all.

Sir Edward Coke (1552–1634) produced in his lifetime commencing in 1600 eleven volumes of what have come to be designated "Nominate Reports", where the reporter is known and identified and his identity lends authority and marketability to the books.[2] Coke added commentary to his accounts of the cases, which given his stature as a jurist represented added-value to their readership and contributed to his reports being reprinted several times throughout the seventeenth century. With Tottel's monopoly broken and Coke (and in due course, others) supplementing the reports with commentary on the reasons for what the judges were doing, the market for reports expanded, so much so that publishers found it expedient to invent fictitious attributions of particular volumes to noted jurists of the day. There was also a decided shift to the English vernacular for law reporting, the law-French in which English reports had been published for more than four centuries being supplanted at last by the language of the country.

Notwithstanding episodic attempts to establish a tradition of official salaried law reporters, law reporting remained a domain of private entrepreneurship until 1865. Rather like legal translations, consumers of law reports needed to know both what was said by the judge in a case and the reputation for quality of the reporter himself. Observers noted a distinct improvement in the quality of law reporting in the second half of the eighteenth century, especially in the Court of King's Bench, where Lord Mansfield (1733–1821) energetically introduced law reforms that included the appointment of professional reporters who were commissioned to report individual cases for a fee. The remuneration was sufficient to enable rising lawyers to survive and establish a career, eventually moving on to positions of prestige and honor. The reliability of the reports improved accordingly, and during the early nineteenth century most of the other courts at Westminster followed by appointing reporters who were remunerated.

The State became formally involved in law reporting in 1865 when the Incorporated Council of Law Reporting was formed to establish criteria for deciding what cases should be reported and to produce official reports. Although unofficial reports were not abolished in England and continued to find a market because they could be

---

[2] The same later happened in the United States: "Because these early reports were cited by the name of the reporter, a definite feeling persisted that the reporter was far more important than the judges who rendered the decisions". E. C. Surrency, "Law Reports in the United States", *American Journal of Legal History*, XXV (1981), p. 58. This preference was not without foundation. These reporters "actively contributed to the structure and content of their reports, and the quality of the reporter could make a dramatic difference in the quality of the reports". See Susan W. Brenner, *Precedent Inflation* (1992), p. 97, n. 26.

published more rapidly than the official volumes, their continuing commercial appeal has turned more upon specialist collections and targeted audiences.

American Adaptations of British Practices

In the American colonies law reports became essential for local courts just as Sir Edward Coke was publishing his own in England. English reports were available in Virginia during the "latter part of the seventeenth century", although "the common law of England was brought to Virginia at the beginning of 1607".[3] In the courts of Virginia, English law reports "... were regularly used as authority on points of common law and equity".[4] The "published reports of the English courts were widely available in eighteenth century".[5] The same was true in the other colonies, as one would expect. In the seventeenth and eighteenth centuries prior to 1776, "native law books were few and utterly insignificant. There were no printed collections of cases".[6] Colonial Americans acquired English law books for their personal and social libraries for both personal and professional use, including law reports.[7]

Once independence was declared by the colonies the disposition to rely upon American judicial practice was limited only by the paucity of experience, which made reliance upon English case authority essential, at least until a sufficient body and record of relevant precedent had accumulated. To some extent American lawyers did what their English predecessors had undertaken centuries earlier – they prepared their own manuscript notes on local cases and circulated them among colleagues.[8] Ephraim Kirby (1757-1804) published *Reports of Cases Adjudged in the Superior Courts of the State of Connecticut: From the Year 1785 to May 1788; with Some Determinations in the Supreme Court of Errors* (1789) in which he expressed the hope that a "permanent system of common law" would emerge in the United States.[9] The following year Alexander J. Dallas (1759-1817)[10] published *Reports of Cases Ruled and Adjudged in the Courts of Pennsylvania, Before and Since the Revolution* (1790), which included

---

[3] W. H. Bryson, "English Common Law in Virginia", *Journal of Legal History*, VI (1985), pp. 249–256.
[4] W. H. Bryson, "Law Reporting and Legal Records in Virginia", in J. H. Baker (ed.), *Judicial Records, Law Reports and the Growth of Case Law* (1989), p. 329.
[5] Bryson, *Census of Law Books in Colonial Virginia* (1978), pp. xii, 1–17.
[6] L. M. Friedman, *A History of American Law* (3d ed.; 2005), p. 61.
[7] See the law reports listed in M. A. McCorison, *The 1764 Catalogue of the Redwood Library Company at Newport, Rhode Island*, Preface by Wilmarth S. Lewis (1965), pp. 45–47; R. B. Davis, *A Colonial Southern Bookshelf: Reading in the Eighteenth Century* (1979).
[8] Thomas Jefferson being among them. At least five colonial Virginia lawyers made manuscript reports of cases for their own personal use". See Bryson, "Reports of Cases", in Bryson (ed.), *Virginia Law Books: Essays and Bibliographies* (2000), p. 87.
[9] Friedman, note 6 above, p. 242. Kirby printed the volume at his own expense and offered it on subscription. His subscriber list numbered 226, a healthy beginning for the "... first published reports of a court of general jurisdiction in the United States". See M. H.. Hoeflich, *Legal Publishing in Antebellum America* (2010), p. 135.More generally, also see A. V. Briceland, "Ephraim Kirby: Pioneer of American Law Reporting", *American Journal of Legal History*, XVI (1972), p. 297; J. Parrish, "Law Books and Legal Publishing in America, 1760–1840", *Law Library Journal*, LXXII (1979), pp. 355–452.
[10] See H. G. Callaway, *Alexander James Dallas: An Exposition of the Causes and Character of the War. An Annotated Edition* (Dunedin, 2011); R. Walters, Jr., *Alexander James Dallas* (1943). More generally, C. Joyce, "The Rise of the Supreme Court Reporter: An Institutional Perspective on Marshall Court Ascendancy", *Michigan Law Review*, LXXXIII (1985), p. 1291.

cases from 1754 onwards that were furnished by William Rawle (1759–1836) and current cases supplied by sitting judges. The second volume (1798) added cases from the United States Supreme Court, which in those days was seated in Philadelphia nearby. Dallas thereby became the first law reporter of the United States Supreme Court.

By 1810 there were eighteen published volumes of American law reports; in 1848, about eight hundred; by 1885, about 3,798.[11]

The year 1830 more or less marks the point at which English legal experience, both law reports and legal treatises, began to perceptibly recede in favor of American-sourced and published materials. English law reports were actively added to American practitioner law libraries after the Revolution. Peter S. du Ponceau, in Philadelphia, had remarkable holdings, including an early Bracton, that would have been the envy of any London practitioner.[12] But he equally added American reports as they came along, including the Kirby and Dallas.

The transition to relying primarily upon American law reporting for evidence of the law reflected, initially, the volume and comprehensiveness of the materials locally-generated. It was another matter how American practitioners came to have access to this material. Prior to 1876, when *The Syllabi* made its appearance, the

> prompt publication of opinions was practically unknown to the legal profession ... In each State lawyers were compelled to wait in the first instance, on the convenience of their State reporter, whose official duties were more or less subject to exigencies of his private practice; and in the second place, upon the delays incident to the conflicting business demands of the local publisher. The publication of the decisions, which had, from the time of their delivery, become a part of the law of the commonwealth, and concerning which it was legally assumed every citizen had full knowledge, was made subsidiary in turn to the professional obligations of a legal practitioner, and the private business interests of some local publisher or printer.[13]

The Creator

John Briggs West (1852–1922)[14] originated in Massachusetts, the son of a book-keeper, William C. West (1818–1904) and Louisa P. Briggs (1816–1905). The third of

---

[11] Friedman, note 6 above, p. 475.

[12] His holdings are described, and the auction catalog reproduced, in W. E. Butler, *Peter Stephen Du Ponceau: Legal Bibliophile* (2010). Also see H. A. Johnson, *Imported Eighteenth-Century Law Treatises in American Libraries 1700–1799* (1978). Johnson did not include Du Ponceau holdings in his study.

[13] J. B. West, "A Symposium of Law Publishers", *American Law Review*, XXIII (1889), p. 396; quoted from the reprinted text in T. A. Woxland (ed.), *Symposium of Law Publishers* (1991), pp. 155–156.

[14] By far the most accurate and accomplished biography of this surprisingly elusive figure is R. M. Jarvis, "John B. West: Founder of the West Publishing Company", *The American Journal of Legal History*, L (2008-2010), pp. 1–22. Also see William W. Marvin, *West Publishing Co.: Origin, Growth, Leadership* (1969); R. C. Berring, "Full-Text Databases and Legal Research: Backing Into the Future", *High Technology Law Journal*, I (1986), p. 27ff; J. H. Cheskis, "Copyright of Legal Materials: From Wheaton to West – Shaping the Practice of Law in America", *Communications and the Law*, XX, no. 3 (1998), pp. 1–38; T. A. Woxland, "'Forever Associated with the Practice of Law': The Early Years of the West Publishing Company", *Legal Reference Services Quarterly*, V (1985), p. 115–124 . For a précis of what has been produced about West and the difficulties of finding these publications, see Ross E. Davies, "West's Words, Ho!", *Green Bag*, XIV (2d ser; 2011), pp. 303–310.

five children who survived and of eight in all, he grew up in Roxbury and then Malden. A diary that can no longer be located but was apparently accessible to Marvin recorded West's schoolboy struggles with Latin,[15] a passion for reading, and a liking for sport, although after the eighth grade he apparently abandoned schooling to find employment in nearby Boston.

When his father accepted employment in St. Paul, Minnesota, as paymaster with the Lake Superior & Mississippi Railroad Company, John B. West relocated with his parents to St. Paul and joined his elder brother, Horatio, who had found work there as a farm hand. His experience as a grocery clerk in Boston doubtless served him well in securing a position as a sales representative for the D. D. Merrill Book Store in St. Paul. Merrill dealt in sundry office supplies, but among its wares offered medical and legal publications for eastern publishers.[16] Visits to Minnesota law offices persuaded John West that a market opportunity existed for someone who could supply law books on a larger scale together with something that was virtually non-existent – local state law reports.

In 1872 John B. West resigned his position with Merrill and set himself up as a sole proprietorship and began to trade as "John B. West, Publisher and Book Seller". He leased a premise in the heart of the St. Paul business district and devoted himself at once to servicing the legal profession. Although he had no legal education or specialist training in law himself, with the assistance of local lawyers West developed a line of legal stationary and forms which were well received. By then some of the early volumes of Minnesota law reports were out of print, and he arranged for their reissue. With John C. Shaw, a Minneapolis lawyer, and assisted by S. L. Pierce, he collaborated to compile the *An Analytical Index to the General and Special Laws of the Territory and State of Minnesota: from 1849 to 1875* (1876), which he issued under his own imprint and in which he claimed sole copyright; the price in full sheep was $4.00. He actually perceived and addressed a market for a Swedish-language edition of the Minnesota rules of practice, so numerous were Scandinavian lawyers and judges in Minnesota at the time.

His brother, Horatio, in the meantime had left his farmhand position and followed their father by becoming a bookkeeper in a local hardware store. In May 1875 Horatio married a young lady in Malden, Massachusetts, Eliza A. Barney. With his law book business off to a promising beginning, John B. West in 1876 persuaded Horatio to form a partnership with him – a pairing that proved to be well conceived. Marvin described the brothers as follows:

> The two West brothers were a good balance as business associates for the pioneer days. John, the younger brother and founder of the business, was a decisive pushing character, impatient to put into effect expansion plans and a most persuasive salesman, mentally alert and physically robust (the author recalls that he played a good game of handball until he was near 60 years of age) …
>
> Horatio West, in many respects, was John's opposite, with a cautious temperament and a weak physical stature, caused in part by a serious illness in his boyhood and a fall that permanently weakened his back. However, Horatio had a high sense of

---

[15] Marvin, note 14 above, p. 24.
[16] Marvin, note 14 above, p. 26.

> duty and obligation and gave close attention to the manifold duties in the office, including sales, accounting, buying of supplies and also production until these several duties became departmental responsibilities. ... His prudence was a counterbalance to John's lack of interest in detail or in fiscal matters, and was therefore of great importance to the young, struggling company that was in a race against time to occupy the Reporter field, with almost no financial backing.[17]

One of the first ventures, if not the very first, of the new partnership was *The Syllabi*, reproduced in the present volume.[18]

The Syllabi

According to the *OED 2d*, the English-language word "syllabus", plural "syllabi", originates in a corrupt reading of the Greek *syllabus* in some early printed editions of Cicero. A syllabus in this sense is a concise statement of the content of law reports, a "compendium, abstract, summary, epitome".[19] John B. West certainly had the first OED meaning in mind when he entitled his publication *The Syllabi* — the inclusion of the definite article probably demarcating intentionally a terrain in the field of legal publication that he came to dominate.

The name was aptly chosen for what the West brothers had in mind. The first issue was dated 21 October 1876. In all, 26 issues appeared at weekly intervals from that date through 14 April 1877 inclusive, with no Christmas holiday omissions. By now the name of the venture had acquired a different name: "John B. West & Co.". The subscription price was $3.00 per annum in advance. Advertising space was offered at .75 per square inch of column for a week with a sliding scale downward for those who would purchase multiple weeks up to one year. Four St. Paul law firms purchased space for the first issue, of which the firm first listed, O'Brien & Eller, was soon to play a larger role, at least in the person of its partner. West & Co. took the opportunity to offer sets or individual volumes of the Session Laws of Minnesota, some of which at least John B. West had reprinted earlier. This announcement was complemented by a more detailed explanation on p. 7 that the first eleven volumes had been reprinted with notes by the Chief Justice of Minnesota, the Hon. James Gilfallan. Each issue throughout its existence was eight pages, without variation, and pagination was continuous from beginning to end of the entire volume.

The lead editorial of the first issue made the case for the publication and, in so doing, charted the initial course of what would become the world's largest undertaking in the production of law reports. The Minnesota lawyer, John B. West observed, had heretofore had access to the "syllabi" of decisions of the Minnesota Supreme Court only in the daily press insofar as this happened to suit the convenience of a reporter or when the paucity of news persuaded editors to fill up space with case reports, sometimes in one newspaper and sometimes in another. This was a source of "annoyance" among attorneys, which *The Syllabi* proposed to rectify. The original intention was that

---

[17] Marvin, note 14 above, pp. 54–55.

[18] A "limited edition reproduction" of *The Syllabi* was produced in 1991 "after a set of the original Syllabi was discovered".

[19] *The Oxford English Dictionary* (2d ed.; 1989), XVII, p. 446.

each syllabus would be supplied by the judge who wrote the opinion "as soon after the same is filed as may be practicable, accompanied, when desirable to a proper understanding of the points decided", by an abstract of the case itself and of the full opinion when the decision is of general interest and importance.

The decisions of the United States Courts of Minnesota and those of particular interest in the several District Courts of the State would be included. The intention was to "... furnish the legal profession of the State, with prompt and reliable intelligence as to the various questions adjudicated by our own Courts, and at a date long prior to the publication of the regular reports". As for other States, the intention, soon realized, was to furnish digests or opinions which may have special importance for or in Minnesota or which were of more than general interest. New law books would be noticed as they appeared.

The first issue achieved a level of advertising rarely seen thereafter. In addition to the law firms on page one, half of page 7 and all of page 8 was devoted to classified advertisements by a local dentist, tobacconist, coffee house, jeweler, hotel, clothier, music dealer, gun and rifle shop, carpet house, and luggage specialist, together with John B. West & Co. also offering notarial seals and the American reprint of the ninth edition of the *Encyclopedia Britannica*. In its capacity as agent for other publishers, West offered reports from New York, Pennsylvania, California, and Iowa, together with a number of recent treatises, among them: Chitty on Pleading, new edition with American notes in two volumes at $16.00.

Although the initial issue was posted to nearly all the practicing attorneys of Minnesota free of charge, the initial reaction within the space of a week to the next issue cannot have been that great, although the editor and publisher were greatly encouraged. The second issue was embellished with improvements. Homer C. Eller was listed as the Editor and remained in that position throughout the existence of *The Syllabi*, doubtless assuming that role in addition to his law practice as a partner of O'Brien & Eller. A Table of Contents was introduced. The number of advertisers dropped precipitously, although a local bookshop, Houch & Dixon, made its first appearance, as did a Minneapolis attorney, H. A. Partridge. By the third issue, John West is offering the occasional second-hand set, including 62 volumes of the New York Court of Appeals Reports at $132.

Although no specific mention is made, it soon transpires that the judges are not providing their own syllabi of their cases. One must presume that the Wests are securing copies of the decisions and that, in all likelihood, Homer Eller is assuming this task as part of his editorial function. By the sixth issue West is offering "covers for filing and preserving" *The Syllabi*, apparently postpaid at the price of 35 cents. Enough time has elapsed by November for the publication to have been received and noticed elsewhere and for other legal publishers to send their own journals and reports on an exchange basis. These include the *Chicago Legal News*, the *Albany Law Journal*, and the *Insurance Law Journal*. It is not clear that West is acting as agent for these publications, but a fraternity of like-minded publications is plainly being formed and reporting on one another helps fill the columns.

By 2 December 1876 the editors seem to be having difficulty obtaining enough cases to sustain the publication. A plea is published to "attorneys in different parts of the State having cases involving new or important questions of practice or general interest, if they would send us a brief statement of the facts, the points raised, how decided, and authorities cited in support thereof" (p. 49).

Bargain books make their appearance, whether new or secondhand is not entirely clear. The *American Law Register* in fourteen volumes is offered at $40 and a full set of Minnesota Reports in 21 volumes at $145. The Appleton *American Cyclopedia*, normally $96, is offered at $85, and moving outside the field of law, a set of Guizot's France, normally $27, at $20 or a set of the Dore Gallery with 250 engravings in 50 parts, reduced from $50 to $30.

The issue for 9 December 1876 quietly proclaimed a new address for John B. West & Co., although no other notice was taken of the move in the publication. From 60 W. Third Street the Company had moved to No. 1 Wabasha Street, presumably to larger and more suitable quarters.[20]

Cases before the United States Supreme Court, insofar as they involved Minnesota, were noticed, especially if heard on appeal from a Minnesota court. The *United States vs. Larivere, et al.* qualified on this basis and reversed the judgment of the Circuit Court of District of Minnesota. However, the case was merely noted; the decision was not reproduced.

By 23 December 1876 the appeal to local attorneys to provide news of interesting cases began to bring results. An attorney in Rochester, Minnesota, reported on a case decided by the District Court of Olmstead County involving an action on a promissory note. In the last number for 1876 the issue led off with apparently the full text of a Memorandum filed by the Supreme Court in an application for an order to sell a judgment already levied upon. The style of the publication was such that this document was not described in the Table of Contents, although it appeared immediately below that Table.

Other changes came with the new year. Editorial notice was taken of developments in other states and even in Europe. The inclination of a Belgian jury to avoid sentencing to death a man who murdered two wives and instead to hard labor for life because he had a wooden leg was reported with incredulity. So too was the attempt of a St. Louis undertaker to replevin a coffin from the funeral procession on the grounds the casket was not yet paid for. This issue also contained the first syllabus of a Supreme Court other than Minnesota, the choice being Pennsylvania in this instance. The trend continued in the issue for 20 January 1877, which contained case summaries plainly provided by local attorneys, a case from the Circuit Court of the Minnesota District, and for the first time, brief summaries of ten decisions from courts of Missouri, Maryland, Pennsylvania, Virginia, Wisconsin, and Georgia – a practice continued in many issues. The sources for this material certainly included the sundry publications that the editor was receiving in exchange for *The Syllabi*.

By 3 February 1877 West began to publish its own want lists for secondhand books. A set or odd volumes of the New York Court of Appeals Reports was wanted, as were odd volumes of the Early Session Laws of Minnesota. In this same issue the decisions of other states now occupied the lead editorial page, decisions from Kansas and Rhode Island being noted.

---

[20] Marvin throughout gives the address as No. 11, Wabasha Street. *The Syllabi* says otherwise consistently, one of those errors which casts considerable doubt on how accurate Marvin actually is. See Marvin, note 14 above.

Feedback from local attorneys was allegedly responsible for the inclusion of a decision handed down in the Second Judicial District, Ramsey County. Its inclusion was considered remarkable, but necessary, because (a) it was appealed; and (b) the parties settled the case before the appeal was heard. Nonetheless, the decision of the Judge was considered to be of sufficient moment for practitioners to want a copy, and they were duly supplied. This issue also contained a substantial summary of a case from the Supreme Court of Tennessee.

By 17 February 1877 *The Syllabi* had begun to assume its mature form, although the quality of the typesetting suggests hurried production and less than effective proofreading. Typographical errors are rare, but the spacing is often uneven. On 3 March 1877 the editors ventured into legal research and advice for readers. A correspondent inquires whether a notary public may act outside the county of which he is a resident. The editors are "... unable after somewhat extended search, to find any authority upon this question ..." but nonetheless offer a view on the matter. Notice of receipt of the first number of *The Virginia Law Journal* is acknowledged with a warm appreciation of its prospects.

The Supreme Judicial Court of Massachusetts as reported in the *American Law Journal* becomes the center of attention in the issue for 17 March 1877, followed by what is essentially legal gossip from Canada and, what must have seemed unusual and unexpected in Minnesota, the admission of a native of Japan, Eneas Yamada, to the Bar of the Supreme Court of New York. This pattern continued in the issue of 24 March, where "fillers" reported that bankruptcy expenses were much less in Great Britain than in the United States and that the Illinois legislature had asked the United States Congress to abolish copyright on school books on account of the "exhorbatant prices charged for them" (p. 177). The remainder of the lead page was devoted to litigation in Iowa and Nebraska.

In the last issue of *The Syllabi*, dated 14 April 1877, the editors reviewed the previous six months. The name of the publication, while it reflected their original intention, no longer properly represented the character of the publication as it really was or as they wished to make it. They now wanted a larger publication and a change of name. The new paper would be *The Northwestern Reporter*, which would be supplied to all subscribers of *The Syllabi* automatically. The new publication would continue its coverage of Minnesota courts and add in abstracts or in full reports the decisions of the Supreme Court of Wisconsin.

And so *The Syllabi* in its brief time proved, it would seem, to have been a resounding success. It did spawn a larger law reporter of regional scope, which in turn metamorphosed into the spectacular reporter system associated to this day with the West Publishing Co. in its various corporate guises. Financial data is not available to indicate how the Wests were actually doing. Advertising cannot have been a major source of revenue. The number of advertisements declined significantly after the first issue to a small hard core of advertisers who presumably purchased space at a concessionary rate for a longer period of time. Much of the advertising space was occupied by the West company itself. It may well be that John West during this period spent much of his time "on the road",[21] but to the extent he did, it was not reflected in advertising revenues

[21] Marvin, note 14 above, p. 37.

(there were no advertisers from Wisconsin, for example), although this may have been productive in obtaining some copy for local court decisions. Precisely how many subscribers the publication generated is not known, but it must be assumed that subscription revenue was substantial for otherwise there is no explanation as to how the publication succeeded. Derivative revenues from the sale of books, seals, stationary, and the like doubtless helped but would not be sufficient to sustain the publication.

The Epilogue

John B. West and his partners and associates persevered, however, and their accomplishments speak for themselves.[22] The *North Western Reporter* with coverage enlarged to encompass Wisconsin and attention given concisely to other states, lasted until 1879, when it was superseded by a regional reporter of the same name with coverage of Iowa, Michigan, Minnesota, Nebraska, Wisconsin, and the Dakota Territory. Sometime in this period John B. West married a local school teacher, Lillian B. Bronson (1854-1936), originally from Williamsport, Pennsylvania. Five children were born of the marriage.[23]

In 1882 the West partnership incorporated as the West Publishing Company and added two investors.[24] Expansion moved rapidly, as the company added additional regional law reporters, acquired its own building, and commencing in 1887 began to implement John West's "American Digest Classification Scheme". The last, regarded in retrospect as "a radical leap forward",[25] enabled lawyers to locate decisions that had addressed particular issues. As an exercise in indexing, it was soon reinforced by a "key number" scheme that is used to this day. It was at this time that the editor of *American Law Review* decided to invite the five major American law publishers to discuss or comment upon how they believed law books, including law reports, should be published.[26] One of the burning, and enduring, issues was whether all cases should be published or only those that in the opinion of the publisher were worthy of note. James E. Briggs, of Lawyers' Co-op (Rochester, New York) preferred the selective approach, whereas West favored the comprehensive approach, leaving it to individual attorneys to decide what was relevant to their needs.

Sadly, the dialogue was reduced to banal commercial considerations rather than what one might have expected to be an overriding consideration: whether justice in a democratic, rule of law system can ever be done behind closed doors, in this instance the "closed doors" being cases unreported because a law publisher considered them to be "insignificant".[27]

---

[22] "In the last quarter of the century, West Publishing Company, of St. Paul, Minnesota, began a profitable business, which promised to tame the dragons of case law". Friedman, note 6 above, p. 306. In 1880 there were perhaps about 60,000 lawyers in the United States.

[23] See Jarvis, note 14 above, pp. 6–7.

[24] Several versions of the corporate history of West exist which confuse West as a sole proprietorship, partnership, and corporation. The various versions are discussed in Jarvis, note 14 above, pp. 7-8, fn. 49.

[25] Jarvis, note 14 above, p. 8. On the flood of law reports, see J. H. High, "What Shall Be Done with the Reports?", *American Law Review*, XVI (1882), p. 429ff.

[26] See Jarvis, note 14 above, p. 8.

[27] See T. J. Young, "A Look at American Law Reporting in the 19th Century", *Law Library Journal*, LXVIII (1975), pp. 301–302.

The various indexing and key number search tools continued to be refined at West during the 1890s. West had purchased Benjamin V. Abbott's *United States Digest* from Little Brown & Co. (Boston), and John A. Mallory, *Complete Digest*, also acquiring Mallory as part of the "merger".[28] It was intended to produce a comprehensive *The Century Edition of the American Digest* of cases dating from the first in Maryland (1658) up to 1894, then 1896. Marvin recounts how John B. West persuaded the American Bar Association to endorse the product:

> The American Bar Association was due to meet for their annual convention in August 1897, just after the editorial work on Volume 1 was completed. West Publishing Company was desperately anxious to exhibit a completed volume at this convention, to gain expected approval and publicity, but the chances seemed remote that they could meet the deadline of the convention ... Suffice it to say, the volume was completed, taken to the convention by the then President, John G. West, and was the sensation of the meeting. The American Bar Association at its next annual meeting, 1898, formally endorsed the American Classification Plan as the model for modern digesting.[29]

Some months later John B. West sold his stocks and left West Publishing Company: "whether John was pushed out or walked out is not known".[30] He returned to law publishing immediately, within three weeks establishing the Keefe-Davidson Law Book Company.[31] William A. Keefe and Earnest H. Davidson were former West employees. The venture was not successful, and ultimately ceased operations in 1912. A year later, following the pattern of so many Minnesotans, John West moved to California and lived in retirement until his death in 1922. In 1936 his ashes were returned to St. Paul, where they repose in the family plot.

While at Keefe-Davidson, John B. West returned to the issues of reporting, indexing, and classifying in an address to the third annual meeting of the American Association of Law Libraries held at Lake Minnetonka, Minnesota, in 1908.[32] Addressing, as his title indicated, the multiplicity of law reports,[33] he advocated the filing of decisions in numerical order and citation references to those chronological designations. This would create an official number for each case which could be used irrespective of how many systems of reporting may exist and irrespective of the volume number and page of the particular publication — a direct assault upon the approach he had created at West Publishing Co. and had persuaded the American Bar Association to endorse.

---

[28] Marvin, note 14 above, p. 79.

[29] Marvin, note 14 above, pp. 73–74.

[30] Jarvis, note 14 above, p. 11. Two years after John B. West departed his company, West Publishing Company published "an account of the largest law-book house in the world". See *Law Books by the Million* (St. Paul, 1901); reprinted in *Green Bag*, XIV (2d ser.; 2011), pp. 311–339. Davies noted that a shorter version of this promotional brochure appeared under the title: *A Description of the Home Establishment of the National Reporter System, with some account of the Business of the West Publishing Company* (1893), with substantial unattributed excerpts appearing in the June 1894 issue of the *Cornell Law Journal*. See Davies, note 14 above, pp. 305–306.

[31] Jarvis notes that West apparently left his company on 21 August 1899 and that Keefe-Davidson was incorporated on 5 September 1899. See Jarvis, note 14 above, p. 11, n. 68.

[32] For earlier ruminations on the same subject, see *Current Law*, VI (1907), no. 4, with summary and comments in *Green Bag*, XIX (1907), p. 361.

[33] J. B. West, "Multiplicity of Reports", *Law Library Journal*, II (1909), p. 4.

The merits of West's suggestions, regrettably without acknowledging his contribution, were taken up again in the Midwest United States, this time by Wisconsin beginning in the year 2000, which became the first of a still small number of jurisdictions to implement this approach.[34]

[34] See Jarvis, note 14 above, p. 13, n. 80.

THE SYLLABI.

VOL. I. SATURDAY, OCT. 21, 1876. NO. I.

PUBLISHED WEEKLY,

By John B. West & Co.,

60 W. Third Street, ST. PAUL, MINN.

Terms $3.00 per annum in Advance.

The syllabi of the decisions of the Supreme Court of Minnesota have heretofore appeared in the daily papers only as it happened to suit the convenience of a reporter, or when a scarcity of news made them useful in filling up space, sometimes being in one paper, and sometimes in another.

It has been a matter of much annoyance to the attorneys of our State that these decisions have not been published regularly in some one paper, immediately after being filed, and well knowing the importance of such a publication to the profession, we purpose issuing the "Syllabi."

It will contain the syllabus, (prepared by the Judge, writing the opinion,) of each decision of the Supreme Court of Minnesota, as soon after the same is filed as may be practicable, accompanied, when desirable to a proper understanding of the points decided, with an abstract of the case itself, and when the decision is one of general interest and importance, with the full opinion of the Court.

It will also contain abstracts of, and opinions in the more important decisions in the United States Courts of Minnesota, as well as those of particular interest decided in the several District Courts of the State. The general design being to furnish the legal profession of the State, with prompt and reliable intelligence as to the various questions adjudicated by our own Courts, and at a date long prior to the publication of the regular reports.

It is not our purpose to confine our attention exclusively to reports from our own State, but while making those first in importance, also to furnish digests or opinions in cases decided in other States, which may have a special importance here or be of more than general interest.

New law books will be noticed as they appear.

We shall endeavor to make the Syllabi indispensible to Minnesota Attorneys, by making it prompt, interesting, full, and at all times *thoroughly reliable*, and the better to enable us to do so we respectfully request the cordial support of the members of the Bar.

JOHN B. WEST & CO.,

Publishers.

SUPREME COURT OF MINNESOTA.

JAMES H. MANSFIELD, *Respondent*, vs. ALEXANDER M. FLECK, *Appellant*. } Filed June 16, '76.

When an offer of Judgment is made, and is made and served pursuant to Sec. 241, Chap. 66 General Statutes, the plaintiff has ten full days thereafter excluding the day of service, in which to accept or reject the offer, and to give notice thereof in case of acceptance. In case the trial is begun before the expiration of this period, without any action by the plaintiff upon the offer, it thereby becomes ineffectual for any purpose.

Judgment affirmed.

CORNELL, J.

CITED:

Pomeroy vs. Hulin et al., 7 *How. Pr* 161.

JULIUS AUSTRIAN, *Appellant*, vs. WARREN H. DEAN, *Respondent*. } Filed June 23, '76.

The tract of land conveyed by deed, was described as "the W. 1-2 of the N. E. 1-4 of the N. E. 1-4 of Sec. 5, Town 47, Range 4, in the District of Lands subject to sale at Bayfield, Wisconsin, *containing twenty* acres more or less, according to the Government Survey."

Held, that the words expressing the quantity are merely words of description, and do not amount to a covenant as to the quantity.

Judgment affirmed.

GILFILLAN, C. J.

CITED:

Powell vs. Clark, 5 *Mass.* 355.
Jackson vs. Moore, 6 *Conn.* 706.
Jackson vs. Defendorf 1 *Caines R.* 493.
Mann vs. Pearson, 2 *Johns.* 37.

JAMES H. WOOLSEY, et. al, *Appellant*, vs. MICHAEL O'BRIEN, *Respondent*. } Filed June 26. '76.

Under Sec. 241 Chap. 66 of the General Statutes, when the defendant offers to allow judgment to be taken against him for a specified amount and costs, which offer is not accepted, unless the plaintiff recover a more favorable Judgment than that offered him by defendant, he cannot recover disbursments of the action, but theymust be allowed to defendant.

The word "Costs" as used in that section includes disbursments.

Judgment reversed.

GILFILLAN, C. J.

THE STATE OF MINN. *Respondent*, vs. A. B. CROW, *Appellant*. } Filed Oct. 11, '76.

The liability of a person who sells intoxicating liqors, to punishment, under Section 4 Chap. 16 Genl. Statutes, is no way affected by the fact that the town in which such sale is made has voted "in favor of license" under Chap. 32, Laws 1870. Nor by the fact that the Board of County Commissioners of the County in which the sale is made, refuses to grant license to any person whomsoever, to sell such liquors in towns which have not voted against license.

BERRY, J.

CITED;

State vs. Downer, 21 *Wis.* 277.
Mayor of N. Y. vs. Mason, 4 *E. D. Smith* 143.
Com. vs. Blockington, 24 *Pick.* 352.
State vs. Jamison, 23 *Missouri* 330.

STATE OF MINNESOTA, *Respondent*, vs. JACOB LEVY, *Appellant*. } Filed June 29, 76.

The decision of the trial Court upon an objection to a witness on the ground of non age or want of intelligence, cannot be reviewed unless there is a clear abuse of discretion, or the Court admits or rejects the witness upon an erroneous view of a legal principle.

A witness who understands that he is brought to court to tell the truth; that it is wrongful to tell a lie, and that he will be punished if he tells a lie, has, under the statute, sufficient understanding of the obligation of an oath to be competent.

The admission, of a question, to a witness, which, though strictly improper, will only tend to prove, what in the absence of evidence must be presumed, is no ground of error.

Upon a charge of larceny of property which had been lost by the owner, an instruction to the jury, "that to render the finder of the lost property guilty of larceny, two things must concur: 1st, the finder must, at the time of the finding and taking, have and entertain the intention of feloniously appropriating the property to his own use, without the consent of the owner. 2d. he must, at the time of the finding, either know the owner, or have the immediate means of ascertaining him, or have reason to believe, and actually believe, that the owner will be found," states the correct rule.

It is not necessary that the finder should have actual knowledge of who the owner is.

Order affirmed.

GILFILLAN, C. J.

CITED:

Commonwealth vs. Mullins, 2 *Allen* 295.

do vs. Hills, 10 *Cush.* 530.

2 *Bishop Crim. Law*, *Sec.* 850, *and cases cited, note* 7.

Regnia vs. Thurden, 2 *Car. & Kir.* 832.

Mary vs. Green, 7 *M. & W.* 623.

LEWIS G. STEVENSON, *Respondent*, vs. R. N. MCLAREN, *Appellant*. } Filed June 29, '76.

Under Sec. 35 of the United States Bankrupt Act of 1867, transfers of property mentioned by it are as against bankruptcy proceeding, instituted within the prescribed time, absolutely void, and the property so transferred may be taken by the Marshall under a provisional warrant issued in such proceedings.

Judgment modified.

GILFILLAN, C. J.

CITED:

Bolander vs. Gentry, 36 *Cal.* 105.

Hanson vs. Herrick, 100 *Mass.* 323.

Foster vs. Harkley & Sons, 2 *Bankruptcy Register*, 406.

In re Hussenau, *ib.* 437.

In re Mullere E. Bretam, 3 *ib.* 86.

In re Dexter M. Briggs, *ib.* 157.

13*th Amended Order in Bankruptcy.*

PATRICK NASH, *Appellant*, vs. THE CITY OF ST. PAUL, *Respondent*. } Filed July 12, '76.

The estimate required by Sec. 5 of the Act of March 6th, 1871, entitled "An Act to authorize the City of St. Paul to levy assessments for local improvements," as amended by the Act of February 29th, 1872; although such estimate stated the estimated amount of each kind of excavation to be done in the improvement, and although filed with the plans, profile, and specifications for the work in the office of the clerk of the Board of Public Works, was not a part of the plans and specifications to be prepared for the improvement. It did not control the amount of work to be done, and no bidder had a right to rely upon it, except at his own risk, in making his bid.

Sections 27 and 28 of the Act of 1871, as amended in 1872, authorized an advertisement for the bids to do the work, and the making of a contract with the lowest responsible bidder complying with the requirements of the Act to do the work called for by the plan, profile, and specifications on file in the office of the clerk of the Board of Public Works, but there was no authority in any officer to make on such a bidding, a contract that the estimate should govern as to the amount or quality of the work to be done.

The authority conferred by Sec. 1, of the Act of Feb. 21st, 1873, amending the Acts of March 6th, 1871, and Feb. 29th, 1872, upon the Common Council or Board of Public Works, to order a change or modification in a local improvement because of unforeseen obstacles, could be exercised only by formal resolution.

No authority was given to either the Council or Board where no modification or change in the improvement was made, to make or stipulate for any increase in the contract price.

Order affirmed.

GILFILLAN, C. J.

CITED:

Stees vs. Leonard, 20 *Minn.* 494.

ROBERT & BAZILLE, *Respondent*. vs. BROOKS, MCKNIGHT & CO. *Appellants*. } Filed Oct. 10, '76.

The oath to an officer, in whose charge a jury retire to consider of their verdict, in a trial before a Justice of the Peace, required by Sec. 56 ch. 65, General Statutes, may be waived by the parties, and is to be deemed waived if it is omitted and the parties make no objection at the time.

Judgment affirmed.

GILFILLAN, C. J.

HANNAH A. LOVEJOY, *Respondent*, vs. LEVI M. STEWART, et al. *Appellants.* } Filed June 29, '76.

Action for specific performance of the condition of a bond for the conveyance of Real Estate. The facts found by the Court below recapitulated in detail and considered, and held to be equitable circumstances, reasonable and sufficiently explaining the plaintiff's delay in proceeding to secure and enforce her rights under the bond.

A tender in United States Treasury Notes made December 15, 1869, in payment of a liability contracted before the passage of the legal tender act held sufficient; the decision in *Hepboun vs. Griswold*, 8 *Wallace* 603, which held to the contrary, and was subsequently overthrown, not having been promulgated until January 29. 1870.

Order denying a new trial affirmed

BERRY, J.

CITED:
Gill vs. Bradley, 21 *Minnesota.*
Hepboun vs. Griswold, 8 *Wallace*, 603.

UNITED STATES CIRCUIT COURT.

FOR THE DISTRICT OF MINNESOTA.

CHRISTIAN THIELMAN, *Plaintiff*, vs. JOSEPH REYNOLDS, *Defendant.*

The owner of wheat surreptitously sold from a warehouse, holds the party buying responsible for its value.

STATEMENT OF FACTS.

The plaintiff brought suit to recover damages for a conversion of his spring wheat, in the year 1874. It appeared at the trial, that on April 20, 1874, the plaintiff held the warehouse certificate of Hoag & Co., of Wabasha, Minnesota, for a special deposit of 1,196 1-2 bushels of spring wheat. He made a demand for the same, and one of the firm informed him the wheat had been sold by them and shipped to Joseph Reynolds, the defendant. Hoag & Co. finally agreed to pay for the wheat at the rate of $1.10 per bushel.

It is undisputed that plaintiff, when he discovered Hoag & Co. had sold the wheat, consented to take $1.10 per bushel, and did receive in cash $300, and for the balance a bill of sale of a bin of winter wheat in their warehouse, which they affirmed belonged to them. On the next, or second day after this arrangement, Hoag & Co. told plaintiff they were the agents of the defendant, and the winter wheat was purchased with his money, and did not belong to them.

It is also undisputed that Hoag & Co. were storing wheat on their own account. When a demand was made for the winter wheat, plaintiff was informed it had been purchased with defendant's money, and he then brought an action of replevin against Hoag & Co. in the State court, and on a trial defendant, being admitted as a party, he, the present defendant, was decided to be the owner.

It is also undisputed, defendant received from Hoag & Co. the spring wheat, and plaintiff has never realized any more than $300 for it. There was evidence to show the market value of spring wheat at the time of the conversion.

Upon these facts disclosed, the Court instructed the jury that the plaintiff was entitled to recover, and the measure of damages would be the actual value of the wheat taken at the time of conversion, and that a deduction from the amount found should be made of $300.

The jury rendered a verdict for the plaintiff. Defendant now moves for a new trial, and urges, that on the undisputed facts the Court erred in giving this instruction, and the defendant was entitled to a verdict; that the plaintiff occupies in this suit a position inconsistent with his previous conduct.

Bigelow, Flandrau & Clark, and S. L. Campbell, For Plaintiff.

Wilson & Taylor, For Defendant.

OPINION.—It is claimed the plaintiff can not maintain this suit; that by the attempt to enforce, under the warehouse receipt, his right to the winter wheat, he elected to ratify the transaction with Hoag & Co., and thereby affirmed the title to the spring wheat in Reynolds, the defendant.

The general doctrine of estoppel by election of remedies, is agreed to, as claimed; but this case does not fall within the rule. At the time plaintiff presented his certificate of special deposit, and demanded his spring wheat, April 20, 1874, Hoag & Co. had wrongfully parted with it. His legal remedies then were, either to sue for the value, or to follow his wheat. He did neither. But Hoag & Co. agreed to allow him $1.10 per bushel, and paid $300 in cash, and "turned out" for the balance a bin of winter wheat in their warehouse, affirming that it belonged to them.

In this transaction, the title to the winter

wheat was warranted when Hoag & Co. gave the warehouse receipt. Subsequently, when informed they were not the owners, plaintiff commenced suit to settle the question. In his effort to obtain possession he failed, and the defendant in this suit was declared to be the owner. This result determined that Hoag & Co. had not fulfilled the conditions of the sale, and had not satisfied the demand of the plaintiff. The sale was not to be concluded until the winter wheat came into his actual possession. If a conditional sale and delivery of chattels is made, and the vendee fails to perform, the vendor can recover his property, or its value; and if the sale and delivery is induced by fraud, the property or its value can be recovered from the vendee, notwithstanding its manual tradition, or from any person claiming title through him. The failure of ownership in Hoag & Co., determined by the result of the replevin suit, remitted plaintiff to all the remedies he posessed when he demanded his special deposit, and this defendant, being equally guilty of a conversion, is liable. It makes no difference, as I can perceive, that legal proceedings were taken to settle the title to the winter wheat. The demand of the plaintiff was not satisfied, as that suit determined, and the title to the spring wheat did not pass from the plaintiff by this transaction with Hoag & Co. It is urged that the acceptance of $300, in part payment, and failure to return it, is inconsistent with the effort to recover in this action.

Ordinarily the party who rescinds a contract should return all he has received upon it. This is only necessary to place himself in his original position. But here it is manifest Hoag & Co. could not restore the spring wheat, and plaintiff was not obliged to tender or return the $300.

The plaintiff should be indemnified to the extent of his loss only, and as Hoag & Co. were the agents of Reynolds, it was proper that judgment should be reduced *pro tanto*. I find no error upon a full review of the case. New trial denied.

NELSON, J.

I concur in the foregoing opinion.

DILLON, Circuit Judge.

STATE OF MINNESOTA, COUNTY OF HENNEPIN, COURT OF COMMON PLEAS.

IN THE MATTER OF THE APPLICATION OF MARTHA ANGLE DORSETT TO BE ADMITTED TO PRACTICE AS AN ATTORNEY AND COUNSELOR AT LAW IN SAID COURT. } *General Term, Sept.*, 1876.

The applicant, Mrs. Martha Angle Dorsett, having been admitted by the Supreme Court of the State of Iowa to practice as an attorney at law in the courts of said State, presents her certificate to this court and asks to be admitted to practice herein: upon such application having been made, Mrs. Dorsett was duly examined as to her qualifications for such admission, under the laws of the State and the rules of practice of this court, by an examining committee in open court, and which said committee, after a very thorough examination, reported that the same was satisfactory and recommended that she be admitted to the bar of said court, if under the statutes of this State and the rules of this court, such admission is authorized.

The statute bearing upon this point reads as follows:

"Any male person of the age of twenty-one years, of good moral character, and who possesses the requisite qualifications of learning and ability, is entitled to admission to practice in all the courts of this State."

The applicant has furnished to the examining committee and court satisfactory proof that she possesses the requisite qualifications as to age, moral character, learning and ability, to entitle her to admission; but she is a *female*, and does not, therefore, come within the scope of the statute above quoted. It is true that the statute does not, in express terms, declare that *females* shall *not* be admitted to practice; still, by affirmatively providing who may be so admitted, limiting the class to *males*, there is an implied inhibition against the admission of *females*, quite as plain and binding as though the section contained an actual prohibition. The statute referred to is precisely like the Territorial statute of 1857, and which has therefore been in operation for twenty-five years.

A quarter of a century ago it was an unheard of thing for a woman to apply to be admitted to practice in the courts of any of the States, and it is scarcely to be inferred that the limiting clause referred to was at that time intended by the legislature to possess any significance as a negative act. During the period referred to, very many important alterations have been made in the laws of this, as also many other of the States, enlarging and defining the powers and liabilities of *married women*, and in a measure, approaching to the recognition of the rights and qualifications of females to exercise the functions of citizenship in the broadest sense. A limited right of franchise has been accorded in this State. In Iowa, Illinois, and possibly some other States, women have, by express statute or by an implied right, where the law is silent upon the subject, been admitted to practice in the courts. In Wisconsin, the Supreme Court, under a statute containing no *positive*, and a very doubtful, if at least any implied prohibition, rejected an application of a woman to be admitted to that court on *general principles*. The arguments of Chief Justice Ryan, in deciding the case referred to, are not without merit and sound reason, and yet it will be claimed that there is a smattering of a conservatism which assumes to exercise a guardianship of advisory protection over females, which is not in accordance with the advanced ideas of unlimited rights of citizenship on the part of such persons.

The law is noted for its conservatism, and especially so is that class of lawyers and judges who have made their profession a life study, and believe that a lawyer can only attain to a standing worthy of his calling by a life-long application thereto. The part assigned to women by nature, is as a rule, inconsistent with this idea.

The work which the wives and mothers of our land are called upon to perform, and the part they are to take in training and educating the young, and which none other can do so well, forbids that they shall bestow that time (early and late) and labor, so essential in attaining to the eminence to which the true lawyer should ever aspire. It cannot therefore be said that the opposition of courts to the admission of females to practice, when such opposition has been manifest, is to any extent the outgrowth of that conservatism, or as it is sometimes styled, "old fogyism," which is opposed to the enfranchisement of women: it arises rather from a comprehension of the magnitude of the responsibilities connected with the successful practice of law, and a desire to grade up the profession, and encourage only those to adopt the same, as from their attainments, natural and acquired, are qualified for, and from their adaptability and earnestness, it may reasonably be expected will, honor the calling. Sex is by no means the *only* criterion by which to determine this question, as is evidenced, by the many *male* persons applying for admission, whose characters, learning and ability, entitle them to take but a low seat in the practice; such is the proportion of this class of applicants received, that the "lower seats" are all full, and for the honor of the profession, it is desirable that every means should be adopted which will tend to raise the standard of legal ability, not forgetting moral worth.

And in this, it is not attempted to underrate or belittle the natural qualifications of females for the profession, as many are unquestionably in such respects fitted to take a high place in any calling or profession, and when such an one possesses such a love for the law as that she is thereby impelled to adopt the profession as a life calling and is willing to give her best years to the prosecution of the same, preferring such a life to that of wifehood and motherhood, in all which these words imply, I do not think the profession would suffer from any such accession.

But the courts have not made, nor will they ever assume to dictate, the law in the premises, and when the people of the State in a legislative capacity, shall remove the disability, I doubt not the profession as now constituted, will heartily welcome to its ranks this applicant and others of like merit, and seek to adapt the practice in all respects so far as possible to the new element thus introduced. For the reason first stated, however, this application must be refused.

So ordered.

A. H. YOUNG, Judge.

ANNOUNCEMENTS.

The Gilfillan edition of Minnesota Reports, vols. 1 to 11.

We take great pleasure in announcing a reprint of the first eleven volumes of Minnesota Reports, with notes by Hon. James Gilfillan, Chief Justice of Minnesota.

These volumes have so long been out of print, and so much called for, that we have decided to reprint them, and have made arrangements as above announced.

Specimen pages will be mailed to the profession early next week.

Prove that you desire the reprint by ordering it.

LATEST PUBLICATIONS.

Shaw's Index to Minn. Session Laws, 1849–1875. Full sheep, - $4 00

Minn. Session Laws, 1876, Gen. and Spec. together, full sheep, - - - - 2 00
Same, half sheep, - - - - 1 75
Minn. Reports, vol. 21, full sheep, - 5 00

Chitty on Pleading.—New Ed., with American notes, 2 vols., - - 16 00

Philosophy of Law, etc., by Herbert Brown. 8 vo. 307 pp., cloth, - 2 50

N. Y. Superior Ct. Reports, vol. 40, by Jones & Spencer. 8 vo. 600 pp., sheep, 7 00

National Bankruptcy Register Reports, vol. 14, by O. F. Bump. 8 vo. 650 pp. sheep, - - - - - - - 6 00

Penn. State Reports, vol. 28, Jan. and May terms, 1875, by P. F. Smith. 8vo. 587 pp., sheep, - - - - - 4 50

The Notary Public, by W. R. Lynch. 8 vo., 178 pp., paper, - - 2 00

N. Y. Weekly Digest of cases decided in the U. S. Supreme and District Courts, Appellate Courts of the several States, State and City Courts of New York, and English Courts. Royal 8 vo., 660 pp., sheep, - - - - - - 6 50

California Supreme Court Reports, vol. 50. 8 vo., 725 pp., law sheep, 5 00

Law of Private Corporations, by John Proffatt. 8 vo., 275 pp., full sheep, 4 50

Journal Entries, by E. N. Wild, of Cincinnati. 8 vo., 428 pp., law sheep, 3 50

Law of the Road, or Wrongs and Rights of Travelers, by R. V. Rogers. 12 mo. 283 pp., cloth, - - - - - 1 50

Probate Law, by Wm. L. Smith, 8 vo., law sheep, - - - - - 2 50

Law of Damages, by Geo. W. Field, 808 pp., law sheep, - - - - - 7 50

Reports of Cases in Law and Equity Determined in the Supreme Court of Iowa, Vol. XLI, by John J. Runnells, Reporter, 784 pp., law sheep - 5 00

BRIEFS.

Briefs printed at short notice.

THE SYLLABI.

VOL. 1. SATURDAY, OCT. 28, 1876. No. 2.

PUBLISHED WEEKLY,

By JOHN B. WEST & CO.,

60 W. Third Street, - ST. PAUL, MINN.

Terms 3 00 per annum in Advance.

HOMER C. ELLER, Editor.

TABLE OF CONTENTS.

THE first number of THE SYLLABI was mailed gratuitously to nearly, if not quite, all the practicing attorneys of the State, and the reports received thus far, are of the most flattering character, assuring us that it not only supplies a want long felt, but that it will meet with a hearty support. The present number will be sent out in the same manner, and we hope that those who have not already done so, will signify their intention to become subscribers, at an early day.

Volume 22 of Minnesota Reports, is now in course of preparation, and will be published sometime during the winter; it will include decisions filed prior to March 1st 1876 and perhaps some of later date. We intend in connection with current decisions to include in this publication all those filed since March 1st, 1876, bringing them down to date as rapidly as time and our space will permit.

A case of special importance, to those purchasing certificates of such school lands as have at any time been occupied by the owner or assignee of such certificate as a homestead, is that of *Wilder vs. Haughey* 21 *Minn.* 101, and the necessity of careful inquiry into the previous history and transfers of such certificates is well illustrated in the facts connected with the next case in same report viz: *Hartman vs. Munch*, for a statement of which we are indebted to Messrs. S. & O. Kipp, of Henderson. In that case, it appears, that in October 1868, L purchased 80 acres of school land receiving Commissioners certificate. He resided upon the land with wife and family, claiming it as a homestead, until November 1868, when he assigned the certificate, his wife not joining to S. S, in 1871, assigned it to Munch, who with his wife and family, resided upon the land as a homestead, until March, 1873, when, without his wife joining he assigned the certificate to Hartman. Shortly after, Munch left for parts unknown leaving his wife and family residing upon the land; Hartman then brought ejectment against Mrs. Munch, but she claiming that it was a homestead, and that the assignment, without her joining therein, was void, decision was for defendant, (21 *Minn.* 107) after that decision Hartman obtained a new assignment of the certificate from L, the original purchaser, L's wife joining therein, and again brought ejectment against Mrs. Munch, and at trial had Sept. Term 1876, Sibley Co., Judge Brown, presiding, it was held that plaintiff was entitled to recover.

SUPREME COURT OF MINNESOTA.

THE MILWAUKEE & ST. PAUL RAILWAY COMPANY, *Respondent*, vs THE CITY OF FARIBAULT, *Appellant*. } Filed Oct 17, '76

Under a general power to lay out and open streets in a city, the city council has no authority to lay out and open a street through the depot grounds of a railroad company in such manner as to destroy, or essentially impair, the value of the company's easement therein, theretofore acquired under, and in pursuance of, an express legislative grant for that purpose.

When the jurisdiction of a Municipal body over a particular subject matter depends, not upon an express grant of power, but upon the existance of an alleged necessity from which the disputed power is to be implied its decision upon the existence of such necessity is not conclusive upon the courts

CORNELL, J.

CITED:

LEGISLATIVE INTENT

Inhabitants of Springfield vs. R. R. Co., 4 *Cush*. 63.
Bridgeport vs. R. R. Co., 36 *Conn*. 255.
Matter of Boston & A. R.R. Co.,53 *N.Y.*574
Hickok vs Hine 23 *Ohio St. R.* 523.

JAMES ORR, *Appellant*, vs WILLIAM BOX, *Respondent*. } Filed April 6, '76.

When an execution under which personal property is seized and sold, appears to be regular on it face, and to have been issued upon a judgment of a court of competent jurisdiction as respects the subject matter, and does not disclose any want of jurisdiction in respect to the person, it furnishes a full protection to the officer executing it whether in fact the court ever acquired any jurisdiction over the person or not.

An absconding debtor who has departed the state without any intention of returning, and becomes a resident of another jurisdiction, cannot avail himself of the benefits of our exemption laws in respect to personal property left behind him and subsequently seized and sold upon execution.

CORNELL, J.

CITED:

AS TO PROTECTION OF OFFICER.

Savacool vs. Boughton 5 *Wend*. 170.

RIGHTS OF ABSCONDING DEBTOR.

Yelverton vs Burton, 26 *Pa. St.*351

GEORGE HEWETT, *Appellant*, vs THE PIONEER-PRESS CO., *Respondent*. } Filed Oct. 23, '76.

The granting of a new trial for misconduct of the jury is in the sound discretion of the trial court, and it requires a clear case against its action to justify this court in reversing the decision of such court.

In an action for libel the defendant, (the fact being properly pleaded,) may, in mitigation of the damages, prove that, prior to publishing the alleged libel, it had seen the same matter published in other newspapers.

GILFILLAN, C. J.

CITED:

PREVIOUS PUBLICATION OF LIBELOUS MATTER IN MITIGATION OF DAMAGES.

Saunders vs. Mills. 6 *Bing*. 60
Huson vs. Dale, 19 *Mich*. 17.

THE STATE OF MINNESOTA, *Respondent*, vs. E. W. MAHONEY, *Appellant*. } Filed Oct. 23, '76.

A single sale to an habitual drunkard made by the clerk of a person authorized to sell spiritulous liquors at his place of business, made in his absence, is not sufficient to raise a presumption that the clerk was authorized by his employer to make such alleged sale.

Judgment reversed.

GILFILLAN, C. J.

CITED:

Parker vs. State, 4 *Ohio St. R*. 563.

JESSE M. HODGMAN, *Respondent*, vs. THE ST. PAUL & CHICAGO RAILWAY COMPANY, *Appellant*. } Filed Oct. 17, '76.

In May, 1869, the city of Red Wing, under legislative authority for that purpose, duly entered into an agreement with the defendant company, for the issue of a certain amount of bonds to aid in the construction of defendant's railway between St. Paul and Winona, one of the stipulations of which, required the company "fully to construct equip and put into successful operation, for the transit of freight and passengers, that portion of its railway from St. Paul to Red Wing" (which crossed the Missisippi river at Hastings,) "on or before the 1st day of January, 1871," as a condition precedent to its right to receive any of such bonds.

Held, that this did not require the Company

to construct a bridge at Hastings, but to provide such facilities for passing the river as at the time of making the contract were usual and customary under like circumstances in railroad transportation across said stream, and as were adequate and reasonably convenient in reference to such mode of transit.

Upon an issue as to the performance of such stipulation, testimony tending to show that all heavy freights received by the Company for transportation from either of the points therein named to the other had invariably been carried over another line of railway under its control, instead of the one in question, was competent evidence and admissible.

In case the stipulation was substantially performed within the required time, any subsequent misconduct of the Company in operating the road would not constitute a breach of the agreement.

Order denying new trial reversed.

CORNELL, J.

CITED :

Penn. vs. Wheeling Bridge Co., 13 *How.* 564-5.

A. F. NORDIN, *Appellant*, vs. THE BOARD OF COUNTY COMMISSIONERS OF THE COUNTY OF KANDIYOHI, *Respondent*. } Filed Oct. 17, '76.

Counties are not liable to Registers of Deeds for keeping Reception Books, under Section 155, Chapter 8, General Statutes.

BERRY, J.

GAINES, COOK & CO., *Respondents*, vs. CLARK & MCCLURE, *Appellants*. } Filed June 26, '76.

If either party to an arbitrament under the Statute has any reason to urge why the award of the arbitrators shall not stand, it is his duty to present such reason to the Court when the application to confirm the award, and for judgment on it, is made, and if he fails without excuse to present it at that time, he cannot afterwards be heard upon it.

GILFILLAN, C. J.

W. S. CONRAD, ET AL. vs. A. MARCOTTE, *et al*.

Prior to the passage of Chap. 44, Laws of 1876, an assignment of personal property in trust for the benefit of creditors, accompanied with such delivery to the assignees as the nature of the property admitted, was not required to be in writing; Sec. 9, Chap. 41, General Statutes, has no reference to the *making* of assignments in trust for creditors.

Parol evidence of a valid and completed verbal agreement is not excluded by the fact that the agreement is subsequently reduced to writing.

BERRY, J

CITED :

VALIDITY OF VERBAL ASSIGNMENT.

Curtis vs Norris, 8 *Pick.* 280.

CHAS. A. DEGRAFF, ET. AL. *Appellants*, vs. THE ST. PAUL & PACIFIC RAILROAD COMPANY, *Respondent*. } Filed Oct. 16, '76.

Chapter 105, Special Laws, 1874, entitled, "An act to secure the payment of certain debts contracted in the construction of certain lines of road of the St. Paul & Pacific Railroad Company," impairs the obligation of the contract between the State of Minnesota and said Company, and is therefore invalid.

BERRY, J.

PANCOST, SAGE & MORSE, *Respondents*, vs. L. M. VALENTINE, *Appellant*. } Filed June, 29, '76.

The general rule is that payment of part of a liquidated and ascertained debt is no satisfac- of the whole; to this rule there is an exception, where the partial payment is made in compliance with an agreement between the debtor and any number of his creditors for a composition; in that case, the engagement of the other creditors to accept a composition on their debts is the consideration for the giving up, by each, of his claim for the residue; mutuality between the creditors, as respects the consideration, is therefore essential to the validity of an agreement for a composition.

BERRY, J.

CITED :

2 *Chitty on Contracts*, 11*th Am. Ed.*, 1191, 1157-8.
Norman vs. Thompson, 4 *Exch.* 755.
Perkins vs. Lockwood, 100 *Mass.* 249.
Pierson vs. McCahill, 21 *Cal.* 122.
Devou vs. Ham, 17 *Ind.* 472.
Addison on Contracts, 998.

BERLINDA SHULL, *Respondent*, vs. DYAR RAYMOND, *Appellant*. } Filed June 26, '76.

Where different requests to charge the jury were refused, and the Court also charged the jury at large, the exception, "Defendant now excepts to each and every part of the charge, and also to the refusal of the court to give requests of defendant as requested "is not a good exception.

In an action for slander a request to charge the jury that "words are not slanderous unless spoken with intent to slander and so understood by the hearers" was correctly refused.

GILFILLAN C. J.

CITED:

DEFINITION OF SLANDER:

1 *Hilliard on Torts*, 228, *criticised.*
3 *Blackstone*, *p* 125.
Maitland vs. Goldney, 2 *East* 426.
Beavor vs. Hides, 2 *Wilson* (*K. B.*) 300.

BERRY, J.—If "each and every proposition in a charge was erroneous," I am of opinion that an exception to "each and every part of the charge," would be sufficient.

This remark is only important with reference to the statement of a general rule, since in the case at bar there is no claim, nor ground for claim, that the charge was in all particulars erroneous.

ROBERT MONTGOMERY, *et al.* executors &c of Lyman Montgomery, deceased, vs THOMAS J. WITBECK, *Respondent*. } Filed Oct. 19, '76.

Where in a suit on a promissory note executed by the defendant before he became of age, his infancy is pleaded as a defense, and there is evidence tending to show that the note was given as a part of the consideration, upon an agreement for the purchase of property, the plaintiff may prove a ratification of the note by introducing the deed conveying the property to the defendant after he became of age, and also show that he afterwards mortgaged the same property.

Order denying new trial reversed.

GILFILLAN, C. J.

CORNELL, J. files a dissenting opinion to the effect, That in this particular case, even had the evidence been admitted, (the rejection of which constituted the error of Court below,) the Court would still have been bound to set aside any verdict in favor of the plaintiff as against evidence; That a proper consideration of the whole evidence in the case, together with that rejected, shows a want of consideration for the note sued on, and therefore the matter of ratification was immaterial.

DANIEL MCARTHUR, *Respondent*. vs. JOHN MARTIN, *et al.*, *Appellant*. } Filed June 27, '76.

So soon as a surety pays the debt of his principal there arises in his favor an equity to have the securities held by the creditor for his debt turned over to him, and to avail himself of them as fully as the creditor could have done. For the purpose of indemnity he is entitled to be subrogated to all the rights, remedies and securties of the creditor, and entitled to enforce all his liens, priorities and means of payment, as against the principal. Payment by a surety although it extinguishes the remedy and discharges the security as respects the creditor does not have that effect as between the surety and his principal; as between the latter, it is in the nature of a purchase by the surety from the creditor. It operates in equity as an assignment of the debt and securities. The right of subrogation and the equitable assignment relate to the date of the suretyship, as against the principal and those claiming under him. When the question is whether the acts of a party have had the effect to keep a security on foot, the court, in the absence of proof to the contrary, will presume that they were done with that intention which is most for the interest of the party doing them.

Where "A" holds security upon two tracts of land one which is a homestead and "B" holds security only upon the tract, not a homestead, "A" will *not* be compelled to resort to the homestead tract first in order to leave the other tract as far as may be to "B."

BERRY, J.

CITED:

EFFECT OF ACT OF PARTY AS KEEPING SECURITY ON FOOT.

***Davis vs. Pierce*, 10 *Minn.* 376.**
***Parcher vs. R. R. Co.*, 14 *Minn.* 297.**
***Horton vs. Maffitt*, *Ibid* 289.**

JOHN J MORELAND, Administrator &c., *Respondent*, vs. PATRICK LAWRENCE, *Appellant*. } Filed June 27, '76.

When it appears that a Probate Court has jurisdiction of the subject of the appointment of an administrator of the estate of a person deceased, the letters of administration issued by such court, are, in a collateral proceeding, conclusive evidence of the due appointment of the person therein named as administrator; consideration of certain documentary evidence in this case, and bearing upon the question of the appointment of an administrator.

When a note draws interest from date at five per cent. per annum, but contains no stipulation as to interest after maturity, it is proper to allow interest by way of damages at the rate of seven per cent., after the maturity of the note.

The defective attestation of a mortgage made May 6th., 1856, attested by one witness only is cured by Chap. 39 Laws 1872.

In impeaching a witness by attacking his character, the inquiry must be confined to his character for truth and veracity.

BERRY, J.

CITED:

ON POINT OF ADMINISTRATION LETTERS.

Emery vs. Hildreth, 2 *Gray* 238.

Mut. Ben. L. Ins. Co. vs. Tisdale, Sup. Ct. U. S. Oct. Tr. 1875 13 *Alb. L. Jr.* 82.

FOUNDATION FOR PAROL EVIDENCE OF CONTENTS LOST INSTRUMENT.

Thayer vs. Barney, 12 *Minn*. 510.

SUFFICIENCY OF EVIDENCE, TN TUSTAIN REFEREE'S FINDINGS.

Humphrey vs. Havens 12 *Minn*. 298.

Brown vs. Gurney, 20 *Minn*. 527.

Berkey, vs. Judd, Apr. Term, '75, *Minn*.

7 PER CENT INTEREST BY WAY OT DAMAGES.

Talcott vs Marston, 3 *Minn*. 339.

Lash vs. Lambert, 15 *Minn*. 416.

IMPEACHEENT OF WITNESS:

Rudsdill vs Slingerland, 18 *Minn*. 380.

GEO. A. WILSON, *Appellant*-
vs.
RED WING SCHOOL DIST. *Respondent*.

The act of March 10 1873 entitled "An act to protect *bonafide* occupants of real estate" was not intended to apply to cases of improvements upon land made before its passage.

GILFILLAN, C. J.

CITED:

Murray vs. Gibson 15 *How* 431.

Johnson vs. Burrell 2 *Hill* 238

Baker vs. Kelly 11 *Minn*. 480.

MARTIN & EASTMAN *Respondents*,
vs
C. A. PILLSBURY & Co., *Appellants*.
Filed Oct. 20, '76.

March 12th, 1875 Judd made a negotiable promissory note, due (allowing grace) June 15th. Prior to June 12th. the note was sold and transferred to defendants. On June 12th, defendants purchased of Judd a quantity of lumber for $452.30, payable June 30th.

On June 14th, Judd being insolvent, made a general assignment of all his property to plaintiffs for the benefit of his creditors. Defendants had no notice of the assignment until after the maturity of the note.

HELD, That in an action brought by the plaintiffs to recover the price of the lumber, the defendants are entitled to set off the note.

BERRY, J.—On March 12th, 1875, Wm. S. Judd, made a negotiable promissory note for $500, payable in three months. Prior to June 12th following the note was sold and transferred to defendants. On June 12th defendants purchased of Judd a quantity of lumber for $452.30 payable June 30th. On June 14th Judd made a general assignment of all his property to plaintiffs for the benefit of his creditors. Allowing grace, the note fell due June 15th. Defendants had no notice of the assignment until after maturity of the note.

The plaintiff's bring this action to recover the price of the lumber. Defendants answer setting up the facts above stated as also Judd's insolvency, and ask to have the amount due them on the note set off against the plaintiff's claim. From an order sustaining a demurrer to their answer, defendants appeal. Our statute (Chap. 66. General Statutes Sec. 27) provides that "in the case of an assignment of a thing in action, the action by the assignee is without prejudice to any set off, or other defence, existing at the time of or before notice of the assignment."

The words "existing at the time of or before notice of assignment," apply to set offs as to other defences.

Harris vs. Burwell et al. 65 *N. C.* 584.

McCabe vs. Grey, 20 *Cal* 509.

As respects his right to interpose a set off or other defence, the effect of the statute is, that until he has notice of the assignment the defendant occupies the same position as if the thing in action assigned was still held by the assignor.

In the case at bar the defendants, were at the time when they received notice of the assignment holders of a matured note against the assignor; the claim assigned to the plaintiffs was not due and the assignor was insolvent.

This state of facts brings the case within the doctrine of *Lindsey vs. Jackson* 2 *Paige* 581. This doctrine is succinctly stated in *Bradley vs. Angel* 3 *Comstock* 475 as follows: "A" having a demand against "B" which is due, and "B" one against "A" not due; "A" may in equity compel a set off if "B" is insolvent. See also *Colyers, Adm'r vs. Craig & Smith* 11 *B. Monroe* 73.

Upon the construction which we have given to the statute the defendants, as respects this equitable right of set off, which occured before notice of the assigment, occupy the same position as if the thing in action assigned, was still held by the assignor.

It is therefore available in their favor against the plaintiff. For the purpose of maintaining his position that no debt or demand, not due at the time of an assignment, can be set off within the meaning of the statue before quoted, the counsel relies upon several cases from New York especially upon *Martin vs. Kunzmullur* **37** *N. Y.* **396**, in New York the statue under which the case cited was decided, is as follows viz: "If the action be founded upon a contract other than a negotiable promissory note, or bill of exchange, which has been assigned by the plaintiff, a demand existing against such plaintiff or any assignee of such contract, at the time of the assignment, thereof and belonging to the defendant, in good faith, before notice of such assignment, may be set off to the amount of the plaintiff's debt, ***if the demand be such as might have been set off against such plaintiff or such assignee, while the contract belonged to him.***

The latter clause (which we have italicised) is not found in our statute which is therefore in our opinion so essentially and materially different from the statute of New York as to render decisions based upon the latter inapplicable so far as the point involved in the case at bar is concerned.

Order sustaining demurer reversed.

ELVIRA E. BARNARD, *Appellant*, vs WILLIAM A. STANCHFIELD, and WILLIAM H. GASLIN, *Respondents*. — Filed Oct. 25, '76

The rule in Levering ET AL, vs Washington 3 Minn. 323. Kern vs Von Phul 7 Ib. 426. First National Bank vs National Marine Bank, 20 Ib. 63 followed

GILFILLAN, C. J.—The defendant Gaslin, who had endorsed a note payable to his order, and which was delivered to the plaintiff, is attempted to be held upon the note, notwithstanding failure to serve him with notice of nonpayment, by oral testimony that the actual contract between the parties was other than that of endorser and endorsee. No fraud or mistake such as to avoid the endorsement or justify a reformation of the written contract is alleged.

The case comes within the rule laid down in Levering ET AL. vs Washington 3 Minn. 323. Kern vs Von Phul 7 Do 426 First Natinal Bank vs National Marine Bank 20 Do. 63, which held that oral testimony was not competent to vary the contract of endorsement.

Order affirmed.

ST. ANTHONY FALLS WATER POWER CO., *Respondent*, vs. THE KING WROUGHT IRON BRIDGE, CO., *Appellant*. — Filed Oct. 26, '76.

An order made upon the application for a removal of a cause from a state court to the circuit court of the United States is not appealable.

When a party has complied in time, with the acts of congress, the state court, without entering any order, at once loses jurisdiction to proceed in the cause.

The requirements of the acts of congress in reference to the removal of causes from state to the federal courts, must be complied with before the trial in the state court is commenced.

The calling of a jury to try a cause is a part of the trial and producing the security required by the acts of congress after a jury is called, to try the cause, is too late. When the complaint alleges that the defendant is a corporation, and the answer denies, each and every allegation in in said complaint contained, and each and every part and portion thereof not thereinafter expressly, admitted, qualified or denied, and then goes on to allege acts done by defendant without showing that they were done in any other capacity than that alleged of defendants in the complaint, the allegation of corporation, in the complaint, stands admitted.

The plaintiff dedicated to public use as a highway, a strip across the land leading to a bridge which the city of Minneapolis contemplated building. The defendant made a contract with the city to construct the bridge, under which contract and the plaintiff's dedication it might claim the right to use in constructing the bridge, the rock necessary to be removed for the purpose of placing the bridge.

After this, defendant made a contract with plaintiff, by which plaintiff agreed with defendant that it might take from plaintiff's land all the rock which it might want to construct the bridge, and by which defendant agreed to pay plaintiff for all the rock so taken at a specified rate per perch, no distinction being made by the contract between rock which it was necessary to remove for the purpose of placing the bridge and rock taken from other parts of plaintiff's land.

Held, that plaintiff might recover at the contract price as well for the rock which it was thus necessary to remove, as the other.

Order appealed from, affirmed.

BERRY. J.

CITED:

RIGHT OF PUBLIC TO USE SOIL &C., ON DEDICATED HIGHWAY.

Jackson vs. Hathaway, 15 *Johns*. 447.

(In the above entitled cause the appellants had performed, before the trial, all the acts necessary to remove the case to the United States Court, *except* offering the security required, within the meaning of the law, which, says the decision, must be actually presented to the court for its approval; Defendants, did or offered to do this after the jury was called, but it was held, to be then, too late.)

STATE OF MINNESOTA, *Respondent*, vs EDWARD LEE, *Appellant*. } Filed, Febry. 26, '76.

Negative evidence of character is competent.

For instance the testimony of a witness who swears, that he has been acquainted with an accused person for a considerable time, under such circumstances that he would be more or less likely to have heard what was said about him, and has never heard any remark about his character—the fact that a person's character is not talked about at all being excellent evidence that he gives no occasinn for censure, or, in other words, that his character is good.

The disposition of a person may be proved as a fact by a witneas who knows what the disposition in question is, from his own personal observation,

Judgment reversed. New trial ordered.

BERRY, J.

CITED:

EVIDENCE OF CHARACTER:

1 *Taylor on Evidence*, §325 *A*.
Regina vs. Rowton, 2 *Bennet* & *Heard's Cr. Cases*, 333 *et seq. and note*.
Gawdolfo vs. Ohio, 11 *Ohio St.* 114.
1 *Bishop Cr. Pro.* §489.
1 *Wharton Am. Cr. Law*, §636.

ANNOUNCEMENTS.

The Gilfillan edition of Minnesota Reports. xols. 1 to 11.

We take great pleasure in announcing a reprint of the first eleven volumes of Minnesota Reports, with notes by Hon. James Gilfillan, Chief Justice of Minnesota.

These volumes have so long been out of print, and so much called for, that we have decided to reprint them, and have made arrangements as above announced.

Specimen pages will be mailed to the profession early next week.

Prove that you desire the reprint by ordering it.

LATEST PUBLICATIONS.

Shaw's Index to Minn. Session Laws. 1849–1875. Full sheep. - $4 00

Minn. Session Laws, 1876, Gen. and Spec. together, full sheep. - - - - 2 00
Same, half sheep. - - - 1 75
Minn. Reports, vol. 21, full sheep - 5 00

Chitty on pleading.—New Ed., with American notes, 2 vols., - - 16 00

Philcsophy of Law, etc., by Herbert Brown. 8 vo. 307 pp., cloth. - 2 50

N. Y. Superior Ct. Reports. vol. 40, by Jones & Spencer. 8 vo. 600 pp., sheep, 7 00

National Bankruptcy Register Reports, vol. 14, by O. F. Bump. 8 vo. 650 pp. sheep, - - - - - - 6 00

Penn. State Reports, vol. 28, Jan. and May terms, 1875, by P. F. Smith. 8vo. 587 pp., sheep, - - - - 4 50

The Notary Public, by W. R. Lynch. 8 vo., 178 pp., paper, - - 2 00

N. Y. Weekly Digest of cases decided in the U. S. Supreme and District Courts, Appelate Courts of the several States, State and City Courts of New York, and English Conrts. Royal 8 vo., 660 pp., sheep, - - - - - 6 50

California Supreme Court Reports, vol. 50. 8 vo., 725 pp., full sheep, - 5 00

Law of Private Corporations, by John Proffat. 8 vo., 275 pp., full sheep, 4 50

Journal Entries, by E. N. Wild, of Cincinnati. 8 vo., 428 pp., law sheep, 3 50

Law of the Road, or Wrongs and Rights of Travelers, by R. V. Rogers. 12 mo 283 pp., cloto, - - - - - 1 50

Probate Law, by Wm. L. Smith, 8 vo., law sheep, - - - - - 2 50

Law of Damages, by Geo. W. Field, 808 pp., law sheep, - - - - - 7 50

Reports of Cases in Law and Equity Determined in the Supreme Court of Iowa, Vol. XLI, by John J. Runnels, Reporter, 784 pp., law sheep - 5 00

BRIEFS.

Briefs printed at short notice.

THE SYLLABI.

VOL. 1. SATURDAY, NOV. 4, 1876. NO. 3.

PUBLISHED WEEKLY,

By JOHN B. WEST & CO.,

60 W. Third Street, - ST. PAUL, MINN.

Terms 3.00 per annum in Advance.

HOMER C. ELLER, Editor.

TABLE OF CONTENTS,

OWING to changes in arrangements in regard to printing, we were somewhat delayed in getting out our last week's edition, some slight typographical errors also crept in, that in the hurried manner in which the proofs were required to be read, escaped notice ; with the present arrangements, however, we trust these matters will not occur again.

Upon the question of right of removal of suits, to United States courts, the case of Lanz vs. Randall recently decided in U. S. Circuit Court, District of Minnesota, Opinion by Judge Miller, of U. S. Supreme Court, (*Cent. Law Journal, Oct. 27th,* 1876,) adjudicates a question of very general importance in this as well as other western States, and the decision will no doubt materially increase the business of the Federal tribunals. The plaintiff Lanz was a native born citizen of the Grand Duchy of Mecklenberg, but emigrated to this conuty many years ago, and shortly thereafter declared in proper form his intention of becoming a citizen of the United States. For fifteen years past he had resided in Minnesota, and frequently voted at State elections, but was never finally admitted to citizenship under the naturalization laws of the United States. Defendants were citizens of the State of Minnesota. The case was originally commenced in a State court, and then transferred to the United States Court, on the ground of the plaiutiff being an alien ; and the question came before that court on a motion to remand to the State Court, which was denied. The court holding that the constitution of the United States (Art. 1, Sect. 8,) having provided that Congress shall have power "to establish a uniform rule of naturalization * * * throughout the United States," its rules when established are the only ones by which an alien can become a citizen of the State or of United States ; and nothing short of complete naturalization under these rules will change his condition from that of an alien, to a citizen; and that the right to vote granted by the constitution of this State to "white persons of foreign birth who shall have declared their intention to become citizens, &c," does not make such persons citizens even if the State has the power so to do. That the right to vote may exist without citizenship, and citizenship without the right to vote.

Supreme Court, State of Minnesota.

William Chandler, *Respondent*, *vs.* William Crooks, et al. *Appellants.* } Filed M'ch. 29,'76.

A contract to furnish ties and other material, and to construct and complete a definate line of single track railroad for a given compensation, payable in installments as the work progresses, upon monthly estimates of the amount of work done and material furnished. is a contract for work and material and not of sale; until placed in the track, the property in ties furnished under such a contract remains in the contractor even though prior thereto they may have been inspected by the Railroad Company and included in the monthly estimates.

Order reversed.

Cornell, J.

Cited:

CONTRACT FOR WORK AND MATERIAL—WHEN TITLE PASSES.

Andrews vs. Durant. 11 *N. Y.* 35.
Tompkins et al vs. Dudley et al. 25 *Ib.* 272.
Adams vs. Nichols et al 19 *Pick.* 275.
School Dist. No. 1 *vs. Dauchy* 25 *Conn.* 530.

John Robson, *Appellant*, *vs.* Conrad Bohn, *Respondent*, } Filed M'ch. 16,'76.

By the terms of a written contract, R. was bound to furnish B. at least 200,000 feet of lumber before August 1st, and B. was to pay R. on account of the contract, $2000, on the first day of August.

R, having failed to furnish the 200,000 feet before August 1st, and having refused to go on and perform his contract, B. had the right if he saw fit, to treat the contract as at an end, and to refuse to make the $2000 payment; B. having elected to treat the contract as at an end.

Held, that R. must recover for the lumber furnished, upon an implied contract upon the part of B. to pay the value of the quantity of lumber received and kept by him.

The effect of the rendition of certain bills as evidence of accounts stated, considered.

New trial ordered.

Berry, J.

Cited:

2 *Smith Leading Cases,* (*6th Am. Ed.*) 30, 40.

[It was contended on behalf of plaintiff in this case, that certain bills of the lumber delivered under the contract. (such bills being rendered daily,) should have the same effect as accounts stated—Court says. if such bills were received and kept by defendant, without objection, they might properly have that effect, as to the quantity of lumber delivered: but could not as to prices. for the reason that they not only contained no prices in dollars and cents, but were furnished under the then existing contract as to prices.]

Jason C. Easton, *Respondent.* *vs.* Benj. F. Goodwin, *Appellant.* } Filed M'ch. 20,'76.

A sheriff levied an attachment on certain goods as the property of defendant, who thereupon gave a receipt and retained possession of the same; Defendant in such receipt admitted the property to be his, and its value, to be $800, subsequently he moved to set aside the levy, on the ground that he had no attachable interest in the property.

Held, that the sheriff had the right to rely upon the admissions in the receipt, and having acted thereon, defendant was thereafter estopped from asserting the contrary.

Order affirmed.

Cornell, J.

Cited:

EFFECT OF RECEIPT TO SHERIFF.

Cornell vs. Dakin 38 *N. Y.* 253.

ESTOPPEL.

People vs. Reeder 25 *N. Y.* 302.
Dezell vs. Odell 3 *Hill* 219.
Scanlan vs. O'Brien 21 *Minn.* 434.

Northern Line Packet Co., *Respondent*, *vs.* Zephaniah Platt, Surv'g Partner, etc. *Appellant*, } Filed March 18, '76.

To enable a plaintiff to recover, as upon an account stated, upon written statements or accounts made out and rendered by defendant, he must declare upon them as such.

If, in his complaint, he sets out the original transactions, and not the account stated, as the grounds of his action, either party may prove what the original transactions were.

Order reversed.

Gilfillan, C. J.

John A. Weide, *Appellant*, *vs.* Nelson T. Porter, *Respondent*. } Filed March 20, '76.

In pleading a contract made by a duly authorized agent, for and on behalf of his principal, it is sufficient to aver it as the contract of the principal, without disclosing the fact of the agency.

On an issue as to the execution of contract by A., proof that it was executed by A. by his duly authorized agent B., is competent evidence.

On an issue as to the ownership of certain personal property by A., it is competent to prove a written assignment of such property from the former owner to him, in trust for the benefit of creditors.

Judgment reversed. New trial ordered.

Cornell, J.

State of Minnesota, *Def't in Error*, *vs.* Pleas R. Davis, *Pl'tf in Error*. } Filed March 20, '76.

The case of the State *vs.* Welsh, decided at April Term, 1874, followed and approved.

It is no valid objection to an indictment that it was found and presented by the Grand Jury at an adjourned regular term of the court, and after the Petit Jury had been finally discharged.

The right to challenge the panel of a Grand Jury, or any member thereof, is only secured by statute to prisoners held to answer a charge for a public offense.

Cornell, J.

Cited:
State vs. Welsh, 21 *Minn.* 22,

Starkey & Scott, *Respondents*, *vs.* DeGraff & Wallace *Appellants*. } Filed March 20, '75.

In a contract between plaintiffs and defendants, for the construction of a certain line of railroad, were stipulations constituting the Chief Engineer of the railroad company an umpire, to determine all questions growing out of the contract, and making him the sole judge of the quality and quantity of the work done and materials furnished, etc.

It appearing from the express terms of the contract, that a certain price was agreed to be paid for a certain kind of work;

Held, that as to that, the Chief Engineer had no authority to fix another or different measure of compensation;

Second.—In case the Engineer refuses to measure or estimate the work done under the contract, the party entitled to compensation therefor may prove the quantity by other competent evidence;

Third—Such stipulations do not extend to extra work done outside of the contract.

It is not error for the Court to refuse a request to charge, which assumes as uncontroverted a fact fairly open to dispute before the jury, though correct in other respects.

Order denying new trial affirmed.

Cornell, J.

Augustus F. Knight *Respondent*. *vs.* Patrick Nash, *Appellant*. } Filed March 23, '76.

An order made, upon a disclosure in proceedings supplementary to execution, directing the assignment of certain claims belonging to the judgment debtor, and appointing a receiver to collect the same, is an appealable order, under *Sub.* 6 *Sec.* 8 *Chap.* 86 *General Statutes*.

An affidavit made and filed for the purpose of procuring an order for an examination of a judgment debtor in such proceedings, is not defective in omitting to state the nature of the relief sought.

A debt due from a municipal corporation to a judgment debtor, even though denied by the corporation, may be reached by a final order, upon disclosure directing the transfer of the claim and appointing a receiver to collect it for the benefit of the creditor.

The rule that a debt due from a municipal corporation cannot be reached by process of garnishment has no application to an order of this character.

Order affirmed.

Cornell, J.

Walter C. Cowles, *Respondent*, *vs.* William P. Warner, *Appellant*. } Filed March 23, '76.

A parol agreement that, by its terms, is not to be performed within one year from the making thereof, is within the statute of frauds, and void; otherwise if its obligations can be performed within that period.

The complaint disclosed a contract terminable at the pleasure of either party.

On the trial, the contract proved by plaintiff was one that, by its terms, was to continue in force for a period of time longer than one year from the making thereof.

Held, a fatal variance.

New trial ordered.

CORNELL, J.

THOMAS ERD, *Respondent*. *vs.* THE CITY OF ST. PAUL *Appellant*, } Filed March 23, '76.

One of the material facts in issue before the jury being whether defendant had knowledge of the defective condition of one of its sidewalks at a particular place, a resolution of the City Council directing such sidewalk to be made passable at such place, is competent evidence tending to show such fact.

When contributory negligence is charged, the question is one of ordinary and reasonable care and caution, such as a prudent man under like circumstances would be likely to exercise, having reference to the degree and kind of danger to be apprehended, and the means of avoiding it. A greater degree of care would be required in avoiding an apparently imminent and reasonably certain danger than one of a less certain or doubtful character;

Hence the degree of care necessary to constitute ordinary care, in any given case, necessarily depends upon the peculiar facts and circumstances of each case, and whenever these facts and circumstances are fairly open to doubt or controversy, from the evidence, the question of negligence is one for the jury under proper instructions from the court.

Upon the facts in this case as stated in the opinion—*Held*, that the question of plaintiff's contributory negligence was properly submitted by the Court to the jury.

When an instruction is given which is open to two constructions, one of which is correct, and the other incorrect as a proposition of law, the former will be presumed to have been the sense in which it was given and understood, unless the ambiguity was particularly called to the attention of the Court, with a request to correct the same.

Order denying new trial affirmed.

CORNELL, J.

THE STATE OF MINNESOTA, *vs.* CHAUNCEY W. GREENMAN, } Filed Oct. 28 '76

One who is held to answer at a term of the District Court, for a criminal offense, must make any objection that he has to the manner of procuring the grand jury by challenge, and cannot move to set aside the indictment against him, upon such grounds.

GILFILLAN, C. J.—The defendant was, upon a criminal charge, bound over by a magistrate, to appear at the General Term of the District Court, to be held in June, in the county of Jackson. At that term the Grand Jury found an indictment against him on the charge. He moved to set aside the indictment on the ground, that the same had not been found, endorsed and presented, as required by *Chap.* 107 *General Statutes*. The facts upon which the objection was based were these:—The Board of County Commissioners, at their session in January, 1876, selected a list of seventy-two names of persons, for Grand Jurors; that this list was not signed nor certified by the Chairman of the Board, nor attested by the Clerk of the Board; that a list of seventy-two names, purporting to be a list of names selected for Grand Jurors, was handed to the Deputy Clerk of the Court; this does not appear to have been filed. In drawing the Grand Jury for the term, it appears that the Deputy Clerk placed in the box seventy-two names from a list, which it appears he supposed, to be the list made by the County Commissioners. The law is watchful, and properly so, of the manner in which jurors are selected; *Sec.* 98 *Chap.* 8 *General Statutes* provides how the names shall be selected in each county to draw the jurors for each term of the court during the year; it provides that at its annual meeting in January, the Board of County Commissioners shall select and make separate lists of seventy-two properly qualified persons to serve as Grand Jurors during the year, and the same number to serve as petit jurors; that these lists "shall be certified and signed by the chairman of the Board, attested by the clerk, and shall forthwith be delivered to the clerk of the District Court;" *Sec.* 15 *Chap.* 107 provides "that on receiving the list of grand jurors, the clerk of the court shall write the names of the persons in it on separate pieces of paper and deposit the same in a box, and (*Sec.* 6) that from this box, he shall, in the presence of the sheriff and a justice of the peace, draw twenty-three names to serve as grand jurors for the term."

Although the Board of County Commissioners may have selected the proper number of names, and had them written down on paper, the list cannot be deemed complete until it is certified, signed and attested as required by *Sec.* 98, *Chap.* 8; the list is then in the nature of a record of the action of the Board, required to be made. The clerk of the court has no authority to draw a grand jury from any list, except such as is made out and certified to him, as required by *Sec.* 98.

The question then arises, How shall a party indicted avail himself of the objection? The first ground of challenge to the panel given by *Sec.* 14, *Chap.* 107, is that "the requisite number of ballots were not drawn from the grand jury box of the county." The jury box is the box in which are placed the names, on separate pieces of paper, of the seventy-two persons named in a properly made out list. The box from which the drawing in this case was had, did not contain such names, it was, for that reason, not a grand jury box, and no ballots could be drawn from it to make up the grand jury for the term; a challenge to the panel would have lain for that reason.

And when we refer to the grounds upon which an indictment may under the statutes be set aside, it is evident that they are all such as arise subsequent to the empanelling of the grand jury; *see Sec.* 1, *Chap.* 110, *General Statutes*. It was the intention of the Legislature that objections to the panel, or to individual grand jurors, should be made by challenge. at the time of empanelling the jury, at least where they are made by one who has the right and opportunity to challenge, as is the case with a person held to answer at the term. It is not necessary to determine whether one not held to answer at the term, could move to set aside the indictment, for this defendant was held to answer, and he had the right and opportunity to challenge, and by not making his objection in that way waived it.

Order appealed from affirmed.

H. M. KNOWLES, *Respondent*, *vs.* SAMUEL D. VAN GORDER, *Appellant*. } Filed Oct. 26, '76.

An application to set aside a verdict and grant a new trial, upon the ground that the jury has been improperly and unfairly influenced by counsel, is largely addressed to the sound discretion of the trial Court.

An objection made by the Court, of its own motion, to the improper conduct complained of, is sufficient to enable the opposite party to take advantage of such conduct.

BERRY, J.--An application to set aside a verdict and for a new trial, upon the ground that the jury have been improperly and unfairly influenced by counsel, is largely addressed to the sound discretion of the trial Court; that Court has far greater advantages than an appelate Court can possibly have for observing the character and effect of the influence complained of. In view of these considerations, and upon looking at the facts appearing in the case, and the grounds assigned by the court below for its action in the premises, we find no reason for doubting that the discretion appealed to in the present instance was properly exercised.

The fact that the improper conduct complained of, was not objected to by plaintiff's counsel becomes unimportant when it is considered that it was objected to by the Court of its own motion; this answered every purpose of an objection taken by counsel and sustained by the Court. If, after being admonished by the Court, defendant's counsel persisted (as he in effect did) in the impropriety to which his attention was called, it was not necessary for plaintiff, in order to save his right, to make a further objection.

Order affirmed.

[NOTE.—The improper conduct complained of, in the above entitled case, was the persistent offers of certain irrelevant and incompetent testimony, and the comments of counsel to the jury thereon.]

JOHN SMITH, *Respondent*, *vs.* THE MOORHEAD MANUFACTURING CO., *Appellant*. } Filed Oct. 14, '76.

First.--The sufficiency of certain evidence to prove the receipt by a party of a letter considered.

Second.--A letterpress copy, the handwriting of which is verified as his by the person who wrote the paper copied, is sufficiently verified to be used as secondary evidence of the contents of such paper, when a case is made for the introduction of secondary evidence.

Judgment affirmed.

GILFILLAN, C. J.

MINNEAPOLIS MILL CO., *Respondent*, *vs.* WILLIAM L. TIFFANY, *Appellant*. } Filed Mar. 24, '76.

A reservation in an allodial grant of a certain sum of money, payable annually, for any length of time. whether in the way of rent for the use of the thing granted. or as a consideration for the grant itself, does not give it a feudal character. Fealty was the essential and distinguishing feature of a feudal tenure.

A grant of a parcel of land with one mill power of water, for manufacturing purposes, subject to a fixed, perpetual, annual rent, is not prohibited by *Art.* 1, *Sec.* 15, *of the Constitution.*

A wooden flouring mill run and operated by water, as a motive power, is not "*per se*" a nuisance.

Order affirmed.

CORNELL, J.

CITED:

FEALTY DISTINGUISHING FEATURE OF FEUDAL TENURE.

Van Rensselaer vs. Hays, 19 *N. Y.* 68.

Wallace vs. Harmstad, 44 *Pa. St.* 492.

White vs. Fuller, 38 *Vt.* 193,

NUISANCE:

Rhodes vs. Dunbar, 57 *Pa. St.* 274.

JOHN B. QUINN, *Respondent*, *vs.* JAMES G. SCOTT, *Appellant.* } Filed March 24, '76.

In in action of slander, facts and circumstances sufficient to create a belief in the truth of the alleged defamatory matter, if neither known nor relied upon as true by the party uttering the slander, cannot be considered in mitigation as tending to repel the inference of malice.

Gross incompetency in a magistrate is not of itself, sufficient evidence of official corruption or personal depravity, and an erroneous judicial decision, unaccompanied by any fact or circumstance indicating a corrupt or dishonest motive, is wholly insufficient upon which to predicate a charge of criminality or corrupt misconduct in office.

When a party makes a false and slanderous statement against another, not believing it to be true at the time, he is not in a position to raise any question as to the privileged character of such statement, nor as to the admissibility or effect of general rumors and suspicions as to its truth.

Judgment affirmed.

CORNELL, J.

CITED:

MALICE:

Gorton vs. Keeler, 51 *Barb.* 475.

WHAT NECESSARY IN CASE OF PRIVILEGED STATEMENTS:

Twogood vs. Spyring, 4 *Tyrwh* 582. 1 *C, M. & R.* 181.

Swan vs. Tappan, 5 *Cush.* 104.

Gassett vs. Gilbert, 6 *Gray* 94.

Klinck vs. Colby, et al., 46 *N. Y.* 428.

Wachter vs. Quenzer, 29 *N. Y.* 553.

A. RICHARDS, *Respondent*, *vs.* JOHN M. SPICER, *et al.* *Appellant.* } Filed Oct. 30, '76.

June 2d, 1874, M. mortgaged a yoke of oxen, a pair of horses and a lumber wagon to S. & L., to secure two promissory notes. In August M. sold the oxen to R.; after this M. executed a second mortgage on the horses and lumber wagon to S. & L. In March, 1875, when the indebtedness secured by the two mortgages amounted to $325, M. and S. & L. entered into an arrangement by which M. made an absolute sale and delivery of the horses and wagon to S. & L., for $358. By the terms of the arrangement, $275 of this sum was applied upon the mortgage debts, so as to pay the debt secured by the second mortgage in full, and so as to pay all of the indebtedness secured by the first mortgage, except $50; the remainder of the $358 was applied to the payment of indebtedness of M. to S. & L. not covered by the mortgage, and which accrued after S. & L. had notice of R.'s purchase of the oxen; subsequently, by virtue of the first mortgage, upon which $50 remained uncancelled, and which was overdue, S. & L. caused the oxen to be taken from plaintiff's possession, and sold in satisfaction of said amount of $50.

Held, that if, under the facts above appearing, R. had any equities which entitled him to insist that the price of the horses and wagon, under the arrangements of March 18, 1875, should be applied to satisfy and extinguish the first mortgage, it was his duty to take seasonable measures to assert his equities and stop the sale.

Held, further, that as he failed to take such measures, and no excuse is found for his failure, and as the sale is to be presumed to have been fairly conducted and clear of fraud, R. cannot now attack it or claim that it subjected S. & L. to any liability to him.

BERRY, J.

CITED:

Johnson vs. Williams, 4 *Minn.* 260.

THOMAS WRIGHT, *Respondent*, *vs.* JACOB LEVY & ESTHER LEVY. *Appelants.* } Filed March 28, '76.

In this case the cause of action arose on the 14th Sept., 1874. It was placed on the calendar for General Term. District Court, commencing October 14th, 1874, and on 29th of same month, an application was made for postponement of trial, on the ground of absence of evidence. Defendants were husband and wife, and the evidence desired was the testimony of the wife, Esther Levy, who was then pregnant, and unwilling to appear in court and testify in the cause; the reason urged was danger to her life and health. The question of danger was referred by the Court to two physicians, who each certified in effect that under the circumstances, it would be dangerous to her life and health to compel her attendance, in court; but that if she was willing to appear in court and submit to an examination, she could do so with safety. The application for a continuance was refused; trial had without her evidence, and judgment for the plaintiff.

The following is the syllabus of the Supreme Court:

Judgment in this case reversed upon the ground of error in refusing to postpone the trial of the action on account of the absence of evidence.

Gillfllan C. J., dissenting, says:

Assuming the good will of the application for a continuance, the case made was a strong one.

But the record shows enough to raise a question, as to its good faith; and when the application fairly presents such a question, I do not think the decision of the trial court upon it, is subject to review, and am therefore of opinion that the judgment should be affirmed.

DANIEL F. McCARTHY, *Appellant*, vs. JOHN GRACE, *Respondent*. } Filed Oct. 24, '76.

When a party claims under a chattel mortgage, the burden is upon him to show any delivery or change of possession of the things mortgaged, which may be neccessary to make the mortgage valid.

When a chattel mortgage is not accompanied by an immediate delivery and followed by a actual and continued change of possession of the things mortgaged, though it appears to have been executed in good faith, and not for the purpose of defrauding any creditor, it is void as against a levying creditor of the mortgagor, (having no notice of the existence of the mortgage) unless it has been duly filed within two years before the levy.

The fact that the sheriff who makes the levy is the mortgagee, in a chattel mortgage upon the things levied upon, is not notice to the levying creditor of the existence of the mortgage.

Judgment affirmed.

BERRY, J.

SHERIFF NOT AN AGENT, BUT OFFICER OF LAW.

Armstrong vs. Vroman, 11 *Minn.* 220.

Horton vs. Maffitt, 14 *Minn.* 289.

ANNOUNCEMENTS.

The Gilfillan edition of Minnesota Reports. xols. 1 to 11.

We take great pleasure in announcing a reprint of the first eleven volumes of Minnesota Reports, with notes by Hon. James Gilfillan, Chief Justice of Minnesota.

These volumes have so long been out of print, and so much called for, that we have decided to reprint them, and have made arrangements as above announced.

Prove that you desire the reprint by ordering it.

LATEST PUBLICATIONS.

Chitty on pleading.—New Ed., with American notes, 2 vols., - -	16 00
Philosophy of Law, etc,, by Herbert Brown. 8 vo. 307 pp., cloth. -	2 50
The Notary Public, by W. R. Lynch. 8 vo., 178 pp., paper, - -	2 00
California Supreme Court Reports, vol. 50. 8 vo., 725 pp., full sheep, -	5 00
Law of Private Corporations, by John Proffat. 8 vo., 275 pp., full sheep,	4 50
Journal Entries, by E. N. Wild, of Cincinnati. 8 vo., 428 pp., law sheep,	3 50
Law of the Road, or Wrongs and Rights of Travelers, by R. V. Rogers. 12 mo 283 pp., cloth, - - - - -	1 50
Probate Law, by Wm. L. Smith, 8 vo., law sheep, - - - - -	2 50
Law of Damages, by Geo. W. Field, 808 pp., law sheep, - - - - -	7 50
Reports of Cases in Law and Equity Determined in the Supreme Court of Iowa, Vol. XLI, by John J. Runnels, Reporter, 784 pp., law sheep -	5 00
Shaw's Index to Minn. Session Laws. 1849–1875. Full sheep. -	$4 00
Minn. Reports. vol. 21, full sheep -	5 00

A Statute Law Against Forfeiture of Life Policies.

Massachusetts alone has this, and the NEW ENGLAND MUTUAL LIFE, of Boston, is the oldest chartered Mutual Life Insurance Company in the United States. Policies issued by this Company on life plan secure two years' insurance for each premium paid. Long term policies, up to age 60 or 70, on good lives, at from 20 to 40 per cent. less than life rates. No Tontine or other fallacious form of policy issued by this Company. Agents wanted throughout the State.

Address,

J. H. McDONALD,
General Agent,
St. Paul.

THE AMERICAN REPRINT

OF THE

ENCYCLOPÆDIA BRITANNICA,

New Ninth Edition.

Volumes 1, 2, 3 and 4 are now ready.

This is the Largest and Best work of the kind in the English Language. Every Article is a Complete Treatise by the most Eminent Writers.

Send for Specimen Pages to

JOHN B. WEST & CO.

HOUGH & DIXON,

BOOKSELLERS AND STATIONERS,

15 East Third St.,

ST. PAUL, - - MINN.

LEGAL BLANKS.

We fill promptly all orders for Legal Blanks and for the convenience of our customers, will put up all orders for two or more dozen of one kind in blocks.

John D. O'Brien. Homer C. Eller.

O'BRIEN & ELLER,

ATTORNEYS AT LAW,

Ingersoll Block, ST. PAUL, MINN.

H. A. PARTRIDGE,

Lawyer and Notary Public,

ROOM NO. 1, HARRISON BLOCK,

MINNEAPOLIS, - - MINN.

WARREN H. MEAD. CYRUS J. THOMPSON.

MEAD & THOMPSON,

ATTORNEYS AT LAW,

Cor. Third and Wabashaw Sts., St. Paul.

Special attention given to Bankrupt Proceedings and Collections. Loans securely placed.

SESSION LAWS.

We have the Session Laws of Minnesota from 1849 to 1875 inclusive, 34 vols., which we offer in sets, or by the volume.

Parties wishing to fill their sets, will do well to send list at once.

We offer:

1849	$4.00	1872	$3.50
1861	2.00	1873	2.50
1862	2.50	1874	2.00
1863	2.00	1875	2.00
1864	2.00	1876	1.75
1871	2.00		

Bound in Half Sheep.

We can supply Seals of any Size or Design.

NOTARIAL SEALS for any County, $675,

JOHN B. WEST & CO,

☞ WE have prepared a new revised list of Law Books, which we will send on application,

THE SYLLABI.

VOL. 1. SATURDAY, NOV. 11, 1876. No. 4.

PUBLISHED WEEKLY,

By JOHN B. WEST & CO.,

63 W. Third Street, - ST. PAUL, MINN.

Terms 3 00 per annum in Advance.

HOMER C. ELLER, Editor.

TABLE OF CONTENTS.

THE question "Who is a laboring man, within the provisions of our statute in regard to exemptions?" is a question that has never yet been decided in the court of last resort. Two decisions have been made, however, in the District Court of Ramsey county, which may aid somewhat in the proper construction of the term.

In *St. P. F. & M. Ins. Co. vs. Leahy, Def't, and R. R. Co., Garnishee*, defendant was a section boss on a railroad; his wages, to the amount of some fifty dollars, earned within ninety days previous, were garnisheed; judgment was rendered against garnishee before a justice, and upon an appeal being taken and the question of exemption coming up before Wilkin, J. the following decision was rendered:

"I do not think defendant is a laborer, within the meaning of the act of 1872, which exempts the wages of any laboring man or woman from execution and garnishment.

"The defendant was a section boss; he had charge of a gang of men and of keeping the track in order upon a section of a railroad, between St. Paul and Stillwater; he testifies that he was appointed to take care of the men, and to keep that section in order; that he kept the men's time; that if the men did not work to suit him, he could discharge them; that he hired the men when the road master told him to, and that he directed the men where to go. He also stated that he was hired by the month; that he received more than the others, because he kept the time.

"Although this defendant worked with the men, it is quite evident that his position was different from that of a common laborer—that is, one who is dependent upon the daily labor of his hands alone, for the support of himself and family. He was in a position of trust, having the oversight of laborers, and the charge, to a certain extent, of a portion of the road; he also received an increased compensation, in view of the care and responsibility required by his position.

"Judgment below must be affirmed."

In *Morand vs. Prentiss, defendant, and R. R Co., Garnishee*, the defendant was an engineer, in charge of an engine, and sometimes working a day or so as machinist in the shops. Against his claim for his exemption, it was urged that the term "laboring man" was to be taken in its strict sense, and that it included those only who were engaged in manual occupations requiring little or no skill, and that he did not come within that class.

Brill, J., however, sustained the claim, accompanying his order with the following memorandum:

"I think the defendant is fairly included in the term *laboring man*, as used in our statutes of exemptions. The Courts latterly have been inclined to give such statutes a liberal construction; and all the reasons for calling into existence such a statute to protect any class of laborers, seem to call for the application of this statute to the class of laborers to which defendant belongs. The case of the *St. P. F. & M. Ins. Co. vs. Leahy*, was not a parallel case. The decision there was expressly placed upon the ground that defendant occupied a position of trust, having charge of a company of men, directing their movements, etc., and was not dependent on the labor of his hands for his support."

SUPREME COURT, STATE OF MINNESOTA.

THE FARMERS & MECHANICS BANK.
Appellant,
vs.
RUFUS J. BALDWIN, impleaded with WILLIAM S. JUDD,
Respondent,
Filed Oct. 28, '76

Prior to the amendment of Sec. 13, of Chap. 33, of the General Statutes, Banks organized under the provisions of that chapter, had no power to purchase or traffic in promissory notes as choses in action, or as a species of personal property.

The power to carry on the business of banking by discounting bills, notes and other evidences of debt, is not, within the meaning of that section, a power to buy such securities, but to loan money thereon, with the right to take lawful interest in advance;

CORNELL, J. It is conceded that plaintiff's only title to the note in question, rests upon its absolute purchase, as a chose in action from one Patterson, the then owner, for a specific sum agreed upon, and paid at the time of the purchase;

Patterson did not endorse the note, nor expressly assume any obligation in connection with the transfer; inasmuch as the ownership of the note by plaintiff is first in issue by the pleadings, the question necessarily arises, whether the plaintiff had the corporate power to make the purchase in the manner it did, and whether by such alleged purchase it acquired any title, which it could enforce against either the maker or Baldwin the indorser;

The doctrine that a corporation can only exercise such powers as are expressly granted, or as are incidental to its existence or necessary to enable it to execute some one or more of its express powers, is too firmly established both upon principal and authority, to admit of any doubt or discussion. This rule by which courts must be governed in all inquiries into the existence of any Corporate power, is aptly and justly declared to be axiomatic in the opinion of the court in *First National Bank vs. Ocean National Bank*, 60 *N. Y.* 288, 4 *Wheat.* 636. 2 *Kent* 299. *School District vs. Thompson* 5 *Minn.* 286.

So when an express power is granted, and the specific mode or manner of its exercise is prescribed, it can only be exercised in that particular way, 13 *Peters* 587, 2 *Kent* 290 299. Plaintiff derives its corporate existence and powers from Chapter 33 of the General Laws of 1866, as it existed prior to the amendment in 1876; and if it had the power in question at all it must be found, in some of the provisions of that Chapter, which relates to Banks and Banking. Section two provides, that "any person or association of persons may establish offices of discount, deposit and circulation, and become incorporated upon the terms and conditions, and subject to the liabilities, prescribed in that Chapter." Section eleven prescribes the manner, in which such corporation shall be formed, and declares that upon such formation, as a body politic and corporate, by its assumed name "it shall by such name have power to contract, and be contracted with, sue, and be sued, and shall have all other powers, privileges and immunities, incident to corporations, and applicable to the ends of such establishments, subject to the restrictions and conditions of said chapter." Section 13, which specifically defines the powers of such corporation, is as follows "such person or association, has the power to carry on the business of banking by discounting bills, notes and other evidences of debt, by receiving deposits, by buying and selling gold and silver bullion, foreign coin, and foreign and inland bills of exchange, by loaning money on real and personal securities, and by exercising such incidental powers, as may be necessary to carry on *such* business." Sec. 33, provides, that such bank or banking association may demand and receive for loans on real and personal securities, or for notes, bills or other evidences of debt discounted, such rate of interest as may be agreed upon by the parties, not exceeding twelve per cent. per annum, subject however to such General Laws regulating and fixing the rate of interest as may hereafter be passed by the legislature, and it shall be lawful to receive the interest in advance according to the ordinary usage of banking institutions and in general to do all things and have all the privileges incident to banking associations or corporations." Sec. 43, prescribes a penalty for any violation of the provisions of the Chapter; These sections contain all the provisions of law having any bearing upon the question under consideration; in construing them, regard must be had to the general nature and purpose of banking institutions and it must be assumed that the language and terms employed in framing the statute, were so used, in this their ordinary and appropriate sense, nothing appearing in the enactment itself to show a different meaning.

Bouvier defines a bank to be "an institution authorized to receive deposits of money, to lend money, and to issue promissory notes." These are its principal attributes,

First Nat. Bank vs. Ocean Nat. Bank, 60 *N. Y.* 288. Banks are of three kinds, known as banks of discount, deposit and circulation, though usually in every American system of banking, all these functions are united in the same institution, as in the case under the present law, *Sec.* 19 *Chap.* 33 *Gen. Laws*. Their chief purpose and designs are to furnish safe places of deposit for money, to facilitate its payment and exchanges between different persons and places, thereby serving as clearing houses, where located, and to accommodate the business public with loans or discounts to such an extent, and on such terms as are compatible with their continued safety and solvency, and the legitimate wants and demands of trade and commerce, (*McCullough Com. Dic. Vol.* 1 *p.* 63; *Am. Cy. Vol.* 2 *Title Banks*) In view of these public purposes, in all legislation authorizing their creation, it has been usual to designate the character of the securities which they shall be permitted to take upon their loans or discounts, to limit the rate of interest, and to prescribe such other wholesome regulations as experience has suggested to be necessary to subserve the purposes of their creation, and to protect alike the banks and the public from the evils of general insolvency, sure to follow the general absorption and employment of the banking capital of a country, in purely speculative enterprises for purposes of private gain alone; Under the act in question the business of banking is authorized to be carried on "by discounting bills, notes and other evidences of debt, and by loaning money on real and personal security," (*Sec.* 13,) and the rate of interest allowed to be charged for such discounts and loans is limited to twelve per cent., taken in advance. (*Sec.* 33.) The obvious intent of this legislation was to secure to the public business, loans and accommodations at what was then regarded reasonable, and not exhorbitant rates of interest; and also to protect the shareholders of banks, and the banks themselves, against the risk of loss from inadequate securities, such as would likely be taken under the tempting influence of high rates of interest, regulated only by the necessities of borrowers, and the cupidity of bank directors. If, however, as is claimed on the part of appellant, associations organized under this enactment, possess the unlimited power of dealing in promissory notes and other evidences of debt as property and choses in action, the same as individuals, then, obviously, this restriction upon the rate of interest, is a practical nullity, as the bank has the power of evading it at any time, by simply buying the paper instead of loaning money upon it; no judicial construction leading to such a result is allowable, unless required by some clear and unmistakable provision of the statute.

It is not contended, and cannot be, that the power to purchase and traffic in promissory notes, as a species of personal property, belongs to any bank as a necessary incident to its existence, or to the exercise of any of its powers as a bank of circulation and deposit alone.

It is not conferred, in express terms, by any provision of the statute; it must exist, therefore, if at all, as an incident, necessary to enable it to transact its business as a bank of discount. A bank of discount alone, is defined to be "one that furnishes loans upon drafts, promissory notes, bonds or other securities;" (*Am. Cyc. Vol.* 2 *Title Banks.*) "The discounting of notes," says Spencer, J., in *People vs Utica Ins. Co.* 15 *J. R.* 391, "is one mode of lending money." In the *Firemen's Insurance Co. vs. Ely*, 2, *Cow* 699 Sutherland, J., adopts the same definition; and Gardner J., in delivering the opinion of Court, in the *Talmage vs. Pell*, 3 *Seld.* 343, declares that "to discount bonds in banking is only mode of loaning money." In *Fleckner vs. The Bank of the United States*, 8 *Wheat.* 338, Story, J. uses the following language, "Nothing can be clearer, than that by the language of the commercial world, and the settled practice of the banks, a discount by a bank means '*ex vi termini*,' a deduction or drawback made upon its advances or loans of money on negotiable paper or other evidences of debt payable at a future day, which are transferred to the bank. We suppose the legislature used the language in this, its appropriate sense." The correct proposition, as we understand it, is concisely stated in the Syllabus to the case of the *Niagara County Bank vs. Baker*, 15 *Ohio St.* 69, as follows, "To discount paper, as understood in the business of banking, is only a mode of loaning money, with the right to take the interest allowed by law in advance."

Discounting a note and buying it, are not identical in meaning, the latter expression being used to denote the transaction "when the seller does not endorse the note, and is not accountable for it;" (1 *Bouv.* 481 *citing Pothier De l' Usure* 128) and it is admitted that such was the character of the transaction in this case. In view of this understanding of the functions of a bank of discount, the legal signification attached to the word "discount," and the distinction between it and the word "purchase;" when applied to the business of banking, it is obvious that the power "to carry on the business of banking by discounting notes, bills and other evidences of debt," is only an authority to loan money thereon, with the right to deduct the legal rate of interest in advance; this right can be fully enjoyed without the possession of the unrestricted power of buying and dealing in such securities, as choses in action and personal property. Though, as is urged by appellant, the bank acquires a title to discounted paper, and hence may, in a certain sense, be said to have purchased it; yet it is a purchase by discount, which is permitted, and does not involve the exercise of a power of purchase in any other way than by discount.

It follows from these premises that the powers claimed cannot be regarded as necessarily incidental to that branch of the banking business, which pertains to a bank of discount alone; except as a bank of circulation, the specific powers conferred upon institutions organized under the provisions of this chapter, are all enumerated and defined by *Sec.* 13; among them is an express grant to deal in certain articles of personal property, to-wit:—"buying and selling gold and silver bullion, foreign coin, and foreign and inland bills of exchange." Promissory notes, however, are not included; Clearly, as is suggested by Justice Gardner, in *Talmage vs. Pell*, the maxim "*Expressio unius, &c.*" is applicable here. If an express grant of power was deemed necessary to enable a bank created under this statute, to deal in "gold and silver bullion, coin and bills of exchange," and to invest its funds therein, it is difficult to see why it was not also given as to promissory notes, if it was intended that the bank might ever exercise such power in respect to them.

In the itemized statement of assets and liabilities, which each bank is required to make quarterly by Sec. 34 of the statute, it made the duty of the bank to report, among other things, the aggregate amount of its loans and discounts, and also, separately, its "prommissory notes." No inference can be drawn from this, that the notes herein referred to, are any other than those lawfully acquired by the bank through the exercise of its conceded powers, in making loans on personal securities, and in discounting commercial paper; in both these ways promissory notes may be lawfully obtained and held, and if knowledge of the amount of such kind of paper was deemed important for any purpose, the provision in question was not only pertinent, but absolutely necessary; for it is apparent that a mere statement of the total amount of its loans and discounts would not disclose the desired information. The obvious purpose of the section was not to define the powers of these institutions, or the manner in which they might be exercised, but to procure a true and correct statement of their condition, at stated periods, for the use and benefit of the public, and hence no power can be implied from any of its provisions unless the implication is rendered necessary and unavoidable, both from the language and the context. All the provisions of this chapter of our laws, having any bearing upon the question under consideration, are essentially the same as these contained in the N. York Stat. upon the same subject, from which ours seems to have been copied; Sec. 13 of our statute, in particular, which relates to the powers of these associations, is identical in substance and nearly in language, with a similar section in the N. York stat. In the case of *Talmage vs. Pell* (*supra*) the question arose whether a bank organized under that statute had any legal capacity to purchase the negotiable bonds of the State of Ohio, for purposes of gain or profit; after full and exhaustive argument, the Court of Appeals decided, in an opinion covering the whole ground, that it had no such powers.

In the case of the *Niagara County Bank vs. Baker et al* decided by the Supreme Court of the State of Ohio, (15 *Ohio St.* 69) the same statute came under review upon a state of facts, presenting the precise point involved in this case; and it was held, that a power to carry on the business of banking by discounting promissory notes, was not a power to purchase such notes, but to loan money thereon; Recognizing the principle of these decisions as correct, it must be regarded as decisive, of the present case.

Having no corporate capacity to make the contract of purchase, the plaintiff never acquired any title to the note in suit, and the attempted act of purchase was strictly "*ultra vires*," and conferred no rights whatever,

Wiley vs. First Nat. Bank of Brattleboro. Am. Law Reg. June No. 1875, *p.* 342.

Matthews vs. Skinker, et al., Ib. Aug. No. 1876, *p.* 488.

Kansas Valley Nat. Bank of Topeka vs. Rowell, 2 *Dillon*, 371.

Hoffman vs. Hancock Mut. Life Ins. Co. in U. S. S. Ct., Oct. Tr. 1875, *reported in Vol.* 3 *Central Law Journal No.* 28, *p.* 448.

Upon this ground, the order denying a new trial is affirmed.

GILFILLAN, C. J., *dissenting.*—I am of opinion that while it may not have been the intention of the statute that banks organized under it shall engage in the business of trading in promissory notes, yet such a bank may, as incidental to its business of banking, invest its surplus funds in the purchase of promissory notes, stocks and similar securities; not for the purpose of trading in them, of buying and selling them, but of investing its unemployed funds, in them. Sec. 34 of the statute seems to contemplate that banks may hold such securities, obtained by purchase, for it requires that the quarterly statements to be made by the bank shall state not only loans or discounts, which would cover notes obtained by loans or discount, but also, stock and promissory notes."

And as it is not to be presumed as against a corporation any more than against a private person, that it has violated the law, (19 *N. Y.* 369, 2; 4 *Hill* 442; 3 *Comstock* 470;) This plaintiff must be presumed to have acquired this note in a lawful manner, until the contrary is shown; that is, that it purchased the note for the purpose of investing its unemployed funds, and not for the purpose of selling again.

I think there should be a new trial.

JAMES TAIT, *et al.*, *Appellants*, *vs.* JOSEPH THOMAS, *et al.* *Respondent.* } Filed April 11, '76.

In an action for trespass in which treble damages may be allowed, and a general verdict is returned, the presumption is that it includes all the damages that the plaintiff is entitled to.

GILFILLAN, C. J.—There are two ways in which the amount to be recovered under the statute allowing treble damages for certain trespasses (*Sec.* 28, *Chap.* 75, *General Statutes,*) may be ascertained.

First.—The court may instruct the jury to assess the actual damage, and render their verdict for treble that amount.

Second.—It may instruct the jury to return the single damage, and the fact whether the trespass was willful or involuntary; and the court may then treble the damage so found. The facts upon which the question of treble damages depend, must be passed upon by the jury, and not by the court. In this case it does not appear what instructions were given to the jury Their verdict was general, and the contrary not appearing, it is to be presumed that after ascertaining the character of the trespass, they have allowed the damages to which the plaintiffs are by law entitled.

Livingston vs. Platner, 1 *Cowen*, 175.

Judgment affirmed.

JOHN KNIGHT, *Respondent*, *vs.* JOHN ELLIOT, *Appellant.*

An affidavit filed to bring an appeal from the judgment of a Justice of the Peace must appear on its face to have been taken before a proper officer.

GILFILLAN, C. J.—According to the decision of this court in *McFarland vs. Butler*, 11 *Minn.*, 72, the filing of an affidavit by a party appealing from the judgment of the Justice of the Peace, is essential to give the appellate court jurisdiction.

In this case the paper filed, had a regular jurat, but there was no official designation to the name of the person before whom it purported to have been sworn.

There may be cases where such a defect can bo supplied by other proof, as in the *State vs. Green*, (3 *Green, N. J.*) 88, where the question was, whether certain officers had duly qualified, and the written oath produced had no official designation of the person before whom it was taken; and the court allowed extraneous proof of an official character. The court referring to a different holding of their court as to affidavits to be used as evidence on the trial of a cause, or as the foundation for some motion or proceeding in court, says: "Affidavits are very different from official or promissory oaths which are not at all in the nature of evidence; an affidavit when offered to be read in evidence, must appear upon the face of it to be what an affidavit ought to be, to entitle it to be read. It must appear to have been taken before the proper officer, and in compliance with all legal requirements."

And especially this requirement should be complied with, when the affidavit is to be presented to an officer for his immediate action upon it, and when he has no other means but the paper itself to determine its character.

The affidavit filed with a Justice to bring an appeal should be complete on its face.

Order appealed from affirmed.

ANDREW WARSOP, *Appellant*, *vs.* CITY OF HASTINGS, *Respondent*. Filed March 22, '76.

In all cases where equitable relief is sought through the extraordinary remedy of an injunction, the facts entitling the party to such relief, must be clearly and positively alleged and shown.

It is not enough that their existence may be inferred from the averments in the complaint.

The complaint in this case held insufficient under this rule.

Chap. 34, Special Laws 1869, authorized the City of Hastings at any time prior to August 1st, 1870, by a vote of the majority of its City Council, ratified by the voters of the city, to create and issue its bonds, &c., in aid of the St. P. and C. Railway Company.

It also enacted "that before said bonds should be issued, the question of their issue should be submitted and passed upon by the voters at any election held for that purpose, at any time, prior to said first day of August; and if such issue was by them approved, then that the bonds should be issued, and the council might make such agreements as they might deem proper with the company for, or relating to the disposal of the bonds or their proceeds.

Pursuant to this law the Council on the 3d May, 1870, duly adopted an ordinance authorizing the issue of a certain amount of bonds, and fully prescribing the terms and conditions upon which they should be issued, among which was one that no bonds should be issued until after the completion of the railway, as specified in the ordinance.

This ordinance was duly ratified by the people at an election held on the 15th of May, 1870, in pursuance of its provisions.

Held, That the ordinance was a proper exercise of power on the part of the City Council under the law in question.

The ordinance in question designated the 15th day of May, &c., as the day for holding such election, and directed the city clerk to give ten days notice, by publication. The ordinance was first published May 5th, when it took effect. The notice of election was given simultaneous with the publication of the ordinance.

Held sufficient.

Order appealed from affirmed.

CORNELL, J.

CITED:

SUFFICIENCY OF PUBLICATION OF NOTICE.

Clark vs. City of Janesville, 10 *Wis.*, 136.

RUSSELL BLAKELY, *Respondent*, *vs.* WILLIAM G. LEDUC, *Appellant*. Filed March 30, '76.

In 1863, B. M. and plaintiff as partners under the name of J. C. B. & Co., were engaged in transporting passengers by stage between La-Crosse and St. Paul.

The defendant and others owned and operated a ferry across the Mississippi River at Hastings in this State. In attempting to cross on the ferry boat on March 27th, 1863, the stage coach fell into the river, and Mathew McLean, a passenger, was drowned. McLean's administratrix thereupon brought an action against the Stage Company, under *Sec. 2, Chap. 77, General Statutes*, and in January, 1868, recovered judgment for $5,496.87.

The plaintiff brought the present action on March 5th, 1869. alleging that defendant for a certain fare to be paid him by said company, undertook safely and securely to transport said company's coach and the passengers therein (of whom McLean was one,) by means of the ferry aforesaid, across the Mississippi River, and that through defendant's failure to perform such undertaking, the coach and passengers were precipitated into the river and McLean drowned.

Held, That the cause of action is defendant's failure to perform his contract with the partnership, and that it is assignable.

Held further, That the two years limitation applicable to the action brought by the administratrax of McLean, under *Sec. 2, Chap. 77, Gen. Stat.*, does not apply to the action at bar, which could be brought at any time within six years after the breach complained of, as an action upon a contract, under *Sec. 6, Chap. 66, Gen. Stat.*

J. C. B. & Co.'s cause of action against defendant was personal property, and the interest of B. & M. therein, and in all its incidents, passed to plaintiff by the operation of a written instrument, executed by B., M. and plaintiff, dissolving their partnership, and providing that all the personal property of J. C. B. & Co. should be "retained by and be the property of" the plaintiff.

Plaintiff's right to recover on account of the recovery and payment of the judgment recovered by the administratrix, was a mere incident of J. C. B. & Co.'s original cause of action against defendant, and as such incident, passed to plaintiff by virtue of the instrument above mentioned.

Held, that upon the pleadings in this case, the substantial issue as respected the question of negligence, was this, viz: "Was the Stage

Company or defendant in charge of the ferry at the time of the accident?"

Certain testimony offered for the purpose of showing negligence held to have been properly rejected as having no relation to this issue. Defect of parties defendant can be objected to only by answer or demurrer.

Order denying new trial affirmed.

BERRY, J.

DANIEL H. ATWOOD, *Respondent*, *vs.* WILLIAM H. LANDIS, *Appellant*. } Filed April 28, '76.

The summons issued and served in this case, described the defendant by the name of "William A. Landers," no suggestion being made that that was not his true name.

Held, That the court acquired no jurisdiction over the person of the defendant, and a subsequent order made in the action amending the proceedings by substituting his true name, in the absence of any appearance on his part, was void.

CORNELL, J.—The similarity between the names "William H. Landis," and "William A. Landers," is not such as to constitute this a case of "*idem sonans*" It is not claimed that defendant was ever known by any other than his true name, nor does it appear from either the complaint or summons, that he was sued by the name of William A. Landers, because his real name was unknown.

Under these circumstances no jurisdiction was acquired over the person of the defendant, by the service and return of the summons in this case, and no appearance ever having been made for him in the action, all the proceedings therein were void. The leading and principal cases upon this point are well considered and distinguished by Allen, J., in *Farnham vs. Hildreth, 32 Barb., S. C. R.* 277, in whose conclusion as therein stated, we fully concur.

3 *Chitty Genl. Pr.* 171 *et seq.*

Cole vs. Hindson, et al., 6 *Durnford & East*, 234.

Judgment reversed.

ANNOUNCEMENTS.

The Gilfillan edition of Minnesota Reports. vols. 1 to 11.

We take great pleasure in announcing a reprint of the first eleven volumes of Minnesota Reports with notes by Hon. James Gilfillan, Chief Justice of Minnesota.

These volumes have so long been out of print, and so much called for, that we have decided to reprint them, and have made arrangements as above announced.

Prove that you desire the reprint by ordering it.

LATEST PUBLICATIONS.

Chitty on pleading.—New Ed., with American notes, 2 vols., - - 16 00

Philosophy of Law, etc., by Herbert Brown. 8 vo. 307 pp., cloth. - 2 50

The Notary Public, by W. R. Lynch. 8 vo., 178 pp., paper, - - 2 00

California Supreme Court Reports, vol. 50. 8 vo., 725 pp., full sheep, - 5 00

Law of Private Corporations, by John Frotiat. 8 vo., 275 pp., full sheep, 4 50

Journal Entries, by E. N. Wild, of Cincinnati. 8 vo., 428 pp., law sheep, 3 50

Law of the Road, or Wrongs and Rights of Travelers, by R. V. Rogers. 12 mo 283 pp., cloth, - - - - - 1 50

Probate Law, by Wm. L. Smith, 8 vo., law sheep, - - - - - 2 50

Law of Damages, by Geo. W. Field, 808 pp., law sheep, - - - - - 7 50

Reports of Cases in Law and Equity Determined in the Supreme Court of Iowa, Vol. XLI, by John J. Runnels, Reporter, 784 pp., law sheep - 5 00

Shaw's Index to Minn. Session Laws. 1848–1875. Full sheep. - $4 00

Minn. Reports, vol. 21, full sheep - 5 00

Minn. Session Laws. 1876, Gen. and Spec. together, full sheep. - - - - 2 00
Same, half sheep. - - - - 1 75

Otto's Reports on the Decisions of the Supreme Court of the United States, Vol. 1. 8vo. - - - - - 5 00

Greenleaf on Law of Evidence Vol. 1. By John Wilder May. 13th Ed. 8vo. 6 00

Redfield on Law of Wills, Vol. 2. 3d Ed., 8vo. - - - - - 6 00

A Treatise on Conveyances by Debtors to Defraud Creditors. By Orlando F. Bump. Second Ed., revised and enlarged. 8vo., 750 pp., Law Sheep. 6 50

Mitford & Tyler's Pleadings and Practice in Equity. By John Mitford (the late Lord Resedale.) & Samuel Tyler, L. L. D. 8vo., 774 pp. - - 6 50

Outlines of an International Code. By David Dudley Field. Second Ed., revised and enlarged. 8vo., 890 pp. 7 50

The Syllabi.

Vol. 1. SATURDAY, NOV. 18, 1876. No. 5.

PUBLISHED WEEKLY,

By JOHN B. WEST & CO.,

60 W. Third Street, - ST. PAUL, MINN.

Terms 3.00 per annum in Advance.

HOMER C. ELLER, Editor.

TABLE OF CONTENTS.

Change of Venue.—In the case of Sherwood *vs.* Nesbitt suit was instituted in the District Court of Ramsey county. Two of the defendants resided in the county of Anoka, and one in the county of Isanti. Summons was served July 7th, and on the 22d of July the defendants appeared in the action and served a demand under the statute, that the place of trial be changed to Anoka county. Issue was joined on the 28th of July following. No stipulation consenting to the change was entered into, and no application for an order changing the place of trial was made. Nothing further was done until 20th October, when notice of trial for General Term District Court Ramsey county, was served by plaintiffs on defendants' counsel, service of which was admitted without objection, and the cause was by plaintiffs counsel placed upon the calendar for that term. On the first day of the term there being no appearance for defendant, the case was at the instance of plaintiffs' counsel marked for trial. On the 23d of October, two weeks after the term commenced, notice was given by defendants that they would at a special term to be held November 4, in pursuance of their previous demand apply to the court for an order changing the place of trial of said cause from Ramsey to Anoka county, No reason or excuse for the delay in making the motion was suggested. Upon the motion coming before the court, Simons J. held that service of demand does not of itself change the place of trial, but it must be followed by a consent of parties or an order of the court. That in this case service of notice of trial by plaintiff was a notification that he did not consent to such change. That the provisions of statute in regard to changing the place of trial were for the benefit of defendants, and could be waived by them, and that under the special circumstance above set forth, the motion for a change came too late, and defendants by their laches must be considered as having waived their right to the change, and for that reason denied the motion.

Supreme Court, State of Minnesota.

Ole O. Moen, *Respondent*, *vs.* Wm. H. Eldred, *Appellant.* } Filed April 13, '76.

"The defendant for answer to plaintiff's complaint respectfully states and shows to this court, that he denies each and every allegation in said plaintiff's complaint contained."

Held, to be a *sufficient* denial though not commendable in form.

Berry, J.—The answer in this case commmences as follows: The defendant * * * for answer to plaintiff's complaint * * * respectfully states and shows to this court that he denies each and every allegation in said plaintiffs complaint contained &c. &c,

As to the sufficiency of this mode of denial the courts differ see *Blake vs. Eldred*, 18 *How. Pr.* 240. *Powers vs. Railroad Company* 3 *Hun.* 286. *People vs Christopher* 4 *Hun.* 805. *Chapman vs. Chapman* 34 *How. Pr.* 282. *Espinosa vs. Gregory* 40 *Cal.* 58. *Munn vs. Taulman* 1 *Kansas* 254. See also *Moaks Van Santvoords Pl.* 526 *Note* 3.

We think the form of answer above quoted is equivalent in effect, as well as in the intention of the pleader, to the following viz: The defendant for *answer* to plaintiff's complaint denies each and every allegation &c.

It is therefore a sufficient denial, although as a matter of course it is better in pleading as elsewhere not to use superfluous words.

Judgment and order for judgment reversed.

Board of County Commissioners of Houston County. *Appellants*, *vs.* The N, E. ¼ of the N. W. ¼ Section 7 Township 101 of Range 3 "W" and other Lands. } Filed April 25,'76.

In proceedings to enforce payment of taxes under Ch. 1 Gen. Laws of 1874, the objection, that the County Commissioners did not designate the paper in which the list of taxes should be published, is not proper matter of answer, but should be made by objection to, or motion to dismiss the proceedings, before answering.

In such proceedings it it good matter of defense *pro tanto*. That the County Commissioners have omitted to remit a part of the taxes on the list as directed by Ch. 10, Gen. Laws 1874.

Gilfillan, C. J.—In the proceedings to enforce against the lands involved, payment of taxes imposed for the year 1874, the owners interposed an answer alleging as matters defence.

First—That the Board of County Commissioners never by resolution designated the paper in which to publish the list of lands upon which the taxes are delinquent, as required by *Sec.* 112, *Chap.* 1, *Gen. Laws* 1874.

The second defence, as we gather it from the answer itself, and what seems to be conceded in the briefs of counsel, amounts to this: That, at its July session, 1874, the Board of County Commissioners equalized the assessments of property, and determined as the amount to be raised by taxes, upon five mills on the dollar of the assessed valuation, as equalized by them; that the State Board of Equalization, in September, increased the assessed valuation one hundred and thirty per cent.; and that the resolution levying five mills on the dollar, not having been modified nor any part of it remitted under *Chap.* 10, *Gen. Laws* 1875, the amount of tax appearing on the list is produced by estimating it at five mills on the dollar on the assessed valuation, as increased by the State Board. To the answer a demurrer was interposed and overruled.

As to the first of these defences, while we have no doubt that the objection goes to the jurisdiction of the Court in a point not cured by the statute, and if properly raised before it has been waived, fatal to the proceedings, we do not see how, under the statute, it is matter of defence or objection to the tax to be set up by answer. The proper way to make it available is by objection or motion to dismiss the proceedings before answering.

If, however, the answer alleges matters which entitle the party answering to relief in whole or in part, against the tax, it is not obnoxious to a demurrer.

The gist of the other defence in the answer is, that, by reason of the omission of the Board of County Commissioners to remit pursuant to *Chap.* 10, *Gen. Laws* 1875, the tax appearing on the list and claimed in the proceedings, is more than it ought to be. If the act referred to applies to the case, and its requirements of the County Commissioners are imperative, the defence is a good one *pro tanto*.

The act contemplates those cases where the County Commissioners had, instead of determining a gross sum to be raised for county purposes, fixed upon a percentage, and where the valuation having been raised by the State Board, the percentage on the valuation as increased would raise a larger amount and impose a heavier tax than was intended when the percentage was fixed, and the act therefore provides that, "the Board of County Commissioners in said counties are hereby empowered and instructed respectively to remit all taxes except the state tax, so as to make the amount of tax to be collected correspond with the valuation of said property at the time such percentage was fixed, and upon which such percentage was established." The intention of this was that the Commissioners should remit, so as to retain as a tax only so much as the tax would have been, had the State Board not raised the valuation.

By not merely empowering, but instructing the Board to remit that part of the tax, the act made it the duty of the Commissioners to remit it, which duty, if performed, would have materially diminished the taxes on this land; and while it is the theory of the act of 1874, that no omission shall render the tax absolutely void, it at the same time intends that the omission shall not prejudice the tax-payer.

The answer presents a defence to part of the tax appearing on the list, and the demurrer was rightly overruled.

Order sustained, and the case will be certified to the Court below for further proceedings.

ABBIE A. POTTS, *Respondent*,
vs.
STEPHEN NEWELL, Sheriff of Dakota Co., Minn., and CARIVEAU & FONTAINE, *Appellants*.
Filed Apr. 28, '76.

Where O'N. contracted to deliver to G., when the crop should be thrashed, one third of a certain crop of wheat, the third to be set apart at the thrashing machine,the right of G., under the contract is assignable, and it not appearing that he has or claims any other right with respect to the crop, it will pass by a chattel mortgage of "all the right, title and interest of the said G. in and to certain crop of wheat," describing it, so that when set apart, the title to the third will at once vest in the mortgagee.

GILFILLAN, C. J.—Conceding, as is contended by defendants, that the contract between Gauthier and O'Neil created the relation of landlord and tenant, and that the title to the entire crops was in O'Neil until the one-third which he was to pay or deliver to Gauthier as rent should be set apart as agreed upon, still the plaintiff, as the case stands, was entitled to recover. In that view of the character of the contract, Gauthier had under it the right to demand and receive one-third of the wheat as soon as it was thrashed, and this right would draw to it the legal title to the third, the instant ths separation should be made, as agreed upon.

This right of Gauthier was as clearly assignable as the right to receive a specified rent in money, and, in case of assignment, the title to the third of the wheat would, upon its being set apart, vest at once in the assignee, precisely as it would vest in the assignor if no assignment were made.

The mortgage describes the property intended by it as "all the right, title and interest of the said Louis Gauthier in and to that certain crop of wheat raised upon the land of the said Gauthier, situated in the town of Egan, county of Dakota, and State of Minnesota, by one Robert O'Neil, during the year 1875." The crop then having been cut, and then standing in the shock on the land.

As it does not appear that Gauthier had or claimed any right, title or interest with respect to the wheat, except the right under his contract with O'Neil, to demand and receive one-third of it, the presumption must be, that he intended to pass the right, although it may not be very accurately described in the mortgage.

This being so, the wheat sued for became the property of the plaintiff, the instant it was set apart.

Order appealed from affirmed.

NOTE.—Gauthier was the owner of certain lands in Dakota county, which in April, 1875, he let to O'Neil, to be "farmed on shares." Under this letting, O'Niel was to furnish everything and deliver to Gauthier at the machine, when thrashed, one-third of all grain raised on the land, as his (the owner's) share for the use of the land. O'Neil sowed the land with wheat, and in the month of August, after the same had been cut, and while it was standing in the shock, defendant Newell, as sheriff of said county, and by virtue of an execution issued out of the District Court of Ramsey county, in a proceeding wherein defendants Cariveau & Fontaine had recovered a judgment against Gauthier, levied upon one-third of this wheat, as the property of Gauthier, and to satisfy said judgment; some days before the levy, however, and while the wheat was still in the shock, Gauthier duly executed a chattel mortgage of all his right, title and interest in and to said crop of wheat, to the plaintiff, to secure an antecedent debt then due. When the wheat was thrashed defendants took possession, and upon demand being made by plaintiff, refused to surrender the same, but proceeded to sell it at execution sale, and apply the proceeds to the payment of their judgment against Gauthier; suit was then brought by the plaintiff for the conversion. At the trial defendants having failed to prove their judgment against Gauthier, claimed that the agreement between Gauthier and O'Neil created the relation of landlord and tenant; that they were not joint owners of the crop at the time of the execution of the mortgage, but that title was absolutely in O'Niel, and therefore nothing passed to plaintiff by virtue of the mortgage; and asked the Court to instruct the jury to find for the defendants, which request was granted and a verdict for defendants entered. A motion for a new trial was then made for error in this instruction, the grounds urged being that Gauthier had complete title, to the extent of one-third of the crop, at the time of the mortgage, which passed directly to plaintiff; or assuming that the position of defendants was correct, that he still had, by virtue of his contract with O'Neil, a contingent interest in the crop that was conveyable, and which passed to plaintiff and culminated in an absolute title as soon as division was made at the machine, and took precedence of defendants' levy. A new trial being granted, defendants appealed to Supreme Court from the order.

JULIUS SEMROW, *Appellant*, *vs.* ALVIRA SEMROW, *Respondent.* } Filed Nov. 11, '76.

Errors appearing upon the face of a judgment, or in the proceedings resulting in a judgment, are to be corrected either by a motion for a new trial or an appeal.

The authority given by *Sec.* 25, *Chap.* 62, *Gen. Stat.* to revise and alter a judgment for alimony, is to be exercised only upon new facts occurring after the judgment, or perhaps also upon facts occurring before the judgment, of which a party was excusably ignorant at the time when the judgment was rendered.

When a gross sum is adjudged to a divorced woman, as her permanent alimony, the fact that subsequently to such adjudication, a child of the divorced parties, the care, custody and education of which was committed to the mother, dies, furnishes no reason for reducing the alimony. Where it is claimed that a mortgage has been procured wrongfully and by duress, in part satisfaction of a judgment for alimony, redress is to be had in a regular action brought for that purpose, and not by a motion in the divorce suit to be heard upon affidavits.

BERRY, J.—Upon the points presented by counsel in this Court, this may be taken to be an appeal from the order of the Court below refusing to "revise and alter" a judgment for alimony, and refusing to direct the plaintiff to release and deliver up a certain mortgage alleged to have been obtained by duress, in part satisfaction of such judgment. It is first claimed that the judgment should have been revised and altered on account of errors appearing upon its face or errors in the proceedings of which it was the result. As with respect to judgments in general. the correction of such errors is to be accomplished either by a motion for a new trial or by appeal. (*Grant vs Schmidt, MSS., May*, 1875.) The authority given by *Sec.* 25, *Ch.* 62, *Gen. Stat.*, to revise and alter a judgment for alimony, is to be exercised only upon new facts occurring after the judgment, or perhaps, also upon facts occurring before the judgment, of which a party was excusably ignorant at the time when the judgment was rendered.

Perkins vs. Perkins, 12 *Mich.* 456.
Blythe vs. Blythe, 25 *Iowa* 266.
Fisher vs. Fisher, 32 *Iowa* 20.
Wilde vs. Wilde, 36 *Iowa* 319.
See also, *Graves vs. Graves*, 108 *Mass.* 314.

In this case there was no fact existing at the time of the rendition of the judgment and bearing upon the matter of alimony, of which defendant was excusably ignorant. The only new fact insisted upon is the death, since the rendition of the judgment, of a child of the parties hereto, the care, custody and education of which was awarded to plaintiff. But as by the terms of the judgment the alimony in question was awarded as "her (the plaintiff's) permanent alimony," and not as an allowance for the child, the fact of the child's death becomes unimportant, since it does not furnish any reason why the amount awarded as *her* alimony—that is to say, alimony awarded for her own use—should be reduced. In passing, we observe further that it is by no means certain that the provisions as to alteration and revision of alimony apply to a case in which alimony is awarded, as in this instance, in a *gross* sum. In Illinois it has been held that a similar authority is to be exercised only with reference to what is styled "stipendary alimony," by which we understand alimony payable in the manner of an annuity. (*Plaster vs. Plaster*, 47 *Ill.* 290.)

This brings us to the other branch of the case; viz: that which respects the mortgage; as to this, we are of opinion that defendant cannot obtain the relief which he seeks in the present form of proceeding. If, as is claimed, the mortgage was obtained wrongfully and by duress, there is no reason why defendant cannot obtain proper redress in a regular action brought for that purpose; but a right of property like that involved in the controversy respecting the mortgage, cannot properly be determined upon a motion like that made in this case, to be heard upon affidavits.

Order affirmed.

A. H. REED, *Respondent*, *vs.* E. C. NEWTON, *Appellant.* } Filed April 20, '76.

In an action of ejectment allegations in the answer that defendant entered under an official deed, has had no notice of any defects invalidating the deed, and has made improvements and paid taxes, are not admitted by failure to reply.

Judgment affirmed.

GILFILLAN, C. J.

A. H. REED, *et al.*, *Appellants*, *vs.* MARY PIXLEY, *et al.*, *Respondents.* } Filed April 19, '76.

In an action against two defendants. upon account stated by them jointly, where the answer puts in issue the stating of the account, it is competent for either defendant to show that the account was not stated by him; but if the plaintiff proves the stating of the account by one defendant, he is entitled to recover against that one alone, under *Chap.* 67, *Laws* 1873.

Order denying new trial reversed.

BERRY, J.

HERMAN BISBEE, *Appellant.* vs. LOUIS E. TORINUS, *et al.* *Respondents.* — Filed Apr. 25,'76.

Where the consideration of a note was a permit to cut timber on lands in Wisconsin, upon an answer alleging a failure of consideration, by reason that at the time of giving the permit the lands had been sold for taxes and bid in by the county, and that the statutes of Wisconsin prohibit the cutting of timber on land so sold while the certificate of sale is held by the county, the introduction merely of the tax deed and certificate of tax-sales does not establish the defence; but the levy of the taxes and the other acts to be done before a tax sale can be had under the laws of Wisconsin, must also be proved.

Judgment reversed and new trial ordered.

GILFILLAN, C. J.

DARWIN STOCKING, *et al.*, Executors, &c., *Respondents,* vs. WILLIAM HANSON, *et al.*, *Appellant.* — Filed Ap. 20,'76

When under section 36, chap. 66, General Statutes, an application for substitution is made within one year, the statute regards the application as *prima facie* in time, and the granting of the substitution is almost a matter of course.

But when it is made after the lapse of a year, the application is *prima facie* too late, and it is for the party applying to excuse his delay.

In such case the supplemental complaint required should set forth not only the grounds upon which the application is based, but should also set forth some sufficient excuse for the delay in making it. If the issue of facts raised by an answer to the supplemental complaint is tried, it is neccessary for the applicant to establish the facts pleaded in excuse for his delay.

The facts appearing in the complaint in this case held to show gross loches on plaintiffs' part in the absence of excuse or explanation of their delay in making their supplemental complaint.

The District Court having jurisdiction of the subject matter of an action, and having acquired jurisdiction of the parties, possesses the power to proceed to the final disposition of the action; and while it ought to cease to exercise its jurisdiction over a party at his death, the neglect to do so is an error to be corrected by some proceeding in the action in which the error occurs, and the judgment rendered after the party's death, though erroneous, is not on that account to be attacked in a collateral action; such judgment is voidable when properly assailed, but not void.

When other persons are substituted in place of a deceased party to an action under the provisions of section 36, chap. 66, General Statutes. it is open to them to move to set aside a judgment entered after the decease of the party whom they succeed on account of error in entering the same after such decease.

If the motion be denied, they may appeal to the Supreme Court from the order of denial as a final order affecting a substantial right made upon a summary application in an action after judgment.

If the action be one for the recovery of real property, they may elect to let the judgment stand, and take a second trial under section 5, chap. 75, General Statutes.

Order allowing demurrer reversed.

BERRY J.

CITED:

EFFECT OF GROSS LACHES:

Beach vs. Reynolds. 53 *N. Y.* 1.
Medbury vs. Swan, 46 *N. Y.* 200.
Pendleton vs. Fay, 3 *Paige*, 204.

JUDGMENT AFTER DEATH OF PARTY VALID.

Hayes vs. Shaw, 20 *Minn.* 405.

CHARLES MCCARTHY, *Respondent*, vs. CITY OF ST. PAUL, *Appellant.* — Filed April 10, 1876.

Defendant under and in pursuance of its charter of March 6th, 1868, by the authorized action of the proper authorities, caused the then established grade of Mississippi street to be altered, thereby rendering it necessary for plaintiff to lower the grade of his residence property, and a certain dwelling house thereon adjacent to such street, in order to conform to the new grade, and to make his said property accessible and fit for use in respect thereto, and also making it necessary to build a retaining wall on one side of said property to protect the same from encroachments certain to occur from adjoining lots by reason of such necessary change in the grade of his own.

Held, That under such charter the city became liable to plaintiff, for all damages necessarily resulting to him, in respect to such property from the change in the established grade of the street.

That an action for the recovery of such damages accrued to plaintiff, and might be maintained by him whenever and as soon as the alteration in the grade of the street became legally and finally determined and fixed.

That his right of action was not taken away nor affected by the amended charter of March 5th, 1874.

Neither the street, nor the lots affected by the alteration of the grade having been actually graded to correspond therewith, the necessary *cost* of conforming the latter thereto, is a proper matter for consideration upon the question of damages, and is not objectionable on the ground of its being contingent and prospective,

The cost of a retaining wall was also properly allowed.

Judgment affirmed.

CITED:

CORNELL, J.

BASIS OF DAMAGES.

Stowell vs. City of Milwaukee, 31 *Wis.* 523.

ENFORCEMENT OF STATUTORY RIGHT.

Lowell vs. Wyman, 12 *Cush.* 273.

2 *Dill. Mun. Corp's, Sec.* 759, *p.* 868.

RETAINING WALL PROPER ITEM OF DAMAGES.

Cahill vs. Eastman, 18 *Minn.* 324.

LUCINDA HOSTETTER, *et al.*, *Respondent*, *vs.* JOSEPH ALEXANDER; *Appellant.* } Filed April 28, '76.

An appeal taken within six months after the *entry* of the judgment appealed from, is in time.

Johnson vs. Carpenter 7 Minn. 176 followed upon the point that the privileged character of a negotiable note does not extend to a mortgage by which the same is secured.

BERRY, J.—This appeal was taken within six months "after the entry" of the judgment appealed from. It was therefore in time.

Gen. Laws 1869, *Chap.* 70.

Humphrey vs. Havens, 9 *Minn.* 318.

The principal question presented by this case was examined and considered in *Johnson vs. Carpenter*, 7 *Minn.* 176. It was there determined that "when a debt is secured by a mortgage and also by a negotiable promissory note, the mortgage is a *chose in action*, as between the mortgagor and any subsesequent assignee, and is taken subject to the state of accounts between the mortgagor and mortgagee at the time of the assignment;" and, in effect, that the privileged character of the note as negotiable paper does not extend to the mortgage by which it is secured, but that the mortgage is exposed to the same defences in the hands of an assignee as in the hands of the mortgagee. If this was not the only ground upon which the decision in *Johnson vs. Carpenter* was based, it is evident that it was the ground which received most consideration in that case from the Court and counsel, and upon which the Court mainly relied. Notwithstanding the doubt which may be thrown around the original soundness of Johnson vs. Carpenter, by the comparatively recent case of Carpenter vs. Longan, 16 Wallace 271, and the considerations there suggested, we are not disposed to disregard or overrule a decision of our own court so distinctly made.

It follows that in our opinion the court below erred in declining to pass upon the issue as to the want or failure of the consideration of the notes and mortgages involved in the action.

Judgment reversed.

JAMES A. LUSK, *Resdondent*, *vs.* E. C. BELOTE, *Appellant.* } Filed March 28, '76.

In August, September and October, 1872, defendant was keeping "The Park Place Hotel," a public inn and boarding house, in the city of St. Paul.

On Sept. 20th, 1872, the plaintiff, his wife, and four children, being inmates of the hotel, a gold watch belonging to plaintiff, and certain articles of jewelry belonging to two of the children mentioned, were stolen from the room occupied by the plaintiff and his family.

The jewelry consisted of "ordinary articles of wearing apparel and ornaments of the plaintiff's two daughters," to whom the same belonged, and was brought to the hotel when they came there.

The plaintiff's wife and six children became inmates of the hotel on August 7th, 1872, and (with the exception of two children who left a few days before the theft,) remained there until some time in October following.

The plaintiff was not a resident of this State, but at the time when they came to the hotel, his wife and children were living, and for three or four years previous had been living, in St. Paul, sometimes keeping house and sometimes staying at the hotel or boarding house, the plaintiff being in the habit of making them an occasional visit as often as two or three times a year. The plaintiff arrived at St. Paul and became an inmate of the hotel about Sept. 10, '72.

An inn-keeper is by the common law responsible for the loss in his inn of the goods of a traveler, who is his guest, except when the loss arises from the negligence of the guest, or the act of God, or of the public enemy.

But this strict liability exists only in favor of travellers; as respects the loss of the jewelry, the defendant's liability depends upon the *status* of the plaintiff's two daughters, to whom the same belonged, and they were not *travellers*.

The evidence showing that the plaintiff came to defendant's inn as a traveller, and was received as such, his *status* as a traveller must be presumed to have continued, unless something appears affirmatively to the contrary.

This presumption is not overthrown by proof of an agreement by which plaintiff was to pay special rates for himself and family, lower than those ordinarily charged for transient guests, nor by the fact that he remained in the inn for a month.

CITED: BERRY, J.

LIABILITY OF INN-KEEPERS.

2 *Kent's Com.* 592–7.
Shaw vs. Berry, 31 *Maine*, 478.
Sibley vs. Aldrich, 33 *N. H.*. 553.
Hulett vs. Swift. 33 *N. Y.*, 571.
Wilkins vs. Earle, 44 *N. Y.*, 172.
1 *Chitty on Contracts*, (11 *Am. Ed.*) 674–677 *and notes.*

CHANGE OF STATUS FROM TRAVELER TO BOARDER.

Jalie vs. Cardinal, 35 *Wis.* 118 *and cases cited.*

[NOTE.—With reference to the jewelry belonging to the daughters of plaintiff, court say that they, not having the *status* of travelers, but rather that of dwellers in St. Paul, although their domicile *in law* might be in another State, defendant was not liable to plaintiff for their loss. Ordered that plaintiff stipulate within twenty days to reduce the judgment to the sum of $200, the value of plaintiff's gold watch stolen, otherwise a new trial would be granted.]

ANNOUNCEMENTS.

The Gilfillan edition of Minnesota Reports. vols. 1 to 11.

We take great pleasure in announcing a reprint of the first eleven volumes of Minnesota Reports, with notes by Hon. James Gilfillan, Chief Justice of Minnesota.

These volumes have so long been out of print, and so much called for, that we have decided to reprint them. and have made arrangements as above announced.

Prove that you desire the reprint by ordering it.

A Statute Law Against Forfeiture of Life Policies.

Massachusetts alone has this, and the NEW ENGLAND MUTUAL LIFE, of Boston, is the oldest chartered Mutual Life Insurance Company in the United States. Policies issued by this Company on life plan secure two years' insurance for each premium paid. Long term policies, up to age 60 or 70, on good lives, at from 20 to 40 per cent. less than life rates. No Tontine or other fallacious form of policy issued by this Company. Agents wanted throughout the State.

Address,

J. H. McDONALD,
General Agent,
13 St. Paul.

THE AMERICAN REPRINT

OF THE

ENCYCLOPÆDIA BRITANNICA,

New Ninth Edition.

Volumes 1, 2, 3 and 4 are now ready.

This is the Largest and Best work of the kind in the English Language. Every Article is a Complete Treatise by the most Eminent Writers.

Send for Specimen Pages to

JOHN B. WEST & CO.

HOUCH & DIXON,

BOOKSELLERS AND STATIONERS,

15 East Third St.,

ST. PAUL, - - MINN.

5

BARGAINS.

One set New York Court of Appeals Reports—62 volumes, - - - $132
Second hand, excellent condition.

American Law Register, 14 volumes, - $40

John D. O'Brien. Homer C. Eller

O'BRIEN & ELLER,

ATTORNEYS AT LAW,

Ingersoll Block, ST. PAUL, MINN.

H. A. PARTRIDGE,

Lawyer and Notary Public,

ROOM NO. 1, HARRISON BLOCK,

MINNEAPOLIS, - - MINN.

WARREN H. MEAD. CYRUS J. THOMPSON.

MEAD & THOMPSON,

ATTORNEYS AT LAW,

Cor. Third and Wabashaw Sts,, St. Paul.

Special attention given to Bankrupt Proceedings and Collections. Loans securely placed.

SESSION LAWS.

We have the Session Laws of Minnesota from 1849 to 1875 inclusive, 34 vols., which we offer in sets, or by the volume.

Parties wishing to fill their sets, will do well to send list at once.

We offer:

1849	$4.00	1872	$3.50
1861	2.00	1873	2.50
1862	2.50	1874	2.00
1863	2.00	1875	2.00
1864	2.00	1876	1.75
1871	2.00		

Bound in Half Sheep.

We can supply Seals of any Size or Design.

NOTARIAL SEALS for any County, $6.75

JOHN B. WEST & CO,

WE have covers for filing and preserving THE SYLLABI, which we will send by mail, on receipt of price, 35 cents.

THE SYLLABI.

VOL. 1. SATURDAY, NOV. 25, 1876. No. 6.

PUBLISHED WEEKLY,

By JOHN B. WEST & CO.,

60 W. Third Street, - ST. PAUL, MINN.

Terms 3 00 per annum in Advance.

HOMER C. ELLER, Editor.

TABLE OF CONTENTS.

FROM the *Chicago Legal News*, we observe that in the case of Spafford vs. Lovejoy, *et al.*, removed from the circuit court for District of Minnesota to the Supreme Court of United States, a decision has been reached by appellate court reversing the judgment of court below, holding that to discharge a member of a firm from the claim of one who has had no dealings with it prior to its dissolution, but who knew of its existence, and who were the members, it is not necessary that either actual notice or public notice in a newspaper be shown, but only that the notice of dissolution be so generally communicated to the business men of the vicinity, as to be likely to come to the knowledge of all, and that a refusal to charge, that if such notice was given, the jury were at liberty to infer knowledge, is error.

AMONG the exchanges that have already put in an appearance, we are glad to greet the familiar face of the *Albany Law Journal*, with its weekly discussion of legal topics and collection of items of interest to the profession. The *Chicago Legal News*, with many valuable and interesting decisions reported in full. The *Insurance Law Journal*, a monthly periodical, published by C. C. Hine, New York, devoted to reporting in full the many current decisions made upon that important subject has also arrived. It is of special value to Insurance men, and lawyers, making that branch a specialty.

IF you desire reliable blanks arranged in the most convenient manner for immediate use, send for some of ours put up in blocks, being fastened together, though easily seperated, blanks of the same kind do not get scattered or mixed up with other papers, but are always ready for use, face up.

Supreme Court, State of Minnesota.

C. C. Spottswood, *Respondent*, *vs.* Mary M. Herrick, *Appellant*. } Filed April 24, 1876.

The complaint in this case though flagrantly indefinite and uncertain held as against a demurrer, to state facts constituting a cause of action.

S. was owner in fee of certain real estate subject to a mortgage to H., on which one hundred and sixty seven dollars was paid on account of interest; H. claiming. in her notice of sale that the full amount of the principal and interest of the mortgage as they appeared upon its face, was due at the date of the notice, foreclosed the mortgage upon the basis that no part of the principal or interest had been paid, and the mortgaged premises were sold for the full amount of the principal and interest, as such amount, and not otherwise. S. in the exercise of his right of redemption having been compelled for the use and benefit of H. to pay the full amount of the principal and interest of the mortgage, without any deduction on account of the payment of the sum of $167, is entitled to recover said sum from H. in an action for money had and received.

Order overruling demurrer affirmed.

Berry, J.

Justus Carpenter, *et al.*, *Respondents*, *vs.* Oscar H. Comfort, *et al.*, *Appellants*.

An order denying a motion to change the place of trial is not appealable.

Gilfillan C. J.—This is an appeal from an order denying a motion to change the place of trial. Such an order does not involve the merits of the action, or any part thereof, under sub. 3, of sec. 8, ch. 86, General Statutes. If reviewable at all, it must be upon an appeal from the judgment (or perhaps from an order denying a new trial) as an order affecting the judgment.

Appeal dismissed.

Elias S. Palmer, *Appellants*, *vs.* Howard W. Bates and Angeline E. Keyes, *Respondents*, } Filed April 11, '76.

On July 2nd, 1867, plaintiff being owner in fee of a one hundred and sixty acre tract of land mortgaged the same to W. to secure three promissory notes W. assigned the notes and mortgage to Birge.

On January 22d, 1869, Birge executed and delivered to plaintiff a sealed instrument releasing one forty of the one hundred and sixty from the operation of the mortgage.

April 15th, 1869, Birge assigned the mortgage and two notes (the other note having been paid and taken up) to Bates; Bates foreclosed by advertisement and at the foreclosure sale on Jan'y. 17th, 1870, the whole one hundred and sixty was sold to the defendant who on the same day received a certificate of sale which together with an affidavit of publication was duly recorded.

The release was not recorded until Sept. 9th, 1871.

The defendant had no actual notice of the release until long after her purchase nor until after she had paid for the land purchased. At the date of the foreclosure sale the plaintiff was in possession of the entire one hundred and sixty.

Held, That the release as an instrument by which the title to real estate might be affected in law or equity was under sec. 26, ch. 40, General Statutes "a conveyance" within the meaning of sec. 21 of that chapter which declares that every conveyance of real estate not recorded in the office of the proper Register of Deeds shall be void as against any purchaser in good faith and for a valuable consideration of the same real estate whose conveyance is first duly recorded.

Held, That notwithstanding the plaintiff's possession of the released forty at the time of the foreclosure sale the defendant was a purchaser in good faith and that therefore as to her, the release was void.

Judgment affirmed.

Berry, J.

Cited:

Possession as notice.

Morrison vs. March, 4 *Minn.* 422.
Groff vs. Ramsey, 19 *Ibid.* 44.

Jane E. Colvill and Wm. Colvill, her husband, *Respondents*. *vs.* Robert B. Langdon, *et al.*, *Appellants*. } Filed April 29, '76.

In an action for a personal tort upon the wife, the joinder of the husband as plaintiff with her, is only an irregularity which may be disregarded or corrected at any time, by striking out the name of the husband.

In an action for an assault and battery committing (*sic.*)

while entering against plaintiff's consent and to overcome her resistance to such entry upon premises occupied by her, it cannot be shown in mitigation of the damages that the defendants were acting under authority of a railroad company, and that there were proceedings by it still pending for condemnation of the premises; an inaccuracy in stating the rule of law to the jury in one part of the charge if corrected by the general scope of the entire charge, so that this court can see that the jury could not have been misled by the inaccuracy, is not ground for reversal.

When on a motion for a new trial, an order is entered below denying the motion *pro forma*, whether the Court will, on an appeal from the order, consider any point upon which there has been only a formal, but no actual consideration and decision of the court below, such as the point that the verdict is excessive, or is not sustained by the evidence, *is doubted*, but not necessary to be decided in this case.

GILFILLAN, C. J.—Action for assault and battery upon the plaintiff, Jane E. By Ch. 63, General Laws, 1869, amending sec. 29, Ch. 66, *Gen. Statutes*, a married woman may bring an action like this without joining her husband. Joining him in this case was an irregularity. But as the complaint clearly shows that the cause of action is in her alone, and as defendants could not be in any way prejudiced or embarrassed, in their defence by the mis-joinder, no substantial right is affected, and the court below might either disregard it or correct it at once, by striking out the name of the husband.

The plaintiff, with her husband, was in June, 1871, residing upon certain premises in the city of Red Wing, and the defendant, McDonald, with a large number of men went upon the premises and commenced digging for the purpose of constructing a railroad track, and upon plaintiff attempting to interrupt the digging, some of the men pushed her away, and afterwards in the prosecution of their work pushed her out of the house; as to the other defendant's who were not present participating in the assault, the plaintiff's theory is, that they had concerted a plan that McDonald and his men should enter upon the premises and construct the track against any opposition which plaintiff or her husband might make, and should use such force as might be necessary to overcome the opposition; that the assault and battery was contemplated by such plan, if it should be necessary to effect the construction of the track, and was made upon the procurement of such other defendants.

None of the exceptions taken during the trial require notice but this one.

The defendants, who claim that they, and McDonald and his men, were, in entering upon the premises acting under the authority of the railroad company, offered in evidence for the purpose of mitigating damages, proceedings of condemnation of the premises up to and including the award of the commissioners, filed Dec. 2d, 1870, and an appeal from that award to the District Court, pending at the time of the assault, and also a tender of the amount of the award in April, 1871, before plaintiff, and her husband moved upon the premises. This evidence would fall short of showing any right, or reasonable claim of right to enter the premises. A condemnation without payment of the compensation awarded would not establish such right, and a tender before the award to be paid was ascertained by determination of the appeal was of no effect, the fact that there were proceedings pending which might result in giving the company the right to use the land, would not excuse nor extenuate the conduct of defendants, and the proof was properly excluded. The court, upon plaintiff's second request, instructed the jury that if the defendants, or either of them were accessory, before the fact to the assault and battery, they should return a verdict against such of the defendants as were accessory, which was correct. On plaintiff's third request, the court instructed the jury "that in order to constitute the defendant's, Dodge, Langdon and Van Slyck, accessories to the said assault and battery, before the fact, it is not necessary that they should have directed, advised, procured or connived, at the forcible entry by McDonald and other persons unknown, upon the premises with intent thereby to take forcible possession of the premises, if what they or either of them directed or procured, naturally or ordinarily produced the assault and battery," the objection made to the instruction, is that the jury might understand from it that the directing or procurement by one of the defendants would render the others liable, and if the instruction stood alone, it would be open to that criticism; but any inaccuracy in one part of a charge, especially a mere general proposition, if corrected by the general scope of the entire charge, so that we can see that the jury could not have been misled by the inaccuracies, is not ground of reversal, except as to this particular instruction, the rule laid down by the charge, is that such defendant's liability depends on his own act, or the act of others under his direction or procurement. It is very explicitly stated in the instruction upon defendant's second request, that if McDonald went in and did what the evidence shows "without the advice or consent of either one of the defendants, then the verdict should be for such of the defendants as did not direct or have knowledge of his acts," we are satisfied that the jury could not have been misled by what appears to be an inadvertent verbal inaccuracy in the general proposition stated in the instruction complained of.

The evidence makes no case for the application of the rule in defendant's fourth request the plaintiff was in possession; it is to be presumed rightfully, and the parties who entered without their consent were presumptively wrong-doers whom plaintiff had a right to eject or resist.

The points that the verdict is excessive and that it is against evidence cannot be considered for the case does not purport to contain all the evidence given at the trial.

The order appealed from states that the motion for a new trial is denied *pro forma* from this we understand that there was no actual decision of the motion, but an order entered denying it as a form and without any consideration of the points raised. The parties to such a motion are entitled to the judgment and decision of the court below on the merits upon all points on which the motion is made and there is an appropriate remedy to enforce the right to such judgment and decision. The theory of the Judicial system in this state is that the parties shall have first a decison of the court below and then a review of that decision in this court. The practice which it getting to be very common of entering a *pro forma* order without consideration deprives the parties of the right to the judgment of the lower court, and in effect would make of this court the court to decide the application in the first instance rather than a court of review as is intended by the constitution. The objection to this court making a first decision upon a point raised in the court below, is peculiarly applicable to the points that a verdict is excessive or that it is not sustained by evidence, to judge of which points correctly the court in which the trial was had, has advantages not possessed by this court; we doubt whether we ought in an appeal to consider here a point involved in the order appealed from, if the record shows that there is no actual decision upon it in the court below.

We do not decide the question now but call attention of courts below, and of the bar to it, so that parties may not be taken by surprise when the question should be decided.

Order affirmed.

HIRAM ROGERS *et al.*, *Plaintiffs in error*,
vs.
THE CITY OF ST. PAUL, *Defendant in error*,
Filed April 8, '76.

The term "local improvements in the constitutional amendment of 1869 (sec. chap. 51 Laws 1869) signifies improvements made in a particular locality by which the real property adjoining or near such locality is specially benefited."

Under the provisions of "An act to authorize the City of St. Paul to levy assessments for local improvements" approved March 6th, 1871, as amended Feb. 29th, 1872, the determination of the question whether the special benefits which will result from a proposed local improvement will be as great as the expense of making it, or, in other words, whether the improvement can be paid for without subjecting the property specially benefited to taxation in excess of the special benefits, as well as the whole matter of ordering the improvement to be made, is submitted to the common council, and their determination in the premises is final and conclusive, unless, perhaps, in case of fraud or mistake.

It was competent for the Legislature to give this final and conclusive effect to the determination of the common council. The act above cited is not unconstitutional or invalid, because it permits a contract for the making of a local improvement to be let without any restriction upon the Board of Public Works, as to the price to be paid. In respect to the assessment of the expense of making a particular local improvement, the Board of Public Works exercises an authority with which it is competent for the Legislature to invest it.

When money is to be raised by taxation, it is for the Legislature in its discretion to determine how much should be raised, and for what purpose, and to mark out the boundaries of the tax district, or to provide for the determination of the amount to be raised, and the purpose of raising it, and for the designation of the tax district by some subordinate authority, it being, of course, necessary that the purpose of the taxation should specially pertain to the tax district.

Under the act above cited, the determination of the purpose for which money shall be raised, is committed to the common council, the determination of how much shall be raised, is to some extent committed to both the common council and the Board of Public Works, while the marking out of the boundaries of the tax district is committed to the latter exclusively; upon the subject thus committed to it, the action of the Board of Public Works is conclusive, and it was competent for the Legislature to make it so.

In the proceedings in this case, the common council's order of reference propounded to the Board of Public Works, the question whether the paving of Third street with a Nicholson pavement or other wooden pavement, was proper and necessary.

The report of the Board answers this question in its own terms in the affirmative; the final order of the council directs that Third street, from the so-called Seven Corners to Sibley street, be paved with a "wooden block pavement."

Held, That these descriptions of the pavement were sufficient; the generality of the description in the final order of the Council, is not an unlawful attempt on the part of the council to delegate to the Board of Public Works the power, and to impose upon it the duty, of determining the character of the improvement. In accepting a bid for a particular kind of pavement, the Board is not performing the functions of the council in determining the character of the improvement, but is discharging its duty to let the work to the lowest bidder, cost and quality considered.

The provisions of section 27, of the act cited in reference to a plan and profile of a proposed improvement in reference to specifications for doing the same, held to have been sufficiently complied with, in this case.

Judgment affirmed.

BERRY J.

CITED:

TAX DISTRICTS—DEFINITION OF LOCAL IMPROVEMENTS.

Cooley on Taxation, 109–110–177–419–423–447–459.

Dillon Mun. Corp's, §§. 400–401–586–596–597–*and cases cited.*

Dorgan vs. Boston, 12 *Allen*, 223.

Stinson vs. Smith, 8 *Minn.*, 366.

POWER OF LEGISLATURE.

Cooley on Taxation, Ch. 2.

LEGISLATURE TO PROVIDE FOR MANNER OF RAISING TAX.

Cooley on Taxation, Ch. 20 *and pp.* 449–51.

THE STATE OF MINNESOTA *ex rel.* LUTHER L. BAXTER, *Relator*, *vs.* LUTHER M. BROWN, *Respondent*, } Filed April 5, '76.

Section 10 Art. VI of the Constitution declares that "in case the office of any Judge shall become vacant before the expiration of the regular term for which he was elected the vacancy shall be filled by appointment by the Governor until a successor is elected and qualified; And such successor shall be elected at the first annual election that occurs more than thirty days after the vacancy shall have happened."

Held, that neither the day on which the vacancy happens nor the day on which the election occurs can be counted as part of the thirty days prescribed by this provision of the Constitution.

BERRY, J.—At the general election in November 1870, Andrew G. Chatfield was duly elected to the office of Judge of the Eighth Judicial District an office which he continued to hold until his death at half past seven o'clock in the forenoon of Oct. 3rd, 1875.

On the 27th day of October, 1875, the respondent Luther M. Brown was appointed Judge of said district and qualified and entered upon the duties of his office.

At the general election held Nov. 2d, 1875 the electors of the Eighth Judicial District cast about 7500 votes for the office of District Judge and the relator Luther L. Baxter having received a majority of the votes cast was declared duly elected upon a canvass by Legislature, and he qualified as by law required; nevertheless the respondent claims to be the Judge of said district and continues to hold and exercise the office of Judge to the exclusion of the relator.

This is a proceeding by *quo warranto* the object of which is to determine whether the relator or respondent is entitled to said office.

Section 10 Art. VI. of our Constitution reads as follows viz: "In case the office of any Judge shall become vacant before the expiration of the regular term for which he was elected the vacancy shall be filled by appointment by the Governor, until a successor is elected and qualified. And such successor shall be elected at the first annual election that occurs more than thirty days after the vacancy shall have happened."

The determination of the present controversy depends upon the meaning to be attributed to the words "more than thirty days after the vacancy shall have happened."

A day is the space of twenty-four hours from midnight to midnight. This is the ordinary and popular meaning of the word and therefore *prima facie* the sense in which it must be taken to have been used in our State Constitution which as it was made by the people should be understood as they undestood it. Applying this definition to the constitutional provision in hand it follows that neither the 3d day of Oct. (the date of Judge Chatfields death.) nor the 2d day of November (the date of the election,) can be counted as one of the thirty days mentioned in the constitution. Neither that portion of Oct. 3rd which remained after the hour of Judge Chatfields death, nor that part of

Nov. 2d which preceded the hour of opening or closing the polls was a space of twenty-four hours from midnight to midnight.

Neither could a space of twenty-four hours from midnight to midnight be made up by putting the fraction of Oct. 3d, and that of Nov. 2d together.

This construction necessarily leads to the conclusion that the election of the relator L. L. Baxter is void. This conclusion is we think sustained by a consideration of the ob, ject of the constitutional provision in question: While the general purpose of the constitution is to make judicial offices elective this purpose is qualified by the provisions of section ten; As a part of qualification the last sentence of the section is evidently inserted in appreciation of the great importance of judicial offices and of the consequent necessity that the electors before being called upon to fill them, shall have such time for inquiry and consideration as will enable them to act with reasonable prudence and good sense in the premises.

The evil sought to be provided against was therefore such as would result from an election occurring *too soon* after the happening of a vacancy rather than such as would follow from deferring an election too long.

If as respects the question of computation of time the language of the constitution were *per se* so ambiguous as to admit of two constructions equally plausible, it is upon the foregoing considerations clear that the construction should be adopted which will beyond an peradventure accomplish this purpose of the constitution.

This will require the construction which would give the electors the longest time for deliberation, that is to say, which would give them thirty clear days between the day when the vacancy happened and the day of the election.

This construction has the further advantage of relieving cases of this kind from the obvious practical difficulties and embarrassments which not unfrequently might arise if it were held to be either necessary or proper to take into consideration fractions of a day in computing the thirty days required by the constitution.

It follows from the foregoing views that the respondent is entitled to the office of Judge of the Eighth Judicial District.

The respondents demurrer to the information is therefore allowed and judgment will be entered accordingly.

STATE OF MINNESOTA, *Respondent*, *vs.* GEORGE LAUTENSCHLAGER impleaded with FRANK RAPP AND SOPHIE RAPP, *Appellants*, } Filed Apr. 10, '76.

The case of State vs. Dumphey followed as to the requisites of an indictment for murder in the first degree;

The trial of a criminal case in the court of Common Pleas of Ramsey County as organized under chapter 69, General Laws of 1875 is not rendered invalid because both the Judges of said court sit together and co-operate in the conduct of such trial.

Neither will the temporary absence of one of the Judges during a portion of the trial, no objection being made at the time, avail the defendant as ground of error.

Interrogating a juror as to his qualifications preliminary to his being challenged is a matter purely discretionary with the trial court.

A challenge made and admitted excuses the juror and such challenge cannot thereafter be withdrawn.

The rule stated in Getchell vs. Hill and Lindley in regard to the examination of an expert approved and followed.

The indictment charged the homicide to have been perpetrated "by cutting the deceased with a hatchet or with some other sharp instrument to the grand jury unknown." Defendant requested an instruction that the jury in order to convict," must be satisfied beyond a reasonable doubt that a cut was given the deceased either with a hatchet or with some other sharp instrument, and that such cut was fatal."

Held, that the request was properly refused. the instruction that a premeditated design is to be presumed from the naked fact of killing held in view of the facts appearing in the bill of exceptions as stated in the opinion not to be error for which a new trial should be granted.

Under chap. 88, General Laws of 1868, it is competent for the jury whenever they find a person guilty of murder in the first degree to determine by their verdict that he shall be punished by death.

Ordered remanded to District Court Ramsey County with instructions to proceed in awarding judgment and sentence upon the verdict.

CORNELL, J.

CITED:

SUFFICIENCY OF INDICTMENT.

State vs. Bilansky, 3 *Minn.* 427.

State vs. Dumphey, 4 *Ibid.* 438.

STATEMENT OF HYPOTHETICAL CASE IN EXAMINATION OF EXPERT.

Getchell vs. Hill & Lindley, 21 *Minn.* 464.

IF PROOF AGREE WITH CHARGE IN ITS SUBSTANCE AND GENERIC CHARACTER WILL BE SUFFICIENT.

State vs. Hoyt, 13 *Minn.* 142.

State vs. Fox, 1 *Dutcher* 601.

WRONG INTENT PRESUMED FROM UNLAWFUL ACT, UNTIL CONTRARY APPEARS.

1 *Taylor's Ev. Sec's.* 103 *and note.*

3 *Greenleaf Ev. Sec's.* 13 *and* 14.

1 *Russell on Crimes*, § 482 *and notes.*

State vs. Brown, 12 *Minn.* 543.

INTENT WHEN EQUIVALENT TO PREMEDITATED DESIGN.

State vs. Hoyt, 13 *Minn.* 149.

State vs. Shippey 10 *Minn.* 223.

H. MORRISH, *Respondent*, vs. JAMES H. MOUNTAIN, *Appellant*, } Filed April 29, '76.

The case of *Washburn vs. Mendenhall*, (April Term, 1874,) followed as to the point that a recovery may be had as in an action for conversion, when the facts stated in the complaint are sufficient, notwithstanding the relief asked for is the possession of the property, or its value.

An erroneous ruling resulting in no prejudice is not ground for a new trial.

CORNELL, J.—The complaint in this action is one in form for the recovery of the possession of personal property; where the facts stated in a complaint disclose a good cause of action for the wrongful conversion of personal property, it has been held by this court that the plaintiff may recover as in such an action, notwithstanding the relief asked for is one for the immediate possession of the property or its value *Washburn vs. Mendenhall*, (*MSS. Oct. T.* 1874, 21 *Minn.* 332.)

No point is made upon the insufficiency of of the complaint in not specifically averring that the plaintiff was the owner of the property at the time of its delivery by him to the defendant or when the demand for its return was made and inasmuch, as the cause was tried upon the theory that the plaintiff was such owner and entitled to the return upon demand, and as the evidence of his ownership introduced without objection was full and not controverted, the sufficiency of the complaint in this regard need not be considered.

There is some evidence tending to show that defendant had the control and possession of the property at the time of the demand and that he neglected and refused to deliver it or account for it to the plaintiff, this in connection with plaintiff's conceded ownership and right of possession was sufficient upon which to submit the question of a wrongful conversion to the jury and to support their finding any verdict.

Plaintiff's cause of action occurred at the time of demand and refusal or of the conversion of which they were the evidence and was not affected by the fact that defendants did not have possession or control of the property at the time of the commencement of the action.

Hence the refusal of the court to charge as requested by defendant upon this point was not error; though the court may have erred in its construction of the complaint in stating that it contained sufficient to support a recovery in trespass or trover it is manifest that defendant could not have been prejudiced by it because the jury was plainly instructed, that upon the facts and evidence in the case a recovery could only be had upon proof of the facts of a conversion.

The order denying a new trial should be affirmed.

Latest Publications.

Sansum's Digest of Law of Insurance. A Digest of all the Fire, Life, Marine, Accident and Guarantee Insurance cases decided in Great Britain and America. By O. B. Sansum. 8vo, 600 pp., Law Sheep. 8 00

Bissell's Reports. Volume VI. Reports of cases argued and decided in the Seventh Judicial Circuit. By Josiah H. Bissell. 8vo 650 pp., Law Sheep. 7 50

Massachusetts Reports CXIX. Reports of cases argued and decided in the Supreme Judicial Court of Massachusetts. By John Lathrop, Reporter. 8vo Law Sheep. . . . 4 50

Otto's Reports on the Decisions of the Supreme Court of the United States, Vol. 1, 8vo. - - - - - 5 00

Greenleaf on Law of Evidence, Vol. 1. By John Wilder May. 13th Ed. 8vo. 6 00

Redfield on Law of Wills., Vol. 2. 3d Ed., 8vo. 6 00

A Treatise on Conveyances by Debtors to Defraud Creditors. By Orlando F. Bump. Second Ed., revised and enlarged. 8vo., 750 pp., Law Sheep. 6 50

Mitford & Tyler's Pleadings and Practice in Equity. By John Mitford (the late Lord Rosedale,) & Samuel Tyler, L. L. D. 8vo., 774 pp. - - 6 50

Outlines of an International Code. By David Dudley Field. Second Ed., revised and enlarged. 8vo., 800 pp. 7 50

California Supreme Court Reports, vol. 50. 8 vo., 725 pp., full sheep, - 5 00

Reports of Cases in Law and Equity Determined in the Supreme Court of Iowa, Vol. XLI, by John J. Runnels, Reporter, 784 pp., law sheep - 005

Probate Law, by Wm. L. Smith, 8 vo., law sheep, . - - - - 2 50

Law of Damages, by Geo. W. Field, 808 pp., law sheep, ... 7 50

Shaw's Index to Minn. Session Laws. 1849-1875. Full sheep. - $4 00

Minn. Reports, vol. 21, full sheep - 5 00

Minn. Session Laws, 1876, Gen. and Spec. together, full sheep. - - - - 2 00

Same, half sheep. . . . 1 75

SESSION LAWS.

We have the Session Laws of Minnesota from 1849 to 1875 inclusive, 34 vols., which we offer in sets, or by the volume.

Parties wishing to fill their sets, will do well to send list at once.

We offer:

1849	$4.00	1872	$3.50
1861	2.00	1873	2.50
1862	2.50	1874	2.00
1863	2.00	1875	2.00
1864	2.00	1876	1.75
1871	2.00		

Bound in Half Sheep.

We can supply Seals of any Size or Design.

NOTARIAL SEALS for any County, $6.75

JOHN B. WEST & CO,

LEGAL BLANKS.

We fill promptly all orders for Legal Blanks and for the convenience of our customers, will put up all orders for two or more dozen of one kind in blocks.

The Syllabi.

Vol. 1. SATURDAY, DEC. 2, 1876. No. 7.

PUBLISHED WEEKLY,

By JOHN B. WEST & CO.,

60 W. Third Street, - ST. PAUL, MINN.

Terms 3.00 per annum in Advance.

HOMER C. ELLER, Editor.

Rates of Advertising.

Spa.	1 w.	2 w.	3 w.	4 w.	3 m.	6 m.	1 y.
1 Sq.	.75	1.30	1.90	2.45	6.00	11.65	22.50
2 Sq.	1.50	2.60	3.60	4.50	11.80	22.50	34.25
3 Sq.	2,10	3.75	4.90	6.00	17.25	33.00	65.25
½ C.	2.65	4.70	6.15	7.50	21.50	41.25	81.50
1 C.	5.00	9.00	11.80	14.45	42.40	81.80	162.25

1 sq, consists of one inch of the column.

TABLE OF CONTENTS.

We have covers for filing and preserving The Syllabi, which we will send by mail, on receipt of price, 35 cents.

We would feel greatly obliged to the attorneys in different parts of the State having cases involving new or important questions of practice or general interest, if they would send us a brief statement of the facts, the points raised, how decided, and authorities cited in support thereof. We desire to make our paper as valuable as possible to the profession of our own State, and assistance of such character will prove a great aid, and be thankfully received and acknowledged.

In the case of Henry Warfield brought before the supreme court on Tuesday last upon a writ *Habeas Corpus* some important questions in connection with proceedings supplemental to execution were discussed and and incidently passed upon.

In this case a judgment had been recovered against Warfield in an inferior court, and execution being returned unsatisfed supplemental proceedings were instituted; upon examination, the debtor disclosed certain property in his possession for which a receiver was appointed, and an order made requiring the debtor to turn over the property to such receiver; this order defendant declined to obey and upon being brought before the court to answer why he should not be punished as for contempt for disobedience, it was urged upon his behalf—citing.

Ex parte Grace, 12 *Iowa* 208.

That proceedings supplemental requiring debtor to transfer his property to receiver were opposed to sec. 4-7-12 Art. 1 constitution of Minnesota that debtor had right of trial by jury as to question whether property was exempt and he in position to transfer it &c.; that the proceedings deprived debtor of his property and liberty without due process of law, and that imprisonment for the failure to apply his property as directed was simply imprisonment for debt.

The objections made to constitutionality of the law being over-ruled, a fine of $25 and penalty of a months imprisonment were imposed. The debtor was then brought before the Supreme Court upon a writ of *Habeas Corpus;* Messrs. Davis, O'Brien and Wilson appearing for the petioner, and James N. Granger, Esq., in opposition thereto. The only question argued upon the hearing was the constitutionality of the law and the right of the Court below to imprison the debtor for his refusal to transfer the property as required by the order.

After full argument and due consideration the Court, without filing any opinion, ordered the writ discharged and prisoner remanded to custody of sheriff to serve out his penalty, thus affirming the validity of the law, and proceedings thereunder.

SUPREME COURT, STATE OF MINNESOTA.

THE CHICAGO MILWAUKEE & ST. PAUL R. R. COMPANY, *Appellant*, *vs.* WILLIAM PFÆNDER, *Respondent*, } Filed Nov. 24, '76.

The act of March 2d 1865, (Sp. Laws) entitled "an act to aid and facilitate the completion of the St. Paul & Pacific R. R. and branches" applies to all the lines of railroad authorized to be built under the charter originally granted to the Minnesota & Pacific Railroad Company by the act of May 22d 1857.

This act of 1865 having been passed, as appears upon its face, on the assumption and belief that the St. Paul & Pacific Railroad Company, then owned and held all those lines of road and the franchises thereto belonging, an acceptance of its provisions and benefits by that company, estops it, and every Company subsequently acquiring title through it to any portion of such lines, from disputing the correctness of such assumption.

The exemption from all taxation and assessment therein contained, was not simply a personal privilege conferred upon the Company, but was in the nature of a conditional grant appurtenant to its several lines of railroad and charged with the perpetual burden of an annual payment of the specified sum therein provided, dating from the time when any portion of such lines equal in extent to thirty miles, should be completed and in operation.

In case of a severance and division of such lines of road and the franchises therto appertaining, among different companies, reference must be had to the time when such first thirty miles of completed road was built and put in operation, in ascertaining and fixing the rate per cent. and amount of gross earnings each Company is to pay during any given year as to its line of road.

CORNELL, J.—It is conceded that the point presented for decision in this case depends entirely upon the true meaning and construction of the fourth and fifth provisos of section one of the act of March 4th, 1865, entitled "An act to aid and facilitate the completion of the St. Paul & Pacific railroad and branches."

It is also admitted that these provisions enacted as amendatory of section 18 of the original charter granted to the Minnesota & Pacific railroad company, May 22, 1857, and if we understand aright the statement of appellant's counsel in regard to the action of the First Division company, under the statute of 1865, it is not seriously disputed that it was intended to apply to the same lines of railroad authorized to be built under such original charter and its amendments. Whether, however, we are correct in this or not is not very material, as it is clear from its title, its express provisions and the whole context of the statute, that it does so apply, and that the St. Paul & Pacific company is therein regarded and treated as holding the ownership and control of all such lines of road and the franchises pertaining thereto, and inasmuch as that company accepted the provisions of the statute and its benefits, neither it nor any company subsequently acquiring title through it to any portion of such lines, is in a position to assert a different state of things than that assumed by the statute, upon the faith of which, apparently, its provisions were framed.

Section eighteen aforesaid, provides that "in consideration of the grants, privileges and franchises conferred on the Minnesota & Pacific railroad company, it should and would, on or before the first day of March, in each year, pay into the treasury of the (then) territory or future state, three per centum of the gross earnings of the said railroad for the year ending on the last day of the preceding December, in lieu of all taxes and assessments whatever, * * the first payment to be made on the first day of March next after fifty miles of said railroad should be completed, and in consideration of such annual payments said company should be forever exempt from all assessments and taxes whatever, upon all its stock, its franchises or estate, real, personal or mixed, held by said company, as well as upon its congressional land grant, till the same should be sold and conveyed." To secure the payment of this per centum of gross earnings, a lien was declared in favor of the state upon all the railroad and other property, estate and effects of the company, that should take precedence of all demands, decrees and judgments against the company.

The only substantial changes effected by the act of 1865 relate to the time when the lands of the company should become taxable, the rate per cent. required to be paid annually upon the gross earnings, and the time when it should first take effect. For the three per cent. required by the original charter, the act of 1865 substituted one per cent. for and during the first three years, two per cent. for the next seven, and and three per cent thereafter; and instead of the first fifty miles of completed road, the first thirty miles of road completed and in operation, was fixed upon as the event which was to determine the date of the first per centum payment.

Whenever privileges and franchises are granted to a corporation in matters concerning and affecting public interests such as an exemption from taxation, a strict construction against the corporation and favorable to the public must be adopted, in case the statute containing the grant gives rise to any reasonable doubt or uncertainty as to its meaning, by reason of its ambiguity or otherwise. 2 *Parsons on Contracts*, 506, *and note;* 3 *Ib.*, 535, *and note. Charles River Bridge vs. Warren Bridge*, 11 *Pet.*, 420. *Rice vs. Railroad*, 1 *Black* 380. So when in a grant of this character, it is doubtful whether a particular provision therein creating an obligation against the donee of the the grant is to be regarded as imposing a condition qualifying it, or not, such question should be resolved as the legislative intent may appear, not alone from the collocation of arrangement of the words, but upon the reason and sense of the thing, as indicated by the entire context and subject matter of the statute. 2 *Pars.* 526-7.

Applying these rules to the case in hand, there would seem to be but little difficulty in arriving at a correct conclusion as to the true meaning of the provisos under consideration.

It is claimed by appellant, and conceded by respondent, that, under the original charter, the company accepting its provisions had the power of effecting a division of its lines of road and franchises, so that several separate and distinct railroads might be created therefrom under the exclusive ownership and control respectively of independent corporations possessed of like franchises, and that in the exercise of this power, no restriction whatever was placed upon the number of roads that might be so brought into existence, nor upon the length of either of such railroads. If the construction contended for by appellant is correct, that each such new corporation is exempt from all taxation in respect to its road, franchises and property, and from the paymemt of any per centum of earnings until thirty miles thereof are actually built and put in operation, provided that much of the completed road had not been finished prior to the division, then had the company so divided its lines of road into sections, each less than thirty miles, before any construction, it follows that under the terms of the statute nothing whatever would ever have accrued to the state on account of the per centum obligation, although in part consideration thereof it had parted with its power of taxation over the entire road or lines of road as originally constituted. It is apparent that no such contingency could have been contemplated by the legislature in granting the charter to the original company. By the terms of the section as amended the exemption from assessment and taxation was granted in consideration of the annual payment of the specified per centum of gross earnings, to commence as soon as, and whenever, the requisite amount of railroad was completed and in operation, and the obligation to make this annual payment rested upon the consideration, not only of such exemption, but the grants made to, and the privileges and franchises conferred upon, the company in respect to its entire road or lines of road. The obligation assumed by the state in making the grant, and that of the company in receiving it, to make the required payment in lieu and in full of all assessment and taxation, were in a certain sense, mutual and reciprocal obligations, and it was obviously the intention of the statute that the grant of immunity from taxation should be treated and regarded as in the nature of a conditional one, charged with the perpetual burden of the annual payment therein provided, and which was to commence whenever and as soon as any portion or portions of the road to which the grant applied, amounting in all to thirty miles, should be completed and put in operation. As this immunity was not merely a personal privilege conferred upon the original company, but a right appurtenant to its lines of road (*Parcher vs. First Div. St. P. & P. R. R. Co.*, 14 *Minn.* 329-30) it follows that the condition thereto annexed always accompanied it as to every part of the road, so that any company in acquiring any portion thereof with the franchises and immunities appertaining thereto took it subject to the condition and burthened with the charge. It follows from these views that the plaintiff company became liable to pay three per cent. of its yearly gross earnings from and after the expiration of ten years computed from the time when the first thirty miles of the original lines of road were in fact completed and put in operation. By what company or companies this was done is a matter of no moment as affects the question under consideration. If, as the fact is claimed to be in this case, the expiration of this ten-year period does not coincide with the commencement of the fiscal year embraced in its annual account to the state treasurer, the company will be required to pay two per cent. of its gross earnings accruing during such fiscal year prior to the expiration of such period, and three per cent. upon that portion thereof accruing thereafter, and its account should be rendered accordingly.

Judgment is affirmed.

CHARLES N. NELSON, *et al.*, *Appellants*, *vs.* ADOLPH MUNCH, *et al.*, *Respondents.* } Filed Nov. 25, '76.

An affidavit for an attachment stating that defendant *has* assigned and disposed of his property with intent to delay and defraud his creditors, and that he *is about* to assign and dispose of his property with like intent, is not necessarily objectionable for inconsistency.

Upon a motion to dissolve an attachment, a defendant may properly use his verified answer as an affidavit, so far as its contents are pertinent.

In the exercise of sound discretion, it is competent for the Court, upon the hearing of such motion, to permit the defendant to read affidavits rebutting the affidavits of the plaintiff read upon such hearing.

BERRY, J.—This is an appeal from an order dissolving an attachment.

I. The writ was issued upon an affidavit stating that defendant, Adolph Munch, has assigned and disposed of his property, with intent to delay and defraud his creditors, and that he is about to assign and dispose of his property with like intent. These statements are not (as claimed by respondents) necessarily objectionable for inconsistency, since it may be true, at any given time that a person *has* assigned and disposed of some part of his property with the intent mentioned, and that he *is about* to assign and dispose of another part with like intent. The case differs from *Hinds vs. Fagebank*, 9 *Minn.* 68, because there the property which the defendant was charged with having disposed of, and being about to dispose of, consisted, as the Court says, of "a single item only."

II. Upon a motion to dissolve an attachment, a defendant may properly use his verified answer as an affidavit, so far as its contents are pertinent.

In the exercise of sound discretion, it is competent for the Court, upon the hearing of such motion, to permit the defendant to read affidavits rebutting the affidavits of the plaintiff read upon such hearing.

In the case at bar there is no reason to suppose that the Court below abused its discretion in receiving the affidavits offered in rebuttal.

III. As respects the merits of the order appealed from, after a careful consideration of the affidavits on both sides, and of the positions taken by counsel, we are of opinion that the court below was justified in dissolving the attachment.

Order affirmed.

STATE OF MINNESOTA, *Respondent*, *vs.* JOHN KLINE, *Appellant.* } Filed Nov. 25, '76.

The case of the *State vs. Cassidy* followed as to the validity of Chap. X, General Laws 1873.

Said law is applicable to the city of Saint Paul as well as the rest of the State. *Prince vs. City of Saint Paul*, 19 *Minn.* 267 followed and approved.

CORNELL, J.—The principal question raised in this case, and very ably and elaborately discussed by the counsel for appellant, was directly presented and fully considered by the Court, in the case of the *State vs. Cassidy*, at the April term, 1875. Upon a careful review of the authorities cited, and full consideration of the arguments of the counsel, no good reason is discovered for doubting the correctness of the decision in that case.

The additional point is presented in this case that the law in question is not operative in the city of Saint Paul, because of the provision in its charter that "no *general law* of this state contravening the provisions of this act, shall be considered as repealing, amending or modifying the same, unless such purpose be expressly set forth in such law." This point is fully met by the decision of this Court in the case of *Prince vs. The City of Saint Paul*, 19 *Minn.*, 267, wherein it was held that a provision contained in a general law to the effect that "All insurance companies doing business it this State under its provisions, shall annually at &c., pay the treasurer of the State two per cent, on all premiums received, and that such sum so paid shall be in lieu of all other taxes or licenses to be collected from said companies in the state," operated as a repeal or modification of the charter of the city, so far as it conferred or purported to confer any authority upon the common council to exact a license fee from any such company doing business in said city, although the purpose so to amend or repeal the city charter in this respect was not expressly and particularly stated in the general law.

The language of the statute under consideration is, "All keepers of saloons * * * or other places where spirituous, vinous or malt liquors are soldor kept for sale within this state, shall, before they shall be permitted to sell or dispose of such * * liquors, take out * * a special license in addition to any or all other license or licenses which they are or may be required by any law, ordinance or municipal regulation to take out."

Being thus alike as to the facts, it is clear that the present case must follow that of *Prince vs. City of Saint Paul*, as to the point under consideration.

Judgment appealed from confirmed.

BERRY, J.—Upon the first point considered in the foregoing opinion, I dissent from my brethren, being still of opinion as in *State vs. Cassidy*, that the purpose and effect of the law in question is the raising of revenue, and not the regulation (under the police power) of the traffic in intoxicating liquors.

CHRISTIAN WILLAND, *et al.* *Appellants*, *vs.* DANIEL G. SHILLOCK, *et al.* *Respondents.* — Filed Nov. 25, '76.

In an action brought by him in the District Court for Hennepin county, S., on April 28th, 1869, recovered a money judgment against W. by default; W. brings the present action in the District Court for St. Louis county, for the purpose of enjoining the collection of the judgment, upon the ground that it was procured by certain alleged fraudulent practices, and false testimony of S. before the referee by whom the damages were assessed in the action wherein the judgment was recovered. The complaint shows that W. did not appear in the action mentioned, and was not present, in person or by counsel, before the referee, and further, that he had no notice whatever of any judgment recovered by S. against him until October 28, 1874.

Held, that upon the facts thus charged, the judgment may properly be said to have been taken against W. through his surprise or excusable neglect.

Held, further, that if entitled to relief from the judgment, W. had a complete and adequate remedy at law by an application to the District Court of Hennepin county, under Section 105, Chapter 66, General Statutes, and that therefore the present action cannot be maintained.

Held, further, that the year within which a party may have relief from a judgment under the section mentioned, commences to run from the time when he has *actual notice* of the judgment.

BERRY, J.—On April 28th 1869, the present defendant, Shillock recovered a money judgment by default in an action brought by him against the present plaintiffs, in the District Court for Hennepin county. The present action is brought in the District Court of St. Louis county, for the purpose of enjoining the collection of the judgment, upon the ground that it was procured by certain alleged fraudulent practices and false testimony of the defendant Shillock, before the referee by whom the damages were assessed in the action wherein the judgment was recovered. The complaint shows that the plaintiffs did not appear in the action mentioned and were not present in person or by counsel before the referee, and further that they "had no notice whatever of any judgment recovered by said Shillock, until Oct. 28, 1874, * * and until that time all these plaintiffs were entirely ignorant that any judgment had been rendered against them or either of them." If the facts are as thus charged, the judgment may properly be said to have been taken against the defendants therein (the present plaintiffs) through their surprise or their excusable neglect.

It is provided in section 105, chapter 66, General Statutes that the Court may, in its discretion, at any time within one year after notice thereof, relieve a party from a judgment taken against him through his surprise or excusable neglect. The meaning of this is that the Court in which the judgment is rendered may afford the relief mentioned within one year after the party seeking the relief has actual notice of the judgment.

To hold, as suggested by plaintiff's counsel, that the personal service of the summons in the action is notice of the judgment, would render the language of the statute meaningless.

This case is then one in which upon the allegations of their complaint, the plaintiffs, if they were entitled to any relief, had a complete and adequate remedy at law, by an application to the District Court of Hennepin county for relief from the judgment.

The case falls within the principle of *Johnston vs. Paul*, (April Term 1875, MSS.) in which it is said by the Court that "upon no principle of equity jurisprudence can a separate action be maintained to set aside a judgment of a Court of competent jurisdiction because it has been procured by means of false testimony in a case where the Court rendering it has full power to afford adequate relief upon an application in the same suit or proceeding, and we know no authority giving countenance to any such doctrine."

The demurrer of the defendant, Shillock, to the plaintiffs' complaint specified several grounds, and among them, that the District Court of St. Louis county had no jurisdiction of the subject of the action, and that the complaint does not state facts sufficient to constitute a cause of the action.

The demurrer was incorrectly sustained upon the first ground mentioned. It should have been sustained upon the second; but the mistake is of no practical importance, since it only presents a case of a wrong reason for a right conclusion.

Order affirmed.

OSCAR HOWES, BYRON C. HOWES and FELIX C. HOWES, *Appellants*, *vs.* HENRY GILLETT, *Respondent.* } Filed Nov. 25, '76.

In an action (under section 142, chapter 11, General Statutes) to recover of the proprietor of town lots the amount of delinquent taxes, penalty and interest for which said lots have been sold at a tax sale which has proved invalid, and taxes subsequently paid, the tax duplicates are not *prima facie* evidence of the levy and assessment of such taxes.

BERRY, J.—"Upon the sale of any land or town lot for delinquent taxes, the lien which the State has thereon for taxes then due is transferred to the purchaser at such sale, and if such sale proves to be invalid, on account of any irregularity in the proceedings of any officer having any duty to perform in relation thereto, the purchaser at such sale is entitled to receive from the proprietor of such land or lot the amount of taxes and penalty and interest legally due thereon, and the amount of taxes paid thereon by the purchaser subsequent to such sale, and such land or lot is bound for the payment thereof." *Gen. Stat. Chap.* 11, § 142.

Under this section of the statute the present action is brought, for the purpose of recovering of the defendant (the proprietor of certain town lots in the city of Hastings) the amount of delinquent taxes, penalty and interest, for which the lots were sold at a tax sale which proved invalid, and the amount of taxes on the same paid subsequent to the sale. Whether in such an action a tax duplicate is *prima facie* evidence of the assessment and levy of a tax is the only question presented in the case.

This question must be answered in the negative, for the reason that there is no statute nor any principle or rule of the law of evidence outside of statute, making a duplicate such *prima facie* evidence. As an official document a tax duplicate is proper evidence of its own existence and contents; but it is not evidence of a step in the tax proceeding anterior to itself, like the assessment and levy of taxes.

The presumption that in making it out and issuing it to the county treasurer, the county auditor did his duty, does not carry with it the presumption that the preliminary steps of assessment and levy were properly taken, since both of these steps are jurisdictional as respects the authority of the auditor to make out and issue the duplicate, and the existence of jurisdictional facts is not a matter of presumption.

Cooley on Taxation, 329.

See also *Hopper vs. Ex'rs of Malleson*, 16 *N. J. Eq.* 382.

Judgment affirmed.

SAMUEL FOX AND SAMUEL F. FOREST, PARTNERS AS FOX & FOREST, *Appellants*, *vs.* THE CITY OF WINONA, A. F. HODGINS, Mayor, and JOHN C. SLATER, Marshal of said City. *Respondents*, } Filed May 4,'76.

By the charter of the City of Winona its Common Council is is authorized by ordinances, resolutions or by-laws * * to prevent the incumbrance of streets, sidewalks, lanes or alleys with carriages, carts, wagons, boxes, sleighs, firewood, lumber or any other material or substance whatever.

Held, that the word "incumbrance" is used in the sense of obstruction and that the authority to prevent the incumbrance of streets is an anthority not only to remove or cause to be removed anything actually obstructing a street, but also to take measures to prevent anything from becoming an obstruction.

Held, further that this authorizes the Common Council not only to forbid the setting of posts in a street to support an awning and to remove or cause to be removed posts already set for that purpose, but on account of their liability to fall, to forbid the erection of wooden awnings and to remove the same or cause them to be removed.

BERRY, J.—Plaintiffs are owners in fee and in possession of certain land in the City of Winona and of a building thereon, the front of which stands on the northerly line of Second street; over the sidewalk in front of the building, the plaintiffs in 1868 erected a wooden awning attaching one end of it to the building and supporting the other end by perpendicular posts set into the earth at the outer edge of the sidewalk at the distance of about ten feet from the building.

The important question presented by this case is whether this awning can lawfully be removed by the city authorities.

By the charter of the City of Winona its Common Council is authorized "by ordinances, resolutions or by-laws * * * to prevent the incumbrance of streets, sidewalks, lanes or alleys with carriages, carts, wagons, boxes, sleighs, firewood, lumber or any other material or substance whatever," *Sp. Laws* 1867 *ch.* 20, *sub. ch.* 4. § 2 *sub. div.* 23.

In September, 1872, the city council passed an ordinance containing among others the following provisions: "Section 21. * * and all wooden awnings heretofore erected so as to overhang or project into or over any sidewalk or street, shall be removed within two years from the passage of this ordinance." "Section 22. Any person who shall violate or fail to comply with any of the provisions of this ordinance * * shall pay a fine of not less than five nor more than fifty dollars."

In October, 1874, more than two years after

the passage of the ordinance, the plaintiffs having failed to remove their wooden awning, the city council by resolution directed the city marshal to remove it.

The word "incumbrance" in the charter is used in the sense of obstruction. The authority conferred to *prevent* the incumbrance of the streets and sidewalks by carriages, lumber, &c., &c., or by "any other material or substance whatever" is an authority not only to remove or cause to be removed anything actually obstructing a street or sidewalk, but also to take measures to prevent anything from becoming an obstruction. This authorizes the common council not only to forbid the setting of posts in a street to support an awning and to remove or cause to be removed posts already set in a street for that purpose, but on account of their liability to fall, to forbid the erection of wooden awnings whether supported by posts or not, and to remove the same or cause them to be removed.

It follows that it was competent for the common council to pass the provisions quoted from the ordinance in question.

The effect of these provisions is to make the plaintiffs' failure to remove their awning within the specified two years wrongful, and to subject them to a penalty therefor.

The continuance of the awning after the two years, and therefore at the time when the marshal was directed to remove it, was the unlawful continuance of an incumbrance or obstruction of the street and sidewalk, as well as of something which the common council, in the legitimate exercise of the authority conferred upon it, had determined it to be necessary to remove in order to prevent it from becoming an obstruction.

The city council, in the exercise of its authority to prevent the incumbrances spoken of, is not confined to the right to direct their removal by the parties who placed or maintain them where they are, nor to the right to impose a penalty for the failure of those parties to remove them.

The authority given is more general. It is "by ordinances, resolutions or by-laws * * * to prevent."

This prevention may be accomplished as it was in this instance through a *resolution* directing the marshal (who is bound to execute the order of the common council, see section 7, sub. chap. 3 of the City Charter) to remove the obnoxious awning.

The maintenance of the awning having been made unlawful by the ordinance, and the defendants having had more than two years notice to remove it, the adoption of the resolution in this case cannot be claimed to be an unreasonable exercise of authority. See *Pedrick vs. Bailey*, 12 *Gray* 161.

The other points made by plaintiffs' counsel appear to be based upon the idea that the plaintiffs had some *right* to erect and maintain their awning in the street, whereas it does not appear in fact or by presumption that the awning was there otherwise than by mere sufferance.

Judgment affirmed.

Latest Publications.

Sansum's Digest of Law of Insurance. A Digest of all the Fire, Life, Marine, Accident and Guarantee Insurance cases decided in Great Britain and America. By O. B. Sansum. 8vo, 600 pp., Law Sheep. - - - - - 8 00

Bissell's Reports. Volume VI. Reports of cases argued and decided in the Seventh Judicial Circuit. By Josiah H. Bissell. 8vo 650 pp., Law Sheep. 7 50

Massachusetts Reports CXIX. Reports of cases argued and decided in the Supreme Judicial Court of Massachusetts. By John Lathrop, Reporter. 8vo Law Sheep. - - - - 4 50

Otto's Reports on the Decisions of the Supreme Court of the United States, Vol. 1, 8vo. - - - - - 5 00

Greenleaf on Law of Evidence, Vol. 1. By John Wilder May. 13th Ed. 8vo. 6 00

Redfield on Law of Wills., Vol. 2. 3d Ed., 8vo. - - - - - - - 6 00

A Treatise on Conveyances by Debtors to Defraud Creditors. By Orlando F. Bump. Second Ed., revised and enlarged. 8vo., 750 pp., Law Sheep. 6 50

Mitford & Tyler's Pleadings and Practice in Equity. By John Mitford (the late Lord Rosedale,) & Samuel Tyler, L. L. D. 8vo., 774 pp. - - 6 50

Outlines of an International Code. By David Dudley Field. Second Ed., revised and enlarged. 8vo., 800 pp. 7 50

California Supreme Court Reports, vol. 50. 8 vo., 725 pp., full sheep, - 5 00

Reports of Cases in Law and Equity Determined in the Supreme Court of Iowa, Vol. XLI, by John J. Runnels, Reporter, 784 pp., law sheep - 005

Probate Law, by Wm. L. Smith, 8 vo., law sheep, - - - - - 2 50

Law of Damages, by Geo. W. Field, 808 pp., law sheep, - - - - - 7 50

Shaw's Index to Minn. Session Laws. 1849–1875. Full sheep. - $4 00

Minn. Reports, vol. 21, full sheep - 5 00

Minn. Session Laws, 1876, Gen. and Spec. together, full sheep. - - - - 2 00
Same, half sheep. - - - - 1 75

THE SYLLABI.

VOL. 1. SATURDAY, DEC. 9, 1876. No. 8.

PUBLISHED WEEKLY,

By JOHN B. WEST & CO.,

No. 1 Wabasha St., - ST. PAUL, MINN.

Terms 3.00 per annum in Advance.

HOMER C. ELLER, Editor.

TABLE OF CONTENTS.

A SOMEWHAT novel, though not entirely new, question of practice arose a few days ago in the case of *State vs. Seward*, pending before the District Court, Washington county, Crosby, J., presiding. In that case Seward had been indicted for libel. The offense complained of being the publication, in the paper of which he was editor, of general charges of fraud corruption and malfeasance, against one Butts, Judge of Probate of that county. Time being granted to plead; the prosecution moved, citing *Commonwealth vs. Snelling* 15 *Pickering* 321, that an order be made requiring the defendant, in case he should determine to introduce evidence tending to show the truth of any of the alleged libelous statements, that he notify the prosecution by a certain time upon which charge he would offer such proof, and also file a bill of particulars of the specific acts in reference to which he would offer such proof, and that he relied upon, as showing the truth of the general statement, charged as libelous. After argument motion was granted and an order entered accordingly.

AMONG the leading periodicals whose receipt we have the pleasure to acknowledge is the *American Law Register*, the last number containing, among other things, an excellent article on the subject of the limitations of the United States constitution on the taxing power of the states; the *American Law Record*, a monthly journal conducted by Moos & Patterson, Cincinnati, O., and devoted largely to the publication of current and important decisions in full; *The Law and Equity Reporter, Philadelphia Legal Intelligencer, Chicago Legal Adviser, Internal Revenue Record* and last but not least the well known and widely circulating *Central Law Journal.*

Supreme Court, State of Minnesota.

State of Minnesota, ex rel Peter Johnson. *vs.* Jno. C. Becht, sheriff of Ramsey county, } Filed May 1, '76.

The provisions of sec. 7, chap. 17, of the General Statutes relating to bastards are not repugnant to sec. 7 or sec. 12, art. I of the constitution.

Cornell, J;—The relator having been found guilty of bastardy on a trial in the District Court of Wright county, was thereupon adjudged to be the father of a bastard child and charged with its maintenance in a sum specified in the judgment, together with the costs of prosecution, and ordered to enter into a bond for the performance of the judgment, pursuant to the provisions of section 7 chapter seventeen of the general statutes. Neglecting and refusing to give the required bond, he was committed to the jail of Ramsey county and is now held under such process of commitment.

The main question raised and discussed upon the argument relates to the constitutional validity of so much of this statute as authorizes the commitment of a defendant prosecuted under its provisions in case he refuses to give the required bond pursuant to the order and judgment of the court.

Our statute upon the subject of bastardy seems to have been borrowed from the state of Wisconsin. The Supreme Court of that state in refering to proceedings under this and similar statutes correctly say: "They are not strictly of a criminal character though they have always been considered as *quasi* criminal, and the view undoubtedly taken of them by courts in modern times is, that they are neither wholly civil nor wholly criminal, but have many of the features and incidents of both." *State vs. Jager* 19 *Wis.* 251 and cases there cited; statutes of this character are in the nature of police regulations having as their principal object and purpose the enforcement, upon the putative father of a bastard child, of the moral and natural duty resting upon him to furnish it adequate support and maintenance and to indemnify the community against its becoming a public charge and burden.

Hawes vs. Cooksey, 13 *Ohio* 242.

Musser vs. Stewart, 21 *Ohio St.* 353.

Lower vs. Wallick, 25 *Ind.* 68 followed and approved in *Ex parte Teague* 41 *Ind.* 278.

The infliction upon the father of a punishment, for the act of begetting a bastard child, as for a criminal offence, is not the purpose of our statute, nor is such its effect;

It is rather against the consequences of the act, both as respects the child and the public, that its provisions are directed and and intended to operate. It follows that the statute is not invalid by reason of any thing contained in sec. 7, art. I of the constitution; Is it repugnant to sec. 12 of the same article which declares that "no person shall be imprisoned for debt in this state, but this shall not prevent the Legislature from providing for imprisonment, or holding to bail, persons charged with fraud in contracting said debt." The term debt in its ordinary and legal acceptance imports a sum of money or something due and owing from one to another arising out of r contract express or implied 2 Cooley Black. Book III p 154. *Denny vs. The Manhattan Company*, 2 *Hill* 223,

That this was the sense in which it was intended to be used in the clause under consideration is apparent from the context; It is difficult to perceive why the power of providing for arrest, holding to bail, and imprisonment was withheld from the Legislature in respect to all cases of personal wrongs and torts, penalties, fines, forfeitures and the like and expressly preserved in respect to the single case of a fraud perpetrated in the contraction of a debt, and yet this is the result of this clause according to the construction claimed on the part of the relator.

The same reasons of policy that justify the retention of this power in the Legislature in cases of fraud, apply with equal if not greater force to all other cases of civil wrongs and injuries analagous in character, and alike injurious in their results.

There is nothing in the section of the constitution under consideration, leading to the supposition that its framers intended to make any distinction between an act of fraud, and other like wrongful acts in respect to the power of legislation over them and we are not inclined to give it any such construction;

The liability imposed by the judgment and statute in this case is not a debt within the meaning of this clause of the constitution; It simply charges the relator with the performance of a duty not founded in any contract but growing out of his natural relation to his illegitimate offspring and terminating with the death of the child.

The defect in the process of commitment in not being properly tested in the name of the District Judge, is one which the relator should have specifically pointed out in his petition, in order to avail himself of it on the argument, and is therefore disregarded.

The demurrer to the return is overruled and the prisoner is remanded to the custody of defendant as sheriff as aforesaid.

JULIUS MARSILLE, *Appellant*, *vs.* THE MILWAUKEE & ST. PAUL R. R. CO. *Respondent*, } Filed May 2, '76.

In taking an appeal from Justices Court, filing with the Justice, the original notice of appeal with proof of service thereof within the time prescribed by statute, is a jurisdictional prerequisite to the allowance of the appeal that cannot be dispensed with nor supplied after the prescribed time.

CORNELL, J.—Among the statutory prerequisites to the allowance of an appeal in a Justice Court not only the notice of appeal must be served upon the opposite party within ten days after the judgment, but such original notice with proof of service thereof, must be filed with the Justice who rendered the judgment within ten days after such service, sec. 104, sub. 13, title 11, chap. 65, General Statutes. The fact that the statute (sec. 102 same title,) especially provides that an appeal allowed by a Justice shall not be dismissed by reason of an omission to comply with one of the conditions of the appeal prescribed by section 104, the execution of a proper bond, necessarily implies that the other conditions jurisdictional to its allowance cannot be dispensed with, nor can their omission be renewed or supplied after the prescribed time within which they must be complied with, has expired.

The entry in the Justices docket in this case shows that the appeal was allowed by the Justice upon the affidavit and bond alone.

It cannot be presumed that any notice of appeal with proof of service thereof was filed with him prior to the allowance of the appeal or within the required time, because the Justice expressly certifies to the correctness of his docket as containing an entry of all the proceedings in the action, together with all the papers on file before him, and no mention is made of the filing of any notice of appeal and proof of service thereof; on this ground the appeal from the judgment of the Justice should have been dismissed. The judgment of the District Court is reversed with directions to dismiss the appeal taken from the judgment rendered by the Justice.

THE ST. LOUIS LIFE INSURANCE COMPANY, *Appellant*, *vs.* THE ALLIANCE MUTUAL LIFE ASSURANCE SOCIETY OF THE UNITED STATES, and MAGDALENA YOUNG, *Respondents*. } Filed May 3, '76.

Where two defendants have properly interpleaded in an action brought by plaintiff to determine as to which he shall pay an acknowledged debt, and the money has been paid into court upon its order for the benefit of the successful litigant defendant, it is not competent thereafter to participate in the litigation between such contesting defendants, nor to object to any ruling or decision made in the action, affecting alone their rights as between themselves.

The report of a referee in such an action will not be set aside or disturbed because it allows costs against the plaintiff when the evidence before him reasonably tends to the conclusion that the action was instituted by the plaintiff in bad faith, rather than with the view of delaying and prejudicing the successful defendant in obtaining his rights than of protecting himself against the risk of payment to one of two conflicting claimants.

CORNELL, J.—The complaint in this action is in the nature of a Bill of Interpleader in Equity, as known and understood prior to the adoption of the Code practice; to determine therefore the status and rights of plaintiff in this action it is neccessary to refer to the nature of a suit in equity, under the former practice commenced by such a bill and the rules and principles governing it.

As to the complainant, the sole office and purpose of such a bill was to relieve him from the risk, uncertainty and expense of determining by litigation or otherwise as to which of several conflicting claimants he was owing and ought to pay an acknowledged debt or duty, his obligation and readiness to pay or discharge the same upon the settlement of such question being fully conceded.

Hence, in a bill of this character, it was necessary for it to appear that the complainant had no personal interest in such debt or duty or the fund in his possession; he could not claim any relief against any of the claimant defendants, but could only ask leave of the court to pay the money, or deliver the property, to the one to whom it rightfully belonged, in order that he might thereafter be protected against the claims of all. The only decree the complainant was entitled to was one of interpleader, and that the bill was properly filed. This being obtained, he was thenceforth altogether out of the suit, the defendants alone being left to contest their conflicting claims without any aid or interference on his part. 2 *Daniel Ch. Pr. and Pl.* 1659–60–75–80, *and notes;* 2 *Barb. Ch. Pr.* 117, *and cases cited in notes.*

It is apparent from these considerations that with the exception of the question of costs, none of the questions sought to be raised and discussed by appellant in this appeal, are properly before us for consideration; they all relate solely to matters in controversy between the defendants, and which they alone are interested in litigating and settling.

The decision of the referee in favor of the Assurance Society against the other defendant, acquiesced in, as it seems, by her, entitles it to the money paid into court by the plaintiff, under its order, for the benefit of the successful litigant defendant, and constitutes full protection to plaintiff against any claim on her part.

Plaintiff has no interest, and is under no duty or obligation to prosecute an appeal in her sole interest and behalf, and will not be heard in the assertion of any of his rights.

In the matter of costs, there was sufficient in the evidence, and the conduct of the plaintiff during the trial to justify the referee in arriving at the conclusion that the controversy nominally litigated between the defendants, had its origin and support with the plaintiff, and that the action was instituted in bad faith, with the view of hindering and delaying the defendant society, in the collection of its claim, and not for the sole purpose of self protection.

Under these circumstances it cannot be said that the referee erred in awarding costs against the plaintiff.

Order appealed from is affirmed.

THOMAS H. SULLIVAN, AND SON, *Respondent*, *vs.* EDWARD MURPHY AND SON, *Appellants*, } Filed May 2, '76.

Where the fact of a partnership between the defendants is in issue, the admission of the fact by one of them is proper evidence against himself.

Where a debtor transfers his property to another who in consideration thereof promises to pay the debts of the former, the promise is not within the statute of frauds.

A corporation created under title 2, ch. 34, General Statutes may execute promissory notes to evidence debts which it may contract.

GILFILLAN, C. J.—Action to recover the amount of a promissory note given to plaintiffs by a corporation created under title 2, ch. 34, General Statutes called the Trades Manufacturing Company; It is alleged by the plaintiffs, and found by the court below, that the corporation transferred all its property to defendants upon their undertaking and promise to assume and pay all its debts.

The case made does not purport to contain all the evidence and therefore we cannot consider whether the findings of fact are sustained by the evidence.

The admissions of Ira T. Murphy, of the fact of the partnership between himself and the other defendant, though they would not of themselves be sufficient to prove the partnership as to the other defendant, were proper evidence of it against him;

The promise of defendants made to the corporation to assume and pay its debts is an original undertaking and not a collateral one, and therefore not within the statute of frauds.

Goetz vs. Foos, 14 *Minn.* 265, *and cases cited.*

The Statute under which this corporation was incorporated, authorizes by implication at least, the corporations contemplated by it to create debts in the ordinary transaction of their business, and since the old rule that a corporation can only contract under its corporate seal has been relaxed so as not to apply to contracts in the daily and ordinary transaction of its business; there is no reason why such debts may not be evidenced by promissory notes. The note in question was therefore valid.

Order appealed from affirmed.

EDWARD MARTIN, *Repsondent*, *vs.* HENRY C. FRIDLEY, *Appellant*, } Filed May 5, '76.

G. and S. held a senior mortgage; plaintiffs junior mortgage; G. and S. foreclosed their mortgage by suit to which plaintiff was not made a party, and at the sale under the decree, bid in the property in separate parcels and after the time to redeem expired, conveyed by quit claim to G. and he conveyed to defendant who is now in possession; Plaintiff offered to redeem one of the parcels sold at the G. and S. foreclosure, by paying the amount bid for such parcel and interest, which offer was declined, and he afterwards foreclosed his mortgage by advertisement, and became the purchaser at his sale, and he brings this suit to eject defendant.

Held, that by their quit-claim deed the entire interest of G. and S. passed to G., and by his deed passed to defendant, so that the latter may, as against plaintiff, claim to stand in the position of a mortgagee in possession, who cannot be ejected without payment of the mortgage. Also that a party having a right to redeem from a mortgage which has been foreclosed, but not so as to bind him, cannot redeem from the foreclosure sale, but must, if he redeem at all, redeem from the entire mortgage by paying the whole of it.

GILFILLAN, C. J.—The facts presenting the questions which we deem it necessary to notice in this case are as follows: In July, 1855 the title to the premises in dispute was in A. M. Fridley and Chas. S. Chase, and they executed a mortgage, dulv recorded, upon the same and other parcels, to one Nash, and the ownership of the mortgage afterwards passed by assignment to Wm. Gemmell and Robt. Salmond, who in 1859 instituted suit against the mortgagors and other parties to foreclose the mortgage; a decree for foreclosure and sale was entered Jan. 19, 1860, and April 28, 1860, the property was, under the decree, sold in separate parcels, the plaintiffs in that suit becoming the purchasers, the premises in dispute being struck off to them at the price of $250. In 1869 they conveyed, by quit-claim deed, to John M. Gilman, and he, in 1871, conveyed by a similar deed to defendant, who at the commencement of this action was in possession of the property.

In April, 1856, A. M. Fridley, being then the sole owner of the premises, executed a mortgage on them and other parcels to Richard Martin, who in October, 1849, assigned it to this plaintiff. The mortgage and assignment were duly recorded, and plaintiff, in October, 1870, under a power of sale in his mortgage, foreclosed it by advertisement, and in the sale became the purchaser.

In October, 1861, the plaintiff, under his mortgage, tendered a redemption of the parcel in dispute from the Gemmell and Salimond foreclosure, by offering to pay the amount for which that parcel was *struck off* at such foreclosure, with interest, *which* tender was refused.

The plaintiff was not made a party to the foreclosure suit, and consequently not bound by the foreclosure decree and sale. Upon these facts the plaintiff claims to be entitled to the possession of the land.

First—As the owner of the equity of redemption under his mortgage and foreclosure, the prior mortgage not having been foreclosed as to him.

Second—As having redeemed by his tender from the mortgage and foreclosure of Gemmell and Salmond, and thus acquired the interest which vested in them upon their foreclosure.

In regard to the first of these propositions. the answer suggested is that the Gemmell and Salmond foreclosure not being absolute as to plaintiff, the defendant, who is their successor in interest, has the rights so far as plaintiff is concerned, of a mortgagee in possession.

To this plaintiff objects, that as to him, defendant is not the successor to the mortgage interest of Gemmell and Salmond, that as to him they had no other than a mortgagee's interest, a mere lien; that such an interest will not pass by mere deed of conveyance of the land; that it did not pass to Gilman, nor to defendant by the quit-claim deed, and that consequently, as to plaintiff, the defendant cannot protect his possession under the mortgage, as a mortgagee in possession.

Gemmell and Salmond had foreclosed their mortgage by a foreclosure. which, so far as appears, barred every interest in the property except plaintiff's mortgage, upon the equity of redemption remaining in the mortgagor after the execution of their mortgage. Prior to such foreclosure, a naked deed of conveyance by them would not, according to the authorities, have passed their interest under the mortgage, for the reason that such interest was merely incidental and collateral to the debt, and necessarily was vested in the owner of, and could pass only upon a transfer of, and as an incident to it, and that a deed purporting merely to convey the land is not evidence of an intent to transfer the debt. Upon the expiration of the time to redeem from their foreclosure, they become the absolute owners of the property, subject to plaintiff's right of redemption under his mortgage; except as to his right of redemption there was a complete merger and union of their mortgage interest and the fee.

This merger and union was prevented as to him only so far as was necessary to preserve his right to redeem and to prevent the extinction of their mortgage interest as against such right to redeem. But even as against that right, the character of their mortgage interest was changed. The foreclosure extinguished the debt so far as it affected the land, and the mortgage interest was no longer only a lien to secure and a mere incident to the debt. Had he redeemed he would have been entitled by such redemption to be subrogated, not to a mere lien to secure a debt and the right to enforce such lien as though no foreclosure had been made, but to the interest in the land which their mortgage and its foreclosure gave them. That interest was the entire title, subject to to his right of subrogation to it by redemption, and subject probably to be affected by failure to make the foreclosure absolute as to him within proper time. As after the foreclosure their interest was not a mere security for a debt, those decisions which hold that the security, the incident, can pass only by transfer of the debt, the principle does not apply. Their deed to Gilman and his to defendant, passed the entire interest in the land which their mortgage and foreclosure gave them. Had they, after foreclosure, entered under it upon the land, plaintiff could not have ejected him without redemption, and defendant occupies the same position.

This makes it necessary to determine the validity of plaintiff's attempt to redeem. This attempt was to redeem, not from the mortgage, but from the sale, by paying for a single parcel the amount bid at the sale for such parcel, with interest. It seems well established by the authorities that one who is not bound by a foreclosure cannot redeem from the sale, but that he must redeem, if he has a right of redemption, from the entire mortgage, by paying the whole amount of it. The rule and principle are concisely stated in *Collins vs. Riggs*. "The party offering to redeem proceeds upon the hypothesis that as to him the mortgage has never been foreclosed and is still in existence; therefore he can only lift it by paying it."

Collins vs. Riggs, 14 *Wall* 491
Bradley vs. Snyder, 14 *Ill.* 263.
Benedict vs. Gilman, 4 *Paige* 58.
Johnson vs. Harmon, 19 *Iowa* 56.
Knowles vs. Rablin, 20 *Ib.* 101.
Gage vs. Brewster, 31 *N. Y.* 218.

The tender was therefore of no effect.
Judgment reversed.

STATE OF MINNESOTA AND THEODORE F. KNAPPEN, *Respondent*, *vs.* GILBERT CLOUGH, *Appellant*, } Filed May 9, '76.

To be eligible to the office of County Attorney a person need not be an Attorney and Counselor at Law nor admitted to practice as such in any of the courts of the state.

GILFILLAN, C. J.—The action is in the nature of *quo warranto* to oust defendant from the office of County Attorney of Isanti county to which he was elected, on the ground of his ineligibility to the office.

The only ground of ineligibility alleged is that he is not an Attorney and Counselor at Law nor ever been admitted to practice as such in any of the courts of the state; Sec. 7, art. 7 of the constitution provides that "every person who by the provisions of this article shall be entitled to vote at any election, shall be eligible to any office which now is, or hereafter shall be elected by the people in the district where he shall have residence, thirty days previous to such election, except as otherwise *provided* in this constitution or the constitution and laws of the United States."

The only offices which by the constitution require additional qualifications are those of Judges of the Supreme and District Courts.

That the provisions of sec. 7, art. 7 are unwise in not requiring proper qualifications for offices, the proper discharge of the duties of which call for the exercise of peculiar learning and skill, there can be no doubt, but it is the constitutional rule and we cannot add to it or take from it.

Order appealed from, reversed.

STATE OF MINNESOTA, *vs.* JOHN BYRUD. } Filed May 22, '76.

Section 1 chapter 76 Laws 1870 provides that if upon the trial of any person who shall be convicted in any District Court * * or if upon any demurrer to an indictment, or to a special plea or pleas to an indictment, or upon any motion upon or relating to an indictment, any question of law shall arise which in the opinion of the Judge of said court shall be so important or doubtful as to require the decision of the Supreme Court, he shall * * report the case * * * and certify the said report to the Supreme Court &c.

Held, that to enable this court to take jurisdiction of a case certified up under this statute, it should affirmatively appear that the question of law certified up arose in one of the ways mentioned in the statute.

Held, further, that to the jurisdiction of this court in cases under this statute, it is indispensible that the question raised, be passed upon and determined by the court below.

BERRY, J.—Section 1 chapter 76 Laws 1870 provides that if upon the trial of any person who shall be convicted in any District Court or in the Court of Common Pleas of Ramsey county, or if upon any demurrer to an indictment, or to a special plea or pleas to an indictment, or upon any motion upon or relating to an indictment, any question of law shall arise, which in the opinion of the judge of such court, shall be so important or so doubtful as to require the decision of the Supreme Court, he shall, if the defendant desires or consents thereto, report the case, so far as may be necessary to present the question or questions of law arising therein, and certify the said report to the Supreme Court of the state, and thereupon all proceedings in said cause shall be stayed until the decision of said Supreme Court shall be made.

In this case, which is attempted to be brought here under the provisions of this section, the certificate of the District Judge is as follows:

(Title of the cause.) "This cause came on for trial at general term held in said (Fillmore) county, Nov. 1875, on an indictment for larceny charged to have been committed in said county. On the trial it appeared by the evidence that the property was stolen in the state of Iowa, and was afterwards found in the possession of the defendant in Fillmore county."

The question was raised whether a person who steals property in an adjoining state and brings it into this, is guilty of larceny here. The court deeming the question important and doubtful, at the request of counsel and with the consent of defendant, decided to report the case to the Supreme Court for its decision, and thereupon all further proceedings were stayed. "There are several reasons why we cannot take jurisdiction in this case.

In the first place the case does not come within the terms of the statute before cited. Though it appears the question of law involved arose *upon the trial* of a person in a District Court, it does not appear that the person was convicted; on the contrary, the certificate appears to show that the proceedings were stayed before conviction. Neither does it appear that it arose upon any demurrer to the indictment or to a special plea or pleas to an indictment, or upon any motion upon or relating to an indictment; on the contrary it appears to have arisen upon the evidence.

In the second place it does not appear that the question raised was in anyway passed upon or determined by the court below. It is indispensable that it should be thus passed upon and determined, because the jurisdiction of this court is (except in certain cases not here important to be mentioned) purely appellate.

The exercise of appellate jurisdiction *Ex vi termini* necessarily calls for something to be appealed from, that is to say, there must be some *action* on the part of the inferior tribunal which the appellate court is called upon to review. In the absence of such action the appellate tribunal therefore has no jurisdiction.

In view of the appellate character of our jurisdiction, the statute itself appears to be open to criticism. When a person is tried and convicted, any question arising "upon the trial" is necessarily passed upon by the court below, and in such case we see no reason why the determination of the question may not properly be reviewed here upon the certificate provided for.

But as respects a question of law arising upon demurrer to the indictment or to a special plea or pleas to the indictment, the statute does not expressly require, as it should have done, that the question raised shall be passed upon by the court below; as, however, the statute does not forbid the court below to pass upon such question before reporting the case to this court, we think the duty to do so is to be implied.

This is in accordance with the presumption in favor of the constitutionality of legislation and with the rule that when a statute is susceptible of two constructions, that should be adopted which will effectuate the manifest intention of the lawmaker.

Proceedings dismissed.

Latest Publications.

Sansum's Digest of Law of Insurance. A Digest of all the Fire, Life, Marine, Accident and Guarantee Insurance cases decided in Great Britain and America. By O. B. Sansum. 8vo, 600 pp., Law Sheep. - - - - - 8 00

Bissell's Reports. Volume VI. Reports of cases argued and decided in the Seventh Judicial Circuit. By Josiah H. Bissell. 8vo 650 pp., Law Sheep. 7 50

Massachusetts Reports CXIX. Reports of cases argued and decided in the Supreme Judicial Court of Massachusetts. By John Lathrop, Reporter. 8vo Law Sheep. - - - 4 50

Otto's Reports on the Decisions of the Supreme Court of the United States, Vol. 1, 8vo. - - - - - 5 00

Greenleaf on Law of Evidence, Vol. 1. By John Wilder May. 13th Ed. 8vo. 6 00

Redfield on Law of Wills., Vol. 2. 3d Ed., 8vo. - - - - - - 6 00

A Treatise on Conveyances by Debtors to Defraud Creditors. By Orlando F. Bump. Second Ed., revised and enlarged. 8vo., 750 pp., Law Sheep. 6 50

Mitford & Tyler's Pleadings and Practice in Equity. By John Mitford (the late Lord Rosedale,) & Samuel Tyler, L. L. D. 8vo., 774 pp. - - 6 50

Outlines of an International Code. By David Dudley Field. Second Ed., revised and enlarged. 8vo., 800 pp. 7 50

California Supreme Court Reports, vol. 50. 8 vo., 725 pp., full sheep, - 5 00

Reports of Cases in Law and Equity Determined in the Supreme Court of Iowa, Vol. XLI, by John J. Runnels, Reporter, 784 pp., law sheep - 005

Probate Law, by Wm. L. Smith, 8 vo., law sheep, - - - - - 2 50

Law of Damages, by Geo. W. Field, 808 pp., law sheep, - - - - - 7 50

Shaw's Index to Minn. Session Laws. 1849–1875. Full sheep. - $4 00

Minn. Reports, vol. 21, full sheep - 5 00

Minn. Session Laws, 1876, Gen. and Spec. together, full sheep. - - - 2 00

Same, half sheep. - - - - 1 75

THE SYLLABI.

VOL. 1. SATURDAY, DEC. 16, 1876. No. 9.

PUBLISHED WEEKLY,

By JOHN B. WEST & CO.,

No. 1 Wabasha St., - ST. PAUL, MINN.

Terms 3 00 per annum in Advance.

HOMER C. ELLER, Editor.

TABLE OF CONTENTS.

IN *United States vs. Larivere, et. al.*, recently decided by Supreme Court of United States. Certain spirituous liquors were seized at Crookston, in the county of Polk, Minnesota, and libeled as being unlawfully introduced into that section of the county in contravention of the terms of Treaty of Oct. 2, 1863, with Red Lake and Pembina Bands of Chippewa Indians. By that Treaty, the section of country where the liquors were seized was ceded to the United States; the seventh article of the treaty is as follows: "The laws of the United States now in force or that may hereafter be enacted, prohibiting the introduction and sale of spiritous liquors in the Indian country, shall be in full force and effect throughout the country hereby ceded until otherwise directed by Congress or the President of the United States." The question in the case was, whether the incorporation of this provision in the Treaty was a rightful exercise of power. If so the seizure of goods was proper, otherwise not, The Circuit Court of District of Minnesota, held that the seizure was wrongful.

The Supreme Court reviews the various cases on the subject, (*Cherokee Nation vs. Georgia* 5 *Peter*, 1; *Worcester vs. same*, 6 *Peter*, 515; *U. S. vs. Haliday*, 3 *Wall.*, 409,) and in reversing the judgment of the Circuit Court say "The Act of Congress imported into the Treaty applies alike to all Indian tribes occupying a particular country, whether within or without State lines; and as it is based exclusively on the Eederal authority over the *subject matter* there is no disturbance of State equality. Besides the power to make Treaty with the Indian Tribes is as we have seen co-extensive with the power to make treaties with foreign nations. And it cannot be doubted that the treaty making power is ample to cover all the usual subjects of diplomacy with different powers. One of these subjects relates to the acquisition and distribution of property belonging to the citizens or subjects of each, in the territory of the other. A treaty embracing this matter may contravene the statùtes of a State; but if it does,the Courts would disregard them and give to the alien the full protection accorded him by the treaty. If this result can be obtained by treaty with a foreign nation, surely the Federal Government can in the exercise of its power to treat with Indians, make provision over a subject like the present, coming as it does within the clause relating to the regulation of commerce."

ONE of the most concise as well as complete law books that has appeared in many a day, is Stephen's Digest of Evidence. Though small in size the immense amount of matter the author contrives to condense into its pages is remarkable. Taking the law of this one subject, he reduces it to a few general rules, grouping them together so that a ready comprehension of the whole is at once attained, at the same time explaining their extent and application by illustrations that are models of brevity and cleverness. It is a work that the practitioner as well as student, can read with pleasure, and study with profit. Price. $1.50. For sale by

JOHN B. WEST & Co.

THE Law of Homestead and Exemptions, by John H. Smyth; Sumner, Whitney & Co., San Francisco, Cal., Publishers—an excellent compendium of the law upon this very important and practical subject. Price, $5.00; for sale by

JOHN B. WEST & Co.

Supreme Court, State of Minnesota.

Henry Rippe, *Respondent*, *vs.* The Chicago, Dubuque & Minnesota Railroad Co., *Appellant.* } Filed May 15, '76.

Where evidence of a proceeding in a cause, is contained in a return on file in this court, made in a former appeal of the same cause, it is competent for the court to refer to such return to ascertain the character of such proceeding.

In condemnation proceedings taken under the general railroad act, an appeal from an award of damages made by Commissioners therein, only brings before the District Court the propriety of the amount of such award, where, as in this case, the petition for the appointment of commissioners particularly specifies the property to be condemned, names the contesting claimant as its sole owner, and and a trial is had and an award is made by them upon that basis, with the consent of both parties.

When the accuracy of a plat is verified by a witness as correctly representing the relative situation and location of certain lots with reference to other property, it is not error to allow such witness, on his examination, to use the plat in pointing out to the jury such (lots,) their situation and location.

An owner of lots abutting upon the Mississippi River possesses the riparian right of constructing thereon suitable landings and wharves for the convenience of commerce and navigation, and to extend such construction out into the river to the point of navigability.

In view of the issue in this case certain evidence tending to show the extent, character and duration of respondent's possession of certain lots and a long continued acquiescence therein, on the part of the original patentee and intermediate grantees, held competent upon the question whether, in fact, they abutted upon the river.

Testimony tending to show that a warehouse erected for the storage and shipment of wheat, &c., possessed superior facilities over other structures of a like character in the same vicinity for transacting such business cheaply, by reason of the manner of its construction and more favorable location with reference to the river, is competeut evidence upon the question of value.

There is sufficient competent evidence in this case to support the amount of the verdict, and to preclude any interference by the appellate court.

Cornell, J.— None of the proceedings herein prior to the report of the Commissioners are contained in the return and paper book now before us; but as this cause has heretofore been before this court on an appeal from an order dismissing the petition, and subsequent proceedings, it is competent and proper to refer to the return thus made and now on file, for the purpose of ascertaining the character of the petition and order which constitute the foundation of these proceedings. By such reference it is ascertained, that the company, claiming to be a railroad corporation organized under the general laws of the State, with power and authority to construct a railroad over a certain line or route therein specified, and desiring to acquire the title to certain lands, &c., which it deemed necessary to take and appropriate for the purposes of its enterprise, sought the appointment of commissioners to ascertain and appraise the amount of damages occasioned thereby to the owners, respectively. It is stated in the petition, "*inter alia*," that "the land, property and real estate which it will be necessary to take, appropriate and use for the purposes of said enterprise, together with the names of the owners of said property, or so far as the same are known," are as follows, namely: "a strip of land one hundred feet wide of each" of certain therein described government subdivisions, and also certain village lots, described as "lots in the village of Brownsville, Minnesota, numbered 140, 141, 142 and 143," of which last numbered lots, Henry Rippe is named as the owner.

The order appointing the commissioners was based upon this petition, and followed it. It appears from their report that they examined the line of the road as laid across these lots, heard the respective parties claiming an interest in the matter, &c., and awarded a certain amount of damages for each of said lots to said Rippe, as such owner. In other words, Rippe was regarded and treated in the controversy before them as the sole claimant and owner of the lots, No other party appearing to claim any interest, lien or estate therein, and the damages awarded were in respect to the entire estate and interest, which the company, under its proceedings, had the right to acquire in, and to, said lots, and for all injuries sustained by the absolute owner of such estate by reason of such taking and appropriation.

From the award thus made, Rippe, as absolute owner, appealed to the District Court, on the ground of its insufficiency in amount.

It nowhere appears, in any of the proceedings, that he ever occupied any other or different relation thereto than the one which the company gave him in its petition, that of absolute owner in fee, of the entire premises, and it must be assumed that his appeal was brought and prosecuted in that character.

On the trial of the appeal, the evidence established the uncontroverted fact, that at the commencement of these proceedings Rippe was, and for a long time prior thereto had been in the actual and undisturbed possession and occupancy of the lots, claiming to be their sole owner in fee, and it did not appear that any one was claiming any adverse estate or interest whatever therein. It was, however, objected by the company, during the trial, that in order to enable the plaintiff to introduce evidence tending to show the value of said premises, it was necessary for him to show title thereto, other than that evidenced by possession; which was over-ruled by the court. Defendant also introduced in evidence a patent from the United States to one McPhail, showing title in fee in said premises in himself, and said plaintiff in reply introduced record evidence of several intermediate conveyances from McPhail to Rippe, whereby, it is claimed, he became invested with the fee of said premises; and several questions were raised and decided in regard to the admissibility of such record evidence.

Upon the issue thus made by the evidence, the jury found the title in fee to said premises to be in the plaintiff, and the question is now raised in this court as to the correctness of the various rulings of the court below in connection with this subject.

In this same case, (20 *Minn.* 187) this court, in speaking of the appeal to the District Court, says "the appeal brought before the court only the question of the propriety of the amount of damages awarded; the whole scope of the appeal was to secure a retrial of the matter submitted to and passed upon by the commissioners." *Citing Turner et al. vs. Holleran et al.*, 11 *Minn.* 253 and *Schermeely vs. The Stillwater and St. Paul Railroad Company*, 16 *Minn.* 506. In the case of *Knauft et al. vs. The St. Paul, Stillwater and Taylor Falls Railroad Company*, similar to the present in respect to the petition, which was decided at the April Term, 1875, but is not yet reported, the point was distinctly presented whether any evidence of title on the part of the claimant to the property taken by the company, and which was the subject matter of the award appealed from, was necessary on his part on the trial of the appeal, and the court held that it was not. So in the case of the *Trogdens vs. The Winona and St. Peter Railroad Company*, recently decided, it was held that on proceedings of this character the sole matter to be submitted and passed upon by the jury is that which was considered and determined by the commissioners in making their award.

These cases are decisive of the present so far as the question now under consideration is concerned. The company had asked for the condemnation of certain lots upon which they had located their road, and which they alleged belonged to Rippe. There was no controversy before the commissioners as to the ownership nor as to the character and extent of Rippe's interest.

The award was made in reference to the entire estate in fee in the lots, and not in respect to any less estate nor to any undivided or other interest therein. The matter for retrial, therefore, before the jury was the propriety of the amount of such award in respect to such estate in fee as an entirety and unincumbered. The submission to the jury of any other question would not have been the one which was submitted to and passed upon by the commissioners. The company, in our judgment, was estopped from denying before the jury that the respondent had any title or estate in the premises, or from asserting that he had any other or different estate or interest than that attributed to him in the proceedings, and in respect to which the commissioners had awarded damages. Hence the issue raised by the evidence and submitted to the jury upon this question was irrelevant. As their verdict, however, was in favor of respondent, no prejudice resulted. In view of these considerations it becomes unnecessary to examine the rulings of the court upon the record evidence offered and introduced on the part of respondent in support of his title, or upon that offered by appellant to controvert the same.

It also follows that no error can be predicated upon the ruling of the court, that possession of the lots in question was *prima facie* evidence of title in fee and sufficient, on his part. It is objected as error that the respondent, on his examination as a witness in his own behalf, was permitted the use of a certain plat of the town of Brownsville, to aid him in indentifying the premises, but for no other purpose, so far as witness from his own knowledge of the premises and their surroundings, was able to verify the accuracy of such plat as being a correct representation of the situation of the lots in controversy in reference to each other, to the river, to contiguous streets, and other lots in Brownsville, and was allowed from such knowledge to point out to the jury therefrom, such lots and their relative situation; there was no error, but the witness seems to have been allowed without any specific objection to testify as to the size of the lots as they appeared from the map; This of course was inadmissible and under proper objection would have been error; but as the same facts shown by the plat were abundantly established by other competent evidence, it could have worked no prejudice and furnishes no ground for a re-trial; Conceding that these lots abutted on the Mississippi river, a legally declared public highway, there can be no question but that their owner possessed the riparian right of constructing thereon suitable landings and wharves for the convenience of commerce and navigation, (*Dutton vs. Strong*, 1 *Black* 23. *Railroad Co. vs. Schurmier*, 7 *Wall* 272.) and to extend such constructions out into the river to the point of navigability, *Dutton vs. Strong*, 1 *Back* 23; whether these lots were in fact so bounded on the river, was a question of fact for the jury upon the whole evidence under proper instructions of the court.

The testimony introduced tending to show how they had always been used, and the extent character and duration of respondents possession, without question and with the full knowledge and acquiescence of the patentee from the government, and the intermediate grantees, was competent evidence bearing upon this point proper to be submitted to the jury under suitable instructions which it must be presumed were given in this case.

That the value of a ware.house in any given locality depends somewhat upon its facilities for accomodating and doing cheaply, the business required of such a structure, at such a place, as compared with other buildings of like character in that vicinity, is too apparent for argument.

The testimony tending to show that wheat could be handled at less expense in plaintiff's warehouse in that place by reason of its construction and more favorable in its location, in reference to the river was unobjectionable.

There is sufficient competent evidence as to the value of the property in question upon which to support the verdict of the Jury as to the amount of damages, and to exclude any inference by the appellate court that it was the result of passion or predjudice. Nor is the amount of the verdict such as to rouse any presumption that the Jury was unduly influenced by any statements or expressions of opinion by Counsel as to the value of certain testimony, or concerning the merits of the case, or by any peculiarity in his manner while addressing the Jury, in summing up the case.

Judgment affirmed.

THE STATE OF MINNESOTA, *ex. rel.* DAVID E. SEIPP, *Relator.* *vs.* NEWTON MCFADDEN, *Respondent.* } Filed, May 29, 1876.

Legislative power over counties is supreme except as retrained by the Constitution either expressly or by necessary implication.

The Act of March 6th, 1876, entitled, "An Act in relation to Cass County and to attach the same to the County of Crow Wing," contravenes no provision of the Constitution, and is a valid law. After the passage of such Act the County Commissioners of Cass County had no power to remove the Tre..surer of such County nor fill the vacancy thereby created.

CORNELL, J.—The main question discussed by Counsel and presented for adjudication. is whether the Act of March 6th, 1876, entitled, "An Act in relation to Cass County. and to attach the same to the county of Crow Wing," which practically disorganizes the former and attaches it to the latter county for Judicial, record and taxing purposes, is within or without the limits of legislative power under the State Constitution. It cannot be doubted that the power of State legislation over counties is plenary and absolute. except as restricted by the Constitution either in express terms or by necessary implication. It is claimed that the act in question contravenes the provision of Section 1, Article 11, which is in these words, "The Legislature may from time to time establish and organize new counties, but no new county shall contain less than four hundred square miles; nor shall any county be reduced below that amount; and all laws changing county lines in counties already organized, or for removing county seats shall, before taking effect, be submitted to the electors of the county or counties to be affected thereby, at the next general election after the passage thereof, and be adopted by a majority of such electors; counties now established may be enlarged but not reduced below four hundred square miles."

It is quite clear that a distinction is here made between an established, and an organized county, while the power in the Legislature to create either is expressly recognized. As to the latter, its boundary lines shall not be changed at all except by a vote of the majority of the electors to be affected, while as to the former, the only restriction is that against reducing its territorial area below four hundred square miles—so that this restriction is observed by the Legislature, the boundaries of an organized county may be altered in any manner according as its wisdom or caprice may suggest without consulting or regarding the wishes even of the resident electors and inhabitants. An established county, in the Constitutional sense, is a territorial sub-division of the State with certain prescribed boundaries, designated and set apart by Legislative authority, for the election and creation of an organized county with the powers and incidents pertaining to a *quasi* corporation of that character, whenever in the judgment of the Legislature it should contain the requisite population for that purpose.

The manifest object sought in the establishment of such counties, in advance of settlements, is to secure to each, a territorial area of sufficient size and with suitable boundaries to accommodate, when settled, its entire population, to obtain efficient county governments, and to avoid the evils supposed to be incident to their formation out of sparsely settled districts, under the influence of local considerations, having reference rather to the interests of some town site expectant, the advantages of a county seat, than the well being of the whole.

In furtherance of this object it was deemed necessary to prohibit it, the Legislature from reducing the area of any county organized or unorganized below the standard fixed by the Constitution, also from removing county seats, and from changing the boundaries of any organized county without the consent of the people to be affected, and this is the whole purport and effect of the limitations upon legislative power imposed by the section under consideration.

Outside these exceptions the whole field of legislative power over counties and county governments is left open, and the authority of the Legislature therein is supreme. It may at pleasure create, alter, modify and abolish without the consent of the people or corporation to be thereby effected. This results from the very character and object of a county organization, and the political nature of the powers and functions with which it is invested, the creation of such an involuntary and *quasi* corporation belongs to and is a part of the general governmental policy of the State, and the powers conferred upon it are given mainly, if not exclusively, for public purposes connected with matters of local administration and concern and can never become vested, as against the sovereign whose right of control over all its civil, political and governmental powers is necessarily supreme in the absence of any Constitutional limitations, *Com's Ham. Co. vs. Mighels*, 7 *Ohio St.* 118. *Dart. Coll. vs. Woodward.* 4 *Wheat*, 518. 1 *Dill Minn. Corps., Sec.* 10, 15, 30, 38 *and* 39, *and cases referred to in the notes.* The whole effect of the act under consideration is to reduce the County of Cass from an organized to an unorganized or established County, by taking from it the powers and functions pertaining to its organized existence, and transferring them to Crow Wing County, to which it is attached for Judicial record and taxing purposes; to be held and used by the latter for the benefit of the people of the former, and the public good as therein provided. This in no way interferes with the establishments of Cass County, nor does it remove its county seat. The locality of the latter still remains unchanged and is the place for the transaction of the business of the County, whenever the law making power shall see fit again to empower it with the capacity to act and do business. It is claimed that the law is defective in omitting to make any proper provisions for returning and canvassing the votes of the electors of Cass County. Conceding this to be so, as to which, however, no opinion is expressed, the Act would not therefore be objectionable as one distranchising the people of that County.

Disfranchising an elector is an entirely different thing from that of failing to afford him an opportunity, or the means whereby he can enjoy his right of voting in the place where he resides. A person residing outside the limits of an election precinct may not be able, for the time being, to exercise all his rights as an elector, but he is not thereby dispossessed of those rights.

By Section four of the Act, "the public records, safes and office furniture of said Cass County" are required "to be transferred to and kept in the possession and custody of Crow Wing County, for the use and benefit, and as the property of Cass County." This property was held by Cass County as a public corporation, solely and exclusively for public purposes, concerning chiefly the people of that County, though beneficial in part to the whole State.

It may be doubted whether such property thus held, is private within the meaning of the constitutional provisions which prohibits the taking of private property for public use without compensation.

Darlington vs. Mayor, &c., 31. *N. Y.* 164.

Whether this is so or not, however, is not and need not be determined, as the law in question does not propose to appropriate the property to any new or different use, but simply to entrust its care and custody to another public agency, for the same public use and purpose, and this clearly violates no clause of the Constitution, either in its letter or spirit. Those provisions of the law which relate to the levy and collection of taxes, specifying their objects and limiting their amount, as well as those providing for a settlement and adjustment of the indebtedness of the County are strictly germain to the subject of the enactment as expressed in its title, and do not render it invalid as embracing more than one distinct subject.

Heenan vs. Sups. Ramsey Co., 2, *Minn.* 330.

The law being a valid one the County Commissioners of Cass County had no authority after its passage to create any vacancy in the office of County Treasurer by removal, nor to fill it by appointment. By the express terms of the Act the "functions of all the officers of such County closed from and after its passage" save as provided by section ten, which merely permits them to continue in office for the period of six months for the specific purposes therein named and of course with such powers only as are necessary to accomplish those purposes.

The peremptory writ of mandamus, is denied and the alternative writ discharged.

GILFILLAN, C. J.—*dissenting*—The Constitution, Art. 11, makes a clear distinction between organized counties and those which are merely established and not organized. As to the latter there is no restriction upon the power of the Legislature except that they shall not be reduced below four hundred square miles in area. as to the former no change can be made in the County lines, nor in the location of the County Seats without a vote of the electors of the County or counties to be affected by the change. This distinction is made clearly on account of, and for the purpose of protecting the rights and interests of the people in organized Counties. From the time of their full organization the people within a county are a *quasi* corporation—a political community for the purposes, and with limited powers of, local self-government, and from that time such people are, as a political community, protected by the Constitution from changes in their component parts, by mere act of the Legislature. The letter of that instrument, it is true, prohibits only changes in the County lines, but I think its intent and spirit goes further. It would be strange if the Constitution for the purpose of protecting these *quasi* corporations should prohibit the moving of a County line a few feet easterly or a few feet westerly, without the consent of the electors; but should allow them to be entirely obliterated, so far as they define the limits of an organized political community by the abolition of such community. I look upon the abolition of an organized County as a change of the lines of such organized County within the meaning of the Constitution. Besides, there is no prohibition to change the lines of merely established Counties except that they should not be reduced below four hundred square miles. Within that restriction the Legislature may reduce or enlarge them ; may divide one into several, or may unite several into one. And if the Legislature may reduce a County from the condition of an organized to that of an established County, all that is needed to allow the Legislature to do what the Constitution prohibits, is to abolish the organization of the Counties with respect to which it may desire to exercise the power to change. Counties come under the protection of the Constitution, from Legislative interference with their boundaries, as soon as organized, and I do not think that this protection can be removed by mere Legislative Act.

In my opinion the Act repealing the Act organizing Cass County is unconstitutional.

MARK D. FLOWER, *Respondent.*
vs.
JOHN GRACE, *et. al.* *Appellant.*
} Filed, May 22, '76.

An order allowing a new trial reversed. It appearing not to have been granted upon any ground upon which it could properly have been granted.

BERRY, J. In this case defendent had a verdict; but upon plaintiff's motion, upon a case settled, a new trial was granted. The record does not disclose the grounds upon which the motion was based. As no exceptions were taken by the plaintiff, and no question of excessive damages is raised it could properly be based only upon the ground that the verdict was not justified by the evidence. And of course it could not be properly granted upon any other ground. The order granting the new trial was accompanied by this memorandum, signed by the Judge, viz: "I grant this motion in the exercise of a discretion with which I deem the law has vested me, and in furtherance of substantial justice. One reason for granting the motion is that I think it probable the Jury were unduly influenced by the testimony of the defendant, commencing at line 145, case, admitted without objection, and not commented upon by the Court." Whatever may have been the grounds upon which the new trial was gaanted it is apparent from this memorandum that it was not upon the ground that the verdict was not justified by the evidence. The reason specially assigned by the Court is unsound. The testimony referred to, was not only not objected to but it was entirely harmless. This was an action of claim and delivery in which plaintiff sought to recover the possession or value of twenty cases of boots. The defence was, that defendant as Sheriff, by virtue of an execution issued upon a judgment against Stewart & Co., levied upon the same and took them into his possession, from the possession of said Stewart & Co. The plaintiff's theory was, that the property in controversy was in his possession when it was levied upon and taken. The defendant's theory was, that it was in the possession of Stewart, who constituted the firm of Stewart & Co. There was testimony in the case having a tendency to sustain each of these theories.

Now the testimony referred to in the memorandum was "that there was no affidavit of the plaintiff's claim of title to these goods served in this case." This testimony was evidently introduced with reference to Sec. 137, Ch. 60, General Statutes, as in effect construed in *Barry vs. McGrade*, 14. *Minn.* 163, and the worst that can be said of it, is that it was superfluous as going to prove something which the law would imply in the absence (as in this case) of evidence affirmatively, showing the service of the prescribed affidavit; as there is certainly evidence in the case upon which the jury might have arrived at their verdict, and as the order allowing the new trial appears not to have been granted upon the insufficiency of the evidence to justify the verdict, we perceive no ground upon which it can be sustained and it is accordingly reversed.

MASON E. CRITTENDEN, *et al.*, *Appellants.* *vs.* DANA WHITE, *et al.*, *Respondents*, — Filed May 17, '76.

If a patentee complies with the laws of Congress on the subject, he has a right to sell hie property anywhere in the United States, and a State Law attempting to regulate the sale of patent rights, granted pursuant to the act of congress is void.

GILFILLAN, C. J.—The only question in this case which is necessary to consider, is the validity of the "act to regulate the sale of patent rights and prevent frauds in connection therewith," passed Mar. 6, 1871. This act requires of the owners of patent rights, the performance of certain acts before they can sell such rights within the state and makes it a misdemeanor to sell such rights without having performed such acts. A similar law of the State of Indiana came before the United States Court in the case *Ex parte Robinson 2 Bissell* 309. and was held invalid for reasons so sound and conclusive that we need do nothing more than copy them from the report of the case. "It is clear that this kind of legislation is unauthorized; to Congress is given, by the constitution, the power to promote the progress of science and useful arts, by securins for limited times to authors and inventors the exclusive rights of their respective writings and discoveries.

This power has been exercised by congress, who has directed the manner in which patents shall be obtained, and when obtained how they shall be assigned and sold. The property in inventions exists by virtue of the laws of Congress, and no state has a right to interfere with its enjoyment or to annex conditions to the grant. If the patentee complies with the law of Congress on the subject, he has a right to go into the open market anywhere within the United States and sell his property. If this were not so it is easy to see that a state could impose terms which would result in a prohibition of the sale of this species of property within its borders, and in this way nullify the laws of Congress which regulate its transfer, and destroy the power conferred upon Congress by the constitution."

The act referred to is invalid, and non-compliance with its terms furnished no defense to the note in question.

Order denying a new trial is reversed.

Latest Publications.

Stephens' Digest of the Law of Evidence; edited, with notes and references, by J. W. May. - - $1.50

Sansum's Digest of Law of Insurance. A Digest of all the Fire, Life, Marine, Accident and Guarantee Insurance cases decided in Great Britain and America. By O. B. Sansum. 8vo, 600 pp., Law Sheep. - - - - - 8 00

Bissell's Reports. Volume VI. Reports of cases argued and decided in the Seventh Judicial Circuit. By Josiah H. Bissell. 8vo 650 pp., Law Sheep. 7 50

Massachusetts Reports CXIX. Reports of cases argued and decided in the Supreme Judicial Court of Massachusetts. By John Lathrop, Reporter. 8vo Law Sheep. - - - - 4 50

Otto's Reports on the Decisions of the Supreme Court of the United States, Vol. 1, 8vo. - - - - - 5 00

Greenleaf on Law of Evidence, Vol. 1. By John Wilder May. 13th Ed. 8vo. 6 00

Redfield on Law of Wills., Vol. 2. 3d Ed., 8vo. - - - - - - - 6 00

A Treatise on Conveyances by Debtors to Defraud Creditors. By Orlando F. Bump. Second Ed., revised and enlarged. 8vo., 750 pp., Law Sheep. 6 50

Mitford & Tyler's Pleadings and Practice in Equity. By John Mitford (the late Lord Rosedale,) & Samuel Tyler, L. L. D. 8vo., 774 pp. - - - 6 50

Outlines of an International Code. By David Dudley Field. Second Ed., revised and enlarged. 8vo., 800 pp. 7 50

California Supreme Court Reports, vol. 50. 8 vo., 725 pp., full sheep, - 5 00

Reports of Cases in Law and Equity Determined in the Supreme Court of Iowa, Vol. XLI, by John J. Runnels, Reporter, 784 pp., law sheep - 5 00

Probate Law, by Wm. L. Smith, 8 vo., law sheep, - - - - - - 2 50

Law of Damages, by Geo. W. Field, 808 pp., law sheep, - - - - - 7 50

Minn. Session Laws, 1876, Gen. and Spec. together, full sheep. - - - - 2 00
Same, half sheep. - - - - 1 75

THE SYLLABI.

VOL. 1. SATURDAY, DEC. 23, 1876. No. 10.

PUBLISHED WEEKLY,

By JOHN B. WEST & CO.,

No. 1 Wabasha St., - ST. PAUL, MINN.

Terms 3.00 per annum in Advance.

HOMER C. ELLER, Editor.

TABLE OF CONTENTS.

WE are indebted to Hon. C. C. Wilson, of Rochester, Minn., for the following decision, recently made by His Honor Judge Mitchell, of the Third District, with reference to the right of *National Banks*, to acquire title to "promissory notes," as choses in action, by purchase.

First National Bank of Rochester. vs. F. M. Pierson. } *District Court. Olmsted County.*

Action on promissory note.

"MITCHELL J.—This cause came up for hearing on motion of defendant, for a new trial, on the ground of alleged errors of law occurring during the trial and duly excepted to. Upon the trial, defendant requested the court to instruct the jury to find a verdict for defendant, for the reason that plaintiff had no authority to purchase or traffic in promissory notes as choses in action or personal property, and that it was undisputed by the evidence that the transaction under which plaintiff, claimed to have acquired the note in question was a "purchase," and not a "discount." The request was refused for the purpose of further consideration of the point.

Upon examination of the evidence, it seems to me undisputed that this transaction was an out and out "purchase" of the note, and not "discounting," nor lending money on the credit of it. The fact that the payee endorsed it does not change the character of the transaction.

On comparison of section 13 of our State law with section 8 of the U. S. Statute, we think the latter gives no greater power in the premises, than was given by the former to our State Banks.

If this be so, then in the absence of any authoritative construction of the U. S. Statutes, by the Federal Courts, we think the decision of our Supreme Court, in the case of *Bank vs. Baldwin*, is decisive of the case.

On this point, and on this alone, I think a new trial should be granted.

Ordered therefore, that a new trial be and the same hereby is granted in this case."

Dated December 5. 1876.

Jones & Gove, Attorneys for plaintiff.
Chas. C. Wilson, Att'y for def't, Pierson.

U. S. CIRCUIT COURT—MINNESOTA DIST.

THE MINNESOTA LINSEED OIL CO. *vs.* THE COLLIER WHITE LEAD CO.

In "contracts by telegraph" the same rule prevails as in contracts by mail; The contract is completed when an acceptance of the proposition made is deposited, for transmission, in the telegraph office.

In case of a proposition by telegraph for the sale of certain goods, the market for which, was subject to sudden and great fluctuations, *held*, that an immediate answer should have been returned, and that an acceptance of such proposition telegraphed after a delay of twenty-four hours from the time of its receipt was not an acceptance within a reasonable time, and did not operate to complete the contract.

This action was removed from the State court and a trial by jury is waived.

The plaintiff seeks to recover the sum of $2,151.50 with interest from September 20, 1875—a balance claimed to be due for oil sold defendant.

The defendant in its answer alleges that on August 3d, 1875, a contract was entered into between the parties whereby the plaintiff agreed to sell and deliver to the defendant at the city of St. Louis, during the said month of August, twelve thousand four hundred and fifty (12,450) gallons of linseed oil for the sum of fifty-eight (58) cents per gallon, and that the plaintiff has neglected and refused to deliver the oil according to the contract; that the market value of oil after August 3d, and during the month was not less than seventy (70) cents per gallon, and therefore claims a set-off or counterclaim to plaintiff's cause of action.

The reply of the plaintiff denies that any contract was entered into between it and defendant.

The plaintiff resided at Minneapolis, Minnesota, and the defendant was the resident agent of the plaintiff, at St. Louis, Missouri. The contract is alleged to have been made by telegraph.

The plaintiff sent the following dispatch to the defendant:

MINNEAPOLIS, July 29, 1875.
"To Alex. Easton, Secretary Collier White Lead Co., St. Louis, Mo.:
Account of sales not enclosed in yours of 27th. Please wire us best offer for round lot named by you—100 barrels shipped.
MINN. LINSEED OIL CO."

The following answer was received:

ST. LOUIS, MO., July 30, 1875.
"To Minn. Linseed Oil Co.:
Three hundred barrels 55c here, 30 days, no commission, August delivery, answer.
COLLIER CO."

The following reply was returned.

MINNEAPOLIS, July 31, 1875.
Will accept (58c) fifty-eight, on terms named in your telegram.
MINN. LINSEED OIL CO.

This dispatch was transmitted Saturday, July 31, 1875, at 9:15 P. M., and was not delivered to the defendant in St. Louis, until Monday morning, August 2, between eight and nine o'clock.

On Tuesday, August 3d, at 9:53 A. M., the following dispatch was deposited, for transmission, in the telegraph office:

"ST. LOUIS, MO., Aug. 3, 1875.
To Minnesota Linseed Oil Company, Minneapolis:
Offer accepted—ship 300 bbls. as soon as possible.
COLLIER CO."

The following telegrams passed between the parties after the last one was deposited in the office at St. Louis:

"MINNEAPOLIS, Aug. 3, 1875.
To Collier Co., St. Louis:
We must withdraw our offer wired July 31st.
MINNESOTA LINSEED OIL CO."

Answered.

"ST. LOUIS, Aug. 3, 1875.
Minnesota Linseed Oil Company:
Sale effected before your request to withdraw received. When will you ship?
COLLIER CO."

It appeared that the market was very much unsettled, and that the price of oil was subject to sudden fluctuations during the month previous, and at the time of this negotiation, varying from day to day, and ranging between 55 and 75 cents per gallon.

It is urged by the defendant that the dispatch of Tuesday, August 3, 1875, accepting the offer of the plaintiff transmitted July 31st, and delivered Monday morning, August 2d concluded a contract for the sale of the 12,450 gallons of oil.

The plaintiff, on the contrary, claims, 1st, that the dispatch, accepting the proposition, made July 31st, was not received until after the offer had been withdrawn; 2d, that the acceptance of the offer was not in due time; that the delay was unreasonable, and therefore no contract was completed.

Young & Newel, Attorneys for plaintiff.

Geo. L. & Chas. E. Otis, Atty's for def't.

NELSON, J.—It is well settled by the authorities in this country, and sustained by the later English decisions, that there is no difference in the rules governing the negotiation of contracts by correspondence through the post office, and by telegraph, and a contract is concluded when an acceptance of a proposition is deposited in the telegraph office for transmission. (See Am. Law Reg. Vol. 14, No. 7, p, 401 "Contracts by telegraph" article by Judge Redfield, and authorities cited; also *Trevor vs. Wood* 36, *N. Y.* 307.)

The reason for this rule is well stated in *Adams vs. Lindsell*, 1 *Barn and Ald.* 681. The negotiation in that case was by post. The court said "That if a bargain could not be closed by letter before the answer was received, no contract could be completed through the medium of the post office. That if the one party was not bound by his offer when it was accepted, (that is at the time the letter of acceptance is deposited in the mail,) then the other party ought not to be bound until after they had received a notification that the answer had been received, and assented to, and that so it might go on *ad infinitum*." (See also 5 *Penn. State Rep. p.* 339; 11 *N. Y. Rep.*, 441; *Mactier vs. Frith*, 6 *Wend.*, 103; 48 *New Hampshire, page* 14, *and* 8 *English Common Bench, page* 225.) In the case at bar the delivery of the message at the telegraph office signified the acceptance of the offer. If any contract was entered into the meeting of minds was at 8:53 of the clock, on Tuesday morning, Aug. 3, and the subsequent dispatches are out of the case. 1 *Parson on Contracts*, 482-3.)

This rule is not strenuously dissented from on the argument, and it is substantially admitted that the acceptance of an offer by letter or by telegraph, completes the contract, when such acceptance is put in the proper and usual way of being communicated by the agency employed to create it; and that when an offer is made by telegraph, an acceptance by telegraph takes effect when the dispatch containing the acceptance is deposited for transmission in the telegraph office, and not when it is received by the other party. Conceding this, there remains only one question to decide, which will determine the issues: Was the acceptance of defendant deposited in the telegraph office Tuesday Aug. 3d, within a reasonable time, so as to consumate a contract binding upon the plaintiff?

It is undoubtedly the rule that when a proposition is made under the circumstances in this case, an acceptance concludes the contract if the offer is still open, and the mutual consent necessary to convert the offer of one party into a binding contract by the acceptance of the other is established, if such acceptance is within a reasonable time after the offer was received,

The best opinion is, that what is, or is not a reasonable time must depend upon the circumstances attending the negotiation and the character of the subject matter of the contract, and in no better way can the intention of the parties be determined.

If the negotiation is in respect to an article stable in price, there is not so much reason for an immediate acceptance of the offer, and the same rule would not apply as in a case where the negotiation related to an article subject to sudden and great fluctuations in the market.

The rule in regard to the length of the time an offer shall continue, and when an acceptance completes the contract, is laid down in *Parsons on Contracts* (Vol. 1. page 482.) He says, "It may be said that whether the offer be made for a time, certain or not, the intention or understanding of the parties is to govern. * * * If no definite time is stated, then the inquiry as to a reasonable time, resolves itself into an inquiry as to what time it is rational to suppose the parties contemplated; and the law will decide this to be that time which as rational men they ought to have understood each other to have had in mind." Applying this rule it seems clear that intention of the plaintiff in making the offer by telegraph to sell an article which fluctuates so much in price, must have been upon the understanding that the acceptance, if at all, should be immediate, and as soon after the receipt of the offer as would give a fair opportunity for consideration. The delay here was too long, and manifestly unjust to the plaintiff, for it afforded the defendant an opportunity to take advantage of a change in the market and accept or refuse the offer as would best subserve its interests.

Judgment will be entered in favor of the plaintiff for the amount claimed.

Supreme Court, State of Minnesota.

WARREN CARPENTER, *Plaintiff in error*, *vs.* THE CITY OF ST. PAUL, *Defendant in error*, } Filed Dec. 12, '76.

The case of Rogers vs. the City of St. Paul, (MSS., Oct. 7th, 1875), followed as to the extent of the Legislative power of taxation under sec. 1, art. 9, of the constitution in matters of local improvement, and the delegation of such power to local tribunals.

It is competent for the Legislature to authorize a city council or other local tribunal to determine what property is benefited by any proposed local improvement and to assess the cost thereof upon such property, according to the benefits conferred. The decision of a tribunal invested with such authority, that certain property is so benefitted cannot be impeached by parol evidence showing no benefit in fact.

Sec. 60, title 1, chap. 7 of the act of March 5th, 1874, being chap. 1, special laws of that year, relate as well to cases of defective assessments originating prior to the passage of the statute, as to those occurring thereafter.

The conclusive effect of a final determination made in the matter of opening a public street and condemning land therefor by the proper authorities of the city of St. Paul, under its charter, cannot be questioned in a collateral proceeding for defects and irregularities not going to the jurisdiction.

An advertisement for bids to be put in on the 23d of June, 1873, which was published in the official paper of the city on the 12th, and continued in each successive daily issue of the paper until the 22d, inclusive, of the same month, was a full compliance with the charter provisions requiring it to be given and continued in such paper, for at least ten days, though one of such intervening publications occured on Sunday, and no paper was issued on the Monday following, as was the custom of such official paper.

CORNELL, J.—Whether in exercising the power of taxation, under sec. 1, art. 9, ofthe constitution, it is competent for the Legislature to confer upon the Common council or Board of public works of a city, authority to decide upon the local character of any contemplated public improvement within said city, to fix the amount necessary to be raised by taxation for that purpose, to ascertain what property will be benefited by the improvement, to prescribe the tax district within which the amount shall be raised, and to apportion the same by an assessment upon the property therein embraced and benefited, as also to give a final and conclusive effect to such, its decision, except in case of fraud or mistake, was fully considered and affirmatively settled in the case of *Rogers vs. The City of St. Paul Oct. Term,* 1875.

Instead of prescribing in terms the limits of the tax district for any such local improvement the legislature may, in its discretion, authorize the assessment to be made on such property as shall appear to be benefited, and empower such subordinate tribunal to ascertain and report as a matter of judgment upon actual inspection, what property will be so benefited, in which case the property so designated in the report is regarded as constituting the tax district as prescribed by legislative authority—*Cooley on Tax.* 451—*Matter of Ward, 52 N. Y.* 395—*Appeal of Powers, 29 Michigan* 504.

Those principles are decisive of the main question raised and discussed by the counsel for appellant in this case as to his right to show by parol evidence upon the application for judgment in the District Court, that the property in question was not in fact benefited by the proposed improvement, as well as the constitutional validity of the statute in question.

It follows that the proceedings upon the reassessment in this case must be sustained, unless there has been some material departure from the provisions of the statute under which the judgment was rendered.

It is claimed by the petitioner that sec. 60 of the act of March 5th, 1874, compiling the several acts relating to the incorporation of the City of St. Paul, and amending the same, (*ch.* 1, *Special laws*, 1874.) gives no authority for a reassessment in any case originating prior to the passage of such act, The language of the section is, "In all cases where application has been, or shall be made, for judgment under secs. 36, 37, 38 *and* 39 of this chapter," &c. This clearly recognizes the fact that in some cases application for judgment" has been "or may have been made under the provisions of these sections prior to the passage of the act, and when we consider that the statute is but a codification of the then existing law relating to this subject, with such amendments as experience had suggested, and that these sections were substantially taken from the act of 1871, as amended by the act of 1872 and 1873, relating to the same subject, there is no reasonable doubt that it was the intention of the Legislature by this section, not only to provide for future, but past defective assessments. It appears from the admitted facts that the application for judgment upon the original assessment was refused because of some defect, in the final order of the Common Council ordering the improvement, and because the Board of Public Works had never specially reported to the Council whether in their opinion real estate to be assessed for said improvement could be found benefited to the extent of the damages, costs and expenses necessary to be incurred in making it.

This by the very terms of the section, authorized the council to direct a new assessment, in case it should appear to it, that the said lots affected thereby, had been or would be, benefited by the improvement. In the order made by the council for the re-assessment it is expressly recited that this fact had been made so to appear, and from the record before us, it must be taken as true, as nothing appears therefrom to the contrary. The order is in all respects regular.

The point was made in opposition to the application for judgment, on the hearing in the court below, and overruled, that the street in question, concerning the grading of which the proceeding herein were being had, was not a legally established public highway, inasmuch as the land over which it run, the fee of which was in the petitioner, had never been lawfully condemned and appropriated to the public use, as such.

It was admitted that proceedings for its condemnation had theretofore been properly instituted, and that the same had been prosecuted to a final determination under the charter, but it was objected that they "were *irregular*," because of certain specified irregularities and defects; and therefore invalid The ground of the objection did not go to the jurisdiction of the tribunal charged with the proceedings, but to irregularities and defects occuring during their prosecution. Conceding their character to be such as would have affected the validity of the final adjudication, an objection properly taken in that proceeding, or on appeal, it is clear that they are not proper subject of inquiry in this proceeding. It cannot be attacked collaterally in this proceeding on any such ground.

Under a provision in the charter it was made the duty of the City Clerk "to advertise for proposals for doing the work" and "to continue such advertisement for at least ten days, in the official paper of the city." The advertisement in this case, inviting the submission of proposals for the 23, June 1873, was first given by publication in the official paper of the city on the 12th and continued in each successive daily issue of such paper until the 22d day, inclusive, of that month. This was a compliance with the statute, although, as is claimed, one of these intervening publications occurred on Sunday. and no paper was issued the following Monday, as was the custom with such official daily paper. In the case of *Sewall vs. City of St. Paul*, cited by counsel, the statute required "the notice to be given by six days publication," and the court held it to mean six distinct publications on as many different, lawful days of publication. The statute in this case only required the advertisement to be given and continued in the official paper for the space of ten days, and if it was published in every legal issue of such paper during such period, it was sufficient.

The question raised by the sixth point of the petitioner, does not appear to have been made in the court below, and is not properly before us for consideration.

Judgment affirmed,

ELIHU M. BENNETT, *Appellant*, vs. JAMES A. ELLISON, *Respondent*. } Filed Dec. 15. '76

An assignment by a debtor of his property, purporting to be for the benefit of his creditors, and fair on its face, if in fact executed by the assignor with the intent and for the purpose of thereby effecting a compromise with his creditors, is void even though the assignee have no notice of such intent.

GILFILLAN C. J.—This is an action for taking and converting personal property. The plaintiff claims title to property under an assignment to him by James P. McClelland, for the benefit of the creditors of the latter. The defendant was sheriff and had levied upon the property as the property of McClelland upon executions against him. The issue was as to the validity of the assignments. It was in the usual form of such assignments, authorizing the conversion of the property into money by sale as soon as the assignee should be able, and after paying debts and taxes due the United States, and the State, and the expenses &c. of executing the trust, to distribute and pay the remainder *pro rata* among the creditors of the assignor, and it there should be any surplus after paying such creditors, to pay over such surplus to the assignor.

The jury found a general verdict in favor of the defendant, and the court also submitted to them for their special finding this question: "Did the assignor, McClelland make this assignment with the intent and for the purpose of thereby effecting a compromise with his creditors?" To which the jury returned the answer: "Yes."

The proposed compromise which the evidence tended to prove, and to which the special verdict relates, was this: "Prior to the assignment McClelland made an effort to compromise with all his creditors upon his paying fifty per cent in full of their demands except the firm of which the plaintiff was a member, who where to receive their demand in full. A majority of the creditors had agreed to accept the propósed compromise. but others had refused to do so."

By the schedules attached to the assignment the debts of McClelland are stated at $19,982.40, and the value of his assets at $13,675.00.

After the proofs closed the plaintiff submitted to the court certain requests for instructions to the jury, mainly abstract propositions so far as regards the fact found by the special verdict, which fact must control the result of the controversy. So far as these propositions have any application to the fact as found, they are in substance these:

First—That the fact that the assignment was made with the intent and for the purpose of thereby effecting a compromise with McClelland's creditors, did not render the assigment fraudulent.

Second—That to render the assignment void as to the assignee by reason of fraudulant intent on the part of the assignor, the assignee, when he took the assignment, must have had notice of such intent.

It is the intent with which conveyances of property are made, and not the terms in which they are expressed, that determines their validity as against the creditors of the assignor. If such intent be in any manner to hinder, delay, or defraud the creditors, they are void as against the creditors intended to be hindered, delayed, or defrauded, although they may be so expressed as, if carried out according to their terms, there would be no such effect. Assignments of all the debtors' property for the payment of his debts are tolerated, although there is incidental to them the delay necessary to the conversion of the property into money, and its distribution among the creditors. In this respect they may be regarded as an exception to the rule. But no other delay than such as is reasonably necessary to the application of the property to the payment of debts is permitted. On this ground a provision in an assignment allowing the assignee to sell on credit, renders the assignment void *Greenleaf vs. Edes*, 2 *Minn.* 264, *Nicholson vs. Leavitt*, 6 *N.Y.* 510, *Brigham vs. Tillinghast*, 13, *N. Y.* 215.

Also the sole purpose of the assignment must be to immediately appropriate the debtors property to the payment of his debts. The reservation of any benefit or advantage, to the debtor before his debts shall be fully paid, will avoid the assignment. A discharge from his debts without full payment is such a benefit, or advantage to the debtor, as if the assignment exact it as a condition of participating in the distribution, it will void the assignment. *Grover vs. Wakeman*, 4 *Paige* 23, *and* 11 *Wendell* 189. The case goes so far as to hold that if a release of the debt is exacted as a condition to the right to a preference provided in the assignment, it renders the assignment void. Mr. Justice Sutherland says, (11 *Wend.*, 202,) "But where instead of directly distributing his property among his creditors as far as it will go, he places it beyond their reach by an assignment not merely for the purpose of saving it from one particular creditor to be given to another, or to be equally divided among all, but for the purpose of enabling him to extort from some, or all of them, an absolute discharge from their debts, as the condition of receiving a partial payment, he perverts the power to a purpose which it was never intended to cover and which the principle on which the right to give preference will not justify."

The assignment in this case was executed as found by the jury, with the intent and for the purpose of thereby effecting a compromise with the assignor's creditors. The purpose in executing it then was to place the property beyond the reach of creditors in order to give the assignor time, and to place him in a position. to be able to bring the creditors to compound their debts. To effect this, delay in appropriating the property to the payment of his debts, would of course be necessary. The immediate application of the property to the demand of the creditors would be inconsistent with the purpose to effect a compromise by means of the assignment, and *vice versa*. The intent to effect a compromise by means of the assignment, includes intent to delay the execution of the trust expressed in it, at least so long as might be necessary for the assignor to ascertain if the creditors would compromise. This was an intent to delay which might be necessarily incident to the execution of the trust to sell the property and pay the proceeds to the creditors, and was therefore fraudulent. The intent was also thereby to secure a benefit to the assignor, to-wit: A discharge from his debts without full payment and without even the application of all his property upon those debts. For these reasons the assignment was, as between the assignor and his creditors void. It has been decided by this court that an assignee in all assignments for the benefit of creditors is not regarded as a purchaser for a valuable consideration,when the assignment is assailed for fraud upon the creditors, and that knowledge in the assignee of the assignor's fraudulent intent is not necessary to enable the creditors to avoid the assignment. *Gere vs. Murray*, 6 *Minn.* 305. That decision is in accordance with the weight of authority and with principle. The judgment is affirmed.

WILLIAM H. GASLIN, *Appellant.*
vs.
OVID PINNEY and JANE BROCKWAY, Partners as Pinney & Brockway, *Respondents.*
Filed, May 20, '76.

Defendants were partners in a general lumber business, under the firm name of Pinney & Brockway. The partnership articles contained the following provisions, viz: "The said Pinney, party of the first part, agrees to furnish a capital of from six to ten thousand dollars, in such sums and at such times as may be drawn for by the operating agent of said parties. No single draft to exceed one thousand dollars in amount unless previous arrangement has been made to the contrary. The money so furnished, as well as that received from the sale of lumber or other products of the mill, to be used for stocking the mill with logs, erecting piers or booms, purchasing or hiring teams, the payment of running expenses and the payment of firm debts. * * * And it is mutually agreed that neither party, nor the agent of the parties, shall sign the firm name to any note or other evidence of indebtedness, except with the concurrence of both parties; nor shall the firm name be used in any case except in necessary connection with the legitimate business of the mill."

The articles further appointed William Brockway as the operating agent of the concern, providing that he should "use his best skill and judgment in purchasing logs."

In part payment for logs purchased of plaintiff, William Brockway drew five orders for the payment of money, in favor of plaintiff, directed to defendant, Pinney. Two of the orders were signed "Pinney & Brockway, by William Brockway, agent." The other three, "Pinney & Brockway, by William Brockway, agent for the firm of Pinney & Brockway." It appeared that all money, for which William Brockway ever drew upon Pinney, did not amount to $6,000.

Held, that William Brockway was authorized to draw the orders, and that they were in proper form.

California Supreme Court Reports, vol. 50. 8 vo., 725 pp., full sheep, - 5 00

Reports of Cases in Law and Equity Determined in the Supreme Court of Iowa, Vol. XLI, by John J. Runnels, Reporter, 784 pp., law sheep - 5 00

Probate Law, by Wm. L. Smith, 8 vo., law sheep, - - - - - 2 50

Law of Damages, by Geo. W. Field, 808 pp., law sheep, - - - - - 7 50

Minn. Session Laws, 1876, Gen. and Spec. together, full sheep. - - - 2 00
Same, half sheep. - - - 1 75

The American Reprint

OF THE

ENCYCLOPÆDIA BRITANNICA,

New Ninth Edition.

Volumes 1, 2, 3 and 4 are now ready.

This is the Largest and Best work of the kind in the English Language. Every Article is a Complete Treatise by the most Eminent Writers.

Send for Specimen Pages to

JOHN B. WEST & CO.

SESSION LAWS.

We have the Session Laws of Minnesota from 1849 to 1875 inclusive, 34 vols., which we offer in sets, or by the volume.

Parties wishing to fill their sets, will do well to send list at once.

We offer:

1861	2.00	1872	$3.50
1862	2.50	1873	2.50
1863	2.00	1874	2.00
1864	2.00	1875	2.50
1871	2.00	1876	1.75

Bound in Half Sheep.

We have covers for filing and preserving The Syllabi, which we will send by mail, on receipt of price, 35 cents.

John D. O'Brien. Homer C. Eller.

O'BRIEN & ELLER,

ATTORNEYS AT LAW,

Ingersoll Block, ST. PAUL, MINN.

H. A. PARTRIDGE,

Lawyer and Notary Public,

ROOM NO. 1, HARRISON BLOCK,

MINNEAPOLIS, - - MINN.

WARREN H. MEAD. CYRUS J. THOMPSON.

MEAD & THOMPSON,

ATTORNEYS AT LAW,

Cor. Third and Wabashaw Sts., St. Paul.

Special attention given to Bankrupt Proceedings and Collections. Loans securely placed.

We can supply Seals of any Size or Design

NOTARIAL SEALS for any County, **$6.75**

JOHN B. WEST & CO,

A Statute Law Against Forfeiture of Life Policies.

Massachusetts alone has this, and the NEW ENGLAND MUTUAL LIFE, of Boston, is the oldest chartered Mutual Life Insurance Company in the United States. Policies issued by this Company on life plan secure two years' insurance for each premium paid. Long term policies, up to age 60 or 70, on good lives, at from 20 to 40 per cent. less than life rates. No Tontine or other fallacious form of policy issued by this Company. Agents wanted throughout the State.

Address,
J. H. McDONALD,
General Agent,
St. Paul.

THE SYLLABI.

VOL. 1. SATURDAY, DEC. 30, 1876. No. 11.

PUBLISHED WEEKLY,

By JOHN B. WEST & CO.,

No. 1 Wabasha St., - ST. PAUL, MINN.

Terms 3.00 per annum in Advance.

HOMER C. ELLER, Editor.

TABLE OF CONTENTS.

THE question of the right of a sheriff to levy on a judgment is one the Supreme Court has not yet authoritively settled. It however came up before Wilkin, J., in the case of Bell vs. White, *et al* upon an application for an order to sell a judgment already levied upon. A motion to vacate the levy upon the ground that a judgment could not be levid upon being also made the whole matter was submitted on that question alone. The court affirmed the validity of the levy and granted the order of sale. The following is the memorandum filed:

"The plaintiff in this action having obtained judgment against the defendants and levied upon a judgment in favor of defendant White against Grant & Brosseau has applied to this court for an order to sell the judgment so levied upon.

The attorney for White contends that a judgment is not the subject of levy under execution. Our statute sec. 269, ch. 66 of the General Statutes provides as follows, viz: 'All goods, chattels, real or personal, and all property real, personal or mixed including all rights and shares in the stock of any corporation, all money, bills, notes, bank accounts, debts, credits, and other evidences of indebtedness, belonging to the defendant, may be levied upon and sold on execution.' The language of the statute is very broad and comprehensve and I do not see how upon any reasonable construction a judgment can be excluded from it operation; It is easy to see that much difficulty and confusion may arise, and great hardship result,from the enforcement of the statute in the case of judgments but the remedy must be sought from the Legislature and not from the Courts. The decisions in Iowa which have been referred to as supporting the views of the defendant's counsel are based upon a statute which is quite different in its terms from our own. In the case in the Court of Common Pleas, of this county, which was mentioned upon the argument, I find upon examination, that Judge Hall, in a passing remark, simply suggested a doubt as to whether a judgment was the subject of levy and sale under execution. It was suggested upon the argument that a sale of the judgment, under an order of this Court, would be an interference with the execution of the process of the Court of Common Pleas, in which the judgment levied upon was rendered. I do not so understand it. This Court does not attempt by its order to stay the execution, or in any way interfere with the process of the Court in which the judgment was rendered; but simply subjects this defendant's right of property in that judgment to the payment of his debts in the manner provided by law. All questions in reference to the execution of the process and the disposition of the proceeds of the execution, must be submitted to that Court as before. I conclude, therefore, that the plaintiff is entitled to the order of sale asked for. The sale, however, must be made subject to the lien of the attorney of the plaintiff in the judgment against Grant & Brosseau.

The motion to set aside the levy must be denied without costs."

Supreme Court, State of Minnesota.*

Theodore Crane, *Respondent.*
vs.
Geo. Braun, *Defendant*, J. Hauenstein, *Garnishee*, and J. B. Karl, *Claimant. Appellant,* } Filed Dec. 14, '76.

Under sec. 157, ch. 66, General Statutes, when a debt from the Garnishee to the defendant is disolosed and it appears that any person not a party, to the action is interested, or claims any interest, in the debt by an agreement or matter which existed prior to the service of the garnishee summons, such person may be permitted to appear and be made a party to the proceeding.

An instrument under seal in this form, "I, George Braun do hereby certify and acknowledge that I have on this first day of March, A. D. 1876, given up all claims I have against John Hauenstein in favor of John B. Karl," is sufficient to pass to Karl the title to any debt due from Hauenstein to Braun.

Gilfillan, C. J.—The plaintiff in a suit against the defendant instituted garnishee proceedings against Hauenstein; pending the proceedings Karl applied to be admitted as a claimant of the debt disclosed, and was so admitted; judgment was rendered in favor of the plaintiff against the garnishee for the debt disclosed, and Karl as claimant appeals; on the examination it appeared that Braun before the commencement of the garnishee proceedings, executed to Karl an instrument under seal in the words and figures following:

"State of Minnesota, County of Brown,—ss. New Ulm March 1st, 1876. I, George Braun do hereby certify and acknowledge that I have on this first day of March, A. D. 1876, given up all claims I have against John Hauenstein in favor of John B. Karl."

Two questions are raised on the appeal.

First.—Was Karl entitled to be admitted in the proceedings as a claimant of the debt garnished.

Second.—Was the instrument proved, a sufficient assignment of the debt to Karl?

It is contended that because sec. 157, of ch. 66, General Statutes which prescribe, when a claimant may be made a party to garnishee proceedings, provides that, "If it appears from the evidence or otherwise, that any person not a party to the to the action is interested or claims any interest in, any of the *property or effects* in the hands of the garnishee by virtue of any agreement or matter which existed prior to the service of the summons, the examining officer upon application, may permit such person to appear in the action" &c. and does not specifically mention the case of an *indebtedness* from the garnishee to the defendant, the latter case was not intended to be covered by the provisions of the section. It is true that most of the sections relating to garnishment preceding section 157 use the words "indebtedness to the defendant or property, money or effects" in the hands of the garnishee as though the words "property or effects" were not sufficient to cover the case of indebtedness. But we think as used in that section those words were intended to cover every case where a garnishee could be held.

They are clearly so used in other sections of the act. Sec. 164 uses the *language.* "When any person is charged as garnishee by reason of any property or effects, *other than indebtedness payable in money*" &c., which implies that the words "property or effects" as used in other parts of the act, may include an indebtedness from the garnishee: Sec. 174, provides that "If any such person is adjudged, chargeable as garnishee, his said costs and allowance shall be deducted and retained out of the *property money or effects* in his hands and he shall be accountable only for the balance" &c., and sec. 178 that "the judgment against a garnishee shall acquit and discharge him from all claims of all parties to the process, in and to the property money or effects, paid, delivered or accounted for by such garnishee by force of such judgment, no reason could be assigned why in sec. 174 the garnishee should be allowed to retain his costs and allowances out of the property by reason of which he is held, and not out of any indebtedness by reason of which he is held, nor why under sec. 178 the judgment should acquit him of any claim for property, money or effects and should not acquit him for any indebtedness for which the judgment should be rendered. It is clear that both of these sections include the case of garnishee's held by reason of indebtedness and when it is considered how careful the entire act is to guard the rights of the garnishee it cannot be doubted that sec. 157 which is intended for the protection of the rights were intended to apply to all cases of garnishment. We think therefore Karl was properly admitted as a party to the proceedings.

The instrument of assignment is certainly unskillfully drawn; But no matter how unskillful the parties to such an instrument may be in selecting terms to express their intention it is sufficient if it fairly appears that the intention was that the title to the thing should pass from one to the other and that it was upon a sufficient consideration. In this case the seal imports a sufficient consideration and although the words "given up all claims" are not the most apt terms to express a sale they certainly do show an intention that the title to the debt shall pass from Braun to Karl, and as that intention is based on a sufficient consideration it makes a valid contract of transfer.

Judgment reversed, and the court will enter judgment discharging the garnishee.

THOMAS SHEREN, *Respondent*, *vs.* R. J. MENDENHALL, and R. J. BALDWIN *Appellants*, } Filed June 27, '76.

A savings association formed for the pecuniary profit of its members is not a benevolent or charitable society within the meaning of sec's. 56, 57, ch. 17, Pub. Statute.

BERRY, J.—Section 56, ch. 17, Pub. St., (which is amended by ch. 58, Laws 1863,) authorizes any three or more persons desirous of forming any benevolent or charitable society to become a corporation upon taking certain steps prescribed therein, and in section 57, of the same chapter; Under these provisions of statute the defendants and one Murphy undertook to form a corporation the business of which is described in the "articles" as "such as is usually transacted by saving institutions," the articles provide that the "corporation shall be a joint stock company with a capital stock of twenty-five thousand dollars, divided into two hundred and fifty shares of one hundred dollars each."

By section 57 authority is given to make such by-laws and regulations as may be deemed "proper or best for the good order of the corporation," rules and regulations were adopted providing among other things for the receiving of deposits and for semi-annual payments of interest thereon at first "at the rate of six per cent per annum or such rate of interest as the profits of the association for the preceding six months will justify," and subsequently at the rate of seven per cent per annum; There is no provision in the articles by which the business of the association, is required to be conducted for the sole benefit of the defendants and for their sole profit, deducting expenses only.

It is then apparent, especially in view of the current rates of interest in this state, that this was an association for the pecuniary profit of the stock-holders; This fact is decisive against the defendants, claim that their association is a benevolent or charitable society; The leading purpose of an association is the purpose which determines its character *ex vi termini*; a benevolent or charitable association must be one whose leading purpose is benevolence or charity, and not the pecuniary advantage of its members; The fact that a savings association formed for the pecuniary profit of it stockholders will if well managed promote economy and providence in depositors is a mere incident to its characteristic purpose; any useful employment directly or indirectly benefits others than the persons employed, but if it be carried on for the pecuniary profit of such persons, it is never spoken of as benevolent or charitable.

It follows that the court below was right in holding that the association in question was not authorized by sections 56 and 57 before cited, and was therefore not a corporation.

Order refusing a new trial affirmed.

JOSEPH G. BEMIS, *Respondent*, *vs.* THE COUNTY COMMISSIONERS OF RICE CO., *Appellants*. } Filed June 26, '76.

A Sheriff has no power to bind his county by the offer of a reward for the re-capture of a person charged with crime who has escaped from the county jail.

GILFILLAN, C. J.—Two prisoners confined in the county jail of Rice county upon a criminal charge having escaped, the Sheriff of the county offered a reward for their recapture.

They were re-captured and delivered to the Sheriff, by the plaintiff, who brings this actioa against the county to recover the reward.

It was admitted by the defendant on the trial, that if the sheriff could under any circumstances offer a reward for the apprehension of a felon binding upon the public, the offer in this case was right and proper and reasonable in amount.

The sole question in the case is, can a Sheriff bind his county by an offer of a reward for the arrest of persons charged with criminal offences. escaping from his custody? No such authority, either express or implied is to be found in the statute.

At common law the powers and authority of a Sheriff were much more extensive than they are now. But no decision or text book is cited and we think none can be found which even hints at any power in the Sheriff to bind either his county or the crown by the offer of a reward for the apprehension of criminals. It was his duty and he had authority to pursue and take all traitors, murderers, felons and other mis-doers, and commit them to jail for safe custody, and for this purpose he might command all the people of his county to attend him.

No other means for the performance of his duty in arresting ciminals, seem to have been placed at his disposal, except the *posse comitatus*.

As the power to bind the county by such an offer is not to be found in the statute nor the commoa law it does not exist.

Judgment reversed.

PETER THOMPSON, *Appellant*, *vs.* C. Z. SUTTON and JAS. LINNLY, Partners as C. Z. SUTTON & CO., AARON P. MILLER and R. F. HUMISTON, Partners as MILLER, HUMISTON & CO., *Respondents*, } Filed June 14, '76.

If under sec. 269, ch. 66, General Statute a judgment can be levied upon and sold upon execution the sale can only be made "if the court so order" as provided in sec. 284 of the same chapter.

BERRY, J.—If for the purposes of this case it be admitted that under the provisions of sec. 269, ch, 66, General Statute, a judgment can be levied upon by execution. Still as it is a thing in action (*Fore vs. Manlore*, 18 *Cal.* 437. *Burtis vs. Cook*, 16 *Iowa* 194,) the sale can be made only "if the court so orders," ch. 66, General Statute § 284.

Order affirmed.

Chief Justice Gilfillan having been of counsel took no part in this case.

MARY JACOBS, *Respondent*, *vs.* JOHN FOUSE, *Appellant*,

In sec. 7 of art. VI of our constitution it is declared that "a Probate Court shall have jurisdiction over the estate of deceased persons and persons under guardianship, but no other jurisdiction except as prescribed by this constitution," the word "estates," is used only with reference to deceased persons so that the proper reading of the constitutional provisions is that a Probate Court shall have jurisdiction over the estates of deceased persons and over persons under guardianship &c; The jurisdiction over persons under guardianship embraces jurisdiction over their affairs in general, including the management and disposition of their property.

The constitutional provision quoted has the effect to invest the Probate Court with a general jurisdiction over the subject of guardianship; To this end they possess authority to put persons under guardianship, jurisdiction over persons already under guardianship, and so far as matters of guardianship are concerned, jurisdiction over persons who have been under guardianship; and it follows that they have jurisdiction to settle the accounts of the guardian of a minor ward after the ward becomes of age.

Before a guardian account is allowed notice personal or by publication is required to be given to all persons interested, of the time and place of examining and allowing the same, this notice unless effectually waived is jurisdictional;

In the absence of such waiver or notice a settlement and allow ance of a guardians account is void. The proper place to seek for an accounting is in the Probate Court.

The theory of the law of guardianship is that the guardian shall settle with the Judge of Probate or with the ward if of full age, or with his legal representatives and UPON SETTLEMENT pay over and deliver all the property in his hands belonging to the ward, including all moneys due, or that the ward shall have his action upon the guardians bond for breach of the condition to settle and pay over and deliver.

BERRY, J.—In Section 7, of Article VI of our Constitution, it is declared that "A probate court shall have jurisdiction over the estate of deceased persons, and persons under guardianship, but no other jurisdiction except as prescribed in this Constitution." The word "estates" is used only with reference to deceased persons, so that the proper reading of the Constitutional provision is that a Probate Court shall have jurisdiction over the estates of deceased persons and over persons under guardianship &c. The jurisdiction over persons under guardianship embraces jurisdiction over their affairs in general including the management and disposition of their property.

As the jurisdiction conferred, is over persons under guardianship, it is contended in the case at bar that when the guardianship ceases the jurisdiction ceases, so that it is not competent for a Probate Court to settle the account of the guardian of a minor ward, after such ward has became of age; if the words "persons under guardianship" were to be understood in the strictly literal sense of persons under guardianship at the precise time when the jurisdiction is exercised this result would appear to follow; But this construction would be impractically narrow. It would deprive the Probate Courts of large and important portions of the jurisdiction which at the time of the adoption of the constitution and prior thereto they possessed and exercised under the statutes passed in in pursuance of the organic act, and which they have without challenge continued to exercise down to the present time under the same statutes or others from time to time, enacted; This construction would deprive the Probate Courts of power to appoint a guardian where none had been appointed or one had been removed; It would deprive them of the power of authorizing a guardian bond to be prosecuted under ch. 55, General Statutes after a ward had reached majority; It would deprive them of the power to compel a guardian—a creature of their own appointment--to settle his account after the ward had become of age, and what is perhaps equally or more important it would after the same event deprive the guardian of the privilege of making a final settlement of his accounts in the court by which he was appointed, and under the direction of which he had acted; Indeed, unless possibly by some proceeding in chancery, the guardian would be unable to effect a settlement at all, after his ward had become of age, except at the latters pleasure. It is not necessary to multiply instances of other inconveniences and hardships which would follow from the construction suggested; we do not think such is the proper construction of the constitutional provisions or that it was intended to have any such effect; If it was, the course of legislation upon the powers and duties of Probate Courts and the uniform practice of the eighteen years which have elapsed since the adoption of the constitution are simply unaccountable;

In our opinion it is the design and effect of the constitutional provision under consideration to invest the Probate Courts with a general jurisdiction over the subject of guardianship; To this end they possess authority to put persons under guardianship, jurisdiction over persons already under guardianship, and as far as matters of guardianship are concerned, jurisdiction over persons who have been under guardianship. From this construction of the constitution as applied to the ease at bar it follows that a Probate Court has jurisdiction to settle the account of the guardian of a minor ward after the ward has become of age, see. *Woodbury vs. Hammond*, 54 *Me*, 344.

The present appeal is taken from an order overruling a demurrer to the complaint. The complaint alleges the appointment, by the Probate Court of Nicollet county, of the defendant as the guardian of plaintiff then a minor, that after plaintiff came of age defendant presented to said Probate Court, a false and fraudulent account of his guardianship showing that no money belonging to plaintiff remained in his hands, and caused the same to be settled and allowed by said court, and himself to be finally discharged as guardian, that in truth and in fact the defendant, at the time of said fraudulent settlement, had in his hands $751.42 belonging to the plaintiff as his ward, which he has converted to his own use. The complaint further alleges that the fraudulent account was rendered by defendant "without giving or causing to be given any notice whatever to this plaintiff, and that though she was then of age, of which fact the said defendant then and there had notice, and that the rendition of the accounts and the allowance and settlement thereof, and the defendants discharge were all without the knowledge of the plaintiff;" By sec. 18, ch. 59, General Statutes, and sec. 14, ch. 54, General Statutes, it is provided in effect that before a guardian's account is allowed notice, personal or by publication, as the Court may direct, shall be given to all persons interested, of the time and place of examination and allowing the same. This notice, unless effectually waived, is jurisdictional.

Wood vs. Myrick, 16 *Minn*. 494.

As no waiver appears in this case the want of the notice required rendered the settlement and allowance of defendant's accounts void. There is no reason then why the defendant may not now be cited into the Probate Court and compelled to settle his accounts. The relief prayed for in the plaintiff's complaint is that the allowance and settlement of the said account and the defendant's discharge be set aside and declared null and void; that defendant account for the money and interest in his hands belonging to the plaintiff, and judgment for whatever sum shall be found due. From the views before expressed it follows that there is no necessity in any event for setting aside the allowance and settlement of the account or the defendants discharge. As to a future accounting the proper place to seek it is in the Probate Court; that tribunal having already acquired and still retaining jurisdiction of the guardianship for the purpose of settling the guardian's account, a familiar rule of law requires that it should be permitted to proceed, and that its juriadiction should not be interfered with by another tribunal. As to whether irrespective of this rule it would be competent for a District Court to grant the relief prayed for in the complaint, we have no occasion to express an opinion in this case. If the plaintiff's counsel had anticipated the present aspect of this case he might possibly have claimed that irrespective of any accounting or neglect to account the defendant would be liable to the plaintiff for this *conversion* of her money.

But this is not in accordance with the theory of the law of guardianship; That theory manifestly is that the guardian shall settle with the Judge of Probate or with the ward if of full age or with his legal representatives and *upon settlement* pay over and deliver all the property in his hands belonging to the ward including all moneys due, or that the ward shall have his action upon the guardians bond for the breach of the condition to settle and pay over and deliver, *General Statutes, ch.* 59 *sec.* 17.

If a case should occur in which the guardian refused to bring in his account and make settlement of the same and in which there is no remedy upon a bond, (either for want of such bond or otherwise,) we are not to be understood, as determining that the ward could not come into the District Court for a remedy.

The order overruling the demurrer is reversed.

JACOB M. HAUBRICK, *Respondent*, *vs.* JOHN JOHNSTON, *Appellant.* — Filed Dec. 14, '76.

The sufficiency of evidence to sustain a verdict considered.

GILFILLAN C. J.—This was an action to recover the possession of various articles of personal property in the possession of defendant, at a tannery in St. Peter. A verdict was rendered for defendant, and a new trial granted on the ground that the verdict was not justified by the evidence and from the order granting it, the defendant appeals to this court.

The property, or the greater part of it, orginally belonged to one Paul, who assigned it, by an instrument in writing to plaintiff; defendant claimed to own the property, or on interest in it, and claimed to have acquired such ownership under an agreement between him and Paul, by which he was to work for Paul in the tannery, for a fixed salary, and one-half the profits of the business, and by which as he claimed he was to own an interest in the property when his half of the profits should equal half the cost of the property; and he claims that his half of the profits amounted to enough to entitle him under the agreement to be an owner of the property.

It appears, however, beyond queston, that he and Paul had submitted the matters growing out of the agreement to arbitrators, who made an award, afterwards confirmed by the court, in which they found that there had been no profits in the business of the tannery. This disposed of defendant's claim to the property which he set up under the agreement.

He also contended that the assignment of the property by Paul to plaintiff, was not a *bona fide* assignment. So far as any part of the property did not belong to Paul, of course the assignment, whether made in good faith or bad faith, could not affect such property and as the assignment appears to have been good between the parties to it, defendant cannot object to the property of Paul to which he had no title, passing by it. The good or bad faith of the assignment as to such property is a matter in which he has no interest and he therefore cannot raise the question.

Order affirmed.

CITY OF WINONA *Respondent*, *vs.* JAMES BURKE, *Relator.* — Filed Dec. 15, '76.

In a prosecution under an ordinance of a City, the ordinance should be pleaded and proved. Courts do not take judicial notice of them.

GILFILLAN, C. J.—The defendant was convicted in the court below, for the alleged violation of a city ordinance; on the trial no proof of the ordinance was made and defendant moved to dismiss the prosecution on that grouud, which motion was denied.

It is claimed on behalf of the City that because of chapter 68, laws of 1873, which provided that when the "by-laws, ordinances, &c., of any City, have been or hereafter shall be printed and published by authority of the corporation, the same shall be received in evidence in all courts and places without further proof," the court will take judicial notice of the existence of the ordinance without proof; such was not the intention of the act as is clear from its language, and does not affect the necessity of proving the ordinance. Courts do not take judicial notice of City ordinances.

Garvin vs. *Wells*, 8 *Iowa* 286.

Goodrich vs. Brown, 30 *Iowa* 291.

Such ordinances should be pleaded and proved.

Judgment reversed.

U. S. CIRCUIT COURT, MINNESOTA DIST.

JAMES A. OWENS, assignee of, MURPHY & ROWE, bankrupts, *vs.* CONRAD GOTZIAN and CHANNING SEABURY, partners &c., — Dec. Term, 1876.

The judgment of a State Court will be regarded by the Federal Courts sitting within the territorial limits of the State in which the same is rendered, as a domestic judgment.

The service of summons by a party to the action is an irregularity that is cured by entry of judgment, and will not avail when the judgment is attacked in a collateral proceeding.

"Party to the action," as used in section 47, chapter 66, p. 456 R. S. Minn., held to extend only to parties to the record.

This action was brought to recover damages for the conversion by the defendants to their own use ol certain personal property alleged to belong to the bankrupts' estate. During the trial the record of a judgment rendered in a District Court of the State of Minnesota, in an action in which the present defendants were plaintiffs, and the bankrupts were defendants, was introduced in evidence,and proof was made that the defendants purchased the property in question at a sheriff's sale under execution issued upon such judgment. The plaintiff offered to prove that the service of summons in that suit was made by a silent partner of the firm of Gotzian & Seabury, and urged that such service was invalid, and the judgment void, by virtue of the following Statute of the State of Minnesota;

"The summons may be served by the sheriff of the county where the defendant is found, or by any other person not a party to the action," R. S. Min. Sec. 47 pg. 456. The testimony offered was objected to by the defendants.

Davis, O'Brien & Wilson, for plaintiff.
Geo. L. Otis and Rogers & Rogers, for defts.

NELSON, J.—Two propositions are involved in the objection:

I. Is the judgment of the State Court a foreign or domestic judgment?

II. If a domestic judgment, can the plaintiff attack it in this suit?

In nearly every instance where the judgment of a federal court sitting within the same territorial limits, has been the subject of consideration in a state court, it has been regarded as a domestic judgment. *Thomson v. Lee Co.* 22, *Iowa,* and cases cited. For obvious reasons the judgment of a state court would be regarded as domestic by the federal courts in the same state; both federal and state courts enforce and give effect to the same laws; summon jurors from, and their judgments operate upon and compel seizure and sale of the property of, the same citizens, and are not, therefore, foreign to each other.

Being a domestic judgment it may be shown void upon its face if the court rendering it had no jurisdiction of the defendants' persons, and it is equally true that except for errors affecting the jurisdiction of the court, its validity cannot be questioned. If jurisdiction of the persons was obtained in this case in the state court, this court must regard it as conclusive of the question determined, and give it full force and effect. The record discloses personal service upon the defendants, yet the plaintiff urges that the service was made by one of the parties to the action and that such service is not permitted, and renders the judgment a nullity as to strangers to the action. This proposition is not without force. If the statute prescribes the mode and manner of service of summons, and authorizes it to be made by any person except a party to the action, the question may well be asked why a judgment entered up without any appearance of the defendants thus served is not beyond the authority of the court rendering it? Why should strangers to the judgment be prevented from establishing, perhaps a prior lien, or a superior incumbrance, on showing the service of summons was by an incompetent person? The answer is, that this error in the service did not affect the jurisdiction of the court,and is only an irregularity. The actual service upon the defendants appears in the record, and no objection being made before judgment is rendered, the defect is cured by the entry. Such is undoubtedly the rule as between parties to the suit, and it is reasonable that strangers to the record should not impeach it in a collateral action. The service shows a defect in obtaining jurisdiction, not a want of jurisdiction, and it is presumed the court when judgment was rendered determined the service attempted sufficient and passed upon that question. (22 *Iowa*, 380; 2 *Abb. P.* 344.) Again, an inspection of the record shows that the person who served the summons, although perhaps a silent partner of plaintiffs, was not by name a party to the suit. There has been no authoritative construction of this statute, but I think the term "not a party to the action" extends only to parties named in the proceedings, and not to a party in interest whose name does not appear. The objection at least should have been made before judgment was entered.

ANNOUNCEMENTS.

The Gilfillan edition of Minnesota Reports. vols. 1 to 11.

We take great pleasure in announcing a reprint of the first eleven volumes of Minnesota Reports, with notes by Hon. James Gilfillan, Chief Justice of Minnesota.

These volumes have so long been out of print, and so much called for, that we have decided to reprint them. and have made arrangements as above announced.

Prove that you desire the reprint by ordering it.

LEGAL BLANKS.

We fill promptly all orders for Legal Blanks and for the convenience of our customers, will put up all orders for two or more dozen of one kind in blocks.

Latest Publications.

The Law for the Formation of Business Corporations, with Forms, By-Laws. etc., by R. Bach. McMaster; 12mo. 50 pp. Paper, . . . $0 50

Smith's Reports, Vol. XXIX, being Vol. LXXIX of Pennsylvania State Reports; by P. Frazer Smith. 8vo. 579 pp., Law Sheep, . . . 4 50

Reports of Cases argued and determined in the Supreme Court of Appeals of West Virginia, Vol. VIII. By Henry M. Mathews. 8vo., 944 pp. Sheep, ... 4 00

Stephens' Digest of the Law of Evidence; edited, with notes and references, by J. W. May. . . $1.50

Sansum's Digest of Law of Insurance. A Digest of all the Fire, Life, Marine, Accident and Guarantee Insurance cases decided in Great Britain and America. By O. B. Sansum. 8vo, 600 pp., Law Sheep. 8 00

Bissell's Reports. Volume VI. Reports of cases argued and decided. in the Seventh Judicial Circuit. By Josiah H. Bissell. 8vo 650 pp., Law Sheep. 7 50

Massachusetts Reports CXIX. Reports of cases argued and decided in the Supreme Judicial Court of Massachusetts. By John Lathrop, Reporter. 8vo Law Sheep. . . . 4 50

Otto's Reports on the Decisions of the Supreme Court of the United States, Vol. 1, 8vo. 5 00

Greenleaf on Law of Evidence, Vol. 1. By John Wilder May. 13th Ed. 8vo. 6 00

Redfield on Law of Wills., Vol. 2. 3d Ed., 8vo. 6 00

A Treatise on Conveyances by Debtors to Defraud Creditors. By Orlando F. Bump. Second Ed., revised and enlarged. 8vo., 750 pp., Law Sheep. 6 50

Mitford & Tyler's Pleadings and Practice in Equity. By John Mitford (the late Lord Rosedale,) & Samuel Tyler, L. L. D. 8vo., 774 pp. . . 6 50

Outlines of an International Code. By David Dudley Field. Second Ed., revised and enlarged. 8vo., 800 pp. 7 50

THE SYLLABI.

VOL. 1. SATURDAY, JAN. 6, 1877. No. 12.

PUBLISHED WEEKLY,

By JOHN B. WEST & CO.,

No. 1 Wabasha St., - ST. PAUL, MINN.

Terms 3.00 per annum in Advance.

HOMER C. ELLER, Editor.

TABLE OF CONTENTS.

IN the case of *Merchants' Nat. Bank of St. Louis v. Sells*, decided at the November term, 1876, of the St. Louis, Mo., Court of Appeals, the question arose as to the liability of one, who identifies an individual as the payee of a draft to enable him to receive payment, to answer for a mistake. The facts were these: A stranger presenting himself at the plaintiff bank, and requesting the payment of a draft to one J. H. B., whom he represented himself to be, was told by the teller that he must first be identified. Shortly after he returned with the defendant's clerk, who had been sent by the defendant to identify the stranger, and stated this to the teller: "This is J. H. B.; it is all right; he (the defendant) knows him." Relying upon this, the teller paid the money to the stranger, who turned out to be an impostor. Defendant was honestly mistaken, and acted in good faith. The court held that he was not liable as a guarantor, or subject to an action for deceit. The leading case involving the question is *Pasley v. Freeman*, 3 T. R. 51. There the person making the false representation was held liable on the ground that he intended to do an injury thereby. See, also, *Eyre v. Dunsford*, 1 East, 318; *Haycraft v. Creasy*, 2, id. 92; *Ormrod v. Huth*, 14 M. & W. 651; *Russell v. Clark*, 7 Cranch, 70; *Lord v. Goddard*, 13 How. 198; *Young v. Covill*, 8 Johns. 19; *Espy v. First Nat. Bk. of Cincinnati*, 18 Wall. 604; *Litchfield v. Hutchinson*, 117 Mass. 195.—[Albany Law Journal.

A SPECIAL term of the Supreme Court will be held Tuesday, January 30th, 1877, at 10 A. M. Certain causes on the Calendar, in which present members of the Supreme Court are unable to act by reason of having formerly been counsel therein, will probably then come up for argument before the Court, organized as provided for in the amendment to section 3, article VI, of the Constitution, adopted at last election.

MITFORD & TYLER'S Pleadings and Practice in Equity, pub. by Baker, Voorhis & Co., New York; for sale by John B. West & Co., St. Paul, Minn.; 1 vol., 750 pp.—$6.50. This is an admirable work upon the subject indicated. It consists of Mitford's original treatise on Pleading in Equity, of which it has been said, ' That to no authority can reference be had with more propriety for correct information respecting the principles by which Courts of Equity are governed." To this treatise is added the copious notes of Jeremy and Smith, and several valuable chapters prepared by Hon. Samuel Tyler, of the Law Department of Columbian University, upon the general subjects of parties, forms of proceedure and practice in Courts of Chancery, especially with reference to suits in equity in United States Courts. The work is eminently practical and contains many forms and precedents of value to those practicing in the Federal Courts.

Supreme Court, State of Minnesota.

Albert Patridge, *et al.* *Appellants.* *vs.* Joseph Blanchard, *Respondent,* } Filed June 26, '76.

A complaint alleging a contract for the sale and delivery of personal property, a breach of the contract and that plaintiff has sustained damages to a specified amount, by reason of the breach is sufficient although the special damages alleged are not recoverab e.

This was an appeal from an order of District Court for county of Fillmore reversing the judgment of a Justice of the Peace, on the ground that the complaint did not state facts sufficient to constitute a cause of actions. The complaint in substance alleged pl'ffs were co-partners and engaged in the butcher business at the village of Spring Valley: That on or about the 25th day of June 1875, desiring to engage mutton, for the 4th of July next ensuing, they purchased of defendant. fourteen head of sheep at $3 per head, to be delivered by defendant to plaintiffs during the summer at their residence. and when plaintiffs should call for and want them. That in pursuance of this agreement defendant delivered three head of sheep for which plaintiffs paid him nine dollars. That on July 1st, 1875, plaintiff demanded the balance of said sheep. and though they then were, and ever since had been ready and willing to receive and pay for said sheep, defendant refused to deliver the same; That plaintiff were put to great trouble of time and expense in hunting up other sheep to supply their customers for the 4th of July, ensuing, "to-wit: two days time with horse and buggy." That they had sustained damage in the sum of twenty-five dollars by reason of defendants failure to perform his agreement, and demanded judgment for that sum.

J. Q. & J. D. Farmer, att'ys for appellants.
Dryden Smith, att'y for Respondent.

Gilfillan. C. J.—The complaint sets out a contract for the sale and delivery of the sheep and a breach of the contract. In such a case the general allegation of damage is sufficient to admit proof of, and a recovery for general damages, and it is not ground of demurrer that the allegation of special damage is insufficient.

Judgment reversed.

John H. Welch, *Respondent.* *vs.* Elizabeth J. Huntington and Benj. T. Reynolds, *Appellants,* } Filed June 27, '76.

Holly vs. same defendants decided at April Term, 1874, followed and the rules of law therein stated applied to the facts in this case.

Cornell, J.—There is not a particle of evidence tending to show that the defendant Elizabeth J. Huntington ever became a party to the contract set forth in complaint, had any knowledge of its existence, or of the erection of the block of buildings in question, or that the legal title to any portion of the land whereon it was erected had been conveyed to her, till long after the alleged transaction. It is affirmatively shown that the deed from Holly and Welch was made at the suggestion of Reynolds and her husband without any knowledge on her part, that it was not delivered to her, nor was she informed that any such deed had been made till more than two years had elapsed after the erection of the buildings under the alleged agreement. It also appears, that the interest in the land so conveyed to her, was bought and paid for by her husband and that she contributed nothing toward the purchase. or the erection of the buildings.

There is no evidence showing that she was living with her husbund at the time of the alleged transaction, or that her residence or situation was such as would be likely to afford her an opportunity of acquiring any information concerning them. It is affirmatively shown that her husband was in fact. the party to the agreement, and that in entering into it and carrying it out, he acted, and claimed to act, solely for himself. and not for, or on behalf of his wife, and there is no competent evidence whatever tending to show that he even acted as her agent in the matter either by her authority or otherwise.

From this statement of facts disclosed by the testimony and concerning which there is no conflict of evidence, it is evident that no recovery can be sustained against the defendant E. J. Huntington, (*Holly vs. same defendants*, 21 *Minnesota*, 325,) and hence as respects her, the sufficiency of the findings of fact to support the conclusion of law arrived at by the District Court need not be inquired into.

As to the defendant Reynolds, under the pleadings and upon the findings of fact as presented here, it is equally clear that no separate judgment can be rendered against him.

The cause of action relied upon in the complaint is a joint liablity against both defendants arising out of the agreement therein specified.

The separate answer of defendant Reynolds while fully traversing the matters stated in the complaint in respect to the alleged agreement the parties thereto, and the character of its obligations discloses no admission of any seperate liability from him to plaintiff, nor of any facts from which any such separate liability can be inferred and the decision of the District Court contains no finding of any facts upon which a separate judgment can be supported.

The judgment must be reversed.

STATE OF MINNESOTA, *Respondent*, *vs.* C. H. A. RICHTER, *Appellant*, } Filed June 27, '76.

Section 10, ch. 16 of the General Statutes was not repealed by ch. 61 of the General Laws of 1872.

Besides intemperate persons or habitual drunkards, the only persons referred to by sec. 11 of said ch. 16 as amended by the said act of 1872, as those to whom a sale or other disposition of spirituous or other liquors is made unlawful, are minors who are pupils or students in any public school, seminary, academy or other institution of learning within the state.

Appeal from Municipal Court, City of Minneapolis.

Arctander & Reynolds, attorneys for appellant.

E. M. Wilson, attorney for respondent.

CORNELL, J.—Chapter 61 General Laws of 1872, entitled, "An act to amend ch. 16 of the General Statutes relating to the sale of intoxicating liquors, "expressly amends section one, three and eleven of said last named chapter, adds two new sections and declares, "all acts and parts of acts inconsistent with such amendatory" act as repealed. The question pre ented calls for the construction of section eleven as amended ; as chapter 16 stood prior to the act of '72, it was declared by section ten, a misdemeanor punishable by fine not less than ten, nor more than fifty dollars, or by imprisonment, not less than ten, nor more than fifty days, for any saloon keeper, or other person therein designated to furnish intoxicating liquor to any "minor, minor servant or ward," within one year next after receiving written notice forbidding the same, from the parent, master or guardian of such minor, minor servant or ward; sec. 11 declared it a like offense subject to like punishment for any such person to furnish intoxicating liquor to any intemperate person or habitual drunkard within six months next after receiving a like notice from any member of the family of such intemperate person or habitual drunkard or from any overseer of the poor or guardian of such intemperate person &c. Each of these sections defined a separate and distinct offense though of the same grade; In respect to each of the two classes of persons therein mentioned, the power of proper self-control was presumed to be wanting, because of immature age in the one case and of mental weakness produced by habits of self-indulgence in the other and therefore both were alike regarded as fit subjects for legal protection.

Sec. 11, as amended makes it "unlawful for any person to sell or dispose of any spirituous, vinous, fermented or malt liquors, in any quantity, to any minor person, pupil or student in any public school, seminary, academy or other institution of learning within the state. or to any intemperate person or habitual drunkard," and declares such offense a misdemeanor punishable by fine "not less than fifty, nor more than one hundred dollars; or by imprisonment in the county jail not less than thirty, nor more than ninety days, or until such fine is paid. It also makes null and void the license of a person convicted of such offense and declares that no license &c. shall be construed as authorizing any sale of such liquors to the classes of persons therein named.

The true construction of this section as amended must be reached by determining what portions of ch. 16 of the General Statutes remain unaffected by the amendatory act of 1872, as it is a cardinal rule in the interpretation of Statutes, so to construe a law relating to the same general subject, as to harmonize all its provisions and give force and effect so far as possible to all its parts; sections ten and twelve are not repealed in terms and as repeals by implication are not favored in law, they must be regarded as still remaining in force, unless their provisions are so necessarily repugnant to those of the amended section that both cannot stand together; There is no such repugnancy however if we regard the sentence "a minor person, pupil or student in any public school," &c., as here used, as an elliptical one, the true meaning of which is made apparent by supplying the omitted words; Reading the sentence with the ellipsis supplied—"a minor person" (who is a) "pupil or student"—while violating no grammatical rule accords with the obvious intention of the legislature in amending the section in this particular; minor students during their absence at school are to a great extent deprived of the care and counsel of their natural and lawful guardians and the restraining influence of home at a period in life when such influence and counsel are of the most vital importance in the development of character and the formation of correct habits; To shield the inexperience of this class of pupils from any exposure to intemperance and its consequent evils, while thus helplessly situated and deprived of all parental aid and influence was manifestly the main purpose of this provision of the amended statute which prohibits the sale or disposal of any intoxicating liquor to "any minor person, pupil or student while attending school." As respects students who have reached the full legal age of discretion and responsibility no good reason occurs why any discrimination of this character should be made between them and other adult persons. The law recognizes both as alike possessed of the same legal rights and subject to like responsibilities. If the latter require no statutory restraints to prevent them from becoming inebriates the former by reason of superior educational advantages would seem to stand in still less need of legislative aid in their behalf. The conclusion which we reach then is, that section ten applies to minor persons of all classes without reference to business or occupation, while section eleven as amended applies only to students under age in attendance upon some public school, college or other institution of learning, and intemperate persons or habitual drunkards.

Under the former no offense can be committed except after notice given as therein specified while under the latter no notice whatever is required. And inasmuch as the complaint in this case does not state facts sufficient to constitute an offense under either section the decision of the Municipal Court was erroneous and the order appealed from must be reversed.

R. & J. M. WARNER, *Appellants*,
vs.
HIRAM ROGERS, *Respondents*,
} Filed May, 26, '76.

In August 1872 the owner of a lot in St. Paul leased the same to plaintiffs for a term of twenty years to commence May 1st 1873; The leased lot adjoined on the west a lot owned by Brown; on June 28 1873, plaintiffs being about to erect a brick store on the leased premises entered as parties of the first part into a sealed agreement with Brown as party of the second part, which after reciting the lease, the plaintiffs intention to erect the store, and Browns ownership of the lot adjoining proceeds as follows:

"Therefore in consideration &c. * * it is mutually agreed * * that the centre of the westerly wall of the buiding so to be erected, shall be the dividing line between the aforesaid leasehold premises * * and the said real estate of the party of the second part * * and said wall shall be and remain a party wall between the parties of the first and second part, their heirs and assigns forever; and it is further mutually agreed that whenever the party of the second part, his heirs and assigns, shall desire to use said wall they shall have the right to do so upon first paying to the parties of the first part, their heirs and assigns, one half the actual cost thereof and the parties of the first part agree to leave proper openings in said wall for the support of joists or timbers for the use of the party of the second part.

The plaintiffs proceeded to erect the wall and completed it by June 1st 1873; There was evidence tending to show that they put two windows in the wall and did not leave the proper number of places for joist; Early in June 1873 defendant entered into a written contract with Brown for the purchase of his lot and in August 1873, Brown conveyed the same to him with full covenants of warranty and seizin.

The evidence in the case tended to show that aside from the effect of the wall itself as notice the defendant before he contracted for the lot received actual and express notice of the arrangement between Brown and plaintiffs.

Shortly after receiving the conveyance from Brown the defendant erected a brick building upon the lot purchased by him using the wall built by plaintiff as the easterly wall thereof.

HELD, that under the agreement betwen plaintiffs and Brown, the plaintiffs acquired in Browns lot a right of support for the westerly half of the westerly wall of their building and that right is an easement, an incorporeal hereditament and an INTEREST in the servient estate. As such interest the agreement by which they acquired it is a conveyance by the definition found in sec. 26, ch. 40 General Statutes. As the Conveyance contains no EXPRESS covenant on the part of Brown his heirs or assigns, to pay for any part of tha party wall and under the provisions of sec. 6 ch. 40 General Statutes no covenant can be implied, the question whether defendant is liable to plaintiffs for one half of the cost of the wall upon a covenant running with the land which he purchased of Brown does not arise in this case.

The action having been dismissed by the court below upon the ground that plaintiffs had failed to establish their claim to recover of defendant, it is to assumed upon the evidence that defendant prior to his purchase had notice of plaintiffs easement in the Brown lot, and and of plaintiffs rights in respect to the same, from which it follows that defendant took the Brown lot, subject to the easement and to plaintiffs rights respecting it;among which was the right to insist that whenever Brown his heirs or assigns should desire to use the wall they should pay plaintiffs their heirs or assigns, half its actual cost.

HELD, further that defendant having used the wall cannot set up plaintiffs alleged failure to construct it according to the precise terms of the agreement as respects windows and joist holes in BAR of plaintiffs recovery.

Appeal from an order of District Court of Ramsey county, denying the motion for a new trial.

Geo. L. & C. E. Otis, and Smith & Egan, attorneys for appellants.

T. R. Huddleston, att'y for respondent.

BERRY, J.—In August 1872 the owners of a lot in St. Paul leased the same to the plaintiffs for a term of twenty years, to commence May 1st, 1873. The leased lot adjoined on the west a lot owned by Brown.

On January 28th, 1873, the plaintiffs being about to erect a brick store on the leased premises, entered as parties of the first part into a sealed agreement with Brown as party of the second part, which after reciting the lease, the plaintiffs intention to erect the store and Browns ownership of the lot adjoining, proceeds as follows, viz: "Therefore in consideration of the premises and of one dollar each to the other paid, it is mutually agreed between the said parties of the first and second part hereto, that the centre of the westerly wall of the building so to be erected shall be the dividing line between the aforesaid leasehold premises of the parties of the first part and the said real estate of the party of the second part; that said wall shall be constructed, and of the dimensions following, viz: The basement shall be of stone and not less than twenty-four inches thick and above the basement said wall shall be of brick and shall not be less than sixteen inches thick for first story and twelve inches thick above first story, and said wall shall be three stories high above the basement, and which said wall shall be and remain a party wall between the parties of the first and second part, their heirs and assigns forever; and it is further mutually agreed that whenever the party of the second part, his heirs and assigns, shall desire to use said wall, they shall have the right to do so upon first paying to the parties of the first part, their heirs and assigns, one half of the actual cost thereof; and the parties of the first part agree to leave proper openings in said wall for the support of joists or timbers, for the use of the said party of the second part; the said wall shall, after it shall become used by both of the said parties, from thence forth be kept in repair by the parties respectively, at their joint cost and expense, and in case of destruction by fire or the elements, shall be rebuilt at joint expense of both parties."

The plaintiffs proceeded to erect the wall, and completed the same by June 10, 1873: the defendant claims that they did not construct the wall in compliance with the agreement, because, as the evidence tended to thow, they put two windows in the wall, and did not leave the proper number of places for joist.

Early in June, 1873, the defendant, Rogers. entered into a written contract with Brown for the purchase of his lot, and in August, 1873, Brown conveyed the same to him with full Covenants of warranty and seizin.

Aside from the effect of the wall itself as notice to Rogers, the evidence in the case tended to show that before he contracted for the lot, he received actual and express notice of the agreement between Brown and the plaintiffs.

Shortly after receiving the conveyance from Brown, Rogers erected a brick building upon the lot purchased by him, using the wall in question as the easterly wall thereof.

The question in the case is, whether the plaintiffs can recover of Rogers one-half of the cost of the wall.

The agreement between plaintiffs and Brown "that the center of the westerly wall of the building * * to be erected (by plaintiffs) shall be the dividing line" between the leasehold premises and Brown's adjoining lot, must be taken to be an agreement that the center of the wall should be placed upon such dividing line.

This confers upon the plaintiffs the right to erect the westerly half of the wall upon Brown's lot.

Taking this in connection with the further provision that the wall, when constructed, "shall be and remain a party wall between the parties of the first and second part, their heirs and assigns, forever," the evident result is that the plaintiffs acquired in Brown's lot a right of support for the westerly half of the westerly wall of their building—a right which might continue during their term, at least. This right of support is a right to use so much of Brown's lot as is covered by the wall, for the purpose of support; it is, therefore, an *easement,* which has been defined, "To consist of a right in the owner of one parcel of land, by reason of such ownership, to use the land of another for a special purpose not inconsistent with a general property in the owner. [2 *Washburn, R. P.* 25, 78; *1 Ib.* (397); *Washburn on Easements,* 2-5; *Brewster's Dict., Title Easements,*] As an easement it is an incorporeal hereditament an *interest* in the servient estate 1 *Washburn R. P.* (398)

2 *Ib;* (25) *Washburn Easements*, 5. As the easement which the pl'ffs acquired is an interest in real estate, the instrument through which they acquired it, *i.e.* the agreement with Brown,, is, by the express definition found in Section 26, Chapter 40, General Statutes, a "conveyance," as the word is used in that chapter.

By Section 6 of such chapter, it is enacted that "no covenant shall be implied in any conveyance or mortgage of real estate whether such conveyance contains special covenants or not."

In this case it will be observed that the agreement mentioned contains no *express* covenant upon the part of Brown his heirs or assigns to pay for any part of the party wall; as none can be implied it is at once apparent that the question mainly discussed at bar, viz. Whether Rogers was liable to the plaintiff's for one half the cost of the wall *upon a covenant running with the land* which he purchased of Brown, cannot arise in this case.

This action having been dismissed by the court below. upon the ground that the plaintiffs had failed to establish their claim to recover of the defendant, it is to be assumed that the testimony introduced by plaintiffs proved all that it tended to prove. It is therefore to be assumed upon the evidence before mentioned, that the defendant had notice of the plaintiffs easement in the Brown lot and of the plaintiffs rights in respect to the same.

From this assumption it would follow that the defendant took the Brown lot subject to the easement and to the plaintiffs' rights respecting it. Among the latter was the right to insist that whenever Brown, his heirs or assigns, should desire to use the party wall they should pay the plaintiffs. their heirs or assigns, one half of the actual cost

This is equivalent to saying that the defendant (an assignee of Brown) was entitled to use the wall only upon condition of paying the plaintiffs half its cost. If he used it (as is undisputed) he is to be taken to have elected to use it, upon this condition and to have made himself liable accordingly.

It is argued by the defendant, that the plaintiffs cannot recover because they did not construct the wall according to the agreement with Brown.

This has reference to the fact that there were two windows in the wall, and to the failure to leave the proper number of places for joists. It does not appear that any objection was made to the windows. As respects the places for joist the agreement is, "to leave proper openings in said wall for the use of the said party of the second part." It appears that so far as the stone portion of the wall was concerned, "joist holes were left;" but for the purpose of making a better wall, filled up with stones that could easily be found and removed.

In the back portion of the wall it appears that no joist holes were left; but as brick could be easily removed whenever and wherever necessary, we are not able to say that this was not a sufficient compliance with the agreement, to leave *proper* openings.

Besides, it does not appear that any objection was made by defendant, to the want of sufficient joist holes, until after he had used the wall. And, irrespective of these considerations, we are of opinion that if the defendant used the wall he could not set up the plaintiffs alleged failure to construct it according to the precise terms of the agreement in *bar* of a recovery. His remedy (if any) in the premises, would be by recoupment.

Order denying a new trial reversed,

DOMESTIC SEWING MACHINE CO., *Appellants.* *vs.* ANTON ANDERSON, *Respondent,* } Filed June 14, 1875.

The rule forbidding the use of parol evidence to affect a written instrument does not apply to a case in which a part only of the dealings between parties in respect to a particular subject matter is reduced to writing, except as respects such fact.

In case of an absolute sale and delivery of personal property an agreement by the purchaser to pay the vendor for the future use of the same, or to deliver it up to him on demand, is repugnant to the contract of sale and is void.

The receipt of the property by the purchaser furnishes no valid consideration for such agreement.

This was an appeal from the Municipal Court, of the City of St. Paul.

The plaintiff, claiming to be the owner of the property mentioned in the agreement set forth in the opinion, and that the same had been delivered to the defendant solely upon the terms set forth in said agreement, and that the conditions thereof had been violated by defendant, demanded its return; and upon return being refused brought suit to replevy the the same; upon the trial it appeared that the plaintiffs canvassing agent visited defendant's house in the forenoon of the day, upon which the machine was delivered and had a verbal negotiation with defendant in regard to the machine; that in the afternoon of the same day he delivered the machine; and that at the time of such delivery the defendant executed the contract and the plaintiffs 'agent received a second hand-machine and five dollars in money, in part payment thereon. The defendant testified that the negotiations had with plaintiffs' agent were for a purchase of the machine; that he signed some paper when the machine was delivered, but did not think that this was the one. Additional payment had been made on the machine to the amount of $25.

On the part of the plaintiffs it was urged that the negotiations had in the forenoon, the delivery of the machine and execution of the contract in the afternoon were all parts of one transaction, and that whatever may have been the character of previous verbal negotiations, the written agreement was the sole evidence of the final conclusions of the parties; or that even if testimony of def't was admissable, that the circumstances showed at least a conditional sale with title in plaintiffs' until the full price of the machine was paid.

The court below held the agreement void as unconscionable and against public policy, and that title was in defendant.

O'Brien & Eller, attorneys for appellants.

W. J. Parsons & C. S. Bryant, attorneys for respondent.

BERRY, J,—Plaintiff delivered to defendant a sewing machine and at the time of the delivery, defendant executed and delivered to plaintiff the following instrument viz:

$75. ST. PAUL, Aug. 13, 1873.

Received of the Domestic Sewing Machine Co., one Domestic Sewing Machine, style H. C., plate, No. 96.853, with the following parts, viz: 1 Hemmer, 1 Quilting guage, 1 Braider, 1 Thumb Screw and guage, 1 Doz. needles, 6 Bobbins, 1 Wrench, 1 Screw driver, 1 Oiler, 1 Bottle oil and one book of instructions to be returned to them on demand, and until such demand, I agree to pay for the use of them forty-five dollars in hand and five dollars per month for the next seven months if I shall keep the same so long, payable on the thirteenth of each month at their office, 264 Third Street, and agree to take good care of the same while in my possession, and not remove it from my residence, No. ——corner Broadway and Mt. Airy, without their written consent.

[Signed.] ANTON ANDERSON.

The defendant having refused to deliver the plaintiff on demand the Sewing Machine and other articles, plaintiff brought the present action to recover the possession or value of the same.

The plaintiff claimed that the instrument contained the contract between the parties in relation to the Sewing Machine and other articles, and that it was therefore the exclusive evidence of their rights as respected the same. The defendant claimed that the instrument and the contract evidenced by it was only one of two transactions between the parties by which their rights as respected the machine and other articles were determined; for the purpose of showing what the other transaction was so far as material in the case the plaintiff was permitted to introduce oral evidence; this was not an infringment of the rule which forbids the use of paral evidence to affect a written instrument. That rule does not apply to a case in which a part only of the dealings between parties in respect to a particular subject, matter is reduced to writing except as respects such part, 1 *Gr. Ev.* § 284.

The evidence thus introduced tended to show an absolute sale and a delivery of the machine and other articles by the plaintiff to the defendant, and such sale and delivery were accordingly found by the court below to have been made. The absolute sale and delivery of course invested the defendant with the absolute and general ownership and property of the machine and other articles;

The instrument above recited was therefore not only repugnant to the contract of absolute sale and therefore void, but was so far as appears without consideration.

The receipt of ones own property from a person having no right to the possession of it cannot be a valid consideration for an agreement to pay for the future use of the property or to deliver it up to such person upon demand.

For these reasons we are of opinion that the general result arrived at by the court below was correct.

Judgment affirmed.

Latest Publications.

The Law for the Formation of Business Corporations, with Forms, By-Laws, etc., by R. Bach. McMaster; 12mo. 50 pp. Paper, - - - - $0 50

Smith's Reports, Vol. XXIX, being Vol. LXXIX of Pennsylvania State Reports; by P. Frazer Smith. 8vo. 579 pp., Law Sheep, - - - 4 50

Reports of Cases argued and determined in the Supreme Court of Appeals of West Virginia, Vol. VIII. By Henry M. Mathews. 8vo., 944 pp. Sheep, - - - - - - 4 00

Sansum's Digest of Law of Insurance. A Digest of all the Fire, Life, Marine, Accident and Guarantee Insurance cases decided in Great Britain and America. By O. B. Sansum. 8vo, 600 pp., Law Sheep. - - - - - 8 00

Bissell's Reports. Volume VI. Reports of cases argued and decided in the Seventh Judicial Circuit. By Josiah H. Bissell. 8vo 650 pp., Law Sheep. 7 50

Massachusetts Reports CXIX. Reports of cases argued and decided in the Supreme Judicial Court of Massachusetts. By John Lathrop, Reporter. 8vo Law Sheep. - - - - 4 50

Otto's Reports on the Decisions of the Supreme Court of the United States, Vol. 1, 8vo. - - - - - - 5 00

Greenleaf on Law of Evidence, Vol. 1. By John Wilder May. 13th Ed. 8vo. 6 00

Redfield on Law of Wills., Vol. 2. 3d Ed., 8vo. - - - - - - 6 00

A Treatise on Conveyances by Debtors to Defraud Creditors. By Orlando F. Bump. Second Ed., revised and enlarged. 8vo., 750 pp., Law Sheep. 6 50

Mitford & Tyler's Pleadings and Practice in Equity. By John Mitford (the late Lord Rosedale,) & Samuel Tyler, L. L. D. 8vo., 774 pp. - - 6 50

Outlines of an International Code. By David Dudley Field. Second Ed., revised and enlarged. 8vo., 800 pp. 7 50

Reports of Cases in Law and Equity Determined in the Supreme Court of Iowa, Vol. XLI, by John J. Runnels, Reporter, 784 pp., law sheep - 5 00

THE SYLLABI.

VOL. 1. SATURDAY, JAN. 13, 1877. No. 13.

PUBLISHED WEEKLY,

By JOHN B. WEST & CO.,

No. 1 Wabasha St., - ST. PAUL, MINN.

Terms 3.00 per annum in Advance.

HOMER C. ELLER, Editor.

TABLE OF CONTENTS.

THE *Central Law Journal* comes to us this week much changed in appearance and decidedly for the better. Its pages reduced from their former quarto size, to a more convenient octavo, are increased in number, and the subject matter as usual full of interest is in no manner reduced in quantity, but rather increased. The *Journal* certainly deserves the success it has met with, and we congratulate it, not only upon its fine appearance, but its evident financial prosperity.

THE peculiar influences that operate upon the minds of jurors, as well as the conclusions sometimes reached by them, are often subjects of comment; and their ability to find "extenuating circumstances" in cases that arouse their sympathy, is quite remarkable. One of the greatest efforts of this kind, however, was in the recent case of a Belgian jury, who, after finding a prisoner guilty of having murdered two wives, recommended him to mercy on account of his having a wooden leg; a recommendation that resulted in a sentence to hard labor, for life, instead of an infliction of the death penalty.

ST. LOUIS undertakers evidently have an eye single to collections these times. Recently in that city a funeral procession, just about to move, was delayed by an officer, who, with a writ of replevin on behalf of the undertaker, proceeded to take possession of the coffin, finding however that it contained more than the writ called for, and fearing that if he took it with its contents a *habeas corpus* might be desirable on his own behalf, he appealed to the mourners to take out the body or raise the money to pay for the casket, the result of which was a liquidation of the undertaker's claim.

FREEMAN ON EXECUTIONS. Published by Sumner, Whitney & Co., San Francisco, Cal. For sale by John B. West & Co., St. Paul. 950 pp. Price, - - - - - $7.50

To those who have had occasion to consult "Freeman on Judgments," the author of this book needs no commendation; it is properly a sequel to that work, and the author, under the general heads of executions against the person of defendants, against the property of defendants, and for the recovery of specific property, gives a complete *resume* of the law upon this important subject, and incident thereto considers at length other matters more or less associated with the general subject, such as, homestead rights property exempt from execution, rights and duties of officers, supplemental proceedings, &c., &c. It is exhaustive in citations, and of great practical value.

Supreme Court, State of Minnesota.

Casper Fritz, *Respondent*, *vs.* The First Division of the St. Paul & Pacific R. R. Co., *Appellants*. } Filed Feb'y 26, '76.

An ordinance of the City of St. Paul provides, that "cows may run at large during the day time, from five o'clock in the morning to nine o'clock in the evening, from the first day of April to the first day of December."

Held, that this ordinance authorizes the owners of cows to permit the same to make highway use of the public streets unattended, and therefore that to permit a cow to use a public street in such manner, even though she may be liable to stray upon a railroad track at a crossing, is the exercise of a lawful right, and not *per se* negligence; and that a railway company (unless expressly privileged by Statutes,) is to exercise its right to cross a public street, with reference to this right of the owner of a cow, so that notwithstanding a cow at large and unattended in a public street may be liable to stray upon the track, it is the duty of the company to exercise reasonable diligence to avoid injuring her, with reference to the fact that she is a brute and not a rational being.

The foregoing propositions applied to this case upon the question of negligence with special reference to evidence that at the time when the plaintiff's cow was struck by defendant's train, such train was running at a speed prohibited by a city ordinance and without the ringing of a bell, as by such ordinance required.

Appeal from an order of District Court, Ramsey county, denying motion for a new trial.

Bigelow, Flandrau & Clark, attorneys for appellant.

G. Seigenthaler, attorney for respondent.

Berry, J.—The plaintiff brings this action against defendant for killing his cow by negligently running into her with a locomotive; at the time she was struck the cow was in Rice street, a public street of St. Paul, at the crossing of same by defendant's railway: The accident occured Aug. 29, between seven and eight o'clock in the morning, and it appeared that the plaintiff, who resided about a hundred rods from the crossing had milked her that morning, and turned her out to "hunt her feed" according to his usual custom, and there was evidence in the case tending to show that at the time she was struck, she was passing along the street, and over the crossing, on her way out into "the country to feed."

An ordinance of the city of St. Paul provided "that cows may run at large during the day time, from five o'clock in the morning to nine o'clock in the evening, from the first day of April to the first day of December."

For the purposes of this case, it is unnecessary to construe this ordinance further than to say, that it authorizes the owners of cows to permit the same to make highway use of the public streets, unattended; and it follows that to permit a cow to use a public street in this way, even though she may be liable to stray upon a railroad track or crossing, is the exercise of a lawful right, and not *per se* negligence.

Alger vs. M. & M. R. Co., 10 *Iowa* 268.

Galpin vs. C. & N. W. R. Co., 19 *Wis.* 640.

And it further follows that a railway company unlesss expressly privileged by Statute, is to exercise its right to cross a public street, with reference to this right of an owner of a cow, so that notwithstanding a cow at large and unattended in a public street may be liable to stray upon the track, it is the duty of the company to exercise reasonable and at least ordinary diligence to avoid injuring her, with reference to the fact that she is a brute, and not a rational being.

With these views of the rules of law applicable to this case, we are of opinion that the jury were, upon the evidence, at liberty to find that plaintiff was guilty of no negligence in the premises.

Ordinance No.54 of St. Paul,(compilation of 1875) provides (with exceptions not here important) "that no railroad company or corporation, or their agents or employees, shall run a locomotive or train of cars or single car, within the limits of the city of St. Paul, at a greater speed than four miles per hour, nor without having and ringing a bell of sufficient size at all times while so in motion."

On the part of defendant, the testimony was that the locomotive crossed Rice street at a speed of "about six miles an hour" while witness called by plaintiff testified that the rate of speed was much higher.

There was also a conflict of testimony as to whether or not the bell was rung as required by the ordinance, and the testimony of the witnesses called by plaintiff was so contradictory in several respects of the testimony of defendants that the jury was at liberty to credit the former to the discredit of the latter. In this condition of the case, we are of opinion that the jury was at liberty to find that the defendant, whose train was running at an unlawful speed, was not only guilty of negligence in the premises, but of proximate negligence the direct consequence of which was the killing of plaintiff's cow.

Correll vs. B. C. R. & M. R. Co., 38 *Iowa* 120.

And considering the unlawful speed at which defendant's train was running, and its obligation to run its train with reference to plaintiff's rights in the highway, we do not regard the fact (if such it be) that the plaintiff's cow had passed over the track, when the locomotive had reached Rice street and was subsequently "shoved" or "driven back" on to the locomotive, as defendants fireman testifies, as by any means decisively showing that her death was not caused by the negligence of defendant or its employees.

Order denying a new trial affirmed.

O. P. HAWKINS, *Appellant*, vs. THE M. E. CHURCH OF COTTAGE GROVE, *Respondent*. } Filed Jan'y 5, '77.

The definition of an estoppel IN PAIS given in Pence vs. Arbuckle (MSS. Oct. Tr. 1875,) followed and applied to this case.

Appeal from an order of the District Court of Ramsey county vacating a judgment.

The action was one brought by plaintiff as assignee in bankruptcy, for goods, &c., furnished, and work and labor performed by the bankrupt for defendant—a religious corporation.

The summons was served by a person other than an officer, on September 25th, 1871, upon one Morgan L. Sproat, as a trustee of said defendant, and there being no appearance, on the part of the defendant, judgment was entered by default Oct. 16, 1875; February 25th, 1875, the judgment was assigned to C. D. Strong, Esq., who after demanding payment and making efforts to have the same amicably paid and settled, in August, 1875, caused an execution to be issued thereon and certain property to be levied upon.

The ground of the motion was alleged insufficiency or want of service of the summons.

Sproat, the person upon whom service was made, had at one time been a trustee of the defendant and the certificate of his election was duly recorded in the office of the Register of Deeds, for Washington county. The affidavits on the part of the defendant showed however, that he ceased to act as such trustee, in the year 1868, It was claimed on behalf of the appellant that in as much as the rules of the church, by which defendant was governed, provided that trustees should hold their office until their successors were elected, and that as there was no record evidence of any successor to Mr. Sproat ever having been elected he was, so far as the judgment is concerned, to be regarded as still being in office at the time of the service of the summons. That the question of his title to the trusteeship could not be litigated in these proceedings, and, independent of any election, that defendant having held Sproat out as such trustee by causing the certificate of his election as such to be recorded, and never having given any notice that his powers and functions had ceased either by election of a successor or otherwise were estopped from denying his trusteeship; other grounds of estoppel consisting of certain alleged acts and declarations of defendants agents and trustees during Strong's negotiations for a settlement were urged, and are considered at length in the opinion.

Henry A. Castle and C. K. Davis, attorneys for appellant.

Lamprey & James, attorneys for respondent.

BERRY, J.—Upon the affidavits in this case we think the court below properly found that Morgan L. Sproat was not one of the defendant's trustees at the time when the summons was served upon him; It follows as was correctly held that for want of jurisdiction of the defendant the judgment and the proceedings under it are void.

The plaintiff insists however that the defendant is estopped from objecting to the validity of the judgment by the conduct of its trustees and agents and by receiving benefits (upon the basis that the judgment was valid) and then waiting until the Statute of limitations had barred the original cause of action before moving to set aside the judgment.

In *Pence vs. Arbuckle*, (*MSS. Oct. Tr.* 1875.) this court defines an estoppel *in pais* as follows, viz: "An estoppel *in pais* arises when one by his acts or representations, or by his silence when he ought to speak out, intentionally or through culpable negligence induces another to believe certain facts to exist, and such other rightfully acts on the belief so induced in such manner that if the former be permitted to deny the existence of such facts it will prejudice the latter.

In this case the matters appearing in the affidavits and which are not denied, and are important with reference to the claim of estoppel are these: The original cause of action upon which the judgment was based, was barred by the statute of limitations in January 1874; The judgment was assigned to its present holder (C. D. Strong,) on Feb. 26, 1875; Strong in his affidavit says, "that on April 6th, 1875. he wrote to John Laramy, (one of defendant's trustees,) notifying him of the purchase of said judgment and demanding payment; That in response to said letter Rev. S. Bolles then preacher in charge of defendant and to the best of affiants recollection and belief, said Laramy came to affiant and commenced negotiation for the payment of said judgment that thereafter and on June 19th, 1875, at a regular quarterly meeting, called by Rev. D. Cobb, Presiding Elder, of the pastor, official members, and trustees of defendant; affiant met with them as owner of said judgment and at said Cobbs request, said Laramy and others of said trustees being present and participating in the proceedings; that in said meeting various plans for liquidating said indebtedness to affiant and satisfying said judgment were discussed but no claim was made that the said judgment was void and no offers of compromise, based on the invalidity of said judgment were made; but affiant was asked to make and did make his best terms of payment as a favor to defendant and the subject of discussion, was the best means of raising the money without sacrificing the property of defendant.

Strongs affidavit contains further allegations as to the action of the defendant through its trustees and agents but these allegations are met on the other side by positive denials; The trustees (with the exceptions of one who has deceased and whose dying declaration to the same effect is referred to,) all depose that they had no knowledge of the existence of the judgment or of the institution or pendency of the action in which the judgment was rendered until after Strong claimed to be the owner thereof and not till after M'ch '75 and that they had no knowledge as to the person upon whom the summons was served until after or about the time of the execution sale on Oct. 22d and 23d, 1875, but supposed that the service was made and could lawfully be made by publication.

This state of facts fails to make out an estoppel within the definition above quoted. The negotiations and discussions do not appear to have resulted in any definite conclusion or in any agreement or even proposition on the part of defendants trustees; We are unable to perceive how the defendant could properly be said to have been induced by them to believe any fact upon his belief on which he acted in the premises; It is claimed that the negotiations and discussions proceeded upon the basis of the existence of a valid judgment and were therefore an admission of its validity; But in the first place there is no reason to suppose that Strong's belief in the validity of the judgment was in any way induced by anything which appears to have taken place at the the time of the alleged negotiations and discussions; On the contrary the presumption is that he believed the judgment to be valid at the time when he purchased it; In the second place if it were admitted that Strongs belief in the validity of the judgment was induced by the failure of defendant's trustees "to speak out" such failure could not be attributed to "culpable negligence" because the ground of invalidity was not then known to the trustees; as respects the matter of prejudice it can hardly be said that anything alleged to have taken place at the negotiations and discussions could have induced him to *wait* until the Statute of limitations had run against the original cause of action, more than a year before he purchased the judgment; It might be urged that if he had been made aware of the invalidity of the judgment he would not have incurred the expense of the execution sale but even if this were an admitted fact it would not for reasons before suggested bring the case within the principles of estoppel *in pais*.

The burden of making out the estoppel being upon Strong we are thus reluctantly forced to the opinion that the action of the court below in setting aside the judgment and all proceedings thereon, must be sustained; Reluctantly we say for upon perusing the papers in the case we cannot resist the conclusion that the result arrived at is in morals, though not in law, a practical injustice to the holder of the judgment; If the action of Mr. Bolles had not been repudiated as it seems to us it ought not to have been, the result might have been entirely different.

Order affirmed.

John Rogers, Appellant, vs. John McCauley and Theresa McCauley his wife. Respondents. } Filed Feby. 10, 76.

Where a debtor bargains for and purchases real estate, and pays the consideration, and causes the conveyance to be made to his wife, there attaches to the land presumptively a trust in favor of his creditors at the time, and proof that the debtor made the purchaser, and caused the title to be vested in his wife, for the purpose of making the real estate the plaee of residence of himself and family, does not tend to disprove the fraudulent intent, nor does the proof that after making the contract of purchase he placed a house upon the real estate, and always afterwards resided with his family npon it.

Ths homestead right of the wife in such a case will not protect her interest from the claims of the creditors; Sumner v. Sawtelle, 8 Minn. 109, followed.

Appeal from order of Court of Common Pleas of Ramsey county, denying motion for a new trial.

Morris Lamprey, attorney for appellant.

Harvey Officer, attorney for defendants.

Gilfillan, C. J.— In 1861, the defendant, John McCauley, was indebted to the plaintiff and Mathew Flood, who transferred his interest in the debt to plaintiff. The debt was put in judgment January 18th, 1868, an execution afterwards issued and was returned unsatisfied.

After the debt accrued and before the judgment, John McCauley, bargained for and purchased from one Bullen one lot, in St. Paul, at the price of $950, and on said purchase took from said Bullen a bond to the defendant Theresa, then and now his wife, conditioned to convey the lot to her.

The entire consideration was paid by the defendant, John; July 8th, 1868, part of the consideration having been paid the lot was conveyed by Bullen to Theresa, and she and John gave back a mortgage for the balance of the purchase money, which John paid about July 3, 1871. These facts are admitted by the pleadings.

Upon these facts there presumptively arose a trust in favor of the creditors of the defendant John, under Sec. 8, Ch. 43, of the General Statutes.

Section 7 provides that when a conveyance is made to one person, and the consideration paid by another, no trust shall result in favor of the latter. Section 8, proceeds, "every such conveyance shall be presumed fraudulent as against the creditors, at that time, of the person paying the consideration; and when a fraudulent intent is not disapproved, a trust shall result in favor of such creditors, to the extent that may be necessary to satisfy their just demand."

The court below found as a fact "that said John McCauley, Jr., so purchased said real estate, for the purpose of making the same the place of residence of himself and family, and not with intent to defraud his creditors."

That a debtor who buys real estate, and pays for it and causes the title to be vested in another, whether a wife, a child, or another person, does so "with the purpose of making the same the place of residence of himself and family" does not tend to disprove the fraudulent intent.

The only evidence in the case offered upon the question of intent was to the effect, that about the time the bond for a deed was made, the defendant moved a house from an adjoining lot to the one in question, and has ever since with his family continuously resided in the house, and that he has no other real estate.

This does not even tend to remove the presumption which the statute attaches to the transaction, is no evidence that he paid the consideration himself, and took the title in the name of his wife, without an intent to defraud his creditors.

The finding of fact as to the intent cannot be sustained.

It is claimed that from 1870 to '72 the defendant John was solvent, and that plaintiff might then have collected his debt out of the property; This fact, if it is a fact, is immaterial; for it would not relieve the land from the trust which attached by reason of the character of the original transaction, and to enforce which is the object of this suit, The argument is made that as John McCauley might have taken the title in his own name, and held it as a homestead exempt from the claims of his creditors, his causing the title to vest in his wife, instead of himself, could not have operated as a fraud upon his creditors.

This proposition would open a very wide door; For notwithstanding the conveyance of land, purchased by him, to his wife, his right to acquire and hold a homestead would be the same after as before the conveyance; and if the fact that he might have taken title to the land, and held it as a homestead, would protect the conveyance to his wife, it would as well protect successive similar conveyances to her or to any other person. He could claim no rights in this lot as a homestead, for he did not own it. She, having acquired it by gift from her husband, made in fraud of his creditors, took it subject to their rights, and no homestead right in her would protect it against those rights. The homestead laws were not enacted as a shield for any such transactions.

The case does not differ in any material respect from

Sumner v. Sawtelle, 8 *Minn.*, 309.

The order appealed from, is reversed, and a new trial ordered.

WILLIAM SPOONER, *Respondent*, *vs.* LYDIA E. FRENCH. *Appellant.* } Filed, June, 1875.

In proceedings under Ch. 84, General Statutes, by a landlord against his tenant, to recover possession of premises for non-payment of rent, no previous demand of the rent is required.

In such proceedings the Justiee may proceed to hear the case at the time appointed in the summons without waiting an hour as required in Section 19, Ch. 65, of the Statutes.

This was an action of forcible entry and detainer, brought under the provisions of Chapter 84, General Statues, to recover possession of certain premises situated in Minneapolis. The complaint recited the ownership of plaintiff and leasing of premises to defendent, failure to pay the rent as agreed, that rent was then due, and that plaintiff was entitled to possession of the premises and defendant wrongfully detained the same. There was no averment of any demand for rent due or for possession of the premises. Summons was personally served, returnable Nov. 11th, 1873, at 10 o'clock, A. M. Case was called at ten o'clock on return day, and defendant not appearing then, judgment was entered for plaintiff. At 42 minutes past ten o'clock defendant appeared and offered to file answer, but judgment had then been entered. An appeal was then taken to the District Court of Hennepin county, upon questions of law alone. In the District Court a motion was made to dismiss the action upon the ground that complaint did not state facts sufficient to constitute a case of action; also to reverse the judgment for alleged irregularity on the part of the Justice in not waiting an hour for defendant to appear, both of which were denied and action of Justice affirmed. An appeal was then taken to this court.

Pierce & Farmer, attorneys for appellant.

J. Guilford, attorney for respondent.

GILFILLAN, C. J.—The only questions in this case are:

First.—It is necessary that a landlord proceeding against his tenant under the provisions of Chap. 84, General statues, for holding over after rent has become due, shall have first demanded payment of the rent.

Second.—Is it necessary in those proceedings that the Justice should wait one hour after the hour mentioned in the summons for the parties to appear, before going on with hearing.

The Statute, Sec. 11, gives the right to these proceedings when the tenant "holds over" * * after any rent becomes due, according to the terms of the lease; no other thing is required by the Statute. It gives the remedy in all cases, whether the right to re-enter for non-payment of the rent is reserved or not, and it could not have been intended that it should be governed by the requirements at common law, of those cases where the landlord proceeds under the reserved right to re-enter; no demand of the rent is contemplated by the statute.

Sec. 5, provides that "at the time and place appointed" in the summons, the Justice shall proceed to hear the case. In the statute regulating the proceedings in ordinary actions before Justice Courts, Ch. 65, General Statutes, Sec. 19, it is provided that "the parties are entitled to *one hour* in which to make their appearance *after the time* mentioned in the summons for appearance. To add the words of Sec. 19 to those of Sec. 5, would be going further than we are authorized to go; and without doing that, we cannot hold that under Sec. 5, the parties are entitled to one hour, or any time after the time mentioned in the summons. If the summons mentions ten o'clock, that, and not eleven o'clock, is the time appointed for appearance. Doubtless the Justice may for good reasons, for instance, to allow for difference in time-pieces, or when he is at the time engaged in other official business, or if he should see the absent party actually approaching, wait a reasonable time after that mentioned in the summons; but he is not required to do so.

The judgment appealed from is affirmed.

—o;o—

SUPREME COURT OF PENNSYLVANIA.

WOODS. *vs.* PEOPLES' NAT. BANK OF PITTSBURGH. } Filed Nov. 20, '76.

A mortgage given to a National bank to secure a pre-existing debt by the mortgagor, and to secure a future loan to him, is as to the latter ULTRA VIRES.

If the mortgaged premises be sold, the proceeds arising therefrom must be applied in discharge of such pre-existing debt, notwithstanding such proceeds arose from a sale by the sheriff.

An indorser of notes held by a National bank, secured by a mortgage, has a right to have the proceeds arising from a judicial sale of the mortgaged premises by the bank, applied to the payment of such notes in his relief.

Fowler v. Scully, 22 P. F. Smith, followed.

Error to the Court of Common Pleas No. 1 of Allegheny county.

In the early part of 1870 the Peoples' National Bank discounted for R. L. McAboy three notes, amounting to $7000, which were indorsed by Robert Woods. The bank had also loaned to Mr. McAboy $5,055, taking his own unindorsed note. These notes were renewed several times, until about August, 1870, when Mr. McAboy applied to the bank for a loan of $8,000. The bank agreed, provided he secured by mortgage the four notes above, including enough to cover the $8,000 loan, to lend him the additional amount taking his own unindorsed notes for $4,000 each. Accordingly, about the 1st day of September, 1870, Mr. McAboy gave the bank a mortgage on his wife's property, the same being her separate estate, for $40,-000, conditional for the payment of $20,000; and the same was placed on record. On the 8th of September, seven days after the mortgage was recorded, the bank placed $8,000 to Mr. McAboy's credit, and he delivered then the two notes for $4,000 each. None of the notes having been paid, proceedings were commenced by the bank to foreclose the mortgage. The property was sold for $13,816.66, and the bank subsequently sued Robert Woods, the indorser, on his three notes. The case was tried in the Common Pleas No. 1, and was defended on the ground that the bank could only take the mortgage for the three notes, and the $5,055 McAboy note; that it was bound to apply the proceeds of the sheriff's sale to their discharge, and that the proceeds could not be applied to the liquidation of the $8,000 loan, because that was not a pre-existing debt as provided by the Act of Congress.

The court charged the jury the defence was not sufficient, and directed a verdict to be found for the plaintiff, for the amount of three notes with interest.

John H. Hampton, Esq., for Woods.

M. W. Acheson, Esq., for the bank.

PAXSON, J.—It was held in Fowler v. Scully, 22 P. F. S. 456, that the loaning of money by a National bank upon mortgage, or other real estate security, is *ultra vires*, and forbidden by the Act of Congress. This, of course does not apply to the case where a bank has in good faith taken a mortgage by way of security for a previously existing debt. Such case comes within one of the express exceptions of the Act of Congress. It follows, therefore, that in so far as the mortgage of Mrs McAboy to the Peoples' National Bank of Pittsburgh was given to secure money thereafter to be loaned to her husband, it was *ultra vires*. It is manifest from the evidence that the loan of $8,000 to Mr. McAboy on or about the 8th of September, 1870, was upon the faith of the mortgage. As to this loan the mortgage was not a valid security. But it was good as to the indebtedness of Mr. McAboy to the bank existing prior to its execution, amounting to about twelve thousand and fifty-five dollars. For $7,000 of this sum, the bank held the indorsements of plaintiff's in error. His contention is, that the bank was bound to apply the money received from a sheriff's sale of the mortgaged premises to the notes held by it at the time the mortgage was given. In this we think he is right. As the indorser of Mr. McAboy's notes held by the bank, he had a right to call upon the latter to apply the money to the payment of the notes for which alone the mortgage was legally held as security.

The mortgage was as much for his benefit as for the bank. The latter had no right to apply the proceeds thereof to the unsecured notes of $4,000 each. Under the authority of Fowler v. Scully, Mr. McAboy could have objected to such appropriation. Whatever he might have done in this respect, the plaintiff in error, as his indorser, may do also.

From what has been said it will be seen that both the assignments of error are sustained.

The judgment is reversed and a *venire facias de novo* awarded.

Latest Publications.

Abbott's U. S. Practice, vol. 1, by Benjamin Vaughan Abbott; 8vo., 640 pp. Law Sheep, - - - - - $7.50

Supplement to Riddle's Supplementary Proceedings. by John F. Baker; 8vo., 128 pp., half sheep, - - - - 2.00

The Law of Evidence, by Simon Greenleaf; vols. 2 and 3, 13th edition, carefully revised by John Wilder May; 8vo., per vol. - - - - - 6.00

The Law for the Formation of Business Corporations, with Forms, By-Laws, etc., by R. Bach. McMaster; 12mo. 50 pp. Paper, - - - - $0 50

Smith's Reports, Vol. XXIX, being Vol. LXXIX of Pennsylvania State Reports; by P. Frazer Smith. 8vo. 579 pp., Law Sheep, - - - 4 50

Reports of Cases argued and determined in the Supreme Court of Appeals of West Virginia, Vol. VIII. By Henry M. Mathews. 8vo., 944 pp. Sheep, - - - - - - - 4 00

Sansum's Digest of Law of Insurance. A Digest of all the Fire, Life, Marine, Accident and Guarantee Insurance cases decided in Great Britain and America. By O. B. Sansum. 8vo, 600 pp., Law Sheep. - - - - - 8 00

Bissell's Reports. Volume VI. Reports of cases argued and decided in the Seventh Judicial Circuit. By Josiah H. Bissell. 8vo 650 pp., Law Sheep. 7 50

Massachusetts Reports CXIX. Reports of cases argued and decided in the Supreme Judicial Court of Massachusetts. By John Lathrop, Reporter. 8vo Law Sheep. - - - - 4 50

Otto's Reports on the Decisions of the Supreme Court of the United States, Vol. 1, 8vo. - - - - - 5 00

Greenleaf on Law of Evidence, Vol. 1. By John Wilder May. 13th Ed. 8vo. 6 00

Redfield on Law of Wills., Vol. 2. 3d Ed., 8vo. - - - - - - - 6 00

A Treatise on Conveyances by Debtors to Defraud Creditors. By Orlando F. Bump. Second Ed., revised and enlarged. 8vo., 750 pp., Law Sheep. 6 50

13

THE SYLLABI.

VOL. 1. SATURDAY, JAN. 20, 1877. No. 14.

PUBLISHED WEEKLY,

By JOHN B. WEST & CO.,

No. 1 Wabasha St., - ST. PAUL, MINN.

Terms 3.00 per annum in Advance.

HOMER C. ELLER, Editor.

TABLE OF CONTENTS.

ON January 12th, one A. W. Dennis was arrested at St. Cloud, Minn., as a fugitive from justice, from the State of Iowa.

A writ of *habeas corpus* having been procured on his behalf he was in pursuance thereof, brought before McKelvey J., of 7th Dist; The person having Dennis in custody, returned in proper form that the prisoner was arrested by virtue of the Executive warrant of the State of Minnesota, granted upon the requisition of the Governor of the State of Iowa, and in pursuance of ch. 103, General Statutes of Minnesota, and that he, the person so having him in custody, was the duly commissioned agent of the State of Iowa, in such proceedings; counsel for the prisoner objected to the sufficiency of this return for the reason that it in no manner exhibited or pretended to exhibit the proceedings or testimony upon which the warrant of the Governor of Minn., was issued; The objection however was overruled and the prisoner remanded to custody, the court holding that the Statute having vested the executive, with the province of examining into: and determining when a warrant for the arrest of a fugitive from justice should issue. It was to be presumed that his action was proper; and that the courts would not in a *habeas corpus* proceeding, where in such a case the warrant of arrest was valid on its face, go back of such warrant and enquire into the circumstances under which it was issued.

Story & Story, for petitioner.

D. B. Searles and A. P. Barker, Contra.

IN the case of *The State vs. Arbuckle*, in District Court Ramsey county the defendant was indicted for an alleged misdemeanor; among the witnesses whose names were indorsed upon the indictment as having been examined before the Grand Jury, was one J. A. Mulbach. Upon the trial the prosecution called as a witness one J. A. Laubach who, upon being examined by the counsel for defendant, stated that his name was Laubach and that he had been examined before the Grand Jury. Counsel for defendant then moved that the further testimony of the witness be excluded upon the ground that his name had not been endorsed, as required by Sec. 59, Chap. 107, General Statutes, which motion, after argument, was granted, The question seems a new one in this State, but the ruling of the Court is evidently in accordance with the rules laid down in the State of Iowa, under a similar Statute see,

Ray vs. State, 1 *Iowa*, 316.
Harriman vs. State, 2 *Iowa* 284.
Smith vs. State, 4 *Iowa* 190.
State vs. Abrahams, 6 *Clark*, (*Iowa*) 120.

Supreme Court, State of Minnesota.

John B. Downer, *Assignee of F. S. Richards Bankrupt.—Respondent* *vs.* The St. Paul & Chicago Railway Company, *Appellant.* } Filed, Jan. 9, '77.

Where the question is whether the owner of land has by acts IN PAIS made a dedication of it to public use, his declarations, made before an acceptance by the public to the effect that he did not intend to dedicate the land are admissible.

Where a town plat not executed pursuant to the statute is used to show the intention to dedicate to public use certain lands appearing on it, and the evidence of acts, declarations and circumstances, some tending to prove, and others to disprove the existence of such an intention, is given, it is not for the Court to determine the force and effect of the plat, but the whole question should be left to the Jury.

Appeal from an order of District Court, Wabasha county, denying motion for a new trial.

In this case plaintiff appealed to the District Court from the award of Commissioners, in certain condemnation proceedings, for the taking by defendant for its use for railroad purposes, of certain lands situate in the village of Reads and bordering upon the Mississippi river. The land taken was not platted into lots, but was vacant and unoccupied, apparently left as a levee, and had been at various times used as a landing and for other public purposes. The Commissioners upon the theory that the property was a public street or levee, awarded damages to the amount of one dollar only. There was no pretence of a statutory dedication, and the only question on the trial in the Court below, aside from the one of damages, was as to the existence of a common law dedication. Upon this point counsel for defendant, with other testimony, introduced in evidence the recorded plat of the town and showed that the proprietors had made conveyances with reference thereto. Upon the other hand, and in connection with this plat, one of the original proprietors, referring to the land in question, testified to a private conversation had with another of the proprietors, about the time the plat was made, in which he objected to dedicating this strip of river frontage to the public, and wanted it left private property, to which they acceded.

The Court among other things charged the jury that the burden of proof was upon the defendant, to make out a common law dedication; that to constitute such dedication three things were necessary: *First.*—An intention to dedicate. *Second.*—Acts of dedication, and, *Third.*—An acceptance by the public. That the acts and declarations on the part of the owners of the land going to establish such dedication must be such as indicate a deliberate, unequivocal and unmistakable intent to permanently abandon the property to a specific public use. That if such acts and declarations taken altogether were equivocal or did not clearly and plainly indicate an intention to abandon the property to the use of the public permanently they were insufficient. He also declined to charge that the plat was *prima face* evidence of an intent to dedicate the property in question. The jury returned a verdict for the plaintiff, assessing his damages at $1946.

Seagrave Smith, attorney for appellant.

Wilson & Taylor, attorneys for respondent.

Gilfillan, C. J.—It was held in this action, in the opinion filed in October, 1875, that the plat of the town of Pepin, was not made in accordance with the requirements of the statute, and that it could not operate as a statutory conveyance or dedication of the land in controversy, to public use. It was necessary therefore, in order to sustain the claim of the Company, that it should prove a dedication *in pais*, that is, prove an intention and offer on the part of the owner and on acceptance of such offer on the part of the public; whether the whole evidence established such a dedication even by estoppel (if the public could claim it) through the conveyance of lots according to the plat, we are unable to say, for the statement of the case does not purport to contain the whole of the evidence. The only questions which can be considered here are those which are presented by the exceptions to the ruling of the Court below, admitting evidence, and to its refusal to give to the Jury the instruction requested by defendant.

The evidence, to the admission of which the exception was taken, consisted in the declaration of the owner of the land, made at the time of making the plat, to the effect that he did not intend to dedicate the land to public use, but to reserve it for private use; such declarations by the owner were held admissible in *Wilder vs. St. Paul*, 12 *Minn.*, 192. They are evidence of the parties intention with respect to the land claimed to be dedicated, and up to a dedication made irrevocable by acceptance on the part of the public, there is no doubt of the propriety of admitting them. The instruction requested includes three propositions. If either of them was incorrect there was no error in refusing to give the instruction. The second of these propositions was to the effect that the plat shows that the land in dispute was by the owner intended to be donated to the public use as a public street or levee, at the time it was made and executed. This assumes that it was the province of the Court to construe the plat and declare, without submitting the question to the jury, its force and effect. Had the plat been made and recorded, pursuant to the statue, so as to operate *ipso facto* as a conveyance of lands dedicated to public use, it would have been for the Court to construe it and determine what was intended to be dedicated by it, just as the Court construes conveyances and contracts between private persons.

Harrison vs. Eastman, 21 *Minn.*, 509.

The rule in regard to construing writings is that if the writing contains the contract, if any was made between the parties, then the Court and not the jury must construe it, but if the contract is shown, partly by writing and partly by oral testimony, then the entire question must go to the jury.

1 *Taylor on Ev.* 58.

Wilkinson vs. Story, 1 *Jebb & Syms*, 509.

Bolckow vs. Seymour, 17 *Com. Bench, N. S.* 107.

Brook vs. Hook, 6 *L. R, Ex.* 89.

The same rule doubtless applies to maps or plats.

The plat in question could not of itself have the effect of a conveyance, contract or dedication to public use. It could only be used to establish a dedication *in pais*, by showing acts, circumstances and declarations, evidencing an intention to dedicate to public use, existing at the time of the alleged acceptance by the public. It might be one of many acts, circumstances or declarations tending to show such intention, and there might be others to disprove such intention. In this case there were, as appears from so much of the evidence as is contained in the return, acts, circumstances and declarations, other than the plat, some going to prove and some to disprove such an intention. Of the evidence as to intention given on the trial, the plat was only a single item. The case was one in which the entire question should be left to the jury and the Court was right in so leaving it.

Order appealed from affirmed.

MARY A. CURTIS, *Appellant.* vs. CORDELIA JACKSON. *Respondent.* — Filed, Jan. 9, '77.

Upon an application by a defendant, brought on by order to show cause, and made upon the records and files in the cause, and an affidavit of the defendants attorney which stated several alleged defects in the proceedings, one of them going to the Jurisdiction of the Court over the person, for an order setting aside a judgment entered on default.

HELD, That as the affidavit did not particularly specify the ground of the application, it must be assumed that it was made upon all the defects alleged in the affidavit. And as some of them called for the decision of questions other than those affecting the jurisdiction the application was a general appearance in the action, and cured the objection to the jurisdiction.

Appeal from an order of the District Court, Washington county.

The judgment in this case was entered upon default, July 8th, 1867, service of the summons being made by publication; certain real estate was attached at the time of commencement of the action, and after entry of judgment and in August, 1867, was sold in satisfaction thereof. Defendant had notice in May, 1868, of the entry of judgment. The proceedings to vacate were not instituted until Dec., 1874. Defendant's attorney in his affidavit used on the motion stated that he was retained for the purpose of having the judgment vacated and generally in the cause, and in addition to certain matters affecting the sufficiency of the publication of the summons and jurisdiction of the Court, he also specified irregularities in the course of the proceedings subsequent to the service of summons, as ground for the relief prayed. It was claimed on behalf of appellants that the proceedings had were sufficient to give the Court jurisdiction, but aside from that, the averment on the part of defendants attorney, of matters other than those going to the jurisdiction, as ground for relief, amounted to a general appearance that cured any defect in the service of summons; and that as to the other alleged irregularities, more than a year having elapsed since the entry of the judgment and notice thereof to the defendant, they could not be inquired into.

McCluer & Marsh, attorneys for appellant.

J. N. Castle, attorney for respondent.

GILFILLAN, C. J.—This was an appeal from an order vacating a judgment entered in favor of plaintiff. The judgment was entered July 8th, 1867, upon a service of summons by publication and default of defendant to answer, and an attachment having been issued at the time of issuing the summons, and levied upon real estate, an execution was issued on the judgment and the real estate sold under it. In December, 1874, the defendant procured an order to show cause why the judgment should not be vacated and set aside, and such relief granted as in the premises might be just, and pursuant to this order, the order appealed from was made. Neither the order to show cause nor the affidavit of defendant's attorney upon which, and on the files and records in the cause, the application was made, specifies distinctly the grounds on which the application was made, but the affidavit states as irregularities, that there was no sufficient affidavit to authorize the order directing service of the summons by publication; that no sufficient bond or recognizance was ever made in the proceeding by attachment, nor sufficient affidavit of failure to answer; that the facts found by the referee did not warrant a judgment, nor does it appear that said referee ever qualified as such, or was qualified to act; that it does not appear that satisfactory security was given to authorize the entry of judgment in cases where the summons is served by publication. The defects or irregularities alleged may be taken as the grounds of the application.

All of these defects, except the insufficience of the affidavit upon which the order of publication of the summons was made, are mere irregularities and the right to have the judgment set aside on account of such irregularities, was lost by the neglect of defendant to make application in proper time.

The objection to the affidavit upon which the order of publication was made, goes to the jurisdiction of the Court over the person of the defendant, and it might be available to her, if she had not cured the defect by a general appearance in the action. In *Grantier vs. Rosecrance*, 27, *Wis.* 488, a motion had been made and granted in the lower Court to set aside a judgment, on the ground that the record did not show a valid service of the summons, and also because the complaint did not state a cause of action. The Supreme Court reversed the order setting aside the judgment and said, "Had he (the defendent) limited the motion solely to defects in the service of the summons, his appearance would have been a qualified one. But he did not ask to have the judgment vacated for that reason alone; but because the complaint did not state a cause of action against him. This was a full submission to the jurisdiction of the Court and general appearance."

Anderson vs. Coburn, *Ib.* 558, was a similar case and the rule in *Grantier vs. Rosecrance*, was re-affirmed. In *Clark vs. Blackwell*, 4, *C. Greene* 441, the rule was stated, "No special appearance can be made except to jurisdictional questions. If a party so far appears as to call into action the power of the Court for any purpose except to decide upon its own jurisdiction, it is a full appearance."

In this case the affidavit on which the application was made set forth several alleged defects besides the jurisdictional one, without confining the ground of application to any one; and it must be assumed that it was made upon all of them; upon the rule laid down in the cases we have cited, in which we fully concur, this cured all objections to jurisdiction over the person, and as the application was too late to take advantage of the other objections it ought not to have been granted.

Order appealed from reversed.

FREDERICK ALLIS, *Respondent*, vs. ISRAEL LASH, *Appellant*. } Filed Jany. 5. '77.

The exclusion of evidence of a fact appearing by other evidence and in no way disputed held in this case to furnish no ground for a new trial.

"A," after commencing a suit as "L's" attorney at law, to foreclose a mortgage held by "L," purchased (with "D,") the mortgaged premises, A and D agreeing to pay the mortgage debt. By this agreement of purchase A and D were to pay a gross sum for the premises, the amount due on the mortgage to be paid to L and the residue to the parties of whom they purchased. There was a dispute between the latter parties and L, as to the amount due on the mortgage, and the foreclosure litigation was carried on for the purpose of determining this dispute.

HELD, that the agreement of A and D to pay the mortgage debt does not preclude A from recovery for his services in conducting the litigation mentioned.

Appeal from judgment of District Court, Ramsey county.

Allis & Allis, Counsel for respondent.

Williams & Davidson, Counsel for appellant

BERRY, J.—This action is brought to recover compensation for professional services rendered to plaintiff's assignor Lorenzo Allis as an attorney and counsellor at law.

I. It appeared that a bill containing an item forming part of the present cause of action was was made out in the name of the law firm of, Allis, Gilfillan & Williams, and before this action was commenced, paid to some member thereof, by defendants agent; at the time when the services represented by such item were rendered, Lorenzo Allis was a member of the firm mentioned; It appeared however that the item spoken of was put into the bill by mistake, as the services represented by it had been rendered by Allis, acting not for the firm but for himself; They were services with which the firm had no connection, and for which it had, therefor, no proper claim for compensation. It further appeared that the "itəm spoken of was charged to defendant upon the firm books," and the bill rendered to and paid by defendants' agent, without the knowledge of Allis; and that as far as the firm books were concerned, the error was subsequently corrected in the account of Allis, Gilfillan & Williams against him; Upon these facts the bill which was offered in evidence by defendant was excluded by the court below; The mistake in entering the charge for services, rendered entirely outside of the partnership business, upon the firm books and in collecting the amount of the same, from defendants' agent was of course entirely unauthorized by the partnership relation ; and there is no pretense that it was in any way authorized or sanctioned by Allis himself or that Allis in any way led the defendant to believe that the services in question were partnership services; under these circumstances the most that could be claimed for the bill would be that it showed payment (for the item in question,) received by a firm of which Lorenzo Allis was a member; a payment by which he might be bound. But as the fact of the payment appeared by evidence other than the bill and was in no way disputed, the exclusion of the bill, could have worked no practical injury, and funishes no ground for a new trial.

II. The services for which this action is brought were rendered in the foreclosure of a mortgage for defendant; soon after the foreclosure suit was commenced Lorenzo Allis and W. F. Davidson purchased the mortgaged property and agreed to pay the mortgage debt; The defendant requested an instruction to the jury to the effect that under this state of facts Allis could not recover for services rendered by him, after his purchase, in the foreclosure proceedings because it was his duty to pay the mortgage without suit. By the agreement and purchase, Allis and Davidson were to pay a gross sum for the mortgaged premises, the amount due on the mortgage to be paid to the defendant and the residue to the parties of whom they purchased; As to the amount due on the mortgage there was a controversy between the defendant and the parties entitled to the residue of the purchase money, and it was for the purpose of determining this controversy that the foreclosure litigation was carried on; what the determination should be was a matter of indifference to Allis and Davidson; The litigation was not carried on for their benefit but for the benfit of defendant and the fact that Allis and Davidson had purchased, with an agreement to pay the mortgage, furnishes no reason why defendant should not pay Allis for his services in conducting the litigation if he saw fit (as he appears to have done,) to continue to employ him for that purpose.

III. With reference to the money which had been received by Lorenzo Allis for the defendant from the Railroad Co. the stipulation of the parties was that the court should deduct *the amount so* received from the verdict; under this stipulation the court was entirely right in deducting the *amount* received without interest.

Judgment affirmed.

(Chief Justice Gilfillan, for reasons appearing in the opinion, took no part in this case.)

U. S. Circuit Court, Minnesota Dist.

THE AMERICAN BUTTON-HOLE OVER-SEAMING & SEWING MACHINE CO.
vs.
JOHN M. MURRAY, JOHN W. BYRNES, JAS. DAILEY JOHN K. SMITH, JOHN H. HARLAN, LYMAN W. GREGG, AND JERRY MULLANE.
} Dec. Term, '76.

This was an action brought to recover on a promissory note signed by the defendants payable to the plaintiff. It was executed in consideration of an extension of time to J. M. Murray and his sureties upon two bonds held by plaintiff.

The facts sufficiently appear in the charge of the Judge.

Simonton & Reid, for plaintiff.

Wilson & Taylor, and S. L. Campbell, for defendants.

NELSON, J.—*Charge to Jury.*—This action is brought upon a promissory note for $770.68, dated March 23, 1876. Five defendants have interposed several defenses. One defendant, Murray, is in default, and submits to a judgment.

Fraud and want of consideration are alleged by all the defendants answering except Mullane who claims the note never was signed by him, or by one authorized by him to do so.

The undisputed facts are briefly these, J. M. Murray had the exclusive right within certain territorial limits to sell Sewing Machines manufactured by plaintiff; and being supplied on credit, he was required to execute a bond with good and sufficient sureties for the payment of notes given on the purchase of the same. He delivered to plaintiff a bond purporting to have been executed March 17, 1875, by himself and defendants Byrnes and Dailey; and another on September 25, 1875, executed by himself and Harlan, Smith and Gregg. Sometime in March 1876, Murray was indebted to plaintiff on several notes which had matured, and was requested to pay, or suit would be commenced upon the bonds. An arrangement was made whereby the plaintiff agreed to extend the time for the payment of the amount due, in case Murray would give it a note executed by himself and the sureties upon his bonds. There was due at that time $240, for which the sureties upon the bond executed Sept. 25, 1875, were liable, if at all. The sureties upon the first bond executed March 17, 1875, were responsible for the payment of the whole amount claimed $770.68 and this was the indebtedness upon which the plaintiff was willing to grant an extension.

In view of these facts the defendants contesting, with the exception of Mullane, who was not upon either bond, can avail themselves of any defense which would defeat a recovery upon the bonds.

If you believe Mullane never authorized his signature to the note, no recovery can be had against him.

Byrnes and Dailey who signed the bond executed March 17, 1875, claim that they signed it at the request of Murray and upon the condition that it should not be obligatory upon them unless three additional responsible names should be obtained. This is a good defense if the condition was known to the plaintiff at the time, but if it was only known to Murray, the principal obligor, and the bond, perfect on its face, was accepted without knowledge of that condition, these defendants Byrnes and Dailey cannot say that they did not intend be bound unless the names of three other persons, not on the bond when they signed, should be obtained. (16 *Wallace pg.* 1; see also article in *Albany Law Journal, on liability of sureties.* If this defense is not available to defeat a recovery upon the bond, it cannot be urged in this suit, for they were bound by their obligation to pay the amount due the plaintiff from Murray, and the execution of the note gave an extension of time for payment, and was no injury to them.

Smith and Gregg, sureties upon the bond executed Sept. 25, 1875, also allege that the bond they signed is void for the reason it was executed at the request of Murray and upon the condition that it should not bind them unless three other responsible sureties should be obtained, and that the plaintiff acquiesced in this condition. It is urged by them as a defense, also, that when the note was signed the agent of the plaintiff falsely represented that they were liable on their bond to the full extent of the note, whereas, if the bond could be enforced, the amount of their liability would be only $240, and that they declined to sign unless three responsible names were obtained in addition to the sureties on the bonds.

It is conceded that their liability was for that amount only, and that when the note was afterwards presented for their signatures, in compliance with their request, it had the name of Mullane upon it, which the defendant Murray told them he signed by the authority of Mullane. They claim to have been induced to sign it by the fact that Mullane, who was a well-to-do farmer had authorized his signature, and insist they are not liable if his signature is a forgery.

If you believe it is a forgery and that Smith and Gregg refused to sign until some other responsible name was secured but mentioned no person whose signature they required, still as Mullane could not read or write and his name appeared to be signed by some other person they should have ascertained before signing it whether his signature was properly to the note, and are not discharged unless the plaintiff had knowledge of the forgery.

And if Smith and Gregg when they signed the bond delivered it to the general agent of the plaintiff, and it was not to be considered obligatory until the names of three other persons were secured, then, as only themselves and one other appear to have executed it, the plaintiff cannot recover against them upon the note, for it was given on an indebtedness which the plaintiff's agent stated was covered by their bond.

Harlan urges that he signed the note upon the condition that Gregg and Smith would also sign it; now as he was only liable upon his bond to the extent of $240, if you believe a recovery cannot be had against them, the plaintiff cannot hold him, for the reason that his signature was obtained upon the condition known to it that Smith and Gregg were to share the liability with him.

The jury gave a verdict against all the defendants except Mullane.

———oo———

Recent Decisions.

Mechanics Lien.—Where a building was erected upon a wife's property under contract made with her husband, it appearing that she did not authorize the work nor appoint her husband her agent to make the contract, and made no ratification, other than an approval of the arrangement of, the house, held, that a material man had no lien that he could enforce against the property; that knowledge and approbation are merely prima facie evidence of authorization, and may be utterly defeated by direct testimony to the contrary, and that to fix the lien the owner must directly or indirectly participate in the contract.

Garnett vs. Berry, St. Louis Ct. of Appeals, C. L. Jr, Vol. 4, p. 24.

Rights of Tax-Payers.—Tax-payers have a standing in a court of equity to restrain the illegal appropriation by a municipality of money raised by taxation.

Campbell v. City of St. Louis, St. Louis Ct. of appeals. C. L. Jr., Vol. 4, p. 24.

Assignment for Benefit of Creditors.—A Deed of trust for benefit of creditors, did not by its terms profess to convey all of grantors property, and provided for his remaining in possession; Held void as to creditors; that retention of the property by grantor, was unmistakable badge of fraud; no debtor has a right to prescribe terms to his creditors, or to interfere with the appropriate collection of their debts.

Price vs. Pitzer, (Sup. Ct. of Md.) L. & E. Rept. Vol. 3, No. 1.

Indictment.—An Indictment charging the fraudulent alteration etc., of "a book and writing, commonly known as a duplicate of taxes" of a school districts, without setting forth either copy or purport of the whole. or the part altered, is a bad indictment at common law.

Commonwealth vs. Beamish (Sup Ct. of Penn. May 1876.)

Perjury.—A person cannot be convicted of perjury upon the mere evidence that he has made under oath two contradictory statements material to the trial in which he was called to testify; Nor is the rule varied by the fact that the accused stated in his second statement that the first was intentionally false.

Schwartz vs. Commonwealth, (Sup. Ct. of Appeals, Va.) L. & E. R. Vol. 3, No. 1.

Eminent Domain.—Private property cannot be taken for public use without just compensation first made for it; and this protection extends to an adjacent owners fee, in a common highway against its use for the track of a railroad,

The provision in the charter of a railroad company delegating the right of eminent domain without providing for just compensation as condition precedent, to the use of private property would be void under the constitution.

Where a railroad company takes possession of land for which it is liable to make compensation, without the consent of the owner and without having ascertained and paid the compensation under the process given by the statute, it is liable to an action of ejectment; or to an action of trespass, in which the owner may recover the damages, occurring before suit brought but not permanent damages as for the taking of the land.

Sherman vs. Mil. L. S. & Western R. R. Co., (Sup. Ct. of Wis.)

Fiduciary debt of Bankrupt.—Where goods are consigned to a bankrupt for sale on commission and he fails to account for the proceeds; a fiduciary debt is created, which will not be released by his discharge in bankruptcy.

Meader vs. Sharp, (Sup. Ct. of Ga.,) Chicago Legal News, No. 429.

Payment after notice of Fraud.—Notes of defendant amounting to ten thousand dollars, procured by fraudulent representations were purchased by plaintiff without notice at the time, of the fraud and for a valuable consideration; $500 of which was paid before such notice was received; an action being brought upon the notes. Held, that he was only entitled to recover the amount paid on the purchase before notice of the fraud and that the case was governed by the rule that the parties to an unperformed contract which is completed after notice of a fraud, is not within the principle which protects a bona fide purchaser.

Dresser vs. Iowa Railway Construction Co., (U. S. Sup. Court,) Legal News, No. 424.

Implied Warranty of Title.—The principle that he who sells property for a valuable consideration guarantees title to the purchaser, and stands bound to make good any loss to the purchaser from a defective title, is undisputed. But this being so does not prevent the purchaser from assuming the risk of such purchase, and then the circumstances of the sale will be a question for the jury to determine.

Corry Saving Bank vs. Bright, (Sup. Ct., Pa.,) Pitts, L. Jr., No. 20.

Equitable Assignment.—A debtor agreed to transfer to a bank, as collateral security, certain shares of stock of that Bank, and accordingly, by power of attorney, appointed the Cashier his attorney to transfer. The Cashier died without executing the power, and the debtor went into bankruptcy. Held, that the power was irrevocable and could be executed by any one and aside from execution, and as against an assignee in bankruptcy operated as an equitable assignment of the stock.

Lightner, Assignee, vs. First National Bank, (Pa. Sup. Ct.) Pitts' Legal Jr., No. 20.

Latest Publications.

Abbott's U. S. Practice, vol. 1, by Benjamin Vaughan Abbott; 8vo., 640 pp. Law Sheep, ... $7.50

Supplement to Riddle's Supplementary Proceedings, by John F. Baker; 8vo., 128 pp., half sheep, . . . 2.00

The Law of Evidence, by Simon Greenleaf; vols. 2 and 3, 13th edition, carefully revised by John Wilder May; 8vo., per vol. 6.00

The Law for the Formation of Business Corporations, with Forms, By-Laws, etc., by R. Bach. McMaster; 12mo. 50 pp. Paper, . . . $0 50

Smith's Reports, Vol. XXIX, being Vol. LXXIX of Pennsylvania State Reports; by P. Frazer Smith. 8vo. 579 pp., Law Sheep, . . . 4 50

Reports of Cases argued and determined in the Supreme Court of Appeals of West Virginia, Vol. VIII. By Henry M. Mathews. 8vo., 944 pp. Sheep, ... 4 00

Sansum's Digest of Law of Insurance. A Digest of all the Fire, Life, Marine, Accident and Guarantee Insurance cases decided in Great Britain and America. By O. B. Sansum. 8vo, 600 pp., Law Sheep. 8 00

Bissell's Reports. Volume VI. Reports of cases argued and decided in the Seventh Judicial Circuit. By Josiah H. Bissell. 8vo 650 pp., Law Sheep. 7 50

Massachusetts Reports CXIX. Reports of cases argued and decided in the Supreme Judicial Court of Massachusetts. By John Lathrop, Reporter. 8vo Law Sheep. . . . 4 50

Otto's Reports on the Decisions of the Supreme Court of the United States, Vol. 1, 8vo. 5 00

Greenleaf on Law of Evidence, Vol. 1. By John Wilder May. 13th Ed. 8vo. 6 00

A Treatise on Conveyances by Debtors to Defraud Creditors. By Orlando F. Bump. Second Ed., revised and enlarged. 8vo., 750 pp., Law Sheep. 6 50

Shaw's Index to Minn. Session Laws, 1849–1875. Full Sheep, . . . 4 00

THE SYLLABI.

VOL. 1. SATURDAY, JAN. 27, 1877. No. 15.

PUBLISHED WEEKLY,

By JOHN B. WEST & CO.,

No. 1 Wabasha St., - ST. PAUL, MINN.

Terms 3.00 per annum in Advance.

HOMER C. ELLER, Editor.

TABLE OF CONTENTS.

AT the present term of the District Court for the county of Dakota. Crosby, J., presiding, a condition of affairs arose that suggests some new as well as peculiar questions. The regular panel of the grand jury was called, sworn and charged, when before their retiring, challenges to the individual jurors were interposed by the counsel for one Jacob Bird, held to answer, and then confined in jail, upon a charge of murder, and as to thirteen of such jurors the challenges were found true; leaving less than a quorum of the regular panel. The court ordered a special venire for thirteen additional grand jurors to enquire into the charge against Bird, returnable the following morning, the regular grand jury in the meantime proceeding with its labors. The following morning the thirteen persons summoned under the special venire appearing, they were severally challenged, which challenges, however, were, with one exception, withdrawn. In this instance a juror being a native of Prussia, was challenged on the ground of alienage, the counsel on behalf of Bird claiming that under the first section of Chapter CVII, General Statutes, the grand jurors summoned *must be citizens.* It appearing, however, that he had declared his intention of becoming a citizen, and was a qualified elector, the Court held that under section three of said chapter, he was a competent juror. These thirteen men were then charged by the Court in substantially the same manner as the regular grand jury, and were further informed that they, with ten of the regular panel whose names were given them, would form a grand jury for the sole purpose of examining into the charges against Jacob Bird. They then retired to the grand jury room, there joining the ten of the regular panel who were to act with them, the other thirteen withdrawing upon their appearance. It was contemplated that as soon as the jury thus constituted had disposed of the case of Bird, that the thirteen jurors summoned under the special venire should withdraw, and the grand jury as originally constituted proceed with its duties.

A case of this character where so many individual challenges are interposed and found true is of but rare occurrence; and the statute upon the subject certainly does not provide for such an emergency in the clearest terms; an omission that should be provided for by legislation; The facts in this case show the existence of two grand juries at the same time, or a panel of more than the statutory number.

WE publish in this number an important decision of Judge Nelson upon the subject of removing controversies from the State Probate to the Federal courts.

SUPREME COURT, STATE OF MINNESOTA.

THIRD NATIONAL BANK OF SYRACUSE, N.Y., *Appellant.* vs. CLARK & TITUS, *Respondents.* — Filed, Jan. 5, '77.

This was an action brought by plaintiff as indorsee of a promissory note made by defendants, payable to the order of The Williams' Mower and Reaper Company, and indorsed as follows, viz: "Pay Third National Bank, Syracuse, or order, for collection for the Williams Mower and Reaper Co., Syracuse, N. Y., O. Welsh, Treasurer." HELD, that the indorsement is "restrictive" and that parol evidence is inadmi sible to show it absolute.

Rock County Bank vs. Hollister, 21 Minn. 385, followed and applied to this case.

Appeal from Judgment of the District Court, county of Olmsted.

H. C. Butler, attorney for appellant.

Start & Gore, attorneys for respondent.

BERRY, J.—The plaintiff brings this action as indorsee of a promissory note made by defendants and payable to the order of "The Williams' Mower and Reaper Co., Syracuse, N.Y." The indorsement through which the plaintiff claims is in these words, viz: "Pay Third Nat. Bk., Syracuse, or order, for collection for the Williams' Mower and Reaper Co., Syracuse, N. Y., O. Welch, Treasurer." The making of the indorsement by Welch, and his authority to make it are undisputed.

The main controversy in the Court below was as to whether the plaintiff took the note subject to the same defences as if it were in the hands of the payee.

With reference to this question the Court below ruled, *First.*—That the indorsement was "restrictive" and that parol evidence was inadmissible to show that it was absolute and, *Second.*—That the plaintiff under the indorsement took the note subject to the defences mentioned.

The first ruling was clearly right. *Ex vi termini* an *indorsement* must be in writing. There can be no such thing as an indorsement wholly or partly in parol.

The indorsement in this case is in fact restrictive and for that reason cannot be, nor be shown to be, absolute.

What the indorser and indorsee may have intended by the indorsement, except so far as it is expressed in the writing, is of no consequence in this action.

The plaintiff being thus compelled to stand upon the terms of the indorsement under which it claims; the case falls within the doctrine of *Rock County Bank vs. Hollister*, 21 *Minn.* 385, in which it was held that an indorsee claiming under an indorsement like that in this instance, was not the *owner* of the note indorsed, and therefore not the real party in interest, for which reason he could not maintain an action upon the note.

It follows that in the case at bar the jury was properly directed to find for the defendants. This conclusion disposes of the case and prevents us from reaching the second ruling of the Court below.

Judgment affirmed.

STATE OF MINNESOTA, *Respondent,* vs. G. LAUTENSCHLAEGER, *Appellant.* — Filed, Jan. 17,'77.

The fact that the record does not show affirmatively that one of the jurors impannelled to try the cause had ever been sworn, or that the jury on coming into court with their verdict, was in charge of an officer, furnishes no ground for a motion in arrest of judgment after verdict.

The division of a trial court, upon an application for a new trial upon the ground of newly discovered evidence can only be received in an appellate court upon a record showing both the after discovered evidence and that introduced upon the former trial.

Appeal from District Court, Ramsey county.

Geo, P. Wilson, Attorney General, for the State.

H. J. Horn and I. V. D. Heard, for the defendant.

CORNELL, J.—Upon the appeal from the judgment herein this court is asked to review the decision of the District Court, refusing defendant's application for a new trial on the ground of after-discovered evidence, and also the decision denying the motion thereafter made in arrest of judgment. This latter motion was made upon two grounds: First, that it did not affirmatively appear from the record that one of the jurors impannelled to try the cause had ever been sworn; and second, that it did not appear therefrom that the jury, upon coming into court with their verdict, was in charge of an officer. Upon the point presented by this branch of the case the ruling of this court in the *State vs. Ryan,* 13 *Minn.,* 370, is decisive. The motion was properly overruled.

The decision of a trial court, upon an application for a re-trial, because of after discovered evidence, generally involves an excise of judicial discretion upon a full consideration of all the evidence given on the trial and the legitimate effect, which the new evidence, taken in connection therewith, ought, upon legal principles, to have towards producing a different result. Hence when the application has been refused, an appellate court can only review the decision upon a record which affirmitively and substantially discloses all the material testimony which was submitted to the jury, as well as the newly discovered evidence which it is proposed to introduce upon a re-trial. In no other way can the exact character and legal effect of such new testimony be determined.

Hilliard on New Trials, Sec. 31 *and* 36. *Chap.* 15. *Anon.* 7 *Wend.* 331.

In the record before us the bill of exceptions does not purport to contain all the evidence given to the jury, but only the substance of so much of it as was deemed essential to a proper consideration of the rulings made by the court during the trial to which defendant excepted.

For aught apparent upon this record the conclusions reached by the trial court as to the nature and legitimate effect of the new evidence may have been fully justified by the testimony submitted to the jury upon the trial. Such is the presumption, in the absence of a contrary showing.

The order denying a new trial and the judgment appealed from is affirmed.

——o||o——

U. S. Circuit Court, Minnesota Dist.

Barbara Craigie, *et. al.* *vs.* Annie McArthur. } Dec., Term, 1876.

A contest in regard to the distribution of the estate, of a deceased person, where the amount involved is sufficient and the citizenship of parties such as would confer jurisdiction, is a "controversy" that may be removed from the State to the Federal Courts under the provisions of act of Congress of March 3, 1875, (Statutes at Large, vol. 18 p.) Such removal however must be before trial in the Court of original jurisdiction and can not be made from a Court to which, after hearing, an appeal has been taken.—[Ed.]

James G. Craigie died in Otter Tail county, in the State of Minnesota, Sept. 8, 1872, leaving real and personal estate, and on petition of Annie McArthur letters of administration were granted to her March 13, 1876, by the Probate Court of that county. On May 18, 1876, the administratrix filed a petition for a final accounting and for distribution of the estate, in which she claimed to be the sole heir at law of said James G. Craigie, deceased, and prayed that a decree be entered assigning to and vesting in her all the real and personal property in her hands or otherwise, belonging to said estate. A citation was issued by the Probate Court fixing June 13, 1876, as the day upon which a hearing would be had of the matters contained in the petition, and notice to all parties interested, was ordered to be given by publication in a newspaper, to show cause on that day why the prayer of the petition should not be granted. Objection was filed in writing on the day fixed for the hearing by Barbara Craigie, John Craigie, Charles Craigie, Alexander M. Craigie, Elizabeth Enslie, Ann Clark and Ellen R. Shephard, and after the hearing and due consideration of the same, a decree was entered June 14, 1876, which, after reciting the proceedings in the administration of the estate, is as follows: "Now therefore it is ordered, adjudged and decreed, that the administration of the estate of said James G. Craigie be and the same is hereby concluded, and that the administratrix of said estate be, and she is hereby discharged, and that all and singular the property and estate which was of the said James G. Craigie at the time of his death and the increase thereof * * * * * * * * * be and the same hereby are distributed, assigned to, and vested in the said Annie McArthur as the heir, and sole heir at law of the said James G. Craigie."

On August 9, 1876, all the persons appearing and contesting the matters set up in the petition of Annie McArthur, with the exception of Alexander M. Craigie, took an appeal by virtue of the statute of the State of Minnesota, to the District Court of the Seventh Judicial District, and the same was perfected, and a certified transcript of all the proceedings had in the matter, and all the papers, petitions, orders, decrees, notices, etc., were filed in the Clerk's office Oct. 10, 1876.

A petition was filed for a removal of the suit under act of Congress, of March 3, 1875, (Statutes at Large, vol. 18,) to the United States Circuit Court, for the District of Minnesota, Oct. 18, 1876, setting up:

1st. That an action has been commenced and is now pending in the District Court of the Seventh Judicial District, on appeal from the judgment of the Probate Court, in which the petitioners are appellants, and Annie McArthur respondent.

2nd. That since the commencement of said action by said appeal in said Court there has been no term at which a trial of said action could be had.

3rd. That the amount in dispute is over $500. exclusive of costs.

4th. That at the time of the commencement of said action all the appellants were and are aliens and subjects of Victoria, Queen of Great Britian and Ireland, and reside in Scotland.

5th. That the respondent is a citizen of the State of Minnesota, and resides therein.

The proper bond was executed, and the action was transfered, and a return was filed in this Court Dec. 8, 1876.

A motion is now made to remand the suit to the State District Court for the reasons:

1st. That it is not such an action as the said United States Circuit Court can acquire jurisdiction of. under any of the acts of the Congress of the United States pertaining to the removal of causes from State Courts.

2nd. That if this Court could have jurisdiction of the cause, the petition and bond for its removal should have been presented to and filed in the State Court of original jurisdiction, to-wit: the Probate Court of Otter Tail county, before or at the term of said Court at which the cause could first be tried, and that the appellants having submitted themselves, by written objection, to the jurisdiction of the said Probate Court and gone to trial there upon the merits, it is too late to first apply for a removal to the United States Court after appeal taken from the judgment of said Probate Court to a higher and appellate State Court."

Chas. D. Kerr, for the motion.

Bigelow, Flandrau & Clark, and E. E. Corliss, contra.

NELSON, J:—Conceding, for the sake of the argument, that the probate of a will and the appointment of an administrator of an intestates estate are not proper subjects to be determined in the Federal Courts. Yet, when the estate is ready for distribution and a claim is made for the whole of the estate or a portion thereof, and contested, if the necessary conditions exist I think a removal is authorized on proper application being made. All the essential elements of a controversy exist. There are parties, and a contest in reference to property, and informal pleadings under which the disputed matters are to be settled by a Court.

The act of Congress authorizes a removal from a Court of limited or general jurisdiction, and a controversy in a Probate Court involving the distribution of an estate between parties who appear and submit to the jurisdiction and litigate therein, is certainly a suit of "a civil nature * * * in equity," 45 *Maine* 571; 4 *Penn. State R.* 301 22 *N. Y.* 421; 20 *Minn. R.* 247; 19 *Wis. R.* 200.

The Probate Court of the State of Minnesota, is a constitutional Court of record, with a seal and regular terms, fixed by law, (*Sec.* 1, *Art.* 6. *Con. Minn.; 2 Bis. Stat.* 739; 1 *do. p.* 672, *Sec.* 169.) Its decrees. orders and judgments are binding upon all persons. and the right of appeal is given to the District Court. and finally to the Supreme Court of the State. Pleadings are not necessary, but all applications made to the Court orally or in writing are embodied in its records. At the time when the proceedings in that Court assume the form of a controversy between parties, and the conditions requisite exist, the suit is removable, (*Gaines vs. Fuentes, et al.*, 2 *Otto R.* 14.)

When in answer to a notice of the hearing of the matters to be determined in the Probate Court, the petitioners filed their objection, and instituted a contest, the right of removal should have been enforced. It is urged that there is no controversy *inter partes* in the Probate Court, and that the appeal is the commencement of a new suit, when for the first time it is known who are the parties interested. I do not so understand the situation of such controversies. The notice authorized to be published by the Probate Court fixed the time when the matters set forth in the petition would be determined by the Court, and specified the several questions which would be settled. If no objection is made a decree in accordance with the prayer of the petition would be conclusive; but opposition being made a hearing or trial must take place, and all the matters at issue litigated.

When the contestants interposed objections certainly the parties to a controversy were known, and the decree was binding upon them as well as all others interested.

It is too late after the determination of the litigated matters in the Probate Court, and an appeal taken to the District Court of the State, to initiate steps for a removal. No such right then exists, and to entertain jurisdiction would be an attempt to exercise a revisory power over the judgment of the Probate Court, which is given by law to another tribunal.

This Court has entertained jurisdiction of

the removal of a suit pending in a State Court on an appeal from Commissioners appointed by that Court to fix the value of private property taken under the right of eminent domain by an incorporated company (3, *Dillon's R.* 465); but this appeal is of an entirely different character. In the former case the appeal was from an appraisement by Commissioners authorized under the charter of the company, which provided for an appeal from the award to the District Court, and upon the appeal being taken the Clerk is authorized to set it down as a cause upon the docket of the Court appointing the Commissioners. A suit then for the first time is instituted in a Court. In the case before me the initiatory proceedings and contest were in a Court recognized as one of the judicial tribunals of the State, and the appeal was from a decree of that Court.

The removal of a suit under the act of Congress of March 3, 1875, must be from the Court of original jurisdiction.

Motion to remand granted.

DILLON, *Circuit Judge*—I am of opinion that the removal was not applied for in time under the act of March 3, 1875, and that the cause should be remanded.

JULINAH P. ATWATER, *vs.* R. S. HADLEY, *et. al.*, and FIRST NAT. BANK OF OWATONNA. } Dec. Term, 1876.

The rule, that courts will carefully scrutinize all transfers of property between those occupying fiduciary relations, and vacate any such transfer that is not entirely fair and equitable on the part of the person holding a position of trust and confidence, applied to the facts in this case.—[Ed.]

Julinah P. Atwater was the owner in June 1875, of notes and mortgages of the value of $3100, which she placed in the hands of "Hadley's Law and Collection Agency" for collection; R. S. Hadley assuming to act for the same.

On the death of one Seely, a brother-in-law, she claimed to own with her brothers and sisters an interest in the farm and farm property previously occupied by the deceased. A claim to the same was also made by the father and brothers of deceased. Propositions and consultations for settlement were frequently had and made during the summer of 1875, and for an amicable adjustment between the claimants, in which R. S. Hadley participated, acting as the attorney and adviser of Julinah P. Atwater representing herself, and the interest adverse to the Seely heirs. C. W. Hadley acted at one time in giving advice to Julinah P. Atwater, and in July the firm of Cogswell & Johnson were also employed as counsel to aid Julinah in a settlement. No arrangement was consummated, although concessions were made by the Atwater claimants, and on the night of July 30th or 31st, Julinah had agreed to an adjustment whereby the interest she represented would be satisfied with the amount of $2500, and a contract on that basis was ready to be prepared for execution, which was finally objected to by the Seelys. When this last interview had broken off, it was communicated to the plaintiff and her brother, that a purchase of this adverse interest would be made by C. W. Hadley for the sum of $2500, including the notes of the value of $3100, and the claim to the other property represented to be of the value of about $5000. This purchase was finally completed, and as it appears from the testimony, R. S. Hadley was a party to the purchase, although not appearing in the papers drawn up. He and C. W. Hadley were to take the property upon the following terms arranged between themselves: R. S. Hadley was to contribute $1300, taking as his share the notes and mortgages admitted to be of the value of $3100, and C. W. Hadley to have the interest in the land for the sum of $1200. The terms of the sale were $1000 cash, the notes and mortgages to be assigned to C. W Hadley immediately, and a certificate of deposit in The First National Bank of Owatonna for the sum of $1500, payable when a quit claim deed was delivered to the bank, executed by the Atwaters, brothers and sisters, and also a power of attorney from Julinah to C. W. Hadley to take possession of the farm and other property. The $1000 cash was paid, and the certificate of deposit, as above, specifying on its face the conditions, was given to the plaintiff, and the other papers were drawn up and taken to be executed by the other parties who were absent.

It appears that this sale was not entirely satisfactory at the time of the transfer of the notes and mortgages by the plaintiff, and is charged to have been assented to on account of the anxiety of mind and distress the plaintiff was in from the repeated failures to accomplish an amicable adjustment with the Seely heirs, and from apprehension of a criminal proceeding being instituted against her by these heirs. Cogswell & Johnson were not consulted in regard to this purchase by the Hadleys, and whenever their advice had been previously given in regard to the manner of a settlement with the Seely heirs, they had not approved of any concessions being made by the plaintiff of her rights, and of those of her brothers and sisters to the Seelys; and they regarded her claim undoubtedly valid to all the property. C. W. Hadley in his interview with the plaintiff gave her to understand that the Seely heirs could recover from her the notes and mortgages which she owned, and that there had been so much talk against her that she did not stand very well in the community. He also intimated that if the Seelys had him for their adviser, he would find a way to obtain possession of the property. R. S. Hadley at the time of the transfer of the notes and mortgages expressed himself as regretting the purchase by his son C. W. Hadley, when in fact he was a party to the purchase, as above stated. The plaintiff after the bargain was closed paid the "Hadley Agency" $50 for services rendered as her attorneys and advisers. She seeks in this suit to set aside this sale to the Hadleys.

It is urged by the defendants;

1st. That the fiduciary relation between the parties had ceased when the purchase was made.

2d. That the sale was a fair and equitable one, and made by the plaintiff with a full knowledge of all her rights, and with no idea of obtaining any advantage over her on the part of the defendants.

Chas. A. Clark, of Iowa, for plaintiff.

Gordon E. Cole, for defendants.

NELSON, J.—It must be conceded that the relationship of attorney and client, or principal and agent, existed, and was so ununderstood by the parties, up to the time of the purchase. The burden is on the defendants to establish the fairness and equity of the transaction. The careful scrutiny which is bestowed by courts upon sales of this character between persons occupying fiduciary positions and their confidents is in accordance with public policy to prevent public mischief.

The testimony in this case in my opinion brings it within the principle where the strict rule should be applied, and calls upon the defendants to establish the following characteristics without which this transaction cannot be sustained.

The sale must have been fair, the price adequate, and the conduct of the defendants equitable; unless such was the case, the decision cannot be doubtful.

That the price paid is wholly inadequate must be conceded. The value of the notes and mortgages is admitted to be $3100, and the title to the realty was evidently considered good by the defendants. The letter of C. W. Hadley written immediately after the sale expresses a disappointment that the deed upon which it was expected the plaintiff's title could be enforced failed to be in conformity with the laws of the State of Minnesota, and shows that at the time of the purchase he regarded it conclusive upon the title. R. S. Hadley participated in the last effort between the plaintiff and the Seelys to settle the controversy, and it is stated by her that she would have yielded to a small demand on the part of the Seelys which broke up the interview, had not opposition been made by him.

The defendants knowing the firm of Cogswell & Johnson had been employed to aid in bringing about an amicable arrangement with the Seelys, never informed them of a contemplated purchase of the property, and did not consult at all with them as to the fairness and equity of the transaction. It was incumbent on the defendants to have fully communicated to these counsel their determination, and a failure to do so was unfair to the plaintiff, and not in accordance with the relationship existing between the parties.

There can be no doubt that an advantage was obtained by the defendants, and so regarded by them.

The plaintiff regretting the step taken, offered to pay a bonus for the surrender of the notes and mortgages and cancellation of the sale, but this was declined for the reason that the notes had been taken by R. S. Hadley to be sold, and had at that time probably passed out of the control of the defendants or either of them. The testimony conclusively shows this statement to have been untrue.

Without further comment I am satisfied upon a full examination of the evidence the complainant is entitled to the relief asked for. Authorities consulted.

9 *Pickering* 231; *Gibson vs. Jeyes*, 6 *Vesey;* 266 40 *Barbour N. Y. Sup. Ct.* |*R.* 521; 2 *Hare* 60; *Leading cases in Equity.* 3*d Am. Ed.* 202; *Story's Equity Jurisprudence*, *Vol.* 1 *Sec.* 311 *to* 314; 63 *Maine* 17; 3 *Edwards Ch. Rep.* 369; *Howell vs. Ransom*, 11 *Paige* 538.

Recent Decisions.

Supersedeas.—In case of appeal or writ of error to the Supreme Court of the United States, service of writ of error or perfection of appeal within sixty days (Sundays exclusive) after the rendering of judgment or passage of decree. is an indespensible pre-requisite to a supersedeas.

Kitchen vs. Randolph, (U. S. Sup. Ct.) Chic. L. News Vol. IX. 131.

Judgment.—A judgment docketed on a day, declared by Statute to be a holiday, is void and confers no lien.

In re Worthington 14 Nat. Bank. Reg. 388.

Bankruptcy.—A person who is insane at the time of the commission of an alleged act of bankruptcy cannot be adjudged a bankrupt for that act.

In re Weitzel 14 Nat Bank. Reg. 466.

Fraud—Receiving Deposit by Insolvent Bank.—Where a check was deposited in a bank which at the time was hopelessly and fraudulently insolvent and contemplating suspension, with the intention on the part of the depositor to pass the title to the check to the bank, the fraudulent concealment by the bank of its insolvent condition vitiated the transaction so that the bank acquired no title to the check upon which it could maintain an action against the maker and endorser. Had the bank acted in good faith it would have been the owner of the check. But the deposit of the check was made on the faith of the solvency of the bank, and it was a fraud on the part of the bank to receive it.

Fisse vs. Dietrich et al. (St. Louis Ct. of Appeal) Cent. L. Jr. Vol. 4, p. 47.

Suicide, Life Insurance.—A policy of Life Insurance contained a provision that if the person whose life was insured should "die by suicide," (sane or insane) the policy should be void. Held, to be a binding provision and that the death of such person from a wound inflicted by himself, when in an insane condition and unconscious of his acts, avoided the policy.

Bigelow vs. Berkshire Life Ins. Co., U. S. Sup. Ct., Oct. Tr. 1876.

Insurance, Death from Illegal Act—Where death resulted from an illegal operation voluntarily submitted to by insured to produce abortion.

Held, that public policy would preclude the company from insuring against the consequences of such an act, and no recovery could be had.

Hatch vs. Mut. Life Ins. Co., (Sup. Ct., Mass,) 5 Ins. Law Jr. 925.

Liability of Municipal Corporations.—A city having power to construct public sewers and to demand and recover pay from adjoining owners for liberty to enter their private drains into such sewers, is responsible for negligently suffering them to occasion a nuisance to the estates of such adjoining owners, if the nuisance does not result from the original plan of construction, and could be avoided by keeping them in proper condition. In maintaining such public sewer a city is bound to exercise the same degree of care and prudence that a discreet and cautious individual would use if the whole loss or risk was to be his alone.

It will not however be liable for injuries caused to individuals by an obstruction in such public sewer not placed there by its own officials or by authority of the city government, until after actual notice of such obstruction, or until by reason of the lapse of time, actual notice may be presumed.

Rowe vs. Portsmouth, (Sup. Ct., New Hamp.,) Am. Law Reg., vol. 12, p. 713.

Insurance by Warehousemen.—A policy of Insurance was taken out by a Warehouseman against loss or damage by fire on "merchandise, their own, or held by them in trust or in which they have an interest or liability contained in" a certain warehouse.

Held, to cover the merchandise itself and not simply their interest therein, and that in case of loss the assured was entitled to recover the entire value of the goods, not exceeding the sum insured, holding the remainder, after satisfying their own loss, as trustees for the owners; and where owners had taken other policies covering the same goods,the several policies constituted double insurance, and should share the losses proportionately.

Home Ins. Co. vs. Baltimore Warehouse Co., U. S. Supt. Ct, Oct Tr. 1876.

Bankruptcy—Discharge.—P. a bankrupt whose assets were not sufficient to entitle him to a discharge, obtained the necessary consent thereto of more than one-fourth in number, and one-third in value of his creditors who had proved their claims and to whom he was bound as a principal debtor. Desiring to obtain the consent of M., another creditor "to strengthen his application for discharge" he gave him a note for forty dollars with security, and in consideration M. signed the paper consenting to the discharge; R. & Co., opposed the discharge because of this transaction with M.

Held, That this transaction was a violation of Sec. 29 of the Bankrupt act, and the discharge must be refused. That perfect equality among creditors is the fundamental principle upon which the bankrupt law proceeds and that anything that defeats that, is a fraud upon the law. That the obligation incurred to one creditor as the price of his assent to a discharge is as much a fraud on those who had before signed the certificate of assent as on those that had not; That the court was not inquire whether the act complained of had been productive of harm but if it had been committed; and if it had. it was its duty to withhold the discharge.

Palmer vs. Rogers, 14 Nat Bank Reg. 437.

Premature Entry of Judgment.—The premature entry of a judgment, where the court has jurisdiction of the subject matter and the parties, is merely an irregularity; and the judgment cannot be vacated on that ground at a subsequent term.

Pier vs. Amony, Ibid.

Latest Publications.

Abbott's U. S. Practice, vol. 1, by Benjamin Vaughan Abbott; 8vo., 640 pp. Law Sheep, ... $7.50

Supplement to Riddle's Supplementary Proceedings, by John F. Baker; 8vo., 128 pp., half sheep, ... 2.00

The Law of Evidence, by Simon Greenleaf; vols. 2 and 3, 13th edition, carefully revised by John Wilder May; 8vo., per vol. 6.00

The Law for the Formation of Business Corporations, with Forms, By-Laws, etc., by R. Bach. McMaster; 12mo. 50 pp. Paper, ... $0 50

Smith's Reports, Vol. XXIX, being Vol. LXXIX of Pennsylvania State Reports; by P. Frazer Smith. 8vo. 579 pp., Law Sheep, ... 4 50

Reports of Cases argued and determined in the Supreme Court of Appeals of West Virginia, Vol. VIII. By Henry M. Mathews. 8vo., 944 pp. Sheep, ... 4 00

Sansum's Digest of Law of Insurance. A Digest of all the Fire, Life, Marine, Accident and Guarantee Insurance cases decided in Great Britain and America. By O. B. Sansum.8vo, 600 pp., Law Sheep. 8 00

Bissell's Reports. Volume VI. Reports of cases argued and decided in the Seventh Judicial Circuit. By Josiah H. Bissell. 8vo 650 pp., Law Sheep. 7 50

Massachusetts Reports CXIX. Reports of cases argued and decided in the Supreme Judicial Court of Massachusetts. By John Lathrop, Reporter. 8vo Law Sheep. 4 50

Otto's Reports on the Decisions of the Supreme Court of the United States, Vol. 1, 8vo. 5 00

Greenleaf on Law of Evidence, Vol. 1. By John Wilder May. 13th Ed. 8vo. 6 00

A Treatise on Conveyances by Debtors to Defraud Creditors. By Orlando F. Bump. Second Ed., revised and enlarged. 8vo., 750 pp., Law Sheep. 6 50

Shaw's Index to Minn. Session Laws, 1849–1875. Full Sheep. . . 4 00

SESSION LAWS.

We have the Session Laws of Minnesota from 1849 to 1875 inclusive, 34 vols., which we offer in sets, or by the volume.

Parties wishing to fill their sets, will do well to send list at once.

We offer:

1861	2.00	1872	$3.50
1862	2.50	1873	2.50
1863	2.00	1874	2.00
1864	2.00	1875	2.50
1871	2.00	1876	1.75

Bound in Half Sheep.

The American Reprint

OF THE

ENCYCLOPÆDIA BRITANNICA,

New Ninth Edition.

Volumes 1, 2, 3 and 4 are now ready.

This is the Largest and Best work of the kind in the English Language. Every Article is a Complete Treatise by the most Eminent Writers.

Send for Specimen Pages to

JOHN B. WEST & CO.

We have covers for filing and preserving The Syllabi, which we will send by mail, on receipt of price, 35 cents.

THE SYLLABI.

VOL. 1. SATURDAY, FEB. 3, 1877. No. 16.

PUBLISHED WEEKLY,

By JOHN B. WEST & CO.,

No. 1 Wabasha St., - ST. PAUL, MINN

Terms 3.00 per annum in Advance.

HOMER C. ELLER, Editor.

TABLE OF CONTENTS.

THE Supreme Court of Kansas, in the case of *Jansen vs. City of Atchison, et al.*, 16 Kan. 358, hold that where injury has resulted from a defect in a sidewalk, which is under the control of a city. and the city is compelled to pay for such injury, it has no recourse over against the owner of the lot in front of which the defect existed, and there is no liability to the party injured on the part of such owner, arising from the mere fact of ownership. Before the owner can be held responsible there must appear some negligence on his part, or the injury must have been caused by some obstruction or excavation created by him. In this case plaintiff was injured by the falling in of a sidewalk in front of premises owned by one of the defendants, but which were leased to and occupied by a step-mother of plaintiff, in whose employ plaintiff was at the time of the injury. The lease provided that the tenant should repair. The court held that there was no right of action against the owner of the premises. The case seems to be in harmony with *Robbins vs. Jones*, 15 C. B. (N. S.) 221, where a highway was raised several feet above the level as it stood when defendant's house was built, and the defendant bridged over the space between the highway and the upper story with gratings, which were used by the public as a part of the highway. Here it was held that the owner was not liable for the non-repair of such gratings, but it was the duty of the parish to keep them in repair. But where private premises are lawfully connected with the highway by excavation or vaults, open or covered, it has been held that if the owner of it fails to use ordinary diligence to maintain such covers or guards in good repair, he is liable to a person injured through any defect therein. *Proctor vs. Harris*, 4 *C. & P.* 337; *Homan, vs. Stanley*, 66 *Penn. St.* 464; *Coupland vs. Hardingham*, 3 *Campb.* 398; *Temperance Hall vs. Giles*, 33 *N. J. Law* 260. See also *Anderson vs. Dickie*, 1 *Robt.* 238; *S. C.*, 26 *How. Pr.* 105; *Davenport vs. Ruckman*, 37 *N. Y.* 568; *Roswell vs. Prior*, 12 *Mod.* 635.—Albany Law Journal.

IN the case of George H. Corliss, the Supreme Court of Rhode Island recently held that the position of centennial commissioner disqualified one from acting as presidential elector: that such disqualification was not removed by resignation of his office of commissioner after election, and that the existence of such disqualification did not result in the election of the candidate receiving the next highest number of votes, but in a failure to elect, thereby creating a vacancy that, in that State, could only be filled by the General Assembly in Grand Committee.

THE reference to the case of *Pier vs. Amory* contained in the column of "Recent Decisions" of last number, from being misplaced by the printer, is erroneous. It should have been "Sup. Ct. of Wis., instead of 14 Nat. Bk. Reg.

U. S. Circuit Court, Minnesota Dist.

Wm. F. Davidson, vs. Lorenzo Allis,

Where in the foreclosure of a mortgage of real estate, the property mortgaged is insufficient to satisfy the indebtedness secured, and the mortgagor is insolvent, the court has the power independent of any contract lien upon the rents and income of such property, to appoint a reciever for such rents and income and apply the same upon the indebtedness, as well for the period allowed by law for redemption from the foreclosure sale as during proceedings pending the sale.

The speeial equity growing out of the inadequacy of security, and insolvency of the mortgagor, is superior to the legal right, given by the Statute, allowing the mortgagor to remain in possession during the period allowed for redemption.—[Ed.

A Receiver of rents and income was appointed pending the foreclosure of a mortgage on productive real estate. A sale was made June 2, 1876, under a decree and the complainant, the mortgagee, was the purchaser, and received a certificate entitling him under the laws of the State of Minnesota to a deed, and the possession of the property at the expiration of one year from the date of the order confirming the sale, unless the premises shall have been previously redeemed.

A deficiency remains after application of the proceeds of the sale, which by the terms of the decree Lorenzo Allis was ordered to pay to the complainant. The Receiver is not discharged. He has collected $2,111.24-100 from the rents of the premises, which has been paid into the Registry of the court, and is deposited to the credit of this suit.

Application by petition is made for an order directing this amount to be paid upon such deficiency, which is resisted by the defendant Allis, the mortgagor.

It is urged that the rents collected after the sale of the property under the decree cannot be applied on the deficiency, as no equitable lien existed after the sale under the decree.

Bigelow, Flandrau & Clark, for petitioner.

H. J. Horn and Lorenzo Allis, contra.

Nelson, J.—The fee of the property was mortgaged, and no contract lien was given upon the rents and income.

A Receiver of rents and income was appointed, on account of the insufficiency of the fee to satisfy the debt and interests and costs, and the inability of the mortgagor in possession, personally liable for the debt, to answer for the deficiency.

When the mortgage became due and payable, an equitable right to the rents was created, growing out of the fact of the insolvency of the mortgagor, and the inadequate security. A sale of the property under the decree demonstrates the justice of the order appointing a Receiver, for a large deficiency exists.

The special equity subjecting the rents to apply upon the deficiency arising upon the sale of the mortgage security, authorizes the Receiver to collect the rents and income until possession is delivered over to the purchaser. True, the law of Minnesota gives the mortgagor the possession of the mortgaged property after sale as before, and until the time for redemption expires; but this does not restrict the power of a court of chancery to take charge of the rents and income and enforce a superior equity. The special equity growing out of the facts, as above stated, is superior to the legal right claimed.

Let an order be entered as prayed for.

———oo———

Supreme Court, State of Minnesota.

State of Minnesota, vs. The Citizens' Nat. Bank of Faribault. } Filed Jan'y 17, '77.

In the exposition of tax lands under our state constitution, which requires equality and uniformity in the imposition of taxes upon property, upon a cash valuation, such a construction must be adopted as will avoid duplicate taxation unless a contrary interpretation is compelled by some express provision or necessary implication of the Statute.

Under chap. 1 General laws of 1874 the banking office and lot lawfully owned and occupied as its place of business by a National Bank created under the laws of Congress, is not liable to assessment and taxation as real estate "eo nomine" against the bank.

This was an application to the District Court, county of Rice, in proceedings to enforce payment of taxes for the year 1874, for judgment against a portion of Lot 3, Block 57, City of Faribault, owned, and occupied for banking purposes, by the Citizens' National Bank of Faribault and assessed in the name of such Bank. The court below, *pro forma,* sustained the assessment and certified the case to the Supreme Court.

Gordon E. Cole, Counsel for the Bank.

Geo. P. Wilson, Attorney General and *Geo. N. Baxter Co. Att'y, Rice Co.*, for the State.

CORNELL, J.—Is real estate property lawfully owned and used as a place for the transaction of its business by a Bank created and existing under the National banking law. taxable "*eo nomine,*" against the Bank under chapter one General laws of 1874; it being conceded that the specific provisions of that statute require the assessment and taxation of all the shares comprising the entire capital stock of the association in the name of the respective shareholders and at their actual cash value without any deduction on account of the real property so held by the Bank and in which a portion of the capital is invested?

This is the sole question for consideration in this case and its determinatian depends upon the character and effect of the statute. The general policy of the law is to avoid duplicate taxation. No one subject of taxation ought to be required to contribute more than once to the same public burden, while other subjects of taxation belonging to the same class are required to contribute but once.

In the exposition of any tax law, therefore, a construction leading to any such result should be avoided, unless the cogency of some express provision or unavoidable implication of the Statute, compels its adoption.

Says Mr. Cooley in his valuable treatise on the law of taxation, "It is a fundamental maxim in taxation, that the same property shall not be subject to a double tax payable by the same party, either directly or indirectly; and when it is once decided that any kind or class of property is liable to be taxed under one provision of the Statute, it has been held to follow as a legal conclusion that the legislature could not have intended the same property should be subject to another tax though there may be general words in the law which would seem to imply that it may be taxed a second time," (*Cooley on Taxation* 164, 165 *and authorities cited in the notes.*)

Especially should this rule obtain in the Courts of a state whose constitution contains an express provision, requiring equality and uniformity in the imposition of taxes upon property, according to a cash valuation.

The aggregate capital stock of any corporation is but the representation of its entire property including the corporate franchise, and the actual cash value of the former depends wholly upon the productive character and real cash value of the latter; intrinsically it possesses no value, and can have none, as separate and distinct from the corporate property it represents; nor is the property, character or value, of such stock increased or in any way affected by its division into a given number of shares unless the proposition be conceded that all the parts are greater or less than the whole.

Each share but represents a proportional interest in the corporate property determined by the equal rate existing between it and the entire stock, and it possesses a like corresponding value.

Sever the connection between the stock and the shares comprising it on the one hand, and the corporation and its property on the other, and nothing remains to the former but a mere shadow to which no real property or commercial value can be imparted by any legislative device whatever. The authorities bearing upon these propositions are very fully collated and cited by Judge Cooley in his work on taxation pages 164 and 166 inclusive and the notes appended thereto, although no authority would seem necessary to establish their correctness.

Any legislation therefore which requires for the purpose of taxation an *ad valorum* assessment of all the shares of stock in a Bank, as property without allowing any deduction on account of the value imparted to them as the representations of the corporate property and franchise of the bank and also a like assessment of the corporate property itself under its own proper designation, necessarily provides for double taxation and in order to give the statute under consideration that effect it must clearly appear to have been intended by some express provision or necessary implication.

The law under consideration (chap. 1, General Laws 1874) contains specific provisions for listing and assessing the property of every incorporated and unincorporated company or association, (sec. 28) and of "every bank (other than a National Bank,) whether of issue or deposit, and of every banker, broker and stockjobber," (sec. 29.) It is not disputed that these specific provisions are so far exclusive in their character that other clauses of the statute relating generally to the assessment and taxation of real and personal property can have no application whatever to cases clearly falling within the purview of these sections, unless made applicable by express reference or necessary implication, and that there might be no doubt as to the legislative intent, it is expressly declared that the "taxation of banking corporations is specifically provided for by this act, (sec. 28). That the phrase, "banking corporations" as here used, is to be understood as including not only every corporate body doing a general banking business, whether under state or national authority, but also all property employed in banking whether owned by corporations or individuals, is evident from the sections immediately following the one containing this declaration of legislative intent. Sec. 29 in terms relates to banks created under state authority, to private bankers, and to property employed in banking by both, while the exception from its provisions, of National Banks shows the latter to have been in the minds of the Legislature while framing the provisions of the Statute. Sections 30 to 34 inclusive refer exclusively and paticularly to these institutions and their duties in respect to the matter of taxation, and no good reason is perceived why these provisions are not to be treated as covering the whole subject of taxation, as affects them, their property or stock-holders. It is made the duty of each National Bank to furnish the assessor a full and correct list of all its stock-holders with the number of shares held by each, and such shares are required to be assessed and taxed at the locality of the Bank, upon their value, subject to the sole restriction, that such taxation shall not be at a greater rate than is assessed upon other capital or property in the hands of individuals. This clearly indicates that such value is to be ascertained with reference to the actual amount and productive character of the entire corporate property and franchise represented by the aggregate number of shares, and without any deduction on account of any portion of the capital of the corporation being invested in real estate or property exempt from taxation. Full and adequate provision is also made for enforcing the payment of every such tax through the instrumentality of the Bank, upon whom the duty is imposed to retain the amount out of the dividends due to the respective stock-holders.

It is obvious from these provisions that the entire corporate property and franchises of these institutions are subjected to assessment and taxation once in respect to every public burden or matter of taxation. This is manifestly just, as respects both the state and the stockholders of the associations; because all the actual property represented both by the Banks and the stock-holders as such, is required to contribute its equal and proportionate share towards the support of the public burden and no more. If however the real property of these associations is liable to assessment and taxation "*eo nomine*" in addition to the tax upon the shares it is quite clear that the banking capital or property represented by the National Banks is subject to duplicate taxation to the extent of that so imposed directly upon the real estate. Moreover, it would violate the principle of equality as between the stockholders of different Banks, for it is obvious that a shareholder in a Bank having a part of its capital invested in real estate would be subjected directly and indirectly to a greater amount of tax upon his investment than one holding stock of like value and amount in an institution owning no real property; a construction leading to such results is repugnant to all correct ideas of justice and equality. No such feature of duplicate taxation is found in any of the provisions of this statute relating to the taxation of other banking or corporate property: as respects the state banks they are taxed only upon the valuation of their taxable property, which is required specially to be listed for that purpose. Their shares of stock are not subject to taxation; as to the companies mentioned in sec. 28 as amended in 1875, (to cure an evident omission,) they are subjected to taxation upon the assessed value of their real and personal property and also their capital stock after deducting therefrom indebtedness for current expenses and the value of such real and personal property. In view of these facts the legislative intent not to require any assessment of the real property of the National Banks "*eo nomine*" as against the corporations, seems too plainly manifest to admit of any reasonable doubt. If such an assessment had been intended it would have been specifically provided for as in the case of the State Banks under sec. 29 and the other companies and associations referred to in sec. 28.

Reference was made in the argument to section one of the statute as indicating an intention to require the assessment and taxation of all real estate "*eo nomine.*"

The evident purpose of this section was to declare in general terms that all property both real and personal within the jurisdiction of the state, unless specially exempted, should be subject to taxation. It does not however require the listing and assessment of the property in specie. Its language is, "such property *or* the value thereof shall be entered in the list of taxable property for that purpose in the manner prescribed by this act." The mode and manner in which this is to be done is to be sought for therefore in the subsequent provisions of the statute; an assessment of corporate property made by assessing its capital stock, or its shares of stock upon a valuation fixed with reference to the actual value of the entire corporate property would not be repugnant to anything contained in this section.

It is further objected by respondent that sec. 3 art. IX, of the constitution requires the legislature to "pass laws taxing all moneys, credits, investments in bonds, stocks, joint stock companies or otherwise, and also all real and personal property according to its true value in money;" that this means the enactment of laws providing for the taxation of these items of property in specie or "*eo nomine*" and as it must be presumed that the legislature intended to conform to this constitutional requirement, the statute in question must receive a corresponding construction; This section must be construed in connection with sections one and four of the same article and also in view of the condition of things existing at the time of the adoption of the constitution. Section one declares that "all taxes to be raised in the state shall be as nearly equal as may be, and all property on which taxes are to be levied shall have a cash valuation and be equalized and uniform throughout the state. Section four provides that "laws shall be passed for taxing the notes and bills discounted or purchased, moneys loaned and all other property, effects or dues of every description of all banks and of all bankers; so that all property employed in banking shall always be subject to a taxation equal to that imposed on the property of individuals." The leading and controlling purpose of these provisions was to subject all property of every kind and nature within the jurisdiction of the state, except such as is specially authorized to be exempted, to taxation upon a basis of a cash valuation, and to secure so far as practicable, absolute equality and uniformity in the apportionment of taxes, so that every piece of property should bear its just and proportionate share of the public burthen, in the exact ratio of its cash value to that of the entire taxable property of the state, To this end, section three is directed as specially applicable to all property not employed in banking nor embraced within the purview of section four.

Though a distinction seems to have been made between the kinds of property mentioned in sec. 3, and that referred to in sec. 4, it is obviously not one founded upon the idea of any discrimination to be exercised between them in the imposition of taxes; for the like rules of equality and cash valuation are clearly recognized as necessary to be observed as to each; it seems rather to have been the result of an abundance of caution and an apprehension on the part of the framers of that instrument that the banking capital of the state might possibly through the oversight or inadvertance of the legislature escape its just and equal share of taxation unless guarded against by some specific provision particularly directing the attention of the law making power to the subject. To this end section four makes it the special duty of the legislature to provide by law for the taxation of all property of every description of all banks and of all bankers, "*So that* all property employed in banking shall always be subject to a taxation equal to that imposed on the property of individuals." The subjection of all such property to equal taxation upon a like basis with all other property is the sole and declared purpose of the section. The mode and manner of accomplishing this, so that these rules are observed and the end attained, are matters left entirely to legislative discretion. It may be done as to state banks by taxing upon a cash valuation and in the name of each, all its taxable property "*eo nomine*" either in the aggregate or in detail, or its entire capital, in case none of it is invested in property exempt from taxation, or what would be eqivalent thereto by taxing all its shares of stock against and in the name of the shareholders upon a like *ad valorum* assessment; either of these modes would accomplish the result aimed at by the constitution. But this imposition of the same tax upon both the capital and the property in which it is invested or upon either, and the shares representing it, would violate the cardinal principle of equality in taxation, which constitutes its distinguishing feature. As to National Banks they were unknown at the time of the adoption of the constitution, They have been brought into existence since, under federal authority partly to serve the purpose of the National Government as convenient fiscal agents and partly to promote the same ends and accomplish the same objects intended to be subserved by the State Banks; In this latter character they have nearly succeeded in replacing all the state institutions and in absorbing the entire banking capital and business of the country so that they represent in fact the principal property interests which were intended to be affected by section four art. IX. of the constitution and to this extent they fall within the spirit, though not perhaps the letter of its provisions. Inasmuch however as the agencies created and established by the Federal government to assist in the execution of its powers are exempt from state taxation save as allowed by Congress, the state can only exercise its taxing powers over the National Banks and the capital they employ, and represent, in the manner and to the extent permitted by Congressional authority; under this authority it is permitted to the state to tax the real property of the bank as such and also the shares of stock, as personal property belonging to the shareholders, provided the rate of valuation and assessment of the latter is no greater than is assessed upon other nominal capital in the hands of individuals; within the limits of this authority the state may fully exercise its taxing powers in strict obedience however to the requirements of its own constitution; As equality in taxation is the constitutional policy of this state, no scheme of taxation can be presumed to have been intended by the legislature, which necessarily involves in its practical result the imposition of a greater proportionate share of its burdens upon nominal capital invested in the business of banking under national laws than is imposed upon capital similarly employed under state authority. The law under consideration provides for the assessment of the real property of the state Banks, "*eo nomine*" but does not authorize its assessment in any other form; Capital thus invested is therefore subjected to taxation but once for any one object. If a like mode of assessment had been intended in respect to to the real property of the National Banks, it must be presumed that some provision would have been made for deducting the value of such property from the total value of the shares in order to fix upon a correct valuation of the latter for the purpose of taxation. The omission of any such provision was manifestly unintentional as the shares are required to be assessed at their true and full value without any deduction whatever; and in this way the real property belonging to these associations is always subjected to its proper share of taxation.

The decision of the District Court sustaining the assessment and tax in question is reversed and judgment ordered in accordance with the prayer contained in the answer of the Bank.

——o||o——

Recent Decisions.

Construction—In construing any written instrument other than pleadings, effect must be given to every word having a meaning in the connection in which it is used; thus where a bond was given, not to sell liquor or beer to any "intoxicated card playing" person, it was held that to constitute a breach, the sale must be to one who was both an intoxicated AND card playing person.

City of Decorah vs. Kessellmeier, Supt. Ct. of Iowa, Oct Tr. 1876.

Insurance—Notice of Loss.—Where a policy of fire insurance, provided that in event of loss, notice thereof should be given to the Secretary "forthwith." Held, that forthwith as used therein, should be construed to mean within a reasonable time, or with reasonable diligence after the fire.

Bennett vs. Lycoming Mutual Ins. Co., N. Y. Ct. of Appeals Nov. 1876.

Mechanics Lien.—The taking of a note of contractor by material man, with the understanding that it was not to operate as payment unless met at maturity, and the discounting of the same by the material man does not suspend his remedy upon his mechanics lien. The note in such case is to be viewed only as collateral security for the debt for which the lien is also security.

Herron vs. Graham, Sup. Ct. Pa. Oct. 1876.

Sunday Contracts—Estoppel.—A contract executed on Sunday though of no effect between the parties may be transfered and if the assignee took no part in its inception and had no notice of its turpitude, he will be protected. Where a party caused a contract, executed on Sunday to be dated on a week day, held, that he was thereby estopped from denying its validity.

Johns vs. Bailey, et al., Sup. Ct. of Iowa Dec. Tr. 1876.

Fraud.—Where a sale is fraudulent, the party defrauded has a perfect right to rescind the contract and to be restored to his former condition in all respects, upon offering to return the property purchased, promptly after the fraud is discovered. The fact that the party defrauded had opportunities to ascertain the fraud and might with reasonable diligence have done so, HELD, not sufficient to bar his right to avail himself of the fraud upon discovering it, knowledge of the fraudulent act is required and bare suspicion is not enough.

Baker vs. Lever N. Y. Ct. of Appeals.

Undue Influence.—To invalidate a will on the grounds of undue influence there must be affirmative evidence of the facts from which such influence is to be inferred. The declarations of the testator alone are not competent evidence of acts amounting to undue influence; but the acts proved, declarations, of testator may be given to show the operation the acts had on his mind. It is not enough to show that a party benefited by a will had the motive and opportunity to exert uudue influence. There must be evidence that he did exert it, and so control the actions of the testator either by importunities which he could not resist or by deception, fraud or other improper means that the will, is not really the will of the testator.

The character of the provisions of the will may however be considered in connection with other evidence in trying the question of undue influence, but is not of itself evidence of such influence.

Cudney v. Cudney, (N. Y. Ct. of Appeals,) January 1877.

CONTRACT—INSANITY.—Where a contract had been executed, one of the parties at the time being insane, but his incapacity was unknown, no advantage was taken and the parties could not be placed in STATU QUO. HELD, that the courts would not set it aside.

Ashcroft vs. DeArmond, Supt. Ct. Iowa.

EVIDENCE—Though an oral agreement if made contemporaneously with a written contract is not admissible to vary it, yet such an agreement, if made subsequently, is, even though such subsequent agreement be the adoption in terms of the contemporaneous agreement,

Courtenay vs. Fuller, Sup. Ct. of Maine.

ESTOPPEL—The defendant having voluntarily signed, as maker, a negotiable promissory note, supposing he was binding himself to some other contract, and relying on the representations of the payee as to the contents of the paper, without examining it sufficiently to ascertain the fact for himself, is estopped by his own negligence from setting up the invalidity of the note against a BONA FIDE holder thereof.

Kellogg vs. Curtis, Sup. Ct. of Maine.

ACKNOWLEDEMENT by a grantor, in a deed, of the receipt of consideration, is not a conclusive estoppel that it has been so received.

Borter vs. Greenleaf, Sup. Ct. of Maine.

CHATTEL MORTGAGE.—A chattel mortgage on a stock of goods allowed of their disposal in the usual course of trade, but stipulated that if the stock was not kept up to a certain amount, as security for mortgagee, the latter might enter; on breach of this condition, a seizure and sale to the amount of the mortgage debt wrs sustained against subsequent purchasers, with notice, though the identity of the goods had been nearly destroyed.

Leland vs. Colver, Sup. Ct. of Mich.

STATUTE OF FRAUDS.—Full payment of the purchase money for real estate verbally agreed to be conveyed is not of itself sufficient to take the agreement out of the Statutes of frauds. There must also be possession taken of the property.

Temple vs. Johnson, Sup. Ct. of Ill.

APPURTENANCES —FIXTURES. — Appurtenances are things belonging to another thing as principal and which pass as an incident to the principal thing. That the term "with the appurtenances" as used in conveyances, passes nothing but the land and such things, as belong thereto, and are a part of the realty. In determining whether anything is a fixture, the controlling consideration is the intention of the party making the annexation.

Ottumma Woolen Mill Co. vs. James Hawley, Supt. Ct. of Iowa.

FORGERY—Where A, for the purpose of defrauding B. procured C. an innocent party, to sign the name of B, to a promtssory note, by falsely representing that C, was authorized by B. so to do; HELD, that A. was guilty of forgery.

Gregory vs. State, Sup. Ct. of Ohio,

LATEST PUBLICATIONS.

Holmes' Circuit Court Reports. — Reports of cases determined in the Circuit Court of the United States for the First Circuit, from July, 1870, to June, 1875: by Jabez S. Holmes. 8vo, law sheep, - - - - - 7 00

The Electors' Manual.—Constitutional Provisions and Statutes of the United States, relating to Presidential Elections, Elections of Senators and Representatives, Citizenship, and the Elective Franchise; with an appendix showing the Method of Counting the Electoral Votes for President and Vice President: by Chas. Sidney Whitman. Small 8vo. 98 pp., paper, - - .50

Abbott's U. S. Practice, vol. 1, by Benjamin Vaughan Abbott; 8vo., 640 pp. Law Sheep, - - - - - $7.50

Supplement to Riddle's Supplementary Proceedings, by John F. Baker; 8vo., 128 pp., half sheep, - - - - 2.00

The Law of Evidence, by Simon Greenleaf; vols. 2 and 3, 13th edition, carefully revised by John Wilder May; 8vo., per vol. - - - - - 6.00

The Law for the Formation of Business Corporations, with Forms, By-Laws, etc., by R. Bach. McMaster; 12mo. 50 pp. Paper, - - - - $0 50

Smith's Reports, Vol. XXIX, being Vol. LXXIX of Pennsylvania State Reports; by P. Frazer Smith. 8vo. 579 pp., Law Sheep, - - - - 4 50

Reports of Cases argued and determined in the Supreme Court of Appeals of West Virginia, Vol. VIII. By Henry M. Mathews. 8vo., 944 pp. Sheep, - - - - - - 4 00

Sansum's Digest of Law of Insurance. A Digest of all the Fire, Life, Marine, Accident and Guarantee Insurance cases decided in Great Britain and America. By O. B. Sansum. 8vo, 600 pp., Law Sheep. - - - - - 8 00

Bissell's Reports. Volume VI. Reports of cases argued and decided in the Seventh Judicial Circuit. By Josiah H. Bissell. 8vo 650 pp., Law Sheep. 7 50

Shaw's Index to Minn. Session Laws, 1849–1875. Full Sheep, - - 4 00

SESSION LAWS.

We have the Session Laws of Minnesota from 1849 to 1875 inclusive, 34 vols., which we offer in sets, or by the volume.

Parties wishing to fill their sets, will do well to send list at once.

We offer:

1861	2.00	1872	$3.50
1862	2.50	1873	2.50
1863	2.00	1874	2.00
1864	2.00	1875	2.50
1871	2.00	1876	1.75

Bound in Half Sheep.

THE AMERICAN REPRINT

OF THE

ENCYCLOPÆDIA BRITANNICA,

New Ninth Edition.

Volumes 1, 2, 3 and 4 are now ready.

This is the Largest and Best work of the kind in the English Language. Every Article is a Complete Treatise by the most Eminent Writers.

Send for Specimen Pages to

JOHN B. WEST & CO.

WE have covers for filing and preserving THE SYLLABI, which we will send by mail, on receipt of price, 35 cents.

THE SYLLABI.

VOL. 1. SATURDAY, FEB. 10, 1877. No. 17.

PUBLISHED WEEKLY,

By JOHN B. WEST & CO.,

No. 1 Wabasha St., · ST. PAUL, MINN.

Terms 3.00 per annum in Advance.

HOMER C. ELLER, Editor.

TABLE OF CONTENTS.

In the case of *Fanning & Shotwell vs. Getchell & Co.*, District Court, Ramsey co., Berry & Co. appeared and filed a complaint as intervenors, defendants did not answer plaintiff's complaint but both plaintiffs and defendants filed answers to complaint of the intervenors. The application of Berry & Co. to be allowed to intervene was denied. Notice of taxation of costs both on behalf of defendants and plaintiffs was served. To which the intervenors objected on the ground that this case was an equitable one and that no costs could be allowed except by order of court; That it was one of 29 cases between same defendants and intervenors, and all submitted in one proceeding; That item of 20 cents for printing plaintiff's answer was unauthorized; That only one bill of costs was taxable, whereas, two were presented; That in no event should there be more than one bill allowed each party. And that if costs were allowed at all they should in equity be apportioned. The objections were overruled by the clerk, and appeal taken to the court, Judge Brill in deciding the appeal filed the following memorandum:

"If these were equitable actions and the right to costs depended upon the provisions of section 5, of chap. 67, of the General Statutes the taxation by the clerk should be set aside; because in such cases he cannot tax costs at all unless previously allowed by the court; but the question of costs in these actions is determined by the statute of 1876 under which the intervention was made. That statute (not remarkable for its clearness,) provides that if the claim of the intervenor is not sustained he shall pay all the costs of the intervention. The meaning of this is that he shall pay the costs of the party whose interest he attacks, whose claim he seeks to defeat, the party whose rights he seeks to litigate. In this original action the plaintiffs were the only parties who made any kind of claim, the defendants made no answer, the intervenors sought only to defeat the plaintiffs claim, they attacked simply the right of the plaintiff to recover of the defendant; They claimed nothing adversely to the defendants on the contrary the sole object of the intervention was to relieve the defendants from the alleged liability. The claim made by the intervenors, was in the direct interest of the defendants, there was nothing to litigate as between the intervenors and the defendants so far as relates to this action, hence it seems to me the defendants are not entitled to costs. The plaintiffs clearly are not entitled to the expense incurred in preparing their answer.

Orders similar to that attached may be drawn by counsel in the other cases and submitted for signature.

AT the request of several attorneys we publish in this number the decision of Judge Simons in *German American Bank vs. First National Bank of Duluth*, holding that funds or property of a National Bank cannot be garnisheed. We understand that an appeal was taken from this decision but that the matter has since been settled by the parties.

SUPREME COURT, STATE OF MINNESOTA.

STATE OF MINNESOTA, *Respondent*, *vs.* FRANK CONWAY, *Appellant*, } Filed Jan'y 26, '77.

In a criminal case a motion in arrest of judgment after verdict cannot be predicated upon matter not appearing upon the face of the record.

A defect in the authentication of the grand jury list, filed with the clerk of the District Court, from which the grand jury finding the indictment was drawn, cannot be taken advantage of, on a motion of this character.

A temporary separation of a juror from his fellows after the withdrawal of the jury, under the charge of the court, for deliberation upon their verdict, is no ground for a new trial, when it clearly and affirmatively appears that no prejudice resulted, and that the facts and circumstances connected with the separation were such as to exclude all reasonable presumption or suspicion that the juror was tampered with, or that the verdict was or could have been in anyway influenced or affected by the irregularity.

Appeal from judgment of conviction of District Court, Waseca county.

B. S. Lewis and Amos Coggswell, attorneys for defendant.

Geo. P. Wilson, Att'y Gen'l, for the state.

CORNELL, J.—A motion in arrest of judgment in a criminal case cannot be predicated upon matter not appearing upon the face of the record, 3 *Whart. Sec.* 3043; 1 *Bish. Crim. Proc. Sec.* 850.

Conceding then, that the list of persons selected by the Board of County Commissioners to serve as grand jurors was not properly certified and signed by the Chairman of the Board prior to its delivery to the Clerk of the District Court, and that the statute in this regard, is anything more than directory, this was a matter of which the defendant could take no advantage after trial, and verdict, on a motion in arrest of judgment.

II. The question which was raised in this case upon the application to continue the trial of the indictment was one addressed to the sound discretion of the trial court and its decision is not reviewable except for manifest abuse of judicial discretion. (*The State vs. McCarthy*, 17 *Minn.* 81.) The record before us presents no such case.

The continuance was sought, for the purpose of obtaining the testimony of one Cullen as a witness to facts testified to by him, on the preliminary examination of defendant before the committing magistrate. Upon the facts disclosed it was at least doubtful whether sufficient diligence had been used to secure his personal attendance or whether it could be procured in case the application was granted. Moreover the testimony which he gave on the examination was read to the jury under a stipulation of the parties from the minutes kept by the magistrate, and no suggestion is made impeaching their accuracy or correctness. In view of these circumstances it is difficult to perceive how defendant was prejudiced by the decision.

III. Appellant claims that a new trial ought to have been granted because of the misconduct of two members of the petit jury After retiring for deliberation Lindley one of the jurors in answer to a call of nature absented himself from the jury room for one or two minutes by permission of the officer having the jury in charge; It affirmatively appears however that he remained in the custody and sight of the officer during the whole period of his absence, and that no communication whatever took place between him and anyone. A separation under such circumstances, raises no suspicion against the conduct of the juror or the purity and integrity of the verdict. and furnishes no ground for a new trial.

The conduct of the juror Brisbane though unaccompanied with any wrongful intent, is not equally free from criticism and censure. While the jury were retiring to consider their verdict and before all had reached and entered the jury room, this juror separated himself from his fellows and returned alone and unattended by any officer, to obtain an order from the court directing the jury to be provided with water; He did this, as stated in his affidavit, because the deputy sheriff having them in charge doubted his right to provide water and declined to make any request of the court for that purpose. It affirmatively appears that he went directly from the jury room through an open hall some forty feet, to a flight of stairs leading into the court room, thence up the stairs, and across the court room about thirty feet to a table, where meeting the Presiding Judge he preferred his request; that the Judge then informed him that he had no right to be away from the rest of the jury. Whereupon he returned at once direct to the jury room, followed immediately by the sheriff under the directions of the court. A large number of persons including defendant and his attorneys, was present in the court room at the time. It is stated in the affidavits of defendant and one of his attorneys that while said Brisbane was coming from the head of the stairs to the said table he spoke to several of the said persons (spectators) standing in the court room, and they to him, but what was said between them, they (affiants) did not learn; In opposition to this Brisbane makes affidavit positively stating that in thus going from, and returning to the jury room, he neither spoke to, nor had any conversation whatever with, any one except with the Judge as hereinbefore stated. In this he is corroborated by the affidavits of the sheriff and the deputy who had the jury in charge. In respect to the conflicting statements contained in the moving and opposing affidavits it was a matter within the peculiar province of the District Court to determine what degree of weight and credit ought under the circumstances to be given to each, and its decision therein must be deemed conclusive upon this court, especially in view of the fact, that the transaction occurred mostly within the immediate presence and observation of the trial court. Hence in considering the question whether the verdict ought to be set aside because of the misconduct of this juror, it must be assumed that the court below was fully and clearly satisfied upon the evidence before it, that during his temporary separation from his fellows, he had no communication whatever with any one, except with the court as hereinbefore stated, and that the facts and circumstances therewith connected excluded all reasonable inference, presumption or suspicion, that he had been tampered with, or that the verdict was or could have been in any way influenced or affected by the irregular conduct complained of. The irregularity, though good ground for censure and perhaps for punishing the juror, could work no possible prejudice to the defendant and therefore did not entitle him to a new trial.

Eich vs. Taylor, 20 *Minn.* 378.

The record before us does not purport to disclose all the testimony; the point made upon the insufficiency of the evidence cannot therefore be considered.

Judgment affirmed.

George D. Phelps, *Respondent*,
vs
City of Mankato, *Appellant*.
} Jan'y 10, 77.

It is immaterial how a public street in a city became such, whether by formal acceptance or official action of the city; or by acceptance and user by the public, so far as regards the duty of the city to keep it in safe condition.

Evidence held sufficient to sustain the verdict.

Appeal from an order of District Court, county of Blue Earth, denying motion for a new trial.

This was an action brought for injuries sustained by plaintiff in consequence of being thrown from a buggy while driving through the streets of Mankato; the accident being caused by running against a post 8 by 10 inches square and some 18 inches in height that stood near the corner of Byron and State streets and inside the inside line of gutter of both streets as well as inside what was termed the tree area of such street. The complaint alleged that it was the duty of the city to keep its streets in good and safe condition and free from obstructions, that Byron street had been for five years last past much traveled and used by the citizens thereof, and others so much so that the said duty of defendant as to said street was and became at the time of the accident a matter of public concern, that the wooden post before mentioned was wrongfully and negligently suffered by defendant to be and stand in said Byron street and that without negligence on the part of plaintiff he ran into such post and in consequence thereof was thrown upon the ground his leg broken and great injury sustained.

The answer denies that the post mentioned was within Byron street, or the roadway of any street, but avered that it was within the area reserved as sidewalk and tree area, and where teams or carriages had no right to pass, and also contributory negligence on part of plaintiff. The testimony showed that the post in question had been standing some three years or more, and that Byron street had been worked by the street commissioner prior to the accident also that subsequent to the accident the post had been cut down by direction of chairman of committee on streets. The jury found a verdict for plaintiff in the sum of $1000.

Thomas Bohan, and Brown & Wiswell, for appellant.

Wait & Freeman and M. J. Severance, attorney for respondent.

Gilfillan, C. J.—There was no error in admitting evidence under the complaint. After stating the duty of the defendant to keep the streets, in its city in good and safe condition, it alleges that a certain street in said city called Byron street has been for five years last past much traveled and used by the citizens thereof, and others, so much much so, that said duty of said defendant as to said street was, and became at the time hereinafter mentioned, a matter of public concern; This is hardly sufficient as an allegation that Byron street was a public street, used as such. by the public generally, so that the duty of the defendant with respect to public streets, would attach to it; The proof however shows sufficiently that it was such a public street, and as such proof was admitted without any tenable objection having been made to it, the defect in the pleading was cured. The objection to the evidence was specifically upon the ground that the complaint does not state that Byron street was ever officially laid out or had ever been opened or offered for public travel by defendant; This assumes that the duty to keep in safe condition does not attach until there has been some official action on the part of the municipal corporation making or recognizing the street. The objection is bad.

How the street became such whether by formal official action of the city in accepting its dedication, or by acceptance by user on the part of the public is immaterial so far as concerns the duty of the municipal corporation to keep it in such condition as to be safe for the public to travel along. From the evidence it was for the jury to determine whether it was negligence for the defendant to allow the post to remain in the street and also whether the post considering its size and location was such that a person traveling along the street in the exercise of proper care would have seen it; The conclusion that a person so traveling would have seen it is not a question of law, and under the circumsances of this case it is not so clear that a court should take the consideration of it from the jury. The question put to the witness, "Did you at one time think of takina off the leg?" though objectionable in form was not obnoxious to the objection stated *i. e.* that it was immaterial and incompetent: The answer would tend to show the character of the injury whether serious or slight. The questions asked tending to show that after the injury the post was cut down by the defendant and that it had previously done work on the street were proper, and so were those tending to show the location of the post, and that other teams had run into it, for such questions were directly to the point of the dangerous character of the obstruction and of negligence on the part of defendant.

Order affirmed.

J. L. Forepaugh and J. B. Tarbox. *Respondent*, *vs.* Caroline Hoffman, *et al.* *Appellant*, — Jan'y 29, '77.

Under sec. 4, ch. 55, General Statute a creditor may in his own name bring an action upon a probate bond, although his claim against the estate has not been ordered, by a decree of distribution, to be paid.

Appeal from an order of District Court, county of St. Louis, overruling demurrers of certain of defendants.

The action was brought by plaintiffs as creditors of the estate of one Sixtus Hoffman deceased, against Caroline Hoffman as principal and other of defendants as sureties upon the bond of said Caroline as administratrix of the estate of said Sixtus Hoffman. The complaint averred among other things the making and terms of the bond; the appointment of administratrix, and fact of her taking into possession all the goods, &c., of intestate, neglect and failure upon her part to make proper disposition of the property and to collect or sell the debts due the estate, refusal to obey the orders of Probate Court or to render any account of her administration, the allowance of plaintiff's claim by commissioners, payment of part thereof and failure to pay the balance, and that by reason of the improper conduct of such administratrix they had been damaged in the amount of such balance, and a permission of the court to sue.

Counsel for defendant relied upon *Wood vs. Myrick*, 16 *Minn.* 494; *Waterman vs. Millard, MSS., Oct. Tr.* 1875.

H. N. Setzer, Esq., att'y for appellant.

Ensign & Cash and Mead & Thompson, for respondent.

Berry, J.—Section 1, ch. 55, General Statutes provides that all bonds required by law to be taken in, or by order of the Probate Court, in case of any breach of the conditions thereof may be prosecuted in the name and for the use or benefit of any person interested therein, whenever the Judge of Probate, directs. Sec. 2, that an action may be brought on the bond of any executor or administrator by any creditor when the amount due to him has been ascertained and ordered by the decree of distribution to be paid, if the executor or administrator neglects to pay the same when demanded. Sec. 3. That such an action may be brought by any person as next of kin to recover his share of the personal estate after a decree of the Probate Court declaring the amount due to him, or the executor or administrator fails to pay the same when demanded. Sec. 4, that when it appears, on the representation of any person interested in the estate, that the executor or administrator has failed to perform his duty in any other particular than those before specified, the Judge of Probate may authorize any creditor, next of kin, legatee, or other person aggrieved by such failure to bring an action on the bond. Sec. 6 provides that on the application of any person authorized by this chapter to commence an action on the bond, the Judge of Probate may grant him permission to prosecute the same and shall furnish him a copy of the bond &c. Section 7. provides that the judgment of the plaintiff in any action on such bond brought for the benefit of any particular person shall be for the amount of damages which he shows himself entitled to in consequence of the breach of the condition of said bond.

There can be no doubt that sections, 2, 3 and 4 as read in connection with sections. 1. 6 and 7 authorizes the bringing of suits upon probate bonds by and in the name of persons other than the Judge of Probate. Section 2, provides for a case in which the amount due a creditor of the estate has been ascertained and ordered to be paid by the decree of distribution and the executor or administrator neglects to pay the same when demanded. Under this section an action was brought in, *Wood, vs. Myrick*, 16 *Minn.* 494. When it is said in that case, among other things that until the amount due a creditor has been ordered by a decree of distribution to be paid, the creditor has no right of action upon the bond; the court is speaking of a right of action under the provisions of section 2. In *Waterman vs. Millard, (MSS. Oct.* '75,) the action was also attempted to be brought under section 2, and it failed because (as was held in accordance with *Wood vs. Myrick.*) it was necessary to a right of action under that section that the amount due the plaintiff or some part thereof should have been ordered to be paid by the decree of distribution. The general language of the court with reference to the right of action upon a Probate bond is to be read with reference to the case before it.

The present action is brought under Sec. 4. For a cause of action the plaintiffs do not allege such a state of facts as would sustain an action under sections 2 or 3, but they allege that the administratrix has failed to perform her duty in other particulars than those as specified in sections 2 & 3. For instance, among other things they allege that after repeated orders of the Probate Court so to do, she has failed and neglected to render any account or file any report of her proceedings on the administration of the estate so as to furnish a basis for a decree of distribution of the funds belonging to the estate and in her hands. By this, her failure to perform her acts as administratrix, the plaintiffs allege that they have been aggrieved to the amount of their claim against the estate; the same having been duly ascertained, and the administratrix having in her hands, funds of the estate, sufficient to pay all claims against the same. besides expenses of administration.

This action having been brought under sec 4, it is not necessary as defendants contend that the complaint should contain an allegation that the amount due the plaintiffs has been "ordered by the decree of distribution to be paid."

The order overruling the appellants' demurrer is affirmed.

SUPREME COURT OF TENNESSEE.

JOHN J. VAUGHN, *vs.* H. J. VALENTINE, } Sept. 30, 1876.

A fixed purpose to change ones domicile to another state will not operate to deprive a party of his rights as a citizen of this state.

FREEMAN, J.— This is an attachment levied on property admitted to be exempt from execution or attachment, in the hands of the head of a family. It is claimed by plaintiff to be liable to this process under the following facts:

The defendant had resided in the town of Humbolt, Gibson county, for a number of years, and was keeping a boarding house at the time. He had, however, made arrangements to remove to the state of Arkansas, rented a house there, and put the goods levied on, on board the cars, with the purpose of sending them to the place to which he proposed removing.

The Circuit Judge held defendant was still a citizen of Tennessee and entitled to the benefits of our exemption laws. In this he is unquestionably correct. A fixed purpose to change one's domicile, is not such a change as deprives the party of his rights as a citizen of the state wherein he has obtained a domicile by previous residence. To do this, he must have carried out that purpose by actual removal from the state.

Judgment affirmed.

——oo——

District Court, 2nd Judicial Dist. Ramsey County, Minnesota.

The German American Bank.
against
The First National Bank, of Duluth,
Defendant,
And The First National Bank, of St. Paul,
Garnishee.
} March 24, 1876.

Property, money or effects belonging to a National Bank cannot be garnisheed prior to the recovery of judgment against such bank. The word "attachment" as used in sec. 5242, Revised Statutes of the United States held to also include proceedings by garnishment.

Motion on part of defendant and garnishee to vacate garnishee proceedings, and dismiss garnishee. The grounds of the motion are sufficiently set forth in the opinion.

Lamprey & James and J. B. & W. H. Sanborn, atty's for plaintiff.

Gilman, Clough & Lane and W. K. Rogers, att'ys for deft.

Simons, J.—In this case a garnishee summons in behalf of the plaintiff was issued in due form under the statute of this state and served upon the Garnishee, The First National Bank, of Saint Paul, for the purpose of securing any money or property in the possession of said garnishee belonging to the defendant; or any indebtedness from the garnishee to the defendant; to be applied in satisfaction of any judgment that may be recovered in the action by the plaintiff against the defendant. The defendant and garnishee now move to vacate and set aside said garnishee summons and to dismiss all proceedings under the same and to discharge said garnishee therefrom.

The defendant is a banking association organized and existing under the act of Congress commonly known as the National Bank Law, and the motion is made under the last clause of section 5242, of the Revised Statutes of the United States, which is in the following words: "And no attachment, injunction or execution shall be issued against such association, or its property before final judgment in any suit, action or proceedings, in any State, County or Municipal court."

The motion is resisted by the plaintiff upon two grounds, first, because Congress had no power to enact said prohibitory clause, and second, if it had, Garnishee proceedings are not expressly prohibited, and are not included in the term "attachment" which is prohibited by the act.

In my judgment neither of these positions are tenable.

The object Congress had in view in passing the law for the establishment of these National Banks was, as is stated in the title of the act of 1864, "To provide a national currency secured by a pledge of United States bonds, and to provide for the circulation and redemption thereof."

The purpose designed to be accomplished, was a governmental purpose, and the power of Congress to effect it through the agency of these banks is not denied, but its authority to enact the prohibitory clause in question is denied.

The constitution of the United States declares that Congress shall have power "To make laws which shall be necessary and proper for carrying into execution the foregoing powers (the powers expressly granted) and all other powers vested by the constitution in the government of the United States, or in any department or officer thereof."

If Congress has the power to accomplish the end, it has the right to select any appropriate means therefor, not prohibited by the constitution, and its authority in this respect, must be absolutely and entirely beyond the control of the state government. It has the same right to prohibit obstacles being thrown in the way of the execution of the desired purpose, by the states, that it has to provide affirmative means for such execution; and if the court can see that the means provided, are plainly adapted to the end in view, or that the thing prohibited, would interfere with or retard the accomplishment of that end, it is manifestly its duty to uphold the act of Congress upon the subject, according to its true intent and meaning.

In the judgment of Congress the end to be reached, to-wit: The circulation and redemption of this national currency, could best be effected through the instrumentality of these banks.

It could not well be effected in this way unless the banks were invested with certain privileges and allowed to do business as banks; This could not be done successfully, if it were in the power of creditors under state laws at any time before judgment to attach the banks and their property, shut their doors, and put their whole property in the custody of an officer.

If creditors or those claiming to be creditors, had this right, it is obvious that it would be in their power at any moment to interfere with and embarass, the operations of the government in so far as they depended upon or were connected with the banks, and doubtless to prevent that was the object of the prohibition in question.

In my judgment the object Congress intended to accomplish by this prohibitory enactment was clearly within its powers and it is just as clear that that object would be in a manner at least, defeated by the attachment and garnishee laws of this state; and the act of Congress and the Supreme laws of the land must be sustained. The act in question prohibits the issuing of an "attachment." The process issued in this case was a garnishee summons, which it is claimed by the plaintiff is not an attachment and it is not embraced in that term. But I am clearly of the opinion that under our laws, a garnishee summons is a species of attachment. True it is issued under different regulations but its object and purpose is the same, which is to secure and hold debts due the defeudant, and money and property belonging to him in the hands of third persons to satisfy the judgment that may be ultimately recovered by the plaintiff in the action.

It is also true that this prohibitory clause is in derogation of a remedy afforded by the laws of the state, and should not receive a lax construction but it seems to me that the intention of the act is so plain that it would be a manifest perversion of it to hold that the garnishee summons in this case was not an attachment.

The motion must be granted.

——o||o——

Recent Decisions.

Franchise—Immunity from Taxation.—The franchises of a railroad corporation are rights or privileges which are essential to the operations of the corporation, and without which its road and works would be of little value; such as the franchise to run cars, take tolls, to appropriate earth and gravel for the bed of its road, or water for its engines, or the like. They are positive rights or privileges without the possession of which the road of the company could not be successfully worked. Immunity from taxation is not a franchise, but a mere personal privilege, and upon a sale of the property and franchises of the corporation, either under process upon a money judgment or upon foreclosure of a mortgage that in terms covers the property and franchises of the corporation, such immunity will not pass to the purchaser. Being a mere personal privilege, it is incapable of transfer, without express statutory direction.

Morgan vs. Louisiana, Sup. Ct. of U. S.

Attachment—Money in Hands of State Officers.—The plaintiff caused an attachment to be issued against defendants as non-resident debtors. The only property attached was a sum of money in the hands of the state treasurer of New Jersey, alleged to be due from that state to the defendant; Held, that as a State cannot be sued in its own courts without its consent, therefore money in the hands of the State's treasurer due to a non-resident debtor, cannot be attached at the suit of a creditor.

Loder vs. Baker, Arnold & Co., Sup. Ct. of N. J.

Mortgage—Priority of Lien.—E., who was in possession of lands under a contract of sale to him, mortgaged such lands to A., and such mortgage was duly recorded; subsequently a deed of the lands was duly executed to E. who thereafter conveyed the same to P., who had notice of the prior mortgage. E. taking back from P. a mortgage which was also duly recorded. E. assigned this mortgage to T., who examined the records back to the date of conveyance to E., and upon inquiry was informed that the mortgage assigned to him was a first lien. Held, that the mortgage from E. to A. was entitled to priority over that of P. to E, which was assigned to T.

Tn assignee of a mortgage must take it subject to the equities attending the original transaction. If the mortgagee himself cannot enforce it, then the assignee has no greater rights. The only effect of recording an assignment of a mortgage is to protect the assignee against a subsequent sale of the same mortgage.

Crane vs. Turner, N. Y. Ct. of Appeal, Dec. 1876.

Surety—When Discharged.—Any suspension or alteration of the rights of a creditor against his debtor, by the consent of the former, will discharge the surety, though the new arrangement may be beneficial to him. The rule is the same where the security is for the whole debt, though its amount is less than that of the whole debt, and arises from the fact that the relation of the parties is governed by contract, the terms of which cannot be altered at the pleasure of one without discharging the other, even though the alteration be to the latter's benefit.

Polak vs. Everett, Q. B. Div. Court of Appeal.

Instructions to Jury—Exceptions.—While it is correct practice for the judge to instruct the jury, in an absolute form on admitted facts, he is not authorized to take from the jury the right of weighing evidence, when the facts are controverted. Instructions to the jury which are not specifiically excepted to, will not be reviewed on appeal; nor can exceptions be taken for failure to give an instruction not specifically asked.

Mut. Life Ins. Co. vs. Snyder, Sup. Ct. of U. S., Oct. 1876.

Latest Publications.

Holmes' Circuit Court Reports.—Reports of cases determined in the Circuit Court of the United States for the First Circuit, from July, 1870, to June, 1875: by Jabez S. Holmes. 8vo, law sheep, - - - - - 7 00

The Electors' Manual.—Constitutional Provisions and Statutes of the United States, relating to Presidential Elections, Elections of Senators and Representatives, Citizenship, and the Elective Franchise; with an appendix showing the Method of Counting the Electoral Votes for President and Vice President: by Chas. Sidney Whitman. Small 8vo. 98 pp., paper, - - .50

Abbott's U. S. Practice, vol. 1, by Benjamin Vaughan Abbott; 8vo., 640 pp. Law Sheep, - - - - - $7.50

Supplement to Riddle's Supplementary Proceedings, by John F. Baker; 8vo., 128 pp., half sheep, - - - - 2.00

The Law of Evidence, by Simon Greenleaf; vols. 2 and 3, 13th edition, carefully revised by John Wilder May; 8vo., per vol. - - - - - 6.00

The Law for the Formation of Business Corporations, with Forms, By-Laws, etc., by R. Bach. McMaster; 12mo. 50 pp. Paper, - - - $0 50

Smith's Reports, Vol. XXIX, being Vol. LXXIX of Pennsylvania State Reports; by P. Frazer Smith. 8vo. 579 pp., Law Sheep, - - - - 4 50

Reports of Cases argued and determined in the Supreme Court of Appeals of West Virginia, Vol. VIII. By Henry M. Mathews. 8vo., 944 pp. Sheep, - - - - - - - 4 00

Sansum's Digest of Law of Insurance. A Digest of all the Fire, Life, Marine, Accident and Guarantee Insurance cases decided in Great Britain and America. By O. B. Sansum. 8vo, 600 pp., Law Sheep. - - - - - 8 00

Bissell's Reports. Volume VI. Reports of cases argued and decided in the Seventh Judicial Circuit. By Josiah H. Bissell. 8vo 650 pp., Law Sheep. 7 50

Shaw's Index to Minn. Session Laws, 1849–1875. Full Sheep, - - 4 00

SESSION LAWS.

We have the Session Laws of Minnesota from 1849 to 1875 inclusive, 34 vols., which we offer in sets, or by the volume.

Parties wishing to fill their sets, will do well to send list at once.

We offer:

1861	2.00	1872	$3.50
1862	2.50	1873	2.50
1863	2.00	1874	2.00
1864	2.00	1875	2.50
1871	2.00	1876	1.75

Bound in Half Sheep.

We have covers for filing and preserving The Syllabi, which we will send by mail, on receipt of price, 35 cents.

THE SYLLABI.

VOL. 1. SATURDAY, FEB. 17, 1877. No. 18.

PUBLISHED WEEKLY,

By JOHN B. WEST & CO.,

No. 1 Wabasha St., - ST. PAUL, MINN.

Terms 3.00 per annum in Advance.

HOMER C. ELLER, Editor.

TABLE OF CONTENTS.

IN the case of *First National Bank of Fergus Falls vs. Michæl Anderson,* recently tried in District Court for county of Otter Tail, a point that arose that is somewhat new in its application to chattel mortgages, so far as this State is concerned. It appeared that one Collins owning a stock of merchandise in said county, executed a chattel mortgage thereon to one Wetmore. The mortgage authorized the mortgagor to retain possession of the property and to dispose of the same in the ordinary course of business, and under the rule laid down in *Horton vs. Williams,* 21 *Minn.* 187, was fraudulent and void as to creditors. After its execution the mortgage was assigned by Wetmore to the Bank. The defendant, as sheriff of said county and by virtue of an execution against Collins, levied upon the stock, and tnis action was brought by the assignee of the mortgage to recover the same. Upon the trial the plaintiff proved the execution and assignment of the mortgage and in addition thereto that before any creditor attempted to question the validity of the mortgage actual custody of the property had been transferred from the mortgagor to the plaintiff upon account of the mortgage, and that at the time of such transfer of custody Collins authorized the plaintiff to sell and dispose of the same and apply the proceeds to payment of the mortgage debt. Upon this state of facts the plaintiffs contended (*citing Brown vs. Platt,* 8 *Bosworth* 324) that the creditors of Collins could not avail themselves of the objection that the mortgage was void. The court held the position well taken and ordered judgment for plaintiff.

Mason & Williams for plaintiff
E. E. Corliss for defendant.

WE are in receipt of the January and February numbers of *American Law Times and Reports* a monthly legal periodical published by Messrs. Hurd & Houghton, N. Y. It presents a neat appearance and its matter and arrangement is such as to make it of great value to the practitioner. Each number is a large octavo of 64 pages, 16 of which are devotedt o rescripts of the current decisions of the Supreme Court of the United States and digests of the decisions of the Supreme Courts of the different States, and the remaining 48 pages to reporting in full, decisions of the different courts that are of general interest and importance. The two parts being so arranged and paged that they can be readily separated and each part be bound by itself, thus giving in the course of a year two volumes of valuable matter, one of reports and the other of digests.

Supreme Court, State of Minnesota.

Henry C. Fogle, Administrator of the Estate of Lewis Fogle, deceased. *Respondent*, *vs.* Jacob Shaeffer *Appellant*, } Feb'y 2, '77.

In an action purporting to be brought by plaintiff as a foreign administrator, allegations in the complaint to the effect that plaintiff has been duly appointed such foreign administrator, and has duly filed in the proper Probate Court of this state a duly authenticated copy of his appointment, are put in issue by answer denying the complaint, and "each and every part and portion thereof." Fetz vs. Clark, 7 Minn. 217 followed.

Under Sec. 6, ch. 77, General St., it is necessary for a foreign administrator to file in the proper Probate Court a duly authenticated copy of his foreign appointment BEFORE the commencement of an action as such administrator.

His failure to file, BEFORE the commencement of an action cannot be cured (if proper objection is taken) BY a filing AFTER such commencement.

Appeal from an order of the Court of Common Pleas, Hennepin county, over-ruling motion on part of the defendent for a new trial. On the trial of this cause no evidence was received showing the capacity of plaintiff to sue, and a motion was made to dismiss the action upon the ground that the complaint was not sustained by the evidence and that plaintiff had not shown himself to have any standing in Court he being a foreign administrator and it not appearing that he had filed an authenticated copy of his appointment in the Probate Court of Hennepin county, as required by law. The court over-ruled the motion and ordered judgment for the plaintiff, holding that the complaint having set forth the appointment of plaintiff, and the filing of a copy thereof in the Probate Court of Hennepin County; that a simple general denial did not put his legal capacity to sue, in issue, and that no proof thereof was unnecessary. This ruling of the court was the ground of motion for new trial.

Shaw & Levi and Wood & Merrill, Attorneys for Respondent.

Cross & Hicks Attorneys for Appellant.

Berry, J.—This is an action brought in the Common Pleas for Hennepin county upon a judgment against the defendant, recovered in Stark county Ohio, by Francis Fogle as administratrix of the estate of Lewis Fogle deceased. The complaint alleges that, after the recovery of the judgment, said Francis Fogle administratrix departed this life, and this plaintiff was thereupon, to-wit: On or about the 14th day of April, 1875, duly appointed and qualified by and in the Probate Court of said county of Stark as administrator *de bonis non* of the estate of said Louis Fogle deceased and has since been and now is such administrator. "That before the commencement of this action this plaintiff duly filed in the Probate Court of said county of Hennepin, a duly authenticated copy of his appointment as such administrator. For answer to the complaint the defendant "denies the same, and each and every part and portion thereof." The question in the case is whether the answer puts in issue the foregoing allegations of the complaint as to the plaintiffs character as administrator and his right to bring this action. The rule upon the subject involved in this question is correctly stated in *Fetz vs. Clark, 7 Minn.* 217, as follows: "The denial in general terms of each and every allegation of the complaint is not confined in any case to a denial of the principal fact on which the complaint is founded but is equivalent to a denial of each material allegation thereof just as though the pleader had traversed the several allegations in detail."

The decision in which this rule is found was made in 1862 and it was preceded by earlier decisions of this court in the same direction; substantially the same rule is laid down in *Kingsley vs. Gilman,* 12 *Minn.* 515. We are not aware that it has been departed from in this court. It is therefore not only a well established rule but we think it is a correct rule. The reasons given for it in *Fetz vs. Clark,* are quite satisfactory, see also *Boston Relief and Submarine Co. v. Burnett* 1 *Allen* 410; *Gott vs. Express Co.,* 100 *Mass.* 320.

It follows that the allegations of the complaint in reference to the plaintiffs character as administrator and his right to bring this action, being material allegations, were put in issue by the answer in this case.

There is another question which was fully argued in this court and which we are requested to pass upon, with references to future proceedings in the case. sec. 6, Ch. 77, General Statute enacts that "any administrator or executor appointed in any other state or county may commence and prosecute any action, in any court of this state in his capacity of executor or administrator, in like manner and under like restrictions as a resident may do. *Provided,* that before commencing any action, an authenticated copy of his appointment as such executor or administrator is filed in the Probate Court of the county in which such action is to be commenced.

The question is whether a failure to file the authenticated copy of appointment *before* the commencement of an action can be cured by filing such copy *after* the commencement of the action so that the action can properly proceed, defendant objecting.

This question must be answered in the negative. As remarked by Mr. Justice Field in *Noonan vs. Bradley*, 9 *Wallace* 394, in speaking of foreign administrators; "In the absence of any statute giving effect to the foreign appointment, all the authorities deny any efficacy to the appointment outside of the territorial jurisdiction of the state within which it was granted. All hold that in the absence of such a statute, no suit can be maintained by an administrator in his official capacity except within the limits of the state from which he derives his authority."

As upon this principle the authority of a foreign administrator as such, to commence an action in this state is wholly dependent upon the statute, it follows, that he must commence his action upon the terms which the statute prescribes and not otherwise. If he commences it without authority, and if proper objection is taken, his action must fail. He must therefore file the prescribed authenticated copy *before* the commencement of his action, and his failure to do so, if properly objected to, is fatal and cannot be cured by a filing after the comment of his action.

Order refusing new trial reversed and new trial awarded.

TRON OLSON, *Appellant*, *vs.* MATHEA JOHNSON and THE BOARD OF COUNTY COMMISSIONERS OF HOUSTON CO. *Respondent.* Feb'y 2, '77.

In proceedings under the bastardy act the plaintiff was adjudgad to be the father of a bastard child begotten upon the body of Mathea Johnson and he was adjudged to pay said defendant or to the clerk for her, "for the support and maintenance of the child," certain sums per week and also to give a bond to the County Commissioners for the faithful performance of the judgment. The bond was executed and plaintiff has duly performed its condition. HELD, that the facts as alleged in the complaint, that since the proceedings in bastardy said defendant has married one Johnson in the state of Iowa and that she "did immediately thereafter leave, desert and abandon, and has ever since left, deserted and abandoned her said bastard child, to the charitable care of strangers in the state of Iowa, where said child yet remains;" and that the plaintiff is willing and able and now offers to care for and suitably rear and educate the said child and adopt and treat it as his own and is willing and offers to give to the defendants the Board of County Commissioners, such security as the court shall deem adequate, that the said child shall never become a county charge, or a public expense and for the perforance of any decree which the court may deem just and equitable, entitles the plaintiff to no relief in this action as respects the judgment or bond above mentioned,or the care and custody of the child.

Appeal from a judgment of the District Court county of Houston.

O'Brien & Smalley, att'ys for appellant.

W. H. Harries, attorney for respondent, Mathea Johnson.

BERRY, J.—At the May, (1871,) Term, of the District Court for Houston county upon a trial under the bastard act, (Ch. 17, Gen'l St.) the plaintiff was adjudged to be the father of a bastard child, begotten upon the body of the defendant Mathea Johnson. Sections six and seven provide that the person so adjudged to be the father of a bastard child may "be charged with the maintenance thereof in such sum or in such manner as the court may direct," and that he "shall give bond to the commissioners of the proper county with sufficient sureties to be approved by the court for the performance of such judgment and order." Under these sections plaintiff was adjudged to pay to the defendant or to the clerk for her, "for the support and maintenance of the child certain sums varying from a dollar to a dollar and fifty cents per week to be paid semi-annually and he was also adjudged to give a bond to the County Commissioners of said county in the sum of $800 conditioned for the faithful performance of the judgment.

The bond was executed and the plaintiff has duly performed its conditions. The complaint which was verified Oct. 9, 1875, alleges that on or about January 19, 1875, the defendant married Ingebright Johnson in the state of Iowa, and did immediately thereafter leave, desert and abandon and has ever since left, deserted and abandoned her said bastard child to the charitable care of strangers in the state of Iowa, where said child yet remains" admitting that plaintiff is father of the child,the complaint proceeds to allege that he is "willing and able and now offers to care for and suitably rear and educate the said child and adopt and treat it as his own and is willing and offers to give to the defendant, the said Board of County

Commissioners such security as the court shall deem adequate that the said child never becomes a county charge or a public expense, and for the performance by him of any decree in the premises which the court may consider just and equitable. For relief the complaint prays, *first*, that be may be decreed. entitled to the possession and custody of the child upon executing a bond running to the County Commissioners of Houston county conditioned to save the county harmless from any costs or liability on account of said child. *Second*, That upon filing said bond the County Commissioners be adjudged to deliver up to plaintiff the bond heretofore executed as aforesaid to be cancelled. *Third*, That upon filing the proposed bond the defendants be forever restrained from attempting to enforce the collection of any money under the judgment aforesaid or the bond given to secure the same and also for general relief. Upon motion of the defendant Mathea Johnson (who alone appeared) the court below dismissed the complaint for failure to state a cause of action. The judgment in the bastardy proceedings not having been appealed from is conclusive. One effect of the judgment is to compel the plaintiff to pay to the mother a specified allowance for the maintenance of the child to the custody of which she as mother, is in law entitled. If she neglects to support and maintain the child this is no reason why the plaintiff should be relieved from the payment of the allowance nor from the obligation of his bond and as for any proposition to substitute something else in the plaoe of the allowance and his bond, there is no authority whatever for entertaining it. Under the judgment the mother is invested with a species of trust as respects the allowance made for the support and maintenance of the child. If she fails to perform the trust, she may be compelled to perform it, or she may be superseded and another appointed in her place, to see to the expenditure of the allowance, and if necessary, the child can be put under guardianship. But as respects any of these remedies it is not for the plaintiff, acting for himself (as in this action) to seek them, but for some one acting in behalf of the child. As respects such remedies the plaintiff would not be the real party in interest. *As father* of the child he has in law, no better title to its custody and no more right to act for it, than any other person.

Judgment affirmed.

THE STATE OF MINNESOTA, *vs.* C. Z. SUTTON & Co., } Feb'y 2, '77.

Notice of an appeal to the Supreme Court from an order of the District Court refusing to set aside a tax judgment must be served upon the county attorney.

Appeal from the order of District Court, county of Nobles, denying motion to vacate and set aside tax judgment.

Daniel Rohrer, att'y for appellant.

M. B. Soule, County Att'y, Nobles Co., for respondent.

BERRY, J.—In the matter of the proceedings to enforce payment of taxes on real estate remaining delinquent on the first day of June, 1875, for the county of Nobles, state of Minnesota. By sec. 110, ch. 1, laws 1874, it in enacted that the filing of the list of delinquent taxes of real estate "shall have the force and effect of filing a complaint in an action by the county against each piece or parcel of land therein described to enforce payment of taxes therein appearing against it, and shall be deemed the institution of such action and the same shall operate as notice of the pendency of such action, "see also, § § 117-120." By sec. 181, ch. 8, General Statutes, the County Attorney is required to "appear in all cases where the county is party and prosecute or defend for the county." Sec. 62, ch. 66, General St. as amended by ch. 72, Laws 1872 provides that when a party whether resident or non-resident has an attorney in the action the service of papers shall be upon the attorney instead of the party."

An appeal from the District to the Supreme Court is made by the service of a notice in writing on the adverse party and on the clerk. Gen. St. ch. 86, §3.

From these provisions of statute it follows that the filing of the delinquent list by the Auditor under sec. 110, of the Tax Law of 1874, has the effect to institute an action in which the county is party plaintiff, and in which the County Attorney is its attorney, upon whom service of notice of any appeal in such action from the District to the Supreme Court must be made.

The case at bar is an attempted appeal from an order of the District Court refusing to set aside a tax judgment. Upon the hearing below, the County Attorney appeared for the county. Service of a notice of appeal was made upon the County Auditor but no notice of appeal was served upon the County Attorney.

Appeal dismissed.

DAVID P. DAVIS, *Respondent*, *vs.* C. Z. SUTTON, *et. al.*, *Appellant*, — Feb'y 2, '77.

This action is brought upon certain claims originally accruing to H. Davis, and by him assigned to plaintiff. HELD, that the fact that defendants have a claim against H. Davis, which they set up in their answer in this action by way of counter-claim, and which accrued to thhm before the assignment to plaintiff, and which exceeds by several hundred dollars the amount claimed by plaintiff, furnishes no reason why H. Davis should be made a party to this action.

Appeal from an order of District Court, county of Blue Earth, denying the application of the defendant for an order requiring one H. Davis, assignor of plaintiff to be made a party to the action.

M, J. Severance, attorney for respondent.

Waite & Freeman, att'ys for appellants.

BERRY, J.—This action is brought to recover upon defendants promissory note made payable to H. Davis, and alleged to have been sold and transferred to plaintiff after maturity; and also to recover a demand of $28.07 for services rendered by Davis to defendants, which is also alleged to have been transferred to plaintiff. Defendants answer admits the existence of the causes of action set up in the complaint. The answer also sets up a claim against Davis accrued to defendants before the alleged tranfers to plaintiff, and exceeding by several hundred dollars, the amount claimed by plaintiff. Defendants moved below that Davis be made a party this action, upon the ground that in this action as it now stands they can set off so much only of their claim as equals the amount of plaintiff's claims, and that as the cause of action cannot be split so as permit them to recover the residue of Davis, such residue will be lost to them unless they can be permitted to recover of Davis in this action.

The splitting of an entire cause of action, is forbidden, because it produces an unneccessary multiplicity of suits, *Farrington vs. Payne*, 15 *Johnson* 432. *Guernsey vs. Carver*, 8 *Wend*. 492. *Badger vs. Titcomb*, 15 *Pick* 409. *Bennett vs. Hood*, 1 *Allen* 47. Where this result does not follow the rule against splitting does not apply, *see Risley v. Squire* 53 *Barb*. 280. *Bennett vs. Hood, supra.* In the case at bar, if the defendants after recovering by way of set-off so much of their claim against H. Davis as equals the amount of plaintiff's claim recover the residue in a subsequent action against H. Davis, there is no *unnecessary* multiplicity of actions, since both recoveries are requisite to the complete assertion of defendant's rights. It is moreover to be observed that the rule hardly applies to this case, for the reason that it is the vexing of the *same person* by an unnecessary multiplicity of actions against which the rule is directed. See authorities *supra*. The ground upon which defendants base their motion is therefore untenable.

To any suggestion that if Davis could be made a party to this action, it would avoid the necessity of another suit to recover the residue of defendant's claim, there are two answers: first, such is not the practice; second, looking at the common sense of the matter, there is no reason why the plaintiff should not be permitted to carry on this action without the intermeddling of any person as a party, with whom he has no concern.

The order denying defendants motion is affirmed.

MINNEAPOLIS & ST. LOUIS R. R. CO., *Respondent*, *vs.* DORILUS MORRISON, *Appellant*, — Feb'y 2, '77.

The plaintiff's charter, (Ch. 10, Laws 1853,) fixes its capital stock at $2,000,000 provides that as soon as $100,000 thereof shall have been subscribed certain persons shall give notice of a meeting of the stockholders to choose directors, and confers upon the directors the usual general authority to manage the business of the corporation, and among other things authorizes them "to receive payment to the subscriptions to the capital stock at such time, in such proportion not exceeding twenty-five per cent. at any instalment, under such conditions as they shall deem fit." HELD, that these provisions authorize the ORGANIZATION of the corporation npon a stock subscription of one hundred thousand dollars and also authorizes the directors UPON SUCH ORGANIZATION to proceed with the business of the corporation, and among other things to collect instalments of the stock.

HELD, further, that the allegation in the complaint in this case that the plaintiff corporation is DULY ORGANIZED involves the fact of a stock subscription to at least the requisite amount of $100,000.

HELD, further, that the mode of subscription provided for in sec. 4, of plaintiff's charter as amended by sec. 2, ch. 117, Special Laws, 1869 relates to subscriptions made BEFORE organization and that as to subscriptions made AFTER organizatlon, the taking of them is left to the corporation acting through its Board of Directors.

Section 6, of plaintiff's charter authorizes the directors "to receive payment to the subscriptions to the capital stock, * * * * * * in such proportion not exceeding twenty-five per cent. at any one instalment, under such conditions as they shall deem fit," and makes it their duty at least thirty days previous to the appointed time of such required payment to give notice thereof "in some newspaper printed in the Territory of Minnesota, and in such other place or places as may be thought advisable." HELD that these provisions do not make it necessary that each payment required should be called for SEPARATELY or that SEPARATE notice should be given of each required payment or that there should be an interval of thirty days between the appointed times of payment; but that it is competent for the directors at any time and in one call to require several instalments to be paid, each at a different future date and to give one notice of all the required payments.

HELD, further, that the allegation in the complaint that payment of the several instalments called "was duly demanded of defendant by publication of notice for thirty days in the Minneapolis Daily Tribune," is as against a demurrer a sufficient allegation that the proper notice was published in a proper newspaper and in proper time.

HELD, further that the giving of the other notice provided for, is left to the option of the directors.

Appeal from an order of District Court county of Hennepin, overruling demurrer to plaintiff's complaint.

Atwater & Babcock, att'ys for respondent.

Bradley & Morrison, att'ys for app'lts.

BERRY, J.—I. The original charter from which, and acts amendatory, the plaintiff derives its existence and powers is found in ch. 10, Laws 1853. By sec. 3, of that act the capital stock of the corporation created is fixed at two millions of dollars. Sec. 5, provides that "as soon as said stock or one hundred thousand dollars thereof shall have been subscribed," certain named persons shall give notice of a meeting of the stockholders to choose directors. Subsequent portions of the act confer upon the directors the usual general authority to manage the business of the corporation and among other things they are authorized "to receive payment to the subscriptions to the capital stock at such time, in such proportion not exceeding twenty-five per cent. at any instalment, under such conditions as they shall deem fit, under the penalty of forfeiture of all previous payments thereon or otherwise." Whatever might have been the case in the absence of the above provision of sec. 5, that provision clearly authorizes the organization of the corporation upon a stock subscription of one hundred thousand dollars. And the subsequent provisions of the act as clearly authorize the directors, upon such organization to proceed with the business of the corporation, and among other things to collect instalments of the stock. And as the authority to organize depends upon the fact that stock to the amount of $100,000 has been subscribed, the allegation in the complaint in this case that the corporation is *duly* organized involves the fact of such subscription and is sufficient against a demurrer.

II. Defendants second point in substance is that the railroad which the plaintiff alleges that it undertook to build and did build, is not the railroad which it was authorized to build, a reference to the map will show that the former is in fact a *portion* of the latter, which is sufficient. See sec. 16 of original charter, chap. 10, Laws 1853.

III. The third point made by defendant is that it does not appear that defendant ever made any legal or valid subscription to the stock of the plaintiff. This point is based upon the fact that the complaint shows that the subscription was not taken under the provisions of section 4 of the charter as amended by sec. 2, ch. 117, Special Laws, 1869, which authorized certain persons named, to open books for subsriptions to the stock. The mode of subscription provided for in sec. 4, as amended is provided with reference only to subscriptions made *before* organization; as respects subscriptions taken *after* organization like the defendants subscription, in this case, the matter of taking them is left to the corporation, acting through is Board of Directors. Under this authority the defendant's subscription is to be presumed to have been taken upon the allegation of the complaint.

IV. Section 6, of the original charter authorizes the directors "to receive payment to the subscriptions to the capital stock * * * in such proportion not exceeding twenty-five per cent. at any one instalment, under such conditions as they shall deem fit," and makes it their duty "at least thirty days previous to the appointed time of such required payments" to give notice thereof in a newspaper. This does not as defendant contends, make it necessary that each payment required should be called for *separately*, or that *separate* notice should be given of each required payment, or that there should be an interval of thirty days between the appointed times of payment; for such is not the *language* of the statute. It was therefore competent for the directors as they did in this case, at one time and in one call to require several instalments to be paid, each at a different future date, and to give one notice of all the required payments.

V. By sections 6 and 4 of the original charter the subscribers to stock are to be notified of payments required thereupon, "by giving thirty days notice in some newspaper printed in the Territory of Minnesota and in such other place or places as may be thought advisable." The complaint alleges that payment of the several instalments called for upon defendant's subscription "was duly demanded of said defendant by publication of notice for thirty days in the Minneapolis Daily Tribune &c." as against a demurrer this is a sufficient allegation that the proper notice was published in a proper newspaper and in proper time. The giving of the other notice mentioned is left to the option of the directors.

VI. Defendants remaining point, to-wit: "that the complaint shows that the subscription was made before the company had an existence" is a technical objection to an inaccuracy which is amply cured by the general tenor of the complaint.

Order overruliug demurrer affirmed.

(Mr. Justice Cornell took no part, having been of counsel.)

—o||o—

Recent Decisions.

Res Adjudicata.—In order that a judgment in a former action may constitute a bar to the pending suit, it is not essential that the name of the present plaintiff should have appeared upon the record as a party thereto. If he was in fact a party, assuming control of the case,and employing attorneys to attend to it in his own interest, he is bound, and the record of the former suit may be pleaded in bar, or offered in evidence with like effect.

Wood vs. Eusel, Sup. Ct. of Mo. Oct. Term, 1876.

Mechanics Lien—Description of Property.—It is a general rule that a description in a notice of mechanics lien, which will enable one familiar with the locality to identify the land intended to be charged with the lien with reasonable certainty to the exclusion of other lands, is sufficient; and as between the owner and a material mon seeking to inforce the lien, no error in the description will defeat the lien, except upon proof that the error has actually misled the owner to his injury.—[Citing Phil. Mech. Lien § 597, Mattock vs. Lane, 32 Mo. 262. Putnam, et al., vs. Ross, 46 Mo. 337. Asler vs. Rubencan, 46 Mo. 396.]

Dewitt vs. Schell, Sup. Ct. of Mo., Oct. Tr., 1876.

Municipal Corporation—Sewers.—A municipal corporation is not liable to individuals for damages sustained by them through its failure to exercise its legislative authority, or through any proper exercise thereof; but is no more exempt from liability than an individual, when that which it does, necessarily or naturaly, results in the invasion of the freehold of a citizen. Therefore, if a city so construct a sewer that the necessary result is that waters are collected by it, and thrown upon the private premises of an individual to his injury, the city is responsible for such injury. The flooding of private premises is just as much an appropriation of private property as would be the taking of an easement in it.

Ashley vs. City of Port Huron, Sup. Ct. of Michigan.

Costs.—An order setting aside a verdict and granting a new trial upon payment of costs, is not an order conditioned upon such payment. The order is absolute and the stipulation with reference to costs may be enforced by execution or as any other order may be.

Heffner vs. Scranton, Sup. Ct. of Ohio.

Slander.—In an action for slander evidence that when the words charged as slanderous were spoken, a general report or rumor existed in the neighborhood that plaintiff was guilty of the offence charged, is inadmissable for any purpose.

Pease vs. Sheppard, Sup. Ct. of Pa.

Will—Restraining Power of Alienation.—A will provided that certain property of the testate should go to executors in trust,the rents,incomes and profits thereof to be paid to testate's brothers and sisters during their joint lives, and after their several deaths to be divided equally among the children of such brothers and sisters, such children to take the parents share; and in case of the death of either of testators brothers or sisters leaving others surviving them the income that would have went to the person so dying to be paid to the representative or issue of such brother or sister. Held, that this provision restrained the power of alienation for more than two lives in being, and was for that reason void, and that the interest of children was future and contingent.

Cotton vs. Fox, et al., Ct. of Appeal, N. Y., Nov., 1876.

False Pretenses.—In a criminal proceeding for obtaining money by false pretenses. Held, that it was not essential that the indictment should expressly aver that the party from whom the money was obtained gave credit to the false pretences if the implication would arise from other averments, that he was induced by such representations to part with his money.

People vs. Jacobs, Sup. Ct. of Mich., Oct. Tr., 1876.

Frivalous Demurrer or Answer.—When an answer or demurrer is of such a character as to admit of a lawyer like argument to prove that a demurrer is not frivalous it is not frivalous and should not be stricken out as such. To warrant this summary mode of dispensing of a defence the mere reading of the pleadings should be sufficient to disclose, without deliberation and beyond doubt, that the defence is sham or irrelevant.

Cottrell vs. Cramer, Sup. Ct. of Wis., Nov., 1877.

Removal to U. S. Court.—In case of removal from State to United States Court when the proceeding for removal are regular the jurisdiction of the state court is ipso facto ousted by virtue of such proceedings. The allegation as to jurisdiction, can be proven on the trial and the proper judgment asked for.

Shaft vs. Phœnix Mut. Life Ins. Co., N. Y. Ct. of Appeals.

Latest Publications.

The Laws and Practice of Bankruptcy.—By Orlando F. Bump. New edition to January 1877. 8 vo. 1040 pp., law sheep - - - - - 7 50

National Bankruptcy Register Reports.—Vol. XIV. By O. F. Bump, 8 vo.. 600 pp., full sheep. - - - - 6 00

Holmes' Circuit Court Reports.—Reports of cases determined in the Circuit Court of the United States for the First Circuit, from July, 1870, to June, 1875: by Jabez S. Holmes. 8vo, law sheep, - - - - - 7 00

The Electors' Manual.—Constitutional Provisions and Statutes of the United States, relating to Presidential Elections, Elections of Senators and Representatives, Citizenship, and the Elective Franchise; with an appendix showing the Method of Counting the Electoral Votes for President and Vice President: by Chas. Sidney Whitman. Small 8vo. 98 pp., paper, - - 50

Abbott's U. S. Practice, vol. 1, by Benjamin Vaughan Abbott; 8vo., 640 pp. Law Sheep, - - - - - $7.50

Supplement to Riddle's Supplementary Proceedings, by John F. Baker; 8vo., 128 pp., half sheep, - - - - 2.00

The Law of Evidence, by Simon Greenleaf; vols. 2 and 3, 13th edition, carefully revised by John Wilder May; 8vo., per vol. - - - - - - 6.00

The Law for the Formation of Business Corporations, with Forms, By-Laws, etc., by R. Bach. McMaster; 12mo. 50 pp. Paper, - - - - $0 50

Smith's Reports, Vol. XXIX, being Vol. LXXIX of Pennsylvania State Reports; by P. Frazer Smith. 8vo. 579 pp., Law Sheep, - - - - 4 50

Sansum's Digest of Law of Insurance. A Digest of all the Fire, Life, Marine, Accident and Guarantee Insurance cases decided in Great Britain and America. By O. B. Sansum. 8vo, 600 pp., Law Sheep. - - - - - - 8 00

Shaw's Index to Minn. Session Laws, 1849–1875. Full Sheep, - - 4 00

SESSION LAWS.

We have the Session Laws of Minnesota from 1849 to 1875 inclusive, 34 vols., which we offer in sets, or by the volume.

Parties wishing to fill their sets, will do well to send list at once.

We offer:

1861	2.00	1872	$3.50
1862	2.50	1873	2.50
1863	2.00	1874	2.00
1864	2.00	1875	2.50
1871	2.00	1876	1.75

Bound in Half Sheep.

The American Reprint

OF THE

ENCYCLOPÆDIA BRITANNICA,

New Ninth Edition.

Volumes 1, 2, 3 and 4 are now ready.

This is the Largest and Best work of the kind in the English Language. Every Article is a Complete Treatise by the most Eminent Writers.

Send for Specimen Pages to

JOHN B. WEST & CO.

We have covers for filing and preserving The Syllabi, which we will send by mail, on receipt of price, 35 cents.

THE SYLLABI.

VOL. 1. SATURDAY, FEB. 24, 1877. No. 19.

PUBLISHED WEEKLY,

By JOHN B. WEST & CO.,

No. 1 Wabasha St., - ST. PAUL, MINN.

Terms 3.00 per annum in Advance.

HOMER C. ELLER, Editor.

TABLE OF CONTENTS.

THE case of *Cowdrey vs. City of Winona*, recently decided by the Supreme Court of the United States, was an action brought upon interest coupons of certain bonds of that city, issued to aid in the construction of the St. Paul & Chicago Railway.

These bonds were deposited with First National Bank of St. Paul, and were to be delivered upon compliance, on the part of the Construction company, with the terms of their agreement with the city. Proof of such compliance being presented to the depository the bonds were delivered and the plaintiff in this action received the coupons after maturity.

The defense set up was a failure on the part of the company to comply with their contract and the improper delivery of the bonds. This contract which was in terms with the Minnesota Construction Company, provided that that company in its own name or that of its successors or assigns or the St. Paul & Chicago Railway Company should within a certain time construct, and put in operation, a good and substantial Railway from St. Paul to Winona, and connect at Winona by bridge or ferry with the La-Crosse, Prescott & Trempleau Railroad; certain portions of this latter road were also to be built as well as a bridge across the river at Winona, about the construction of which there was no question: The road from St. Paul to Winona was built within the time and was equipped and put in operation by the assignee of St. Paul & Chicago Company which the court hold sufficient. The principle point relied upon by the defense however, was in regard to the connection at Winona. which was effected by constructing this road to a point some few feet inside the limits of of the city of Winona, (and distant over a mile from the bridge,) and there connecting with the track of the Winona & St. Peter Railroad Co., which track of the last named company also formed the connection with the bridge and the LaC. P. & T. road.

The Supreme Court says, "In our opinion the contract does stipulate that the contemplated connection may be by means of the Winona & St. Peter railroad. The contract, it is true, does, in one of its early provisions declare that the connection between the St. Paul and the Lacrosse roads at Winona shall be by means of a bridge or ferry; but the stipulation inserted in a subsequent part of the instrument touching the delivery of the bonds, is express that they shall not be delivered until the bridge is constructed across the river at Winona.connecting the St. Paul Railway or the Winona & St. Peter road with the LaCrosse road at the then terminus of the latter. It was therefore optional with the construction company to build the St. Paul Railway over the bridge and form an actual junction with the LaCrosse road, or to build to any point in the city and make the required connection by means of the Winona & St. Peter road. Either of these modes would secure the object desired by the city—an uninterrupted communication by rail from St. Paul, across the river at Winona, to the eastern seaboard.

It is contended that the contract is against public policy and without consideration. The obvious answer is that it was expressly sanctioned by an act of the legislature of the state, and was designed to insure and expedite the construction of a work of internal improvement deemed of vital importance to the material interests of the city. Whether it be expedient to invest municipal corporations with such authority, is a question foreign to the present inquiry; but where it has been conferred and exercised, and the city has secured the advantages of the contract, the law will not suffer her to repudiate her obligations."

———:o:———

SUPREME COURT, STATE OF MINNESOTA.

AUGUSTUS PARSONS, and Wm. J. PARSONS, *Appellants*,
vs.
JOHN R. WEBB, and ANNA M. NOGLE, *et. al*,, *Respondents*.
} Feb'y 6, '77.

The possession of mortgaged premises by either the mortgagor or mortgagee, in no way affects the right of the one to redeem or the other to foreclose.

The time within which an action to redeem must as a general rule be brought, is in analogy to the Statute limiting the time for commencing an action to foreclose, ten years, and the time for the mortgagor to bring his action to redeem is not extended by the fact, that owing to the mortgagor being out of the state, the mortgagee may bring his action to foreclose after the ten years.

Appeal from an order of the District Court, Hennepin county, denying motion for a new trial.

Benton & Benton, att'ys for appellants.

Geo. Bradley and J. M. Shaw, attorneys for respondents.

GILFILLAN, C. J.—This was a suit to vacate, and set aside, a judgment and proceedings,foreclosing a mortgage upon real estate, and to have an accounting of the rents and profits of the real estate while in possession of the purchaser under said proceedings, and of the amount due on the mortgage, and to be permitted to redeem from the mortgage. The mortgage was executed by the plaintiff Augustus to the defendant, John R. Webb. July 12th, 1856, to secure two promissory notes, the last one of which came due in two years f om said date. After the execution of the mortgage, and on the same day Augustus executed to the plaintiff William J., a bond conditioned to convey an undivided half of the premises at a certain price, the whole of which was afterwards paid, so that William J., thereupon became the equitable owner of an undivided half of the premises.

In May, 1859, Webb the mortgagee, instituted and prosecuted suit against these plaintiffs, to judgment of foreclosure and to a sale of the premises to satisfy the mortgage; and the sale being confirmed, the proper deeds upon such sale were executed to the defendant, Webb, and to one Camp, the grantor of the defendant. Harriet Camp Webb purchases April 26th, 1860. Webb and those claiming under him have been in possession of the real estate under the mortgage and foreclosure proceedings since April, 1859. It is claimed that these foreclosure proceedings were void as against both the defendants in them for want of jurisdiction of the court over the persons of the defendants. and it would seem that they were void against Augustus; But whether void or not, is immaterial under the view that we take of another point in the case.

All of the parties except the plaintiff Augustus, appear to have been during all the time residents of this state; Augustus was during all such time a non-resident of the state.

Upon this state of facts, the right to bring an action to redeem, was barred by lapse of time, prior to the commencement of this action. As to William J's right of action to redeem his undivided half, no question can be made upon it.

If the non-residence of Augustus saved his right of action to redeem because it saved the mortgagee's right of action to foreclose against him, such non-residence could not operate in favor of the mortgagee against William J., nor in favor of William J., against the mortgagee.

The mortgage became fully due, and the mortgagees right of action to foreclose, and the right of action to redeem fully accrued in 1858. Under the act of 1870, changing the time for foreclosing by action from twenty to ten years, the right of action to foreclose as to both the mortgagors, except as it was saved by the non-residence of Augustus, was barred four years before this suit was brought; and under the acts of 1871 and 1873, limiting the time within which a mortgagee may foreclose under a power in the mortgage, the right to foreclose by advertisement was barred in October 1873; a year before this suit was brought.

The Statute prescribes no limit to the time within which an action to redeem may be brought. Where there is no statutory limit to an equitable right of action the court apply to it the rule established by Statute in analogous cases.

This court has adopted in the action to redeem, not the statutory rule, in the action of ejectment, but in the action to foreclose, as most nearly analogous.

Holton vs. Meighen, 15 *Minn.* 69.
King vs. Meighen, 20 *Ib.* 264.

It is therefore established as a general rule, that an action to redeem must be brought within ten years after the right of action accrues. Where the Statute allows, in the cases provided for by it, exceptions, to its operation in favor of the plaintiff, the court in applying the statutory rule to an equitable action, adopts in favor of the plaintiff in such action the same exceptions as are provided in the rule adopted from the Statute.

Demarest vs. Wynkoop. 3 *Johns Ch. R.* 129.

The possession of the premises by the mortgagor or mortgagee, under our statute, in no way affects the right to foreclose; nor under the rule adopted by this court, the right to redeem.

Such possession neither takes away, suspends, nor limits, either of those actions.

It is claimed that the defense given by statute being a personal privilege may be waived by the defendant, that the mortgagor may waive his defense and thus revive the right of action to foreclose and the consequent or concurrent right of action to redeem; and that those mortgagors by bringing this action have waived the statutory bar to the mortgagee's right of action to foreclose and revive such right of action, and consequently their right of action to redeem. The same suggestion was made, and by the court rejected, in *Cunningham vs. Hawkins*, 24 *Cal.* 403.

It is true that when sued for a foreclosure, the mortgagor may waive the statutory defense, and in such case the right of redemption would doubtless continue; but it would be a singular feature of the law, if the mortgagor could by his own gratuitous act, and without the consent of the mortgagee, remove a bar to his own right of action.

The point in the case arises as to Augustus Parson's right of action to redeem, and upon the fact that he being a non-resident, the right of action to foreclose, as against him, has never been barred; and it is insisted that where for such reason, the right of action to foreclose, whether asserted or not, continues beyond the general limit prescribed by Statute, the right of action to redeem also continues.

In other words, that when the statute makes an exception to its operation in favor of a mortgagees right of action to foreclose, it shall operate in favor of the mortgagors right of action to redeem. That in every case, as long as there is a right of action to foreclose, there shall be a right of action to redeem, may seem to be indicated by the language of 2 *Hillard on Mortgages*, 2 that "In general the respective rights of mortgagee and mortgagor with regard to foreclosure on the one hand, and redemption on the other, are treated as mutual; that is, the existence of the former, is held to involve that of the latter, and *vice versa;*" and of *Canfman vs. Sayre*, 2 *B. Monroe* 206. *of Koch vs. Briggs*, 14 *Cal.* 256. *Of Cunningham vs. Hawkins*, 24 *Cal.* 403. *Of Holton vs. Meighen*, 15 *Minn.* 69, in which cases the language of Hillard that, "The right to foreclose, and the right to redeem, are reciprocal and commensurable," is adopted, and of *King vs. Meighen*, 20 *Minn.* 264, refering to *Holton vs. Meighen*, that "The application of this principle in that case, is that as the right to foreclose has not expired, the right to redeem remains in existence." Hillard however in the language quoted is merely stating a general rule to which it is admitted there are exceptions, and in neither of the cases cited, was involved the question, whether when one of the causes of action survives by reason of statutory exceptions in favor of the party holding it, the other cause of action also survives. In *Holton vs. Meighen*, the action to redeem was brought within the time generally limited for bringing the action to foreclose, and the court held it was brought in time. In *King vs. Meighen*, the action to redeem was brought after the time generally limited for the action to foreclose, and the court held it barred. In neither case was there any fact to extend the time for bringing either the action to foreclose, or the action to redeem; All that the court assumed to decide in either of these cases, was that the rule of limitation in an action to foreclose applies to an action to redeem.

Courts of equity have never gone so far as to assume the power to fix absolutely, a limit of time within which, an equitable action may be brought and to arbitrarily determine what the limit shall be.

Refusing a remedy in equity to a party because of his *laches* and delay in seeking it, in doing which, the court is governed by the particular circumstances of each case, stands upon a different footing from refusing a remedy merely by reason of the lapse of time, and without regard to the question of *laches*. In the latter case, it is generally said that courts of equity in applying a limit, act in analogy to the Statute, though the propriety of this language has been questioned.

In *Hovenden vs. Lord Annesley* 2 *Sch & Lef* 607—30, the chancellor said, "But it is said that courts of equity are not within the Statutes of Limitations. This is true in one respect; they are not within the words of the Statutes because the words apply to particular legal remedies, but they are within the spirit and meaning of the Statutes, and have always been so considered. I think it a mistake in point of language to say that courts of equity act merely by analogy to the Statutes; they act in obedience to them." The result however will be the same whether it be more strictly accurate to say that the court acts in analogy to, or that it acts in obedience to, the Statute. For if it be a principle of equity jurisprudence, that equitable remedies shall be barred by lapse, of the time prescribed by Statute in analogous cases at law, that principle is just as binding upon a court as though it were enacted in a Statute. If we are required either by a principle of equity jurisprudence, or by the spirit and meaning of the Statute, to apply to the action to redeem, the limit prescribed by Statute to the most nearly analogous case which it provides for, the action to foreclose, then the time within which the action must be brought is ten years, and such additional time as the Statute allows to the plaintiff, by reason of his disability or inability to prosecute his suit effectually.

The absence of the defendant in the action by non-residence is a specified inability of the plaintiff.

As the courts of the state cannot get jurisdiction of the person of the defendant, the statute assumes that the plaintiff will be during such absence unable to have a full remedy by action, and for this reason it is provided that the time of such absence shall not be part of the time limited for the commencement of the action.

But the absence of the plaintiff is not an inability. Should the court in an action to redeem, allow a longer time than ten years, for the reason that during part of that time, the plaintiff in the action was absent from the state, it would not apply the same rule prescribed by statute in the action to foreclose.

For in that action the Statute makes no allowance on account of the plaintiffs absence. To make the action to redeem, and the action to foreclose, precisely analogous so far as respects the limitation, the plaintiff in each action should have the same time and the same exceptions in his favor; and in case of either action the question whether it may be brought after the ten years, must depend on the disabilities or inability of the plaintiff in it and not on the disabilities or inability of the defendant to bring his action; For the time to foreclose is not affected by an inability of the mortgagor arising from the mortgagee's absence, to bring an action to redeem. The conclusion is, that an action to redeem must be brought within ten years after the cause of action accrues, unless the mortgagor can show that there exists as to him, a disability or inability for which, when existing as to the mortgagee, the Statute extends the time to foreclose. As no such case is shown in favor of either of these plaintiffs, their right of action to redeem was barred when this action was commenced.

The order denying a new trial is affirmed.

(Mr. Justice Cornell, having been of counsel, took no part.)

CHARLES L. COLEMAN, *Respondent*, vs. WILLIAM BALLANDI, *Appellant*, } Aug. 23, '75.

Chapter 26 General Laws of 1869, amending Sec. 2, Chapter 68, of General Statutes, relating to homestead exemptions, construed and held not to authorize a lien and the enforcement thereof, against a debtor's homestead, in favor of the claim of a material man for materials furnished in the erection of a building on such homestead, there being no agreement between the parties creating the lien.

It is constitutionally competent for the Legislature to determine the amount of property that shall be exempted from seizure and sale for the payment of any debt or liability, and to increase or diminish such amount from time to time, but it cannot in its exemption laws, discriminate between different classes of creditors and kinds of debts.

Appeal from a judgment of District Court, county of Faribault.

Andrew C. Dunn, attorney for respondent.

Benj. G. Reynolds and C. H. Radford, attorneys for appellant.

CORNELL, J.—Between July 27th and November 12th, 1872, plantiff sold and delivered to defendant at his request certain building materials, of the value of $299.20 for the purpose of being used, and which in fact were used, in the erection of a certain building on a part of a village lot in Winnebago City, then owned and occupied by defendant as his homestead. In May following, plaintiff filed and recorded in the proper Register of Deeds office the requisite notice, affidavit and verified statement of account, to secure a lien upon said building and premises. This action is brought to recover the balance claimed to be due on such account, to-wit: $136.12, and to enforce the same as a lien against said property. On a trial by the court without a jury, upon these facts, a judgment was ordered and entered in favor of plaintiff for such balance and costs, adjudging the amount a lien against said premises buildings, and ordering a sale thereof, to satisfy the judgment &c. The question presented is whether this judgment can be upheld, under the amendment to the Homestead Exemption act, adopted in 1869, which is as follows: "Such exemption shall not extend to any contract for a lien, or upon which a lien would arise under the lien laws of this state, for work done or material furnished in the erection or repair of a dwelling house or other building on said land." (Chap. 26, General Laws 1869.)

The contract alleged in this case is one of sale and delivery by plaintiff, at defendant's request, of a certain quantity of lumber, of a certain value, for the purpose of being used in a building on defendant's homestead. It contains no stipulation giving to the vendor any lien upon the homestead, for the purchase price of the material sold, and cannot be construed "into a contract for a lien."

Is it a contract "upon which any lien would arise, under the lien laws of this state," &c?

The negative of this is apparent from the following considerations: In the absence of any express contract creating it, the lien which a material man or mechanic may become entitled to, "does not arise out of any contract but depends solely on the statute for its existence. It is a preference which he may secure, if he proceeds in a particular way," and fully complies with the statutory requirements upon the subject and not otherwise. *Bailey and Gilman vs. Mason & Craig*, 4 *Minn R.* 546. Having its origin alone in the statute and proceedings taken under it, it cannot be said to "arise out of or upon contract," and hence is not embraced in the terms of the amendment. To determine its existence in any given case, we must look therefore to some statute authorizing it. The lien laws in force at the time the proceedings in this case were had, are substantially the same as those which came under consideration by this court in the case of *Cogel et al. vs. Mickow, et. al* 11 *Minn.* 475, in which it was distinctly held that under the laws then in force, a material man had no claim against his debtors homestead for materials furnished in the erection of a dwelling thereon. It is claimed however, that the decision in that case is not applicable to the present, because the last clause of the above quoted amendment operates as a modification of the then existing lien laws. This is not so, either in terms or in its effect. It is what it purports to be, simply an amendment of a section of the statute relating to homestead exemptions, and purporting to except from its operations cases founded upon "a contract for a lien, or upon which a lien would arise, under the lien laws of the state, etc." It does not purport to give any right to a lien in any case where by the laws of the state then in force, it did not exist, and cannot be so construed. Assuming however that the Legislature intended, by this amendment, specifically to give to a material man, in the absence of an agreement, the right to secure and enforce his claim as a lien upon his debtor's homestead, and that the section as amended is susceptible of such a construction, it could not be upheld as a constitutional exercise of Legislative power under sec. 12 of the Bill of Rights. This provision of the constitution imposes upon the Legislature the duty of "exempting from seizure or sale, for the payment of any debt or liability, a reasonable amount of property," and of "determining such amount by law." In the discharge of this duty and the exercise of its undoubted power, its judgment and discretion as to amount of the exemption, and its reasonableness, is final and conclusive, and it may increase or diminish such amount from time to time, according to its own views of an enlightened public policy. Beyond this, however, it cannot constitutionally go. Discrimination in its exemption laws, between different classes of creditors and kinds of debts or liabilities, is a species of class legislation which is absolutely prohibited. This must be regarded as the settled doctrine in this state. *Tuttle vs. Straut*, 7 *Minn.* 465. *Cogel et. al. vs. Mickow, et. al.*, 11 *Ibid* 475.

So much of the judgment appealed from as decrees a lien upon the premises therein described for the amount thereof, and orders a sale of all defendant's right, title, interest and estate, therein to satisfy the same, is hereby reversed.

FRANK PFIFFNER, *Respondent*, *vs.* THE STILLWATER & ST. PAUL RAILROAD COMP'Y, and THE NORTHERN PACIFIC RAILROAD COMP'Y, *Appellants*. } Feb. 7, '77,

The making of substantial improvements, pursuant to an oral agreement to convey the real estate improved, by a vendee in possession prior to and at the time of the agreement is such a part performance as takes the agreement out of the statute of frauds.

Appeal from judgment of District Court, county af Washington.

McCluer & Marsh, attorneys for respondent.

James Smith, Jr., and *H. R. Murdock*, attorneys for appellants.

GILFILLAN, C. J.—Action in trespass for entering upon, taking possession of, and continuing to use for railroad purposes, a strip of land belonging to plaintiff. The answer sets up as a defense and counter-claim, and asks for the specific performance of, an oral agreement, by plaintiff, to convey the strip in question to defendant.

In 1869 defendant procured the condemnation to its use in constructing its road, of a strip of plaintiff's land, near to that in question, but afterwards concluded to change its its line and run it over the latter, and there upon without the consent of plaintiff run its line and constructed its road over the latter strip, the strip in question. After the road was constructed across that strip, except surfacing, the parties made an oral agreement by which it was agreed, that defendant should abandon the line first adopted by it, and for which it had condemned the right of way, and adopt and use in lieu thereof the line over the strip in question; should pay as compensation a certain sum, larger than that awarded on the condemnation of the abandoned strip; should as soon as the frost should be out of the ground the ensuing spring, fence its railroad across the strip in question, and construct for plaintiff a wagon and cattle pass with cattle guards across its road, on said strip at such place as plaintiff should designate, and that thereupon, plaintiff should convey said strip to defendant. Relying upon said agreement and pursuant to its terms, the defendant at an expense of $300, constucted the fence, wagon and cattle passes, and cattle guards and crossings, at the places designated by plaintiff, and had the same completed by the 28th of July following the agreement; and it also at an expense of $500, surfaced its railroad across said land. It afterwards tendered the compensation agreed on and demanded a conveyance from plaintiff.

As the taking possession by defendant of the strip in question was before the agreement, and without the consent of plaintiff, such possession was not attributable to the agreement and therefore no part performance to take the agreement out of the Statute of Frauds. But as the court below has found as fact that relying upon the agreement, and pursuant to its terms, the defendant made the improvements mentioned, the making of them was directly attributable to the agreement; and if in any case the making of improvements by a vendee in such an agreement, whose possession is merely continued, will take the case out of the statute, this case is taken out. And of the proposition that merely making improvements, may be a part performance sufficient for that purpose, we entertain very little doubt.

The most satisfactory justification of the action of courts of equity in compelling specific performance of agreements within the letter of the statute of frauds, is, that the commission of frauds is thereby prevented. Mr. Justice Story in his *Eq. Jur. Sec.* 761 says, "But a more general ground and that which ought to be the governing rule in cases of this sort, is that nothing is to be considered as a part performance which does not put the party into a situation which is a fraud upon him unless the agreement is fully performed." And *Browne on Frauds, Sec.* 448. "The doctrine of equity is that where an agreement has been so far executed by one party, with the tacit encouragement of the other, and relying upon his fulfilment of it, that for the latter to repudiate it and shelter himself under the provisions of the Statute, would amount to a fraud upon the former, that fraud will be defeated by compelling him to carry out the agreement."

The most frequent cases in which courts interpose to prevent fraud by compelling performance, are those where possession has been taken under the agreement in which, if the agreement is to be disregarded, the party taking possession will be made a trespasser. These cases, however, are not the measure of the rule, but only instances of its application.

Rendering a party liable as a trespasser, by repudiating an oral agreement with him, cannot be a greater fraud than subjecting him by such repudiation to the loss of improvements.

Browne on Frauds, Sec. 487, says: "The propriety of admitting this expenditure of money in improvements as a reason for enforcing the contract, is perhaps, more clear upon the equitable view of preventing fraud, than is that of admitting the taking or delivering of possession."

Story Eq. Juris. Sec. 763, *a*, after considing whether the continuance of a previous possession is to be deemed a part performance, says: "When substantial improvements are subsequently made in faith of the contract, there could be no question it should be regarded as part performance." See also *Wetmore vs. White*, 2 *Caine's Cases* 87; *Parkhurst vs. Van Courtland*, 14 *Johns* 15.

The case made by the defendant entitled it to a conveyance of the strip of land in question, and makes out a defense to the cause of action, certainly so far as covers the damages from the time the oral agreement was made; and if that agreement was intended as a satisfaction for the technical cause of action existing at that time, which the making of the agreement suggests, though the fact is not found by the court, to the entire cause of action. To determine if such was the intention of the parties in making the agreement, there will have to be a new trial.

The judgment is reversed and a new trial ordered.

——o||o——

U. S. Circuit Court, Minnesota Dist.

C. P. Bailey, *Receiver* of The First National Bank of Duluth, *vs.* Andrew J. Sawyer. — Feb'y '77.

In winding up an insolvent National Bank, the Comptroller of the Currency is vested with authority to determine when a deficiency of assets exists, so that the individual liability of the stockholders may be enforced, and no appeal lies from his decision.

The liability of a stockholder of a National Bank is several, and is fixed by his taking stock in the corporation.

When an assessment upon the stockholders is ordered by the Comptroller, a suit at law is the proper remedy to enforce it.

This is a common law action brought to enforce the individual liability of a stockholder in the First National Bank of Duluth and to recover the amount of an assessment ordered by the Comptroller of the currency, to the extent of seventy-five *per centum* of the par value of the shares of the capital stock of said bank, under and by virtue of the act of congress in relation to national banks

A demurrer is interposed to the complaint. Upon the argument it is urged:

1st. That the complaint should set forth the facts and *data* upon which the Comptroller determined that a necessity existed which authorized proceedings to enforce the individual liability of stockholders:

2nd. That the suit should have been in equity, and not in law.

W. W. Billson, for demurrer.

Ensign & Cash, *contra*.

Nelson, J.—The Comptroller of the currency by virtue of the national banking law in winding up an insolvent bank, is vested with authority to determine when a deficiency of assets exists, so that the individual liability of the stockholders may be enforced. This liability is conditional and was so held in *Bank vs. Kennedy*, (17 *Wall. R. pg.* 22,) but the Comptroller in the exercise of a judicial discretion decides upon the *data* before him when "it is necessary," to compel contribution from stockholders to pay the debts of the bank. The law clothes him with this authority and no appeal lies from his decision by a stockholder. He appoints a receiver and resorts to the ultimate remedy whenever in his judgment the condition of the bank requires its enforcement. And as stated in (*Kennedy vs. Gibson et. al.*, 8 *Wall. R.* 504,) a more speedy settlement of the affairs of an insolvent bank is thus obtained. Again — this obligation of the stockholder is fixed when he becomes a member of the corporation by taking stock therein, and is several, not joint. There is no necessity for invoking the aid of a court of chancery to determine the sum each stockholder must pay, for that is regulated by the number of shares of stock owned. When the Comptroller declares and orders an assessment, the precise amount each stockholder must contribute, is a certain exact sum. A suit at law would seem to be the suitable proceeding to collect the asessment.

Demurrer overruled.

Recent Decisions.

Sunday Verdict.—The verdict of a jury rendered on Sunday is valid.

Reid vs. State. Sup. Ct of Ala. (4 Cent L. Jr. 154.)

Joint and Several Liability.—Upon an obligation that is joint and several, the obligors are each liable for the debt in a separate action.

People vs. Harrison, Sup. Ct. of Ill.

Execution of Instrument.— A written agreement which is intended to be signed by several persons as parties thereto, if not signed by all is not completely executed, and does not bind any of the parties.

Barber vs Burrows, Sup. Ct. of Cal. 1876.

Where city authorities have discretion vested in them, and proof of corrupt action is not established, the court will not interfere in regard to the acceptance or rejection of the lowest bidder.

Findly vs. Mayor, etc., Pittsburg, Sup. Ct. of Pa.

Void Covenant -A covenant in a lease to re-rent them to the lessee after the expiration of his present term, without specifying the amount for which they are to be let, is void for uncertainty.

Delashmunte vs. Thomas, Sup. Ct. of Md.,1876.

Partnership—Debts.—The outgoing members of a firm that is dissolved are sureties on a partnership debt for those who remain, but they are discharged if the latter without their knowledge or consent substitute a new debt that increases their liability.

Smith vs. Sheldon, Sup. Ct. of Mich. Oct., 1876.

Claim for Damages for a Tort is not a Debt.—A claim, sounding in tort, for unliquidated damages, as for negligently setting a fire, which spread to claimant's lands and caused him serious injury, is not, before judgment, a debt, and does not constitute such claimant a creditor in the sense contemplated by the statute, making voluntary deeds fraudulent as to creditors.

Hill vs Bowman, Sup Ct. of Mich., Oct. Term, 1876.

Common Carriers.—Where goods intrusted to a railroad company, (as fruit trees) are injured by unnecessary delay on the part of the carrier in transporting and delivering them, the owner is entitled to recover the value thereof. Testimony of a witness in regard to the trees that "if they had been shipped that evening as promised by the agent they would have gone through all right," is not a mere opinion of the witness, but is the statement of a fact.

Vail vs. R. R. Co., Sup. Ct. of Mo., Oct. Term, 1876.

Bankruptcy —Proof of Debts. —Proceedings by creditors to prove their demands against the estate of a bankrupt, are part of the suit in bankruptcy, and not separate and independent suits; therefore the judgment of the Circuit Court upon an appeal from an order of the District Court,rejecting a claim presented by a supposed creditor against the estate of the bankrupt, cannot be re-examined in the Supreme Court, upon a writ of error.

Wiswall vs. Campbell, Sup. Ct. of U. S. (4 Cent. L. J., 149.)

Contradictory Instructions.—When the instructions given by the court below are manifestly contradictory or antagonistic, the judgment will be reversed. Where the record states that the parties offered evidence tending to sustain their respective sides of the issues made, and one of the issues was whether there was an agreement to give bond, an instruction that "there is no evidence that the bond was mentioned" is good ground for reversing the judgment.

Boynton vs. Miller, Sup. Ct. of Mo., Oct. Term, 1876.

Assignment for Benefit of Creditors.—The act of 1859, in regard to assignments for benefit of creditors, (1 R. S. 1876, 142) requires that such assignments shall be recorded within ten days after their execution, and shall convey no interest to the assignee until recorded. Under this statute the assigned property may be legally taken on execution after the date of the assignment, but before the same is recorded.

Forkner vs. Shafer, et. al., Sup. Ct. of Ind., Nov. Term, 1876.

Evidence.—In a trial for an alleged crime, it is not competent for the prosecution to attack the character of the prisoner, unless the prisoner first puts it in issue by offering of evidence of good character; nor can the bad character of the prisoner be shown by putting in evidence of particular acts.

The State cannot be permitted to show that the prisoner has a tendency to commit the offense charged; nor can other crimes of the prisoner be put in evidence, unless they are so connected by circumstances, with the particular crime for which he is on trial that the proof of one fact with its circumstances has some bearing upon the issue on trial, other than as expressed in the foregoing propositions.

State vs. La Page, Sup. Ct. of N. H.

THE SYLLABI.

VOL. 1. SATURDAY, MARCH 3, 1877. No. 20.

PUBLISHED WEEKLY,

By JOHN B. WEST & CO.,

No. 1 Wabasha St., - ST. PAUL, MINN.

Terms 3.00 per annum in Advance.

HOMER C. ELLER, Editor.

TABLE OF CONTENTS.

A CORRESPONDENT sends us a query in regard to the power of a Notary Public, duly appointed and qualified, to take acknowledgements and otherwise act in the State, outside of the county of which he is a resident. We have been unable after somewhat extended search, to find any authority upon this question, though we are informed that a decision has been made by one of the District Courts to the effect that acts of a Notary performed outside of the county for which he was appointed, and within the state, are entirely valid. A careful examination of the statute would seem to leave but little doubt as to the correctness of such ruling. Sec. 4, ch. 27, Gen'l Statutes provides: "That every Notary Public so appointed, commissioned and qualified, shall have power throughout the state, while residing within the county for which he was appointed, to administer all oaths &c." Granting in as plain words as possible the power, "while a *resident* of the county for which appointed," to act throughout the state. Residence, means a place of permanent abode, not where a party may be temporarily stopping, and is not used here in connection with the territorial extent of a Notary's powers; but with his power to act at all. Again a construction that he has power only throughout his county, to perform the acts specified in the statute, necessarily gives a different meaning to the words "throughout this state" from what their natural sense implies, and can hardly be construed to refer simply to the *validity* of their acts when performed within the county; This view of the statute is, we think, the one most generally adopted among members of the bar. A Notary acting outside of the county of which he is a resident should, of course, lay the venue of his acts, in the county where performed, and they should be authenticated by his own seal, and not by that of a Notary of a different county from where he resides.

WE are in receipt of the first number of *The Virginia Law Journal*, a monthly periodical of some sixty odd pages, published at Richmond, Va., devoted especially to the early publication of decisions of the Supreme Court of Appeals and other courts of that state. Each number will also contain one or more original articles upon legal topics of general interest; The first of the series being by Wm. Green, Esq., of Richmond, on the doctrine of "*Res Judicata.*" As a magazine, it is neat in appearance and undoubtedly will secure wide circulation.

Supreme Court, State of Minnesota.

The Northwestern Mutual Life Ins. Co., and Wm. R. Marshall, *Respondents*, *vs.* Lorenzo Allis, and Mary C. Allis, his wife, *Appellants.* } Feb. 6,'77

Under Ch. 56, Laws of 1869, a married woman may make a valid contract binding herself to pay a preexisting debt of her husband.

Where a creditor has security for his debt upon the property of the principal debtor, and other security upon the property of the surety, a court will not require him to first exhaust the security against the property of the principal debtor, if it appear that such property is of no value as security for the debt.

A creditor who by his contract has a right upon default of the debtor as to part of the debt, to treat the whole debt as due before the time fixed for its payment, may make his election, that the whole shall be due by bringing suit for it.

If the facts in a complaint show in the plaintiff, a right of election, to treat the whole debt as due upon several grounds, the election evidenced by the commencement of a suit will be deemed to be made upon all such grounds, unless the contrary clearly appear. A mortgage of real estate contained a clause that upon default of the mortgagors to pay taxes, the mortgagees might pay them and that the amount so paid should thereupon become a part of the mortgage debt; after a trial in an action to foreclose the mortgage, the mortgagee paid taxes on the property and without notice to the mortgagors, upon the production of the tax receipt the amount so paid was included in the judgment entered.

Held, error and that the mortgagors have a right to a trial of the facts upon which the propriety of adding the taxes to the debt depended.

Appeal from judgment of the District Court, county of Ramsey.

Frederick Allis, attorney for appellant, Mary C. Allis.

Geo. L. & Chas. E. Otis, attorneys for respondent.

Gilfillan, C. J.—From the facts found it appears that the defendants are, and at the several transactions involved, were, husband and wife, and that at St. Paul, on the 1st day of June, 1874, they executed their joint promissory note for the payment to the order of Wm. R. Marshall, two years from said day, of ten thousand dollars, with interest semi-annually, at ten per cent. per annum, and exchange on New York, which note contained this stipulation: "It being distinctly understood and agreed that should there be any default in the payment of the said interest, as above mentioned, that then and as often as such default shall be made, the whole of said principal sum, together with all accrued interest thereon, shall immediately become due and payable at the option of the holder of this note, within thirty days from the time of such default;" and at the same time, to secure said note, they executed to Marshall a mortgage upon real estate, the separate property of Mary C. Allis, which mortgage contained this recital in the description of the note which it was given to secure: "Said note also containing a provision to the effect that should any default be made in the payment of the said interest or any part thereof, on any day whenever the same is made payable as above expressed, that then and as often as such default shall be made, the aforesaid principal sum of ten thousand dollars, with all arrearages of interest thereon, shall at the option of the said party of the second part, or his legal representatives or assigns, become and be due immediately thereafter, and payable within thirty days from the date of such default." There was in the mortgage a covenant that the mortgagors should pay all taxes prior and subsequent to its execution, with the stipulation that in default thereof for thirty days the mortgagee might pay them, and the same should thereupon be due and payable by the mortgagors to the mortgagee, and be deemed secured by the mortgage; and in default of such payment by the said parties of the first part, their heirs, executors, administrators or assigns, the whole of the principal sum and interest secured by this mortgage, shall at the option of the said party of the second part, his executors, administrators or assigns, immediately become due and payable." This note and mortgage were in August, 1874, transferred by Marshall to plaintiff, now the holder, as collateral security.

The note and mortgage were in fact given to secure an individual debt of the husband, and the money he received thereon was used exclusively for his benefit. Of these facts, however, Marshall had no notice, but he was led to believe, and did believe, that the note and mortgage were given to secure the indebtedness of both defendants.

At the same time of executing this note and mortgage, and as further security for said note and another note for four thousand dollars, the defendants executed to Marshall a mortgage upon other real estate, the property of the defendant Lorenzo. The property covered by this last mortgage was at the time of the trial so heavily incumbered by prior liens as to make it of no value whatever as a security for the payment of the note for ten thousand dollars. Defendants failed to pay the installnents of interest on the ten thousand dollar note falling due Dec. 14th, 1874, and have never paid it.

Taxes levied upon the property, were due and unpaid August 28th, 1874, and were never paid by either of defendants, but about that time and before the transfer of the notes and mortgages, were paid by Marshall.

On January 11th, 1875, plaintiff served on defendants, notice of its election to declare the principal sum of the note and mortgage due. This notice is not set out in the record. Judgment for the foreclosure of the ten thousand dollar mortgage and sale of the premises was entered, adjudging the amount found due, and that defendants should pay any deficiency. From this judgment it appears that after the trial the plaintiff paid taxes for the year 1874, to the amount of $211.15, which in the judgment was added to the amount found due by the finding of the court. This was done, as it appears, without notice, and simply upon the production of the tax receipt. Upon these facts the defendant, Mary C., claims that no judgment for a deficiency against her should have been rendered, for the reason, that at the time of the execution of the note and mortgage, she, being a married woman, was by statute incapable of making herself liable for the debts of her husband, and that the note and mortgage were given for his debt.

That as she stood in the relation of surety for her husband it was right to have the security for the debt against her husband's separate property exhausted before resorting to the security against her property.

That it was error to add to the judgment the $211.15.

That by the true construction of the note and mortgage, the holder could exercise his option to decree the principal due, by reason of a default in the payment of interest, only within thirty days after such default.

The first of these points depends on Ch. 56, Gen'l Laws 1869. Sec. 3, of that act reads: "No married woman shall be liable for any debts of her husband, nor shall any married man be liable for any debts or contracts of his wife entered into, either before or during converture except for necessaries furnished to the wife after marriage where he would be liable at common law. "It is argued that as this note and mortgage were to secure the debt of the husband she is not liable personally upon them under this section." Apparently a good answer to this is, that the obligation of the note and mortgage is her debt, as well as that of the husband, and unless the section can be construed as disabling her to make a contract, the consideration for which is a prior debt of her husband, this answer must be conclusive. The defendant claims, that as at the common law, the wife was not liable for the husbands debts, the section was not necessary to exclude such liability, and that the section could not have been inserted for that purpose; but must have been for the purpose of disabling her to contract a liability in consideration of such a debt. To give this effect to the section would be to allow inference and conjucture to qualify and restrict the meaning of the clear add precise language of the act removing the wifes common law disability to contract. Section 2 provldes that, "Any married woman shall be capable of making any contract either by parol or under seal which she might make if unmarried, and shall be bound thereby. Then follow clearly expressed exceptions to her power to contract without her husband; relating only to her real estate. Section 4 expressly retains the common law disabilities of husband ahd wife to contract with each other, relative to the real estate of either, or any authority from one to the other to convey real estate and continues "but in relation to all other subjects either may be constituted the agent of the other, or contract each with the other, as fully as if the relation of husband and wife did not exist.

In view of this clear enabling language, and of the clearly expressed exceptions to it, no implication against the force of such language can be allowed from the language of section 3, unless such implication necessarily follows from the presence of the section in the act.

It may not have been strictly necessary to insert the section for the purpose of preventing any question as to the liability of one, for the debts of the other, but in view of the difficulties of the subject, it was very proper to be inserted for that purpose, and we think such was its purpose. The note and the mortgage were therefore valid.

The power of a court of equity to control a creditor in enforcing his remedies so as to protect the interests of a surety, when the creditor has securities for his debt both upon the property of the principal debtor and also upon that of the surety, and to require the creditor to first exhaust the security against the principal is undoubted; But to call such power into exercise there must in fact be substantial security against the principals property. In this case there is no such security for it is found as a fact, that the separate property of the defendant Lorenzo upon which a mortgage was given to secure this same debt, was so heavily incumbered by liens prior to such mortgage as to make it of no value whatever as security for the debt in question. As enforcing the mortgage against this property could result only in costs, and in delay of the creditor, and would be entirely fruitless of any benefit to it or of any protection to the surety, the court below was clearly right in refusing this demand of defendant.

The point made upon the construction of the note and mortgage. as to the time within which the mortgagee should exercise his option to claim the principal due by reason of a default in payment of the interest, would not, if the court held with the construction claimed by defendant, affect the result, and therefore is not passed on; for the mortgagee had the right to claim the entire debt to be due by reason of the default as to taxes. The notice served by the mortgagee upon the defendants, was at a time when the mortgagee's right of action on account of such taxes was complete, and as the contents of the notice are not before us, we cannot say that the election notified by it, was based on any other ground, in such a way as to be a waiver of the mortgagee's right to elect upon the ground of default in respect to the taxes. The right still remaining, it was properly exercised by bringing suit. Where the facts in the complaint clearly show a right of option upon several grounds, the election evidenced by the commencement of the action will be deemed to be made by reason of all such grounds, unless the contrary clearly appear.

The insertion in the judgment of the $211.15 was clearly erroneous. It stands upon an entirely different footing from the case of an installment falling due at any time before the judgment, for the facts upon which said installment may be entered in the judgment are determined by the trial. In respect to these taxes, the facts upon which the plaintiffs' right to recover for them depended, arose after the trial, and the defendants never had an opportunity, as they have a right, to litigate them.

The judgment must therefore be modified by striking out the $211.15, and the case will be remanded for the court below to so modify it.

(Mr. Justice Cornell did not sit.)

THERESA KOEHLER, *Respondent*, vs. MICHAEL CLEARY, *Appellant*. } Feb. 6,'77.

In case of an application for a new trial, for misconduct of the jury, if it does not appear that the misconduct was occasioned by the prevailing party, or any one in his behalf, and if it does not indicate any improper bias upon the juror's minds, and the court cannot see that it had or might have had an effect unfavorable to the party moving for a new trial, the verdict ought not to be set aside.

If the moving party shows such misconduct that prejudice may have resulted to him from it, a new trial will be granted, unless the successful party shows that in fact such prejudice did not result.

Appeal from an order of the District Court, county of Winona, denying motion for a new trial. The action was one for breach of promise of marriage; the complaint also charged the defendant with seduction. The defense a general denial. The testimony offered by both parties was contradictory in its character, and related almost wholly to conversations, facts and circumstances claimed to have transpired in certain rooms and parts of the hotel and boarding house kept by plaintiff's sister and known as the Green Bay House; a full description of the house and rooms, explained by a diagram, was given by several witnesses for both parties, and on part of plaintiff one witness testified as to certain things heard in one room while he was in another, and in argument to the jury it was asserted on the one hand and denied on the other that it would have been impossible for the witness, from his position, to so have heard. The defendant also testified as to certain things he had seen and certain noises he had heard while occupying a particular position in a certain room in the house, all of which was denied. The jury found a verdict in favor of plaintiff for the sum of $2,000, but court below, on the point that the damages were excessive, denied the motion for a new trial on the plaintiff's consenting to reduce the amount of the verdict to $650.

Dyckson & Yale, attorneys for respondent.

Wilson & Taylor, attorneys for appellant.

GILFILLAN, C. J.—There is no necessity to consider any of the grounds upon which the motion for a new trial was made except that of misconduct of the jury.

Bearing on this point, it appears from the bill of exceptions that certain acts and consultations were testified to. as having occurred in certain rooms in the Green Bay House, the hotel at which the plaintiff lived, and which hotel was kept by plaintiff's sister; and that the testimony of these acts and conversations had a material bearing upon the case. These acts and conversations were denied, and it was claimed that from the locality and position of the rooms, it was impossible that the witness testifying could have seen or heard such acts or conversations.

The credibility of the witnesses, therefore, was in some measure affected by such locality and position. From the affidavits used on the motion, and which are not contradicted nor explained, it appears that five of the jurors who tried the cause, during the trial and without leave of the court, went together to the Green Bay House, and spoke to the bar-tender, who thereupon took the key of one of the rooms testified to, conducted them into it, and closed the door, and they therein remained for some minutes; it appears that the bar-tender was a cousin or nephew of plaintiff, and had been a witness for her on the trial. What occurred in the room after he and the jurors entered it, does not appear. It is evident that the jurors, conducted by a relative of, and a witness for the plaintiff, made without leave of court or consent of defendant, an examination of the premises, and it is a fair presumption that they made it in order to test the credibility of the witnesses. That this was misconduct on the part of the jury is not denied, but it is denied that it is such misconduct as to vitiate the verdict.

The proper rule in such cases we deem to be, that if it does not appear that the misconduct was occasioned by the prevailing party or any one in his behalf, and if it does not indicate any improper bias upon the jurors' minds, and the court cannot see that it either had, or might have had, an effect unfavorable to the party moving for a new trial, the verdict ought not to be set aside. *Pettibone vs. Phelps*, 13 *Conn.* 445.

In this case the fact that the plaintiff could easily have explained what was done and said (if anything) at the time of the jurors' visit, and have shown their misconduct to have been harmless, if it was harmless, and that she makes no attempt at such explanation, requires that every reasonable inference which the facts will justify should be made against her. It would be unreasonable to require that the defendant should show that he was in fact prejudiced. He would not be permitted to do this by the oaths of the jurors; he could not be expected to do it by the oath of the relative and witness, who was himself a party to the misconduct. The most that he could be called upon to do, is to show that the misconduct may have had an effect unfavorable to him. That it may have had such unfavorable effect needs only a statement of the facts to show. The jurors evidently deemed the location and position of the rooms of sufficient importance, in their bearing on the case, to justify them in making an examination. The rooms were in her sister's house, in which she lived, and the examination was made under the guidance of her relative and witness, who may be assumed to have acted in her behalf, though perhaps not by her direct procurement; and it is impossible to say that such an examination, made under such circumstances, may not have had a considerable influence on the minds of the jurors, adverse to the defendant.

It is not sufficient to obviate the probability of prejudice from such influence, that there was introduced in evidence a diagram of the premises, showing the location of the rooms. A diagram on paper might, and with most men would, have an effect very different from that caused by actual view of the premises.

Because of the misconduct, there must be a new trial.

Order appealed from reversed, and new trial ordered.

LEONARD DAY & SONS, *Respondents*, *vs.* MINNEAPOLIS MILL CO., and WILLIAM W. HAYWARD, *Appellants*, — Feb'y 6, '77.

Sufficiency of evidence to support a judgment, affirmed.

Appeal by defendant and intervenor from judgment of Court of Common Pleas county of Hennepin.

D. A. Secombe, attorney for respondent.

Shaw & Levi, for the Minneapolis Mill Company.

L. M. Stewart, attorney for Intervenor.

GILFILLAN, C. J.—This action was originally commenced against the Mill Co. alone.

and after its commencement Hayward intervened by complaint, pursuant to the statute, claiming that he, and not the plaintiffs is entitled to the money, to recover which the action is brought. The Mill Co. does not deny its liability to pay the money desiring apparently only a judgment which will protect it, and as the judgment in the case will undoubtedly protect it against any further claim for the same money, it is really, although it has brought an appeal, no party to the controversy in this court.

The controversy is solely between the plaintiff and Hayward, as to who is entitled to receive the money which the Mill Co. is willing to pay.

The facts out of which the conflicting claims of the plaintiffs and the intervenor spring are these; on Jan'y 20th, 1863, the Mill Co. executed to one W. E. Jones, a lease of rectangular piece of the bed of the Mississippi river being part of its dam and pond at Minneapolis, for a term, to continue until the 1st day of May, 1874, with the stipulation that at the end of the term the value of the annual rent for the ensuing five years, and also the value of the improvements erected by Jones, should be appraised, and that within three days after receiving the award of the appraisers, the Mill Co. might elect whether it would renew the lease for the further further term of five years at the appraised rent, or pay the appraised value of the improvements and become the owner of them; and that in case it elected to do the latter, it should make payment within ninety days, and "thereupon the said party of the second part (Jones) shall peaceably and quietly yield and surrender possession of the said demised premises, together with the improvements thereon to the said party of the first part."

This lease was duly recorded. Oct. 1st, 1872, Jones executed to Hayward to secure the sum of $7,000 a mortgage upon "one half of certain leasehold premises more fully described in a certain indenture (referring to the lease of Jan'y 20th, 1863,) together with one half of the mill fixtures and appurtanances including one-half of the mill, and all powers privileges and appurtanances connected therewith."

This mortgage was given in satisfaction or renewal of a prior mortgage upon an undivided half of the leasehold interest, executed Oct. 1st, 1869, to secure $6,000 by Jones and one Groff, and was duly recorded Oct. 4th, 1872.

Nov. 5th, 1872, Jones assigned and transferred to plaintiffs said leasehold interest and the saw mill erected thereon with mill fixtures &c. In this conveyance to plaintiffs the mortgage to Hayward is mentioned as an incumbrance upon the property, but Jones agrees therein to pay the same.

Dec. 1st, 1873, the Mill Co. executed to plaintiffs a lease to continue until Dec. 1st, 1875, of a rectangular piece of the bed of the river with a stipulation that the company might at its election renew the lease for a further term of five years, or pay for and take the improvements erected by plaintiffs at a valuation appraised as therein provided.

Dec. 3d, 1875, Hayward duly foreclosed his mortgage and bid in the property at the sum of $1,475.72 and they have not been redeemed.

Jan'y 19th, 1876, appraisers selected by plaintiffs and the Mill Co. in the preceding Dec. made their award appraising the yearly rental of the property mentioned tioned in the second lease and also appraising the value of the improvements thereon at $16,170.

And April 10th, 1876, the Mill Co. having elected to pay for the improvements, paid plaintiffs $14,657.85, and retained of the amount appraised $1,512.15 on account of the claim made thereto by Hayward.

Under this state of facts the intervenor claims that the rule which subjects a new lease taken by a tenant under an old lease to the rights legal or equitable, of a party entitled to the benefit and advantage of the old one, is applicable to the case.

Upon a careful examination of the case we do not find any evidence either in the descriptions in the respective leases or otherwise, which indicates that the property described in the second is any part of that described in the first lease, although the court in its findings states such to be the fact.

This being so there is nothing to sustain the intervenor's claim, and as his appeal is based on that claim there is nothing to sustain the appeal.

The judgment is affirmed.

(Mr. Justice Cornell, having been of counsel, did not sit.)

STATE OF MINNESOTA, *Respondent.*
vs.
LEO. MILLER and MATTIE STRICKLAND. *Appellants,*
} Feb'y 8, '77.

When the return to an appeal in a criminal case con-

tains the indictment and judgment, but no exceptions settled and allowed as prescribed by sec. 7, chap. 117, General Statutes, the only question to be considered is, as to the sufficiency of the indictment to support the judgment.

Appeal from judgment of District Court, county of Dakota.

The defendants were indicted by the Grand Jury of Dakota county for lewdly and lasciviously cohabitating and associating together, not being married to each other. The cause was submitted to the court without a jury upon the following stipulation, "It is hereby stipulated by and between the defendant Leo. Miller and the state as follows:

First.—"That a jury trial is waived on part of the defendant.

Second.—That the defendant has and now does, and did at the time charged in the indictment live, cohabit and associate, with Mattie Strickland, at the county of Dakota, State of Minnesota, under and by virtue of a contract entered into by and between the defendant and said Mattie Strickland, (a copy of which is hereto attached.) That no marriage ceremony under the laws of the State of Minnesota, or any other State or Territory, has ever been performed; That they have never been married according to the laws of any state, and disclaim what is called a legal marriage.

Third.—That said cohabitation and association between said parties is a conscientious belief of each of them, and they claim the right thus to associate and cohabit under the constitution of the United States and State of Minnesota. which guarantees liberty of conscience to every citizen.

Fourth.—That the question of such right should be submitted to the court upon the foregoing statement, subject to the right of appeal."

The following is the contract referred to in the foregoing stipulation.

"Union—Civil and Conjugal—The undersigned this second day of November, A. D. 1875, enter into a business partnership under the name of Miller & Strickland on the following conditions, to-wit: That all earnings and profits arising from our individual and joint labors, whether in departments of literature, art, science, mechanics, agriculture or trade, shall be shared and held equally.

Believing that the divine principles of love drawing together two kindred souls, is the only binding law in the conjugal union of the sexes, and the only law making right such intimate relations, we are also happy to confess to each other, to God and His Angels and to all the world, the existence of a mutual affection known by that name; and we deliberately join heart and hand in this most sacred of all unions, hoping and praying that the tie that binds us may last through life and survive the grave.

Should this union be blessed by offspring, we jointly and severally pledge ourselves, our assigns and administrators, to foster and support them during the dependent years of infancy and youth, supplying their physical wants and rearing them in principles of virtue and knowledge to the best of our ability and judgment.

This simple form of conjugal union we are constrained to adopt from the deepest conscientious convictions of right and duty; and we sincerely regret that condition of society, which if we would be true to ourselves makes it necessary for us to oppose the opinions of a majority of our fellow creatures. Disregarding the laws and customs which they assume to make for the control of an affection between the sexes which we believe is, and of divine right ought to be, free.

Chicago, Ill., Nov. 2, 1875.

[Signed.] Leo.. Miller.

[Signed.] Mattie Strickland.

The court below found the defendant guilty as charged in the indictment.

Geo. P. Wilson, Att'y General, for state.

L. Van Slyck, attorney for appellants.

Cornell, J.—The question sought to be presented and argued by appellant is not properly before us for consideration. The return to the appeal contains no exceptions taken to "any opinion, direction or judgment" of the court below and settled, allowed and made a part of the judgment roll as prescribed by sec. 7, chap. 117 of the General Statutes.

Hence, the only question which can be considered upon the record before us is as to the sufficiency of the indictment to support the judgment.

As appellant makes no question of this character, and none is apparent to the court.

The judgment is affirmed.

Recent Decisions.

Pleading—Libel—Where plaintiff brings suit in a name that imports that it is a corporation, the fact that it is a corporation need not be avered. In an action of libel if the complaint avers that the libelous matter was printed and published, it is sufficient both at common law and under the code, and it is not necessary to set forth in detail the manner and extent of such publication.

Indianapolis Ins. Co. vs. Horrell, Sup. Ct. of Ind.

Promissory Note—Where a promissory note was executed by several persons in the usual form "we promise &c" and signed by them as "trustees of First Universalist Church." Held, not be an obligation of the church but of the individuals and that the designation as trustees was merely descriptive of these persons.

Hayes et. al. vs. Crutcher, Sup. Ct. of Ind.

Petition in Bankruptcy—In a petition of involuntary bankruptcy it is sufficient if the petition alleges upon belief, without averring information or knowledge, that the creditors joining therein constitute the requisite number.

In re-Mann, 14 Nat. B. Reg. 572.

Promissory Note—Illegal Consideration--A promissory note given for no other consideration than to aid in the suppression of a criminal prosecution is given for an illegal consideration, and this defense of illegally of the consideration may be asserted even where such note is under seal. And if it appears from plaintiffs own showing that the consideration was illegal, court may properly order a non suit.

Merrill vs. Goodenow, Sup. Ct. of Maine.

Garnishment—A failure on the part of a garnishee to appear on the return day after due notice, is an admission of assets; and a motion to vacate a judgment against him, entered upon such default made several terms after the same is entered, must be supported by clear proof of fraud, surprise or irregularity.

Sarlouis vs. Ins. Co., Garnishee, Sup. Ct. of Md. 1876.

Mechanics' Lien—A mechanics lien dates from the commencement of the structure and is paramount to a mortgage executed after the commencement of the structure, though before the particular work was done, or materials furnished, for which the lien is claimed.

Neilson vs R. R. Co., and Larrabee, et. al., Intervenors, Sup. Ct. of Iowa, Sept. 1876.

Injury While on Premises of Another.—A person who goes to the place of business of another not by invitation, is there at his own risk, and if he suffer damage in consequence of a mere negligent act on the part of the proprietor of the premises, he cannot recover.

Victory adm'r etc. vs. Baker, et. al., N. Y. Ct. of App'ls Nov. 1876.

Latest Publications.

Bishop's New Edition of Burrill on Assignments.—Adapted to the Laws of various States. With appendix of Forms. By Alexander M. Burrill. Third edition, revised and enlarged, by James L. Bishop, Counselor at Law. Royal 8 vo law sheep, 800 pp., $7 50

The Law of Mortgages of Real and Personal Property in the State of New York.—With an appendix of Forms. By Abner C. Thomas, 690 pp., law sheep, - - - - - - 6 00

Practice Pleading and Evidence in the Courts of California, in Civil Suits and Proceedings.—By E. F. Buttemer Harston. 8 vo 713 pp., sheep, 6 50

Hents Forms and Use of Blanks—By J. C. Bates. Second Ed. 8 vo 499 pp., sheep, - - - - - 6 50

Life and Accident Insurance Reports.—Cases decided in the courts of America, England, Scotland and Canada, down to Setember 1876, with notes and references. Vol. V. By Melville M. Bigelow, of the Boston Bar. 8 vo. law sheep, - - - - - 6 50

Civil Malpractice.—A treatise on Surgical Jurisprudence, with chapters on Skill in Diagnosis and Treatment, Prognosis in Fractures, and on Negligence. By Milo A. McClelland, M. D. 8 vo. Cloth $3.50, sheep, - 4 50

Story's Equity Jurispudence.—Twelth Ed. By Joseph Story, 2 vols. sheep, 15 00

Bishop's Commentaries on Criminal Law.—By J. P. Bishop. 6th Ed. 2 vols., - - - - - - - - 8 00

The Laws and Practice of Bankruptcy.—By Orlando F. Bump. New edition to January 1877. 8 vo. 1040 pp., law sheep - - - - - 7 50

National Bankruptcy Register Reports. —Vol. XIV. By O. F. Bump, 8 vo.. 600 pp., full sheep. - - - 6 00

Holmes' Circuit Court Reports.—Reports of cases determined in the Circuit Court of the United States for the First Circuit, from July, 1870, to June, 1875: by Jabez S. Holmes. 8vo, law sheep, - - - - - 7 00

THE SYLLABI.

VOL. 1. SATURDAY, MARCH 10, 1877. No. 21.

PUBLISHED WEEKLY,

By JOHN B. WEST & CO.,

No. 1 Wabasha St., - ST. PAUL, MINN.

Terms 3.00 per annum in Advance.

HOMER C. ELLER, Editor.

TABLE OF CONTENTS.

IN the case of *Uline, County Treasurer, vs. Humphreys.* before the District Court, Ramsey county, some time since, the question was fairly presented, as to the validity of tax upon credits secured by mortgage upon real estate, the real estate being already taxed to its full value as unencumbered, and the tax was by that court held valid.

It was claimed on the part of the creditor that taxation of the mortgage securities, as well as the land itself operated as double taxation, and was therefore void. Referring to the provisions of Section 3, Article IX of Constitution, which are as follows: "Laws shall be passed taxing all moneys, credits, investments in bonds, stocks, joint stock companies or otherwise, and also all real or personal property, according to its true value in money," The court says "It is evident that in the view of the framers of the constitution, to tax a credit in the hands of a creditor and to tax property in the hands of a debtor liable to be taken in satisfaction of the credit, is not double taxation. The creditor certainly has a valuable property, as valuable to him and as real as money or merchandise, or lands, * * and a law requiring the creditor to contribute to the public burden in proportion to the value of this property, can certainly work no injustice to him. Indeed any law which should in terms exempt such property would seem obnoxious to the provision of the Constitution requiring equality of taxation, without regard to the provisions of Section 3, which specifically includes credits. It may be true that when the debtor pays upon the full value of his property without regard to the amount of his indebtedness, and the creditor pays upon the value of his credits, the State receives taxes upon a value which does not in fact exist; but if any injustice is done it is not to the creditor, he pays no more taxes than he ought: that the debtor pays upon a fictitious value, is not a sufficient reason for relieving the creditor from payment upon a real value; he is not called upon to pay a double tax; he is not asked to pay upon property which is valueless or which he does not own. To exempt from taxation any citizen who chooses to hold his property in the shape of credits, is clearly unreasonable and unjust; it is discriminating in favor of the class most able to bear the burdens of taxation, and it would be clearly unconstitutional. * * *

In California, with a constitution like our own, it was held at first that debts secured by mortgage on real estate were taxable, and afterwards held that they were not.

In Illinois, where the constitutional provision is that the Legislature shall provide for levying a tax by valuation, so that every person shall pay a tax in proportion to the value of his property, it was held that such credits were properly taxable.

People vs. Worthington, 21 *Ill.* 171; see also 12 *Ill.* 138; 9 *Pa. St.* 361; *Bank vs. Augusta*, 36 *Me.* 255; *Ins. Co. Board of Assessors*, 56 *Mo.* 503.

SUPREME COURT, STATE OF MINNESOTA.

LEVI M. STEWART, *Appellant.*
vs.
EDGAR NASH, GROVE B. COOLEY, ED. J. DAVENPORT, L. T. N. WILSON, EUGENE M. WILSON and J. W. LAWRENCE, *Respondents,* } Feb'y 9,'77.

A complaint which alleges that on &c., at &c., the defendants, six in number, contriving and maliciously intending to injure plaintiff in his good name &c., and to bring him into public scandal and disgrace, and to cause him to be imprisoned, &c., wilfully and maliciously conspired together to cause plaintiff to be charged with, complained of, arrested and imprisoned, for the crime of perjury, without probable cause, as therein fully set forth; followed by proper averments showing that in pursuance of such conspiracy a criminal complaint charging such offense against plaintiff was made by one of the defendants before deft. C., then being a Municipal Judge, who issued a warrant thereon upon which plaintiff was arrested &c., and also showing that the other defendants named, did other acts in aid of the common purpose, to plaintiffs damage &c., states a cause of action.

For acts done in the exercise of judicial authority conferred, no Judge or officer can be held liable to any one in a civil action.

This immunity rests upon the principle that the free exercise of judicial functions uninfluenced by any fear of consequences personal to the officer, is essential to the best interests of society. In determining the character and effect of an allegation in a pleading, an admission claimed to have been made by counsel on the argument of the demurrer in the court below, but not of record, cannot be considered in this court.

A statement by the court in its opinion that such an admission was made, is insufficient to make it part of the record, so as to affect the pleading.

Appeal from an order of the Court of Common Pleas, county of Hennepin, sustaining the demurrer of Grove B. Cooley, Municipal Judge, to the complaint in the action.

This was an action brought by plaintiff against Cooley, Judge of Municipal Court of Minneapolis, Davenport, Clerk of said Court, and the other defendants, for maliciously and wilfully conspiring together to cause plaintiff to be charged with, complained of, and arrested, upon an alleged charge of perjury, the complaint upon which the warrant issued for the arrest of plaintiff was made by defendant Nash, before defendant Davenport as Clerk of said Court, and defendant Cooley, and the warrant was charged to have been, issued by defendants Davenport and Cooley.

D. A. Secombe, attorney for appellant.

Lochren, McNair & Gilfillan, attorneys for respondents.

CORNELL, J.—Eliminating from the complaint the averments, that defendants on &c., at &c., wilfully and maliciously conspired together to cause the said plaintiff to be charged with, complained of, arrested and imprisoned, for the crime of perjury as hereinafter set forth, and that in pursuance of the said conspiracy "the thereinafter recited acts were done," we find no difficulty whatever in agreeing with the court below that no cause of action is stated against the defendant Cooley.

The reception of the complaint, the issue of a warrant thereon, the decision upon its sufficiency, and refusal to discharge the prisoner from arrest; his subsequent omission to take any steps to procure the attendance of the prosecuting witness and dismissal of the action for want of prosecution; were all acts and omission done and omitted in his capacity as Judge, in the performance and discharge of judicial duties in a matter and proceeding clearly within the criminal jurisdiction of the Municipal Court of which he was Judge. No private action could be maintained upon any of these acts, decisions or omissions however erroneous they may have been or by whatever motives prompted. An independent judiciary is justly regarded as essential to the public welfare and the best interests of society.

Hence the doctrine has become settled that for acts done in the exercise of judicial authority clearly conferred, an officer or judge shall not be held liable to any one in a civil action, so that he may feel free to act upon his own convictions uninfluenced by any fear or apprehension of consequences personal to himself.

Gates vs. Lansing, 5 *I. R.* 282; 9 *Id.* 394. *Rochester White Lead Co. vs. City of Rochester,* 3 *Comst.* 464. *Stewart vs. Hawly.* 21 *Wend* 552. *Weaver vs. Deavendorf* 3 *Den.* 117. *Wilson vs. The Mayor, &c.,* 1 *Den.* 595. *Randall vs. Brigham,* 7 *Wall.* 523. *Bradley vs. Fisher,* 13 *Id.* 335.

While we are thus clear that none of the specific acts charged in the complaint, taken singly or together furnished any ground for a civil action or evidence sufficient to support the allegations of conspiracy in the complaint, we cannot concur with the court below in holding the conspiracy averments hereinbefore quoted as merely formal and immaterial allegations. Under them it would have been competent, on the trial to prove, that prior to the institution of the criminal proceedings the defendant Cooley and the other defendants met together and maliciously, and without probable cause actually entered into an agreement and conspiracy with each other to prosecute plaintiff for perjury for the sole purpose of bringing him into disgrace and subjecting him to arrest and imprisonment; and that each and all the acts charged to have been done by the defendants respectively, were done solely in pursuance of this agreement and to carry out this common purpose and not otherwise. It cannot be doubted that such a conspiracy previously formed and carried out by such a gross perversion and abuse of legal process and proceedings wonld subject all the parties engaged in it to liability to the party injured and aggrieved.

The act of entering into such an agreement was not done in the course of any judicial proceedings in the discharge of any judicial function or duty. In the opinion given by the court below in sustaining the demurrer, it is stated that though the complaint alleges that the parties conspired to do the wrongful acts complained of, "it was admitted on the trial that that was but a formal allegation," and that the action was in fact but for false imprisonment." We have no reason to doubt that such was the understanding of the court below, and the basis of its decision. We can only regret that the admission was not made a matter of record in the cause at the time, in such manner as to have operated as an amendment of the complaint, in conformity, with the admission. Inasmuch as this was not done and as counsel for appellant denies the admission in this court and insists upon the determination of the case upon the record before us, we can only look to the complaint and the demurrer, and not to the opinion, to ascertain whether a cause of action is stated or not. The demurrer should have been overruled.

Order appealed from reversed.

LEVI M. STEWART, *Appellant*, vs. ED. J. DAVENPORT, JAMES W. LAWRENCE and L. T. N. WILSON, Impleaded with others, *Respondents*, } Feb'y 8, '77.

Where no exception is taken to a decision dismissing an action on trial for want of evidence, the correctness of such decision cannot be inquired into, on a motion for a new trial, or on appeal from an order denying a new trial.

Appeal from an order of Court of Common Pleas, Hennepin county, denying motion for a new trial.

In this case, (which is the same elsewhere reported in this number, between same parties,) separate answers were put in by defendants, other than Cooley, and upon trial and at close of plaintiff case the suit as to E. M. Wilson was by plaintiff, and as to the other defendants on motion, dismissed. A motion for a new trial was then made upon the ground that the dismissal was not justified by the evidence and was contrary to law.

Lochren, McNair & Gilfillan, Atwater & Babcock and *James W. Lawrence*, attorneys for respondents.

D. A. Secombe, attorney for appellant.

CORNELL, J.—After plaintiff had introduced his testimony and rested his case, defendants moved for a dismissal of the action on the ground that there was not sufficient evidence to go to the jury showing or tending to show a cause of action against them. The motion was granted and no exception was taken.

A motion was subsequently made for a new trial because of this alleged erroneous ruling, not excepted to, and denied, and the case comes into this court on an appeal from this order.

An erroneous ruling of this character not excepted to at the time, cannot be made the subject of review on a motion for a new trial, or appeal from an order denying it.

Order appealed from affirmed.

THE STATE OF MINNESOTA, vs. ANDREW A. WESTON, } Feb'y 12, '77.

The writ of CERTIORARI, will not lie to remove to this court for review, an intermediate decision of the District Court in a criminal case, such decisions must be embraced in a bill of exceptions, when the defendant may bring them before this court for review only by writ of error upon the judgment, or appeal from the judgment, or order denying a new trial.

Certiorari to District Court, county of Blue Earth.

A. R. Pfau and M. J. Severance, attorneys for state.

Waite & Freeman and Brown & Wiswell, attorneys for defendant.

GILFILLAN, C. J.—The defendant was indicted for the crime of murder. In the court below he made an application upon affidavits for an order changing the venue.

This application was denied, whereupon he sued out a writ of *certiorari* to remove the proceedings to this court, for review. A return having been made and the matter coming on for argument in this court, we are met by the preliminary question, will a writ of *certiorari* lie to remove to this court for review, an intermediate order or decision of the District Court in a criminal case?

The statute regulating the removal of causes for review, provides for removal of a criminal case at the instance of the defendant to this court for review.

First.—By writ of error upon the judgment.

Second.—By appeal from the judgment, or from an order denying a new trial.

Sec. 1 Ch. 117, Gen. Statutes as amended by the act of March 8. 1870, provides: "Criminal cases may be removed by the defendant to the Supreme Court by appeal or writ of error at any time within six months after judgment, or after the decision of a motion denying a new trial."

Sec. 6, of the same chap. as amended by the same act provides: "Any person who is convicted of a crime before the District Court or Court of Common Pleas aforesaid, being aggrieved by any opinion, direction or judgment of the court in any matter of law may allege exceptions to such opinion, direction or judgment; which exceptions being reduced to writing in a summary manner and presented to the court any time before the end of the term, or at any special term thereafter which the court may designate for that purpose, and being found conformable to the truth of the case, shall be allowed and signed by the Judge, and may be used on a motion for a new trial, and when judgment is rendered, shall be attached to and become a part of the judgment roll." These two sections wherever they apply, exclude any other mode for thedefendant to remove a judgment, or order denying a new trial, to this court for review. Sec. 6, provides for presenting to this court on such removal to it of a criminal case any decision of the court below, final or intermediate made in the progress of the case, it must be concluded that such questions can be presented only in the mode prescribed. We can review the decisions of the District Court only when they are thus brought before us,

The statute authorizing this court to issue writs of *certiorari*, does not affect the case. That power can be exercised by the court when that writ is the proper mode of removal and in no other case.

The writ is dismissed.

S. CORNELIA ANDREWS, *Respondent*, *vs.* THE TOWN OF MARION IN OLMSTED CO., MINN., *Appellant*, } Feb'y —,'77.

Under ch. 5, laws of 1873, relating to roads, cartways and bridges, a notice of appeal to the District Court from an order laying out a road and assessing damages, need not state that the party appealing has filed the application and bond required by the act to perfect the appeal. The act does not allow costs to the successful party on an appeal from the order of the Commissioners or Supervisors to the District Court.

Appeal from judgment of District Court, county of Olmsted.

Chas. C. Wilson, att'y for appellant.

Start & Gove, att'ys for respondent.

GILFILLAN, C. J.—This case came into the District Court by appeal by this plaintiff from the order of the supervisors of the town of Marion, laying out a road over the land of plaintiff, and assessing her damages therefor under ch. 5, Laws of 1873. A motion was made by the Town in the District Court to dismiss the appeal on the ground that the notice of appeal merely stated that the party had appealed from an order, (describing it,) to the District Court, without stating the other acts necessary to be done to make an appeal, to-wit: The filing an application and bond as prescribed by the act.

The motion was denied correctly. Notice that a party has appealed, is, unless the statute requires further specification, in effect, notice that the party has done whatever was necessary to make the appeal effectual.

On the trial in the District Court the damages were largely increased and the court below allowed the appellant, there, the costs of the appeal which were entered in the judgment.

In this we think the court below was wrong. The proceeding even on appeal, is not a civil action so as to be groverned by the statute prescribing costs in such action. It is a special proceeding controlled by the statute establishing it. This act, sec's 60 and 61 provides for costs on an appeal, to a Justice of the Peace, but section 62, which relates to appeals to the District Court, is entirely silent on the subject of costs; and as it does not provide for costs on such appeal, none can be recovered. It is undoubtedly a defect in the statute but the court cannot supply the omission.

The judgment must be modified by deducting the amount allowed for costs, and the case will be remanded for that purpose.

WILLIAM A. MERRIAM, *Respondent*, *vs.* THE PINE CITY LUMBER CO., *Appellaut.* } Feb'y 6, '77.

Whenever the evidence adduced in reference to any material fact in controversy is sufficient fairly to raise an issue proper for the consideration of the jury, it should be submitted to them, and their decision thereon is final.

Whether in the giving of certain notes by defendant to plaintiff, a certain claim for stumpage was taken into account by them or not cannot be established or disproved by evidence showing the secret intention or understanding of one, of the parties to the notes.

An error committed in overruling a question put to a witness is cured if the witness subsequently by permission testifies fully in regard to the subject of such inquiry.

Upon the breach of a valid promise to pay his debt to a third party such promisee may maintain an action against the promisor without first paying the debt himself. The measure of damages in such case is the amount of the debt agreed to be paid. A defective pleading, clearly amendable in the discretion of the trial court, cannot be taken advantage of in this court by a party who had an opportunity to make his objection to it in the court below, but omitted so to do. In determining the meaning and probable effect upon the jury of a modification by the court of any specific request asked by either party, reference will be had to the entire charge as given upon the subject. A party is liable for an injury occasioned to another by a false statement, the truth of which he positively affirms, when made with intent to deceive and under circumstances inducing a belief in its truth, whether such statement is understood to be made upon personal knowledge or upon information derived from others; otherwise however, if such statement be but the expression of a belief, founded upon information and without any such fraudulent intent.

Appeal from an order of the District Court, county of Hennepin, denying motion for a new trial.

This was an action brought to recover for 1,616,606 feet of logs sold and delivered to the defendant in the spring of 1873, at the agreed price of $7.25 per thousand feet.

The complaint contained five causes of action four of which were based upon four promissory notes of defendant payable to the plaintiff bearing date in Feb'y and April 1874, and amounting in the aggregate to the sum of $4018.75, dollars besides interest and given in part payment for the logs. The remaining cause of action, treating these notes as payments on account of the logs purchased, was for the balance $4041.50 claimed to be due on the original contract.

The defense relied upon was damages sustained by the defendant in consequence of certain false and fraudulent representations made to its agent in regard to the location of the logs and the condition of the dams in the stream where they were landed. It was claimed that these representations induced defendant to make the purchase and that by reason of their falsity it was greatly delayed and put to great additional expense, in getting said logs down the stream. It was also insisted that as the stumpage for these logs, was agreed by defendant to be paid for, by it, to the state, as part of the purchase price of the same, that the defendant was liable to the state for the amount thereof, and though the defendant had not as yet paid the same, the plaintiff had no right to recover that portion of the price. On the part of plaintiffs it was claimed that the representation as to the location of the logs was only as to their approximate location and in that view was not absolutely false, that defendant had waived its right to damages; and the promissory notes given after the transaction and after the logs had in fact been got out of the stream was for the entire balance of the purchase price, less the amount of stumpage, to be paid by defendant. Defendant offered to show that at time of giving these notes it intended to reserve enough from original purchase price to cover the amount of its damages sustained which offer was rejected.

The jury found a verdict in favor of the plaintiff for the full amount claimed.

Lochren, McNair & Gilfillan, attorney for respondent.

Geo. L. & Chas. E. Otis, and George Bradley, att'ys for appellant.

CORNELL, J.— I.—Upon a careful examination of the whole evidence; we are satisfied no such clear case is presented, of an insufficiency in the evidence to support the verdict, as brings this case within the rule governing this court in granting a new trial upon that ground.

Upon each material fact controverted on the trial, there was sufficient in the nature and character of the testimony and evidence adduced, fairly to raise an issue proper for the consideration of the jury, and its decision thereon is final.

II.—The question referred to in appellants

second point was objectionable in that it called for the secret intention and understanding of the party in giving the notes instead of the facts and circumstances connected with the transaction. As to the ruling referred to in his third point, the error, if any, was cured by the subsequent testimony of the witness, which substantially answered the inquiry made of him by the question which was excluded under the objection.

Sanborn vs. Sturtevant, et. als., 17 *Minn.* 200.

III.—It is admitted by the pleadings, and was neither controverted nor sought to be by either party, at the trial, that at the time the agreement sued on was entered into between plaintiff and defendant, the former was indebted to the state in a certain sum for stumpage on the logs so sold by him to defendant, and that as part of the stipulated purchase price, defendant by the terms of the agreement promised the plaintiff to pay the amount of his said debt to the state within a specified time therein named, and though such time of payment had passed, the debt had not been paid by either party, but remained due and unpaid, when the action was brought. Upon these facts it was claimed by the defendant in his answer, and insisted on at the trial as a defense, that the plaintiff could maintain no action upon a breach of this stipulation of the defendant, until he had first paid the debt himself; because under the rule laid by this court in *Sanders et. al. vs. Classon*, 13 *Minn. R.* 379, the defendant was legally holden to the state upon such, his promise to the plaintiff: The refusal of the court so to charge the jury upon this branch of the case is assigned as error in this court. The defendants undertaking was not one of indemnity; It was an affirmative unconditional promise to the plaintiff upon a valid consideration to pay within a specified time a definite sum of money to a third party, the State, for his benefit. Though within the doctrine of the New York cases upon this subject as well as our own, the state might have maintained an action against defendant upon a breach of his agreement, it is well settled both upon principle and authority that he also remained liable to plaintiff upon his promise by priorty of contract, and a cause of action accrued in favor of the latter, which become complete immediately upon its breach, by the failure of the defendant to make the payment at the stipulated time. It is not necessary for the promisee in such a case to discharge the debt before asserting his right of action against the promissor growing out of the breach of his own agreement. The measure of damages in a case of this kind is the amount of the debt agreed to be paid. The ruling of the court below therefor upon this subject was correct.

Port vs. Jackson, 17 *John R.* 239.
Jackson vs. Port, " " 479.
Matter of Negus, 7 *Wend.* 499.
Thomas vs. Allen, 1 *Hill* 145.
Churchill vs. Hunt, 3 *Den.* 321.
Wicker vs. Happock. 6 *Wall.* 99.

The point is made in this court, and for the first time in the case, as appears from the record before us, that plaintiff cannot sustain a recovery for this breach of his stipulation in this action because of the insufficiency of the averments in the complaint. Conceding that the defect, complained of, was of a material character and not cured by the admissions in the answer, which may be well doubted, under the decisions of this court in the cases of *Farnham vs. Estes*, 11 *Minn.* 423, and *Rollins vs. St. Paul Lumber Co.*, 21 *Minn.* 6, clearly to take advantage of it here as good ground of error, defendant should have pointed out and obtained a ruling upon it in the District Court.

In view of the admissions in the answer, it was properly a matter where, in the exercise of a sound discretion, an amendment of the complaint might have been allowed, remedying the defect complained of; instead of this, however, the trial was conducted without objection, upon the theory that the matters in controversy between the parties were properly put in issue by the pleadings, and no suggestion was made of any departure in pleading, or of any variance between the contract set up in the complaint and that proved upon the trial. Having tried the case upon this theory, defendant will not be permitted to take a different one here, when it is apparent it might have been successfully met by the opposite party, had his attention been called to it in the District Court.

IV.—No point is made in this court but that the law upon the subject of false and fraudulent representation, as applicable to the evidence, was correctly given in its general charge to the jury, and in our opinion it fully covered the case. In the light of this charge the jury could not have been misled by the modification of defendant's third request, to believe that the false representations positively made with intent to deceive, would not, when relied and acted upon, constitute good ground of action, even though not made upon personal knowledge.

The purport of the language made use of by the court in explaining and giving to the jury defendant's fourth request was, that the proposition therein contained was correct as confined to representations positively or unqualifiedly made, and that defendant had the right to rely upon them unless he had the means of knowledge to the contrary then in his possession or at hand and available;—as thus understood it was not objectionable.

The second request of plaintiff, as modified by the court, involved no legal error, and there was some evidence in the case in view of which it was properly given.

If plaintiff's alleged misrepresentations in regard to the situation of the logs and the condition of the dams were positively and fraudulently made, under circumstances inducing a belief in their truth by defendant, then plaintiff was responsible for any injury occasioned thereby, whether such statements were understood as made upon information derived from others or from his personal knowledge; otherwise, however, if they were not so made, but made under circumstances indicating only the expression of a belief on the part of the plaintiff, founded upon information alone, and with no intention to decieve nor to vouch for the correctness of such belief. The character of the statement and the circumstances under which they were made were matters for the consideration and determination of the jury. The fair purport and meaning of plaintiff's fourth request, as modifiedby the court, were not, considered, in connection with the whole charge, at variance with these views, and did not, in our opinion, mislead the jury. No error is presented by any of the exceptions taken, for which a new trial should be granted.

Order appealed from affirmed.

———:o:———

Recent Decisions.

Estoppel—Where a contract is entered into with mutual covenants and advantages, a party enjoying those advantages such as they may be, will not be permitted to avoid the contract by a plea that it is ultra vires.

Oil Creek & Alleghany R. R. Co. vs. Penn. Transporportation Co., Sup. Ct. of Pa. 7 Pitts. Legal Jr., p. 111.

Power of Court over Records.—A court of general jurisdiction has power after lapse of time, and where rights have not been acquired that will be injuriously affected thereby, to correct its own actual mistakes, and omissions of its clerks in making up the record.

Low vs. Kennedy, Sup. Ct. of Pa.

Bona Fide Holder.—A purchaser of negotiable papers who takes the same in the usual course of business, before maturity, for a valuable consideration and without knowledge of facts or circumstances that would impeach its validity between antecedent parties, holds it by a good title; and to defeat a recovery thereon it is not sufficient to show that he took it under circumstances that ought to have excited suspicion in the mind of a prudent man, but it must be shown that he took it under circumstances showing bad faith or want of honesty on his part.

Johnson vs. Way, Sup. Ct. of Ohio.

Destruction of Deed.—The destruction or cancellation of a deed after execution and delivery will not operate to divest the title of grantee therein or revest the same in grantor. And this is so as well in cases of "assignments for the benefit of creditors made under statute" as in cases of ordinary conveyance.

Alpaugh vs. Robertson, et. al., Sup. Ct. of N. Jersey.

Eminent Domain.—Incident to the power of eminent domain is the right to abandon the project and the property condemned at any time before actual payment or tender of compensation. The title does not pass until such payment or tender. When the amount of compensation has been settled either by commissioners or on appeal, it must be paid, or the enterprise abandoned and all loss to the owner resulting from subsequent delays may be recovered from the corporation.

Norris vs. Mayor, &c., Baltimore, Sup. Ct. of Appeals of Maryland, 1876.

Misrepresentation.—Where a vendor undertakes to point out to a purchaser the corners and boundaries of land proposed to be sold, he is bound to point them out correctly; and if he fails so to do he is liable for the damages sustained by reason of such misrepresentation; and it is not necessary in such case to show that the misrepresentation was made with fraudulent intent.

Bird vs. Kleiner, Sup. Ct. of Wis. Feb'y 1877.

Contributory Negligence.—In an action against a city for damages sustained in consequence of defective sidewalk, Held, that in the absence of evidence tending to show contributory negligence, the presumption of law was that plaintiff was free from it, and the burden of proofis on the defendant. Where however the evidence of plaintiff tends to show contributory negligence, this presumption does not exist, and he must go on and show thas he exercised due care.

Hoyt vs. City of Hudson, Sup. Ct. of Wis. Feb. 1877.

Promissory Note—Indorsor.—A promise of an indorser to pay the note, made after maturity, with knowledge that the holder has failed to make demand and give notice of nonpayment is a waiver, of the necessity of such demand and notice; and a statement made by such indorser to the holder after the note falls due, to the effect that he is responsible, for it, is in effect a promise to pay it.

An indorsement in blank by payee, makes the same payable to transferee not as indorser but as bearer, and the fact, that the transferee subsequently re-assigns the same to payee, who then delivers it to a third person does not change the rule.

Curtis v. Sprague, Sup. Ct. of Cal.

Latest Publications.

Burrill on Assignments.—A treatise on the Law and Practice of Voluntary Assignments for the Benefit of Creditors. Adapted to the laws of various States; with an Appendix of Forms; by Alexander M. Burrill. 3d edition, revised, annotated and largely rewritten by James L. Bishop, of the New York Bar. 8vo., 800 pp., Sheep 6 50

Institutes of Common and Statute Law. By John B. Minor, L. L. D., Professor of Common and Statute Law in the Uuiversity of Virginia. 2d Ed. 2 vols. 8vo., 672, 1098 pp., Sheep, 17 00

Story's Equity Jurispudence.—Twelth Ed. By Joseph Story, 2 vols. sheep, 15 00

The Laws and Practice of Bankruptcy.—By Orlando F. Bump. New edition to January 1877. 8 vo. 1040 pp., law sheep - - - - - 7 50

The Law of Mortgages of Real and Personal Property in the State of New York.—With an appendix of Forms. By Abner C. Thomas, 690 pp., law sheep, - - - - - - 6 00

Practice Pleading and Evidence in the Courts of California, in Civil Suits and Proceedings.—By E. F. Buttemer Harston. 8 vo 713 pp., sheep, 6 50

Hents Forms and Use of Blanks—By J. C. Bates. Second Ed. 8 vo 499 pp., sheep, - - - - - 6 50

Life and Accident Insurance Reports.—Cases decided in the courts of America, England, Scotland and Canada, down to Setember 1876, with notes and references. Vol. V. By Melville M. Bigelow, of the Boston Bar. 8 vo. law sheep, - - - - - - 6 50

Civil Malpractice.—A treatise on Surgical Jurisprudence, with chapters on Skill in Diagnosis and Treatment, Prognosis in Fractures, and on Negligence. By Milo A. McClelland, M. D. 8 vo. Cloth $3.50, sheep, - 4 50

Bishop's Commentaries on Criminal Law.—By J. P. Bishop. 6th Ed. 2 vols., 8vo. - - - - - 12 00

Shaw's Index to Minn. Session Laws, 1849–1875. Full Sheep, - - 4 00

// THE SYLLABI.

VOL. 1. SATURDAY, MARCH 17, 1877. No. 22.

PUBLISHED WEEKLY,

By JOHN B. WEST & CO.,

No. 1 Wabasha St., - ST. PAUL, MINN

Terms 3.00 per annum in Advance.

HOMER C. ELLER, Editor.

TABLE OF CONTENTS.

THE Supreme Judicial Court of Massachusetts, has just rendered a decision under which one Foster, sentenced to State's Prison for ten years for forgery, was released, after three years confinement. Foster's method of conducting his operations was peculiar. He was in the habit of getting men of no pecuniary means, but whose names were identical with or similar to those of business men of wealth and credit, to sign their name to notes and then to pass them as the notes of the business men. It was contended on the trial that this was not forgery, but the Court held (114 *Mass.* 311—*S. C.* 19 *Am. Rep.* 353.) that it was. Two of these notes described in the indictment were payable to the order of drawers and one to the order of Foster. *In Commonwealth, vs. Dallinger*, 118 *Mass.* 439 the Court held, an instrument purporting to be signed by I. S. payable to the order of the same I. S., not a promissory note, until endorsed, and the indictment for forgery which charges in separate counts, the making and uttering of such a promissory note, without setting out the endorsement, bad. The indictment in Foster's case did not mention the indorsements and the Court, held for that reason the conviction erroneous.—(*Al. Law Jr.*)

TYLER on Fixtures. By Ransom H. Tyler. Published by Wm. Gould & Son, Albany, N. Y. For sale by JOHN B. WEST, & Co., St. Paul, Minn. 1 vol., 768 p., - $7.50

FOR years the want of more full and complete work upon this important topic has been much felt. The little work of Mr. Hills heretofore almost the only one accessible, while very valuable was almost too meagre in detail to be entirely satisfactory, and the growing importance of the subject especially in our larger cities where so much machinery and so many buildings and other improvements are erected upon leased premises, together with the new questions arising in connection therewith, has made such a work almost a necessity; The need in this respect is ably supplied in this work of Mr. Tyler; It does not purport to be a philosophical treatise, but a full collection of the rules of law applicable to the subject, gathered from adjudicated cases and clearly and systematicaly arranged, and is not the less useful for copious quotations from the opinions of the court in the more important cases giving as it does in such instances not the authors version alone of what was decided or what rule was laid down, but the language of the court itself.

THE *quo warranto* proceedings instituted in the Supreme Court, against J. L. MacDonald as Judge of the 8th Judicial District came up before that body on 13th inst., the return day of the writ, when an answer was filed by the respondent, and a reference ordered to the clerk, to take and report the testimony to be presented. The hearing on the merits being fixed as the first case at April General Term. Brown the relator, and former incumbent claims to be entitled to the office upon the ground of MacDonald's alienage, and the principal question attempted to be raised is whether he has been properly naturalized; The case involves some interesting, as well as important, questions in regard to the practice commonly followed in the naturalization of foreign born citizens.

NOVA SCOTIA has just awakened to a realization of the fact that for eight years last past, all public acts requiring the great seal are absolutely void, a wrong seal having been in use during all that period. The province is thus left without a government, with all marriages consumated during that period void, as well as all commissions issued; A state of affairs that will require an act of parliament to remedy.

THE time allowed to members of the electoral commission to prepare and file opinions was at their last meeting held on the 2d inst., extended to March 31st.

A NATIVE of Japan, Eneas Yamada by name, was recently admitted to the bar of the Supreme Court of New York.

———:‡o‡:———

SUPREME COURT, STATE OF MINNESOTA.

AUGUST ANDERSON, *Appellant*,
vs.
R. H. VOSBERG, *Respondent*, } Feb'y 8, 77.

A contract between defendant of the first part, and B. of the second part, purported to provide for the purchase by defendant, and sale, transfer and assignment to him by B. of his, (B's) right, title, interest and claim whatsoever, of the property connected with the Nicollet House, as follows, to-wit: Then followed thirteen, specifications of property to be transferred and then the following: "14th. All contracts for Hotel supplies so far as the same are binding on the party of the second part to be assumed and fullfilled by the party of the first part, and all advances made on the same to be paid to the party of the second part."

15th. The contract for farm supplies to remain in force and to be continued during the term of hotel lease, provided said supplies are as good as have been furnished, and the milk, pure and unadulterated. The milk for the six months to-wit: April, May, June, July, August and September, to be delivered twice a day if so required, to keep the same from souring, at the price of twenty cents per gallon, and during the remainder of the year to be delivered once a day unless the roads are in such a condition that the same are impassable, and in that event the party of the second part, to use all due diligence to deliver the same. The price of the last six months to be twenty-five cents per gallon. And all other supplies, as well as milk shall be taken from the said party of the second, as far as the same are required for the hotel, at such time and in such quantities and upon such prices as may be agreed upon, and if said parties fail to agree upon any price, then at the market price for such supplies at the time the same are delivered."

In regard to the milk and other supplies, the same to be delivered in such quantities as may be ordered, the night before. Settlement and payment, for said supply to be made monthly." HELD, not to be a contract by which B. agreed to furnish, and defendant to receive during the term of the hotel lease all the milk required at the hotel

Appeal from an order of Court of Common Pleas, county of Hennepin, denying motion for a new trial.

Lowrey & Wilson and *C. J. Bartleson*, atty's for appellant.

Bradley & Morrison, att'ys for respondent.

GILFILLAN, C. J.—The complaint alleges that April 1st, 1874, the defendant was lessee of the Nicollet House in Minneapolis, under a lease for the term of five years, from June 1st, 1873, renewable for the further term of five years at the option of the lessee and that on said April 1st, 1874, defendant entered into a contract in writing with one G. A. Burbank, by which it was agreed that during the term of said lease Burbank should furnish and defendant pay for, at certain agreed prices monthly, all milk required for use at the hotel.

That this contract was with defendants consent assigned by Burbank to plaintiff, who entered upon the performance thereof and continued to furnish said milk till about Sept. 1st, 1874, when def't refused to receive milk any further or pay therefor to the great damage of plaintiff &c. It alleges readiness by plaintiff at all times to perform on his part.

The answer denies this contract. On the trial the plaintiff offered in evidence a contract between Burbank and defendant for the purchase, sale, transfer and assignment of his (Burbank's) right, title, interest and claim whatever of the property connected with the Nicollet House within the aforesaid city as follows, to-wit: "Then follows thirteen clauses specifying different kinds or clauses of property and then the following:

14th. All contracts for hotel supplies so far as the same are binding on the party of the second part, (said Burbank,) to be assumed and fulfilled by the party of the first part, (the defendant,) and all advances made on the same to be paid to the party of the second part.

15th. The contract for farm supplies to remain in force during the term of hotel lease, provided said supplies are as good as have been furnished and the milk pure and unadulterated. The milk for the six months to-wit: April, May, June, July, August and September, to be delivered twice a day if so required to keep the same from souring, at the price of twenty cents per gallon;

And during the remainder of the year to be delivered once a day, unless the roads are in such condition that the same are impassable and in that event the party of the second part to use all due diligence to deliver the same. The price for the last six months to be twenty-five cents per gallon and all other supplies as well as milk shall be taken, from the said party of the second part, as far as the same are required for the hotel, at such time and in such quantities and upon such prices as may be agreed upon, and if said parties fail to agree upon any price, then at the market price for such supplies, at the time the same are delivered. In regard to the milk and other supplies the same to be delivered in such quantities, as may be ordered the night before. Settlement and payment for said supplies to be made monthly."

This evidence was objected to as incompetent, immaterial and irrelevant to the issues in the case under the pleadings therein, and was excluded. This contract appears to be the one intended by the complaint; whether standing alone it is such a contract is the only question to be considered. It does not appear that any extrinsic facts or circumstances, in view of which the contract can be construed, were proved or offered to be proved. Had it been the purpose of the parties in their use of language to obscure their meaning they could hardly have made a more effective arrangement of it. It is claimed by plaintiff that the language quoted shows an agreement by Burbank to furnish and defendant to receive during the lease all the milk needed for the Hotel, the defendant claims that the language can be construed only as referring to some real or supposed pre-existing contract and that the intention was to transfer it to defendant to be performed by him on conditions stated. And we think the entire language points more to the latter than the former meaning. It is true the statement as to how the milk shall be delivered, the price stated, the requirement in a certain contingency of due diligence on the part of Burbank to deliver it, and the stipulation as to when settlements shall be made, and the other words, "all other supplies as well as milk shall be taken from the said party of the second part, as far as the same are required for the hotel," indicate an original contract, on the other hand the quantity of milk as that it should be all that might be needed for use at the hotel is not expressly stated, as would be expected in an original contract. There is no clearly expressed promise to furnish and receive the milk as between these parties. The first part of the 15th clause and the whole of the 14th which has some bearing on the meaning of the fifteenth, clearly indicate existing contracts, to be transferred to, and assumed and fulfilled by, defendant, rather than a new contract. The 14th clause reads, "All contracts for hotel supplies so far as the same are binding on the party of the second part to be assumed and fulfilled by the party of the first part, and all advances on the same to be paid to the party of second part.

This language is clear and can refer to nothing but pre-existing contracts and advances made upon them. The first sentence of the 15th clause is the contract for farm supplies to remain in force and be continued during the term of the Hotel lease, provided said supplies are as good as have been furnished and the milk pure and unadulterated." This clearly indicates a pre-existing contract for farm supplies, including milk, which is to remain in force and be continued; provided &c. Then follow stipulations as to how such contract should be carried out, which may or may not change, the obligation that would attach to defendant upon an unqualified transfer to, and assumption by, him of the existing contract.

On the whole we conclude though it is with some doubts, that clause 14 was intended to provide for a transfer to defendant of all binding contracts for hotel supplies including farm supplies and for an assumption by him of Burbank's obligations upon such, contracts and that clause 15 was intended to qualify in some measure defendant Burbank's obligation to fulfill the contract for farm supplies.

The decision of the court below was therefore correct, and the order appealed from is affirmed.

SIMON A. EVANS, *Respondent*, *vs.* THE TOWN OF STANTON, *Appellant*, } Feb'y 13, '77.

The Commissioners of Goodhue county appropriated $200 to the construction of a certain bridge, and directed county orders for the amount to be issued on the order of the chairman of the board of supervisors of the town of Stanton, in which the bridge was constructed.

The town of Stanton at its annual town meeting voted to raise $700, for roads and bridges, especially for the bridge mentioned by the county commissioners and another.

After these appropriations the town entered into a contract with the plaintiff to construct the bridges for the price of $900, to be paid in town and county orders.

Held, that as the parties are presumed to have contracted with reference to the two appropriations, and that the town and county orders mentioned in the contract were those at the disposal of the town under such appropriation, the contract was not one incurring a town debt or making an expenditure of town funds to to a greater amount than was voted at the town meeting, and the contract was therefore valid. The contract provided that one of the bridges should be accepted by the board of county commissioners.

Held, That as the acceptance of the bridge would naturally come within the duties of a committee on roads and bridges appointed by the county commissioners, the act of the committee in accepting the bridge would be PRIMA FACIE the act of the commissioners, and proof of acceptance by a majority of the committee, was proper.

Appeal from an order of the District Court, county of Goodhue, denying defendant's motion for a new trial.

C. McClure with *J. C. McClure*, att'ys for appellant.

Williston & Hall, attorneys for respdt.

Gilfillan, C J.—It appears from the evidence in this case that on the 9th day of March, 1869, the board of county commissioners of the county of Goodhue, in which county defendant town is situate, by resolution changed an appropriation of $200 previously made by the board for a bridge at one place so as to be expended for a bridge at another place, and instructed the County Auditor to issue orders to the amount of said appropriation upon the order of the chairman of the board of supervisors of defendant. On April 6th, following, at the annual town meeting of the defendant, it was voted to raise $700 for roads and bridges especially for two designated bridges, one of them the bridge mentioned in the resolution of the board of county commissioners, said money to be applied at the discretion of the supervisors.

On the 19th of October, following, the town entered into a contract with plaintiff, by which plaintiff agreed to build the two bridges, and the town to pay him therefor $900 in town and county orders, the work to be accepted by the board of supervisors, and one of the bridges, (that mentioned in the resolution of the county commissioners) by the board of county commissioners.

It appears that the county orders were issued and paid to plaintiff on his contract and other payments made, which with the county orders left a balance of the contract price of $216.66 to recover which this suit is brought.

The first and important question in the case is, was the contract valid? It is claimed that the defendant's board of supervisors had no authority to bind the town by a contract to pay for building these bridges, any greater sum than $700, that being the amount voted at the preceding annual town meeting to be expended upon roads and bridges. The proposition is made, that no town can contract a debt for any one year for a specified purpose in any larger sum than the amount of taxes assessed for such year, for such purposes. The assessment for township purposes is based upon the vote at the town meeting. Under ch. 10, Gen. Statutes and ch. 22, laws of 1869, we are inclined to think that is correct and if there was nothing appearing *aliunde* the contract but the vote of the town, we do not see how the contract could be upheld.

The contract however is not void upon its face. It is necessary to prove matters outside to avoid it, and it was competent to show outside matters to sustain it. It was proper also to show the subject matters of the contract, and the circumstances connected with them so that the court in construing the contract may stand as nearly as possible in the position of the parties when they made it. The parties must be assumed to have contracted with reference to those circumstances. The contract by express terms provides for payment, not in money' but in county orders and town orders. It indicates that there are county as well as town orders which the town has the right to use, and which it agrees to use in the work contracted for, what these county orders were, was open for proof, just as is the identification of a subject matter in any contract. The statute prohibits the creation of a town debt, or the expenditure of town money to a greater amount than the assessment for the year. The application by the town, of a county fund, to the to the purposes for which it was appropriated by the commissioners, and the application of which was intrusted to the town would not come within the appropriation. It appears then that at the time the contract was made there were by appropriation of the county commissioners $200 in county orders at the disposal of the town for building these bridges and it does not appear that there were any other county orders at its disposal. Also, that for the same purpose there was at its disposal by the appropriation of the town meeting the sum of $700. Now that the parties must be presumed to have contracted with reference to these facts, and that the county and town orders mentioned in the contract were those at the disposal of the town under these two appropriations cannot be doubted. The county appropriation is indicated by the addenda to the contract providing that one of the bridges, the one for which the county had appropriated $200 of its orders should be accepted by the county commissioners. The contract being then in effect to pay to the plaintiff the amount of the two appropriations in the orders of the county and town respectively, and to pay $900 out of funds raised or to be raised by the town, it is not obnoxious to the objection made to it. The charge of the court below on this point being in accordance with the views we have expressed was correct.

The point that the breach of the contract set up in the answer is a counter-claim is not well taken. The breach was not pleaded as a counter-claim, but only as a defense.

Proof that the bridge which by the contract was to be accepted by the board of county commissionerrs, had been accepted by a majority of the committee on roads and bridges, of the board of county commissioners was proper. Such acts would naturally come within the duties of such a committee and its act would be *prima facie* the act of the board.

Proof that the bridges have stood and been used since their construction was proper; not for the purpose of proving acceptance but as having some bearing upon the answer and testimony on the part of defendant the bridges were constructed in an unworkmanlike manner and of bad materials.

The order is affirmed.

LUCY H. GILL, *Respondent*, vs. THE McLEOD CO. CHEESE MANUFACTUING ASSOCIATION, WILLIAM C. RUSSELL and HARRISON, ROSE & Co., *Appellants*, — Feb'y 12, '77.

Upon the hearing of a case upon evidence taken and reported by a Referee appointed for that purpose alone, a party desiring to avail himself of any objection interposed before the referee, must renew it, and obtain a ruling thereon by the court, and if adverse, take an exception.

B. a corporation duly executed to plaintiff a real estate mortgage for valuable consideration which through mutual mistake of parties, misdescribed the premises intended and agreed to be mortgaged. Plaintiff caused the mortgage to be duly recorded. R. one of the directors, who participated in the giving of the mortgage and in the mistake, afterwards obtained a judgment against the corporation and duly docketed the same so as to make it a lien upon the premises, before the discovery of the error. In an action by plaintiff against the corporation and R. to correct the error and to foreclose his mortgage as a prior lien to R's judgment.

HELD, That R. is estopped from contesting the relief sought.

A party will not be permitted to make use of the Registry act as an instrument of fraud.

Appeal from judgment of District Court, county of McLeod.

H. J. Peck, att'y for respondent.

Baxter & Child, att'ys for appel't Russell.

CORNELL, J.—It appears from the settled case that this cause was tried before Hon. F. M. Crosby, Judge of the District Court, upon the pleadings and evidence, taken and reported to the court by a Referee, appointed for that purpose.

The report shows that whenever any question was put or evidence offered by either party, which was objected to by the opposite party, the objection was noted and overruled as well as the exceptions, if any, and the testimony was received. Undoubtedly the correct practice in such cases is for the Referee to note the objections and receive the testimony subject thereto, and if the party making an objection desires to insist upon it he should renew it after the report of the Referee, and upon the introduction of the evidence to the court, obtain a ruling upon it and take his exception. If he omits to do this he will be deemed to have waived his objection.

Dartnell vs. Davidson, 16 *Minn.* 530. It does not appear that any of the objections interposed to any of the testimony taken before the Referee in this case was ever brought to the notice of the court or any decision obtained thereon to which any exception was taken.

Hence no question is properly before us in regard to the admissibility of evidence.

The point made by appellant that the court below erred in overruling the defendant's objections to the amendment of the complaint offered before the Referee. This assumes what was undoubtedly the fact that the amendment was allowed by order of the the court, but it nowhere appears that any exception was ever taken to the decision of the court allowing it.

The only exception disclosed by the record is that taken to the decision of the Referee in receiving the amendment at the time of taking the testimony.

The objection then made, admits that the amendment had been authorized by the court at the May term 1875, but claims that it should have been served prior to the taking of the testimony. This objection does not appear to have been presented to the court nor any ruling obtained upon it. The case shows a submission upon the evidence and pleadings before the Referee and by him reported to the court, and as no objection was interposed at the hearing, it must be presumed that the decision was based upon such evidence and the pleadings as amended and reported by the Referee.

The objection to the complaint urged in this court "that it does not describe the premises intended to be conveyed or what the mistake was" is fully met by the amended complaint which is sufficient in this regard. As this is the only point made in this court or in the record as to the sufficiency of the complaint, the only question left for consideration relates to the sufficiency of the evidence and findings of facts to support the conclusion of law. The facts are briefly and substantially as follows:

During the time of the alleged transaction the defendant association was a corporation of which defendant Russell was one of the Directors who were charged with the administration and management of its business and affairs. The corporation being indebted to the plaintiff agreed to give its note for the amount, payable in six months secured by a mortgage upon certain premises which it then owned free and unincumbered and occupied in doing its business, consisting of a certain two acre tract of land with the cheese factory and other buildings thereon, situate as described in the complaint.

Pursuant to this agreement the note was given and the mortgage was duly executed, acknowledged and delivered to the plaintiff, in the full belief that it corresponded with the agreement and covered the identical premises intended by all the parties and the plaintiff thereupon caused the same to be duly recorded in the proper recording office. Russell, as one of the Directors participated in the making of the agreement, and the giving of the note and mortgage, and witnessed the execution of the latter; through the mistake and inadvertance of all the parties including Russell, the description of the premises as inserted in the mortgage was erroneous so that in fact it did not cover the property intended and owned by the corporation.

After this and before the discovery of the error, Russell obtained a judgment against the corporation of which he was such Director and member, and proceeded to enforce the same against the premises as a prior lien to plaintiff's mortgage.

This action is brought to reform the mortgage, to make the corresponding alteration and correction ot the record, and to foreclose the same as thus reformed and as a prior incumbrance to defendant Russell's judgment.

This, Russell resists, claiming his judgment to be a prior lien under the recording act which declares "every mortgage conveyance of real estate void as against any judgment lawfully obtained at the suit of any party against the person in whose name the title to such land appears of record prior to the recording of such conveyance."

It is not denied that the defendant corporation was under every legal and moral obligation to plaintiff to consent to the correction of the mortgage and the record as of the dates when originally made, so that plaintiff would be able to receive the benefit of his security as a lien upon the intended property as fully as though the mistake had not occurred, and the court in the exercise of its equity jurisdiction possesses ample power to render this obligation effectual by causing the correction to be made as between the parties.

Upon the Directors of the corporation charged with the general conduct and management of its affairs, the law imposed the duty of causing all the admitted obligations of the company to be honestly and faithfully observed and to use their best exertions to that end.

Richards vs. New Hampshire Ins. Co., 43 *N. H.* 263.

Belknap vs. Davis, 19 *Me.* 457.

This duty rested upon Russell as one of the Directors, equally with the others, and he will not be permitted in plain disregard of such, his duty to take advantage of a known mistake for which he was in part responsible, to set up the lien of a judgment subsequently acquired in his own favor so as to overreach the prior conceded equity of plaintiff. The Registry Act cannot avail him; for though valuable as a protection and a shield, it cannot be used as a weapon or instrument of fraud.

Judgment affirmed.

U. S. Circuit Court, Minnesota Dist.

In Equity.

David C. Price, vs. James E. Kelly, } February 1877.

Patent numbered 172, 269, compared with patents numbered 125, 329—134, 486 and 163, 537 and HELD that the construction of show seats pursuant to the former is not an infringement upon the latter patents.

Bill in equity to restrain defendant from infringing complainant's Patent and for an accounting.

Davis, O'Brien & Wilson, counsel for complainant.

Palmer & Bell, for defendant.

Nelson, J.—The complainant obtained two patents, numbers 125, 329 and 134, 486, dated respectively April 2d and December 31st, 1872, as the original inventor of an "improvement in show and portable show seats." He also secured patent number 163, 537 to be issued to himself as the assignee of the original inventor, Wm. H. Shuey, and dated May 18, 1875, "for an improvement in circus seats." He brings suit against James E. Kelly because of an infringement of his patents.

The complainant declares his invention number 125, 329 has for its object "to provide an improved arrangement of seats for use in circus and other shows, the same being constructed with a view to the comfort of the spectator, while possessing the necessary qualities of security when erected and compactness when packed for transportation." He claims as new an "improvement consisting of notched supports, straps or bars, and boards and chairs constructed and arranged as shown in a diagram." Also chairs provided with slots or recesses through which boards can pass and "the seats be shoved along to the required position." Also "the combination with the supports and boards of the binding bars or straps and stakes to secure the supports."

The diagram of this invention shows the ordinary stringers used in circus and outdoor portable seats elevated and adjusted on an inclined plane, the stringers being notched for the support of boards and elevated at the back by means of trestles. Every alternate board has a chair seat upon it, and the board immediately in front is used as a foot rest. The boards upon which are the chairs or seats, as well as the foot rests, are secured in place at each end by a zigzag shaped strap passing from the top of each stringer over the boards to the bottom, and terminating in an eye, through which a stake is driven into the ground.

In number 134, 486, every alternate board is suspended at each end from the under side of the stringer by a band of metal running the length, or nearly so, of each one, and by forming the shape of a clevis, upon which the ends of the board rest, secures it in position like a hanging shelf and is called a foot rest. The complainant claims as new "the series of foot boards or rests in combination with the supports (stringers) and braces" (trestles).

In number 163, 537, the invention is claimed as a "show seat consisting of the frame, the back formed of a single piece of bent wood, pivoted to the side of the frame, and jointed braces, the back being constructed to fold around and closely embrace the seat frame in order that the upper surfaces may be flush.

The defendant alleges want of novelty; denies that the patents are for original inventions, and denies that he has infringed either of the inventions and patented improvements.

It is admitted that there is no novelty in using stringers and trestles to form portable show seats, nor in making every alternate board on the stringers a foot-rest; but the combination of all these in connection with a chair seat and folding back, and straps to secure the ends of the seat boards in position, is urged by the complainant's counsel as new and patentable, and the infringement of this combination is charged.

An examination of the manufacture of the defendant shows that it has nothing in common with that of the complainant except the notched stringers and the trestles, and the metal straps used to secure the seat boards, the space between the strap and the stringer at the notches being sufficiently open to allow the ends of each board to pass easily through.

The chair seat proper has nothing in common except a cushion. The Price or Shuey patent has an open back in the shape of a yoke, pivoted to the side of the seat and with braces attached and jointed to permit its being folded about the seat. The Kelly seat is composed of two leaves upholstered and connected at one edge by a hinge joint, so as to hold the back when open and allow it to be folded upon the top of the seat. The hinged edges are rabbeted so that the back when open bears against the seat proper, and prevents the seat board from splitting. Price suspends every alternate board in the ordinary circus seat, by a stirrup of metal fixed below the stringers, for a foot rest. He is thus enabled to bring his seat boards nearer together and accommodate more spectators with no inconvenience, the knees and feet of the persons when seated being below the seat boards, do not interfere with those seated in front.

Kelly uses notched stringers and raises his seat boards so they have the appearance of a high bench upon which he puts his chair seats, and then uses for a foot rest every alternate board on top the of the stringers as in the old and ordinary circus seats. When the seat board is raised the board in front used as a foot-rest falls below the back of the seat immediately in front of it, and the persons seated do not interfere with those in front. The security and comfort of the spectators are attained by each, and the mechanism permits the seats to be packed in a small compass for transportation, and rapidly and easily adjusted; but the arrangement in each is different. The only device used by Kelly not found in the old and ordinary circus seat is the upholstered chair seat and back and the metal strap or clamp fastened to the stringers which holds the seat board in position. Price describes this strap in his patents and claims it as new. The testimony of the mechanics and architects is, however, that this mode of securing boards or underlying axles by a clamp or clevis in a firm and fixed position, is a common and ordinary device and "is on the general principle of holding stairs or steps in their place and securing windlasses," etc.

The complainant, therefore, cannot maintain his suit on account of the use of this device, and as defendant constructs substantially the ordinary circus seat, which is old and common, and upon every alternate board of which when elevated he puts a chair seat which is not an infringement, his bill of complaint must fall.

It is unnecessary then to examine the other issues raised by the pleadings. Decree will be entered dismissing the bill of complaint.

LATEST PUBLICATIONS.

THE SYLLABI.

VOL. 1. SATURDAY, MARCH 24, 1877. No. 23

PUBLISHED WEEKLY,

By JOHN B. WEST & CO.,

No. 1 Wabasha St., - ST. PAUL, MINN.

Terms 3.00 per annum in Advance.

HOMER C. ELLER, Editor.

TABLE OF CONTENTS.

BANKRUPTCY expenses average much less in Great Britain than in this country being £65 per £1000 in England and £93, per £1000 in Scotland.

THE Illinois Legislature has adopted a resolution asking congress to abolish the privilege of copy right on school books on account of the exhorbatant prices charged for them.

A SOMEWHAT peculiar litigation with reference to the subject matter, was recently determined by the District Court of Iowa county, Iowa. In 1875 a meteor passing over the county burst to pieces; a man named Maas found a large fragment of it in the public highway where the same passed over the lands of the Amana Society, and claimed title to it by right of discovery and possession. The society claimed that, it being found in the highway over their land, it belonged to the realty by accretion from natural causes, and the court held their claim well founded and that the title to the fragment was in the society.

THE Supreme Court of Nebraska has recently decided some questions of interest to those acquiring title to government lands under the homestead acts. In the case of *Bellinger vs. White* they hold that such homestead becomes subject to taxation as soon as the settler's right to make his final proofs and perfect his title is complete whether he in fact makes such proofs or not; that after that time the United States do not own the land but simply hold it as trustee, having no interest therein except a special one, for the amount of fees that may be unpaid. In *Cheney vs. White* the court held that a mortgage of such homestead executed after the right to perfect the title in the settler had become complete, but before final proofs were made or patent applied for was entirely valid; and in *Jones vs. Yoakam* that it was entirely immaterial that the debt which such mortgage was given to secure was contracted previous to the perfecting of the mortgagors title, and that all congress could have intended by section 4 of the homestead act which provides that "No lands acquired under the provision of this act shall in any event become liable to the satisfaction of any debt or debts contracted prior to the issuing of the patent therefor" was, that the owner of such homestead should not be deprived of the land by virtue of the legal process founded on a debt contracted before the patent issued, to simply protect him against compulsory payment of such debt.

Supreme Court, State of Minnesota.

The Board of Co. Commissioners of Mower Co. *Respondent*, *vs.* Sylvester Smith. *Appellant*, } Aug. 11,'75.

First.—The Board of County Commissioners may sue the County Treasurer either on the Bond, or independent of it, for the conversion of funds belonging in the County Treasury, and in such suit may recover for all the funds converted, state, county, town, school and other funds.

Second.—In such a suit for conversion the defendant is not entitled to demand a bill of particulars. If the allegations in the complaint, are not sufficiently specific, his remedy is by motion to have it made more definite and certain.

Third.—It is not necessary in such suit that the complaint should allege that there was an accounting and settlement by the Treasurer, nor to state wherein the accounts of the Treasurer are incorrect. If there has been such an accounting or settlement as the law requires, it is a matter of defense and it may be impeached for fraud or mistake.

Fourth.—Where there has been a fraudulent conversion, the time limited for the commencement of an action, is to be counted from the discovery of the fraud.

Fifth.—Memoranda of the receipt of taxes made in the margin of the assessment books with the name of the defendant signed to them, are not admissible to charge him with such taxes, unless in some way authenticated as his entries. They are not "written instruments" within the meaning of ch. 64, of the Laws of 1867.

Sixth.—Where the Judge of the District in which an action is pending is disqualified to act in the cause, a motion in it may be made before the Judge of an adjoining District, without regard to the distance from the residence of the Judge of the District in which the action is pending.

Appeal from an order of District Court, county of Mower, denying defendants' motion for a new trial.

E. O. Wheeler and Batchelder & Buckham, att'ys for respondent.

D. B. Johnson, Gordon E. Cole and R. A. Jones, att'y for appellant.

Gilfillan, C. J.—This is an action against the defendant Ex-Treasurer of the county of Mower, for failing to account for and pay over, and for converting, monies belonging in the treasury of the county.

In the complaint are five causes of action or counts; the first four relating to as many different terms of office of defendant, and the fifth covering all of them.

The aggregate amount claimed in the complaint is forty-one thousand dollars, alleged to have belonged to the various funds in the treasury, state, county and school funds, the amount belonging to each not being stated.

The referees find by their report, that during his terms of office, the defendant appropriated and converted to his own use $17,144.97, from the county treasury; but at what particular times, or from what particular fund or funds, they say they are unable to determine.

The defendant makes and argues with great ability the objection that the Board of County Commissioners is not the proper party plaintiff in a suit of this kind; and this we deem the most important question in the case.

The Statute ch. 8, Sec. 75, Gen. St. makes each organized county a body politic and corporate, with capacity to sue and be sued, without any specification of the cases in which it may sue and be sued, and by sec. 80, the name by which it is to sue or be sued, is "The Board of County Commissioners" of the county. The case is different from that of *Hunter vs. The Commissioners of Mercer County*, 10 *Ohio St.* 515, for in that state, counties are not bodies corporate, and general authority to sue and be sued is not conferred on them by statute; but the statute of that state expressly specifiies the cases in which the Boards of County Commissioners may sue or be sued. In this state the county may sue and be sued, in any matter pertaining to the county, with no limitation other than would be applied to any corporation.

That the County Commissioners may sue a defaulting Treasurer without reference to his official bond, is held in the *County Commissioners of McLeod County vs. Gilbert*, 19 *Minn.*, 214.

The principal argument used to show that the county is not the proper plaintiff, is that the monies abstracted from the County Treasury belong, not to the county but to the state, towns and school districts; and that therefore the county is not the reel party in intererast; and that because the statute prescribes that the Treasurers bonds shall run, not to the county but to the state the latter, and not the former, is the trustee of the various funds in the treasury; and that if suit is to be brought by any but the real parties in interest; that is the various corporations or *quasi* corporations to whom the various funds belong, then it must be brought by or in the name of the state as the trustee of an express trust.

This suit is not upon the bond but upon the

defendant's liability independent of it. This liability does not arise upon the bond, nor are the rights of the county, as against the defendant created by it. It is required not for the purpose of defining the rights and liabilities of the parties, but as security to rights and obligations that would exist if no bond were given.

But the provisions of statute in regard to such bond, and the enforcement of them, are material and controling, as showing the relations of the state, county, towns, school districts, &c., to the monies intended to be secured by them, we think that whoever would be a proper plaintiff in a suit upon such a bond, would be a proper plaintiff in a suit, not on the bond, to enforce the liability which the bond is given to secure.

By sec. 126, ch. 8, the bonds of County Treasurers are "payable to the State of Minnesota, and conditioned for the safe keeping and paying over, according to law, of all monies which come into his hands, for state, county, township, school, road, bridge, poor, town and all other purposes."

Sec. 1, of ch. 78, provides that "the official bond or other security of a public officer, to the state, or any municipal body or corporation, whether with or without sureties, is to be construed as security to all persons severally, for the official delinquencies against which it is intended to provide as well as to the state, body or corporation designated therein; provided that when no other provision is made by law, it shall run to the State of Minnesota."

Sec. 2, "When a public officer by official misconduct or neglect forfeits his official bond, or renders his sureties liable upon an official security, any person injured thereby, or who is by law entitled to the benefit of the security may bring an action thereon in his own name," &c.

This statute makes the decisions cited from 2 *Ind.* 40 and 21 *Ind.* 70, inapplicable because in that state, so far as we can discover from those cases, there is no provision of the statute, like the one we have just quoted, and suits on official bonds which are required to run to the state as obligee, must be brought in the name of the state, being governed wholly by the rules of the common law.

According to the provisions of these statutes, the state in the greater number of official bonds, is only a nominal, and not the actual obligee. This however, shows no more than that the state need not, simply by reason of its being named as obligee in the bond, be the plaintiff in a suit on it. Any person entitled to its security may sue upon it, after obtaining leave of the court.

It is not necessary to determine whether the state or any city, town or school district, may, by reason of its interest, and not by reason of the statute, directing suit to be brought, sue either on the bond or independent of it, forthe portion of the abstracted monies to which it is entitled. The question is, does the statute intend that the county may sue to enforce a restoration to its treasury of all monies un-lawfully taken or withheld from it? It does not follow that because one may sue, the other cannot.

The right of the general owner of property, and of one having a special property in it, to sue for a conversion of it, is an instance of a right at common law in two different persons to sue for the same thing. Nor does the right of the county to sue depend on its being strictly the trustee of an express trust within the meaning of sec. 28, ch. 66, of the General Statutes.

The county is expressly authorized by statute to bring suits, and if the recovery to its treasury of monies belonging in it, comes within the legitimate business of the county, it is a person expressly authorized to sue mentioned in sec. 28. That the care over the County Treasury and all the monies in it is intended by statute to be part of the business of the county organization, is evident from the different provisions made in regard to it. All taxes when collected belong in the county treasury. The treasurer is required (sec. 86, ch. 11, Gen. Statutes,) to "place the same when collected to the credit of the county." They are to remain in the treasury, until drawn out according to law. The accounts of the treasurer are rendered to the County Commissioners, and County Auditor, if the Commissioners are in session, if they are not in session then to the Auditor alone.

All the treasurer's books, accounts and vouchers, and all monies in the treasury, are to be at all times subject to the inspection, and examination of the commissioners or any committee thereof. Sec. 132, ch. 8. The settlements are to be made with the County Auditor, or County Commissioners. Sec. 103, 133, 134, ch. 8, sec. 102, ch. 11. They may require treasurer to give a new bond and if he fail to do so, his office is declared vacant. Sec's 141, 142, ch. 8. When an action is commenced against him, they may remove him. Sec. 137, ch. 8. They may order suit to be commenced on his bond. Sec. 136, ch. 8. And in such suit judgment may be rendered against him and his sureties, not for the amount due the county fund alone, but for the whole amount due from the treasurer. When the money is collected in such suit, it is to be paid into the treasury of the county in which it is due, sec. 138, ch. 8.

It is provided that the state shall, except where otherwise expressly provided, be the obligee in all official bonds. But that it was thereby intended to make the state the trustee of an express trust, in all such cases, so as to be the only proper party plaintiff in a suit on such bond, is negatived, by the provisions that the bond shall be construed as security to all persons severally for the official delinquencies against which it is intended to provide, as well as to the state, &c. And that any person entitled to the security may bring an action thereon in his own name &c. Such bonds are required to run to the state, only as a matter of convenience, to establish a uniform rule, and prevent doubt or mistakes.

That the State Auditor may instruct the County Auditor to cause an action to be commenced on the bond, does not show that the action must be in the name of the state, but rather tends to show the reverse.

For if it was intended by the statute that the action can only be brought by the state, and in its name, we would naturally expect that the State Auditor should cause, or should direct the Attorney General, or some otheristate officer to cause it to be commenced, and that the control over and prosecution of it, should be entrusted to some officer of the state. The purpose of this provision was undoubtedly to prevent the prosecution of such bonds being in the uncontrolled discretion of the Board of County Commissioners.

If it had been intended that the state as trustee of an express trust, must sue for all the funds, provision would have been made for payment of the monies collected on the judgment into the State Treasury, and for distribution of it by the *trustee* among the *cestui que trusts*. And had it been intended that each corporation or *quasi* corporation interested in the funds must sue for the portion to which it is entitled, provision would surely have been made for commencement of the action by some officer of such corporation, or *quasi* corporation, and for the payment to it, of the money, when collected by means of the action.

Instead of this, the legislature has provided for an action to be commenced by county officers, to recover monies belonging in the County Treasury, and for the restoration to that treasury of such monies when collected. The only connection which any but county officers can, under the statute have with such action, is that the State Auditor may instruct the County Auditor to cause it to be commenced.

The great multiplicity of suits that would have been made necessary by it, and the difficulty in many instances of proving what portion of any sum abstracted from the treasury, each plaintiff would be entitled to, make it highly improbable that the legislature intended it is a general rule, that the state, county, cities, towns and school districts, must necessarily sue, each for its own portion of the funds, for such delinquency by County Treasurers.

We have no doubt that it was intended that the county may sue in such cases, and recover the whole amount of the delinquency, unless perhaps where the state or some of the corporations or *quasi* corporations has recovered for its portion.

The only case to which we have been referred, which really covers the point, is the *Supervisors of Albany Co. vs. Durant*, 9 *Paige* 182.

That was a suit, in the nature of a creditors bill, to enforce the payment of taxes. It was held that although the taxes, when collected, were to be paid into the County Treasurer, the Supervisors were the proper parties to enforce the payment. Certainly if the Supervisors or County Commissioners may bring suit to collect the taxes, and bring them into the treasury, they can sue and compel a return of the money, upon an unlawful abstraction of it.

Within the proper time after the service of the complaint, the defendant demanded a bill of particulars, which demand was not complied with, and at the commencement of the trial, the defendant moved to dismiss the action on that ground, and also objected to the admission of any evidence on the same ground. The motion was denied and the objection overruled.

The action is not one in which the defendant is entitled, of right, to a bill of particulars. It is an action of conversion of monies and not on an account alleged, and if the complaint does not set forth sufficient particulars of the monies alleged to have been converted to enable defendant adequately to defend himself, his remedy was by motion to make it more definite and certain.

Blackie vs. Neilson, 6 *Bosw.*, 681.

On the trial the defendant moved to dismiss and also objected to any evidence being given, because as claimed by defendant, the action is substantially one to impeach the accounts or settlements of the treasurer, and the complaint does uot state the particulars in which it is claimed the accounts or settlements are incorrect. The action as we have stated is for the conversion of monies and the complaint does not allege any accounting or settlement such as the law requires of the treasurer. If there was any, it was matter of fact to be pleaded, and because it did not appear from the complaint, it was for the defendant, if he relied upon it, to set it up in the answer which he has done; such a defense requires no reply, and from proof of the defense being offered at the trial, the plaintiff might controvert it, or avoid it by proofs impeaching the account or settlement for fraud or mistake.

It could not avail as a defense at law, if founded in fraud or mistake; an account stated or settled, is a mere admission that the account is correct. It is not an estoppel. The account is still open to impeachment for mistakes or errors. *Lockwoord vs. Thorne*, 18 *N. Y.*, 292.

If the defendant occupying as he did a fiduciary relation to the county, converted the monie's it was a fraud within the rule in *Cock vs. Van Etten*, 12 *Minn.*, 523, and the time limited for the commencement of the action began to run upon the discovery by plaintiff of the fraud, or notice to it of such facts and circumstances as, if investigated, would lead to such discovery.

To charge the defendant with money received, the plaintiff offerred a great number of what were called "grand duplicates," but which appear to have been the assessment in tax books of towns; opposite many of the items of tax, in which was written in the margin the word "Paid" and the name of defendant. These marginal entries were objected to because there was no evidence that the name of defendant written in connection with the word "Paid" opposite the various items was his signature. The entries were received in evidence.

There is no law requiring such entries to be made and therefore they do not stand as official records.

There was no proof that the entries were in the books when in custody of defendant, and so there could be no presumption of their genuineness from the fact that they came from his possession. Such memoranda are not "within instruments," within the meaning of ch. 64, of the laws of 1867. The written instruments meant by that statute are formal instruments, or agreements and do not include mere entries made only for the use or convenience of the party making them. It was error to admit these entries without proof of their authenticity.

We have carefully examined the case to ascertain if there is any evidence curing this error, and find none, and for this reason a new trial must be had.

Judge Paige was Judge of the District (the 10th,) in which the action was pending, and resided at Austin, the county seat of the county in which the action was pending. The motion for a new trial was noticed for hearing at Mankato before Judge Waite, of the 6th (an adjoining) District.

The respondent makes the objection that the latter had no jurisdicton to hear the motion. Sec. 4, ch. 67, of the session laws of 1867, provides that "motions must be made in the district in which the action is pending, or in an adjoining district. Provided that no motion shall be made in an adjoining district which shall require the hearing of such a motion at a greater distance from the county seat where the action is pending in which the motion is made than the residence of the Judge of the District wherein such action is pending, from such county seat."

The act of 1867, does not in terms repeal sec. 5, ch. 64, Gen. Statutes. That section provides that "Whenever a District Judge is a party or otherwise interested in any cause, another District Judge, in an adjoining district shall within his district, transact any *ex parte* business hear and determine motions &c."

Except under this provision the parties in a cause where the Judge of the District in which it is pending is disqualified to act, can make no applications in vacation. We cannot hold by implication that the act of 1867 was intended to take away their right, to make such applications; and the right given in sec. 5, ch. 64, is preserved.

Judge Paige was disqualified by reason of having been attorney in the cause.

Many other questions of little importance are made by the appellant, but as a new trial must be had for the reason stated, upon which trial those questions are not very likely to arise, we pass them over.

The order denying a new trial is reversed.

———:o:———

U. S. Circuit Court, Minnesota Dist.

In Chancery.

E. Sarah Goldsmith and John Nininger, *vs.* Mary Greve, Herman Greve, Nathan Schwarzenberg and Moses Lowenstein. } Dec. Term '76.

Application of the doctrine of res judicata, to the facts in this case.

The complainants bring suit, and ask that their title set forth to certain real estate described in the bill of complaint be declared good, and superior to the claim of title urged by defendant Mary Greve, and that a decree be granted ordering and requiring Mary Greve and her husband Herman Greve, to release and convey to them all the title and interest which they or either of them acquired and hold under and by virtue of a deed made to Mary Greve by Levi Greve, July 5, 1855, or by virtue of any subsequent deed from him. They also ask for an accounting.

Mary Greve and her husband answer the bill of complaint, and among other things, charge, in substance, that neither of the complainants ever had any right, title or interest at law, or in equity, in or to any of the real property described therein.

COMPLAINANTS' CASE.

Levi Greve was the owner of the property June 26, 1855, and sold and conveyed the same on that day to Nathan Schwarzenberg by deed executed for him by his attorney Moses H. Schwarzenberg, which deed was properly recorded in Ramsey county, Minnesota, June 27th, of that year.

Previous to July 5, 1855, at Milwaukee in the State of Wisconsin, where Levi Greve, at that time resided, Moses H. Schwarzenberg paid him the proceeds of the sale, which he received, and expressed himself satisfied, and ratified the action of his attorney. The complainants' title to the property was derived through Moses Lowenstein, the grantee of Nathan Schwarzenberg, by deed recorded April 17th 1857, and they have conveyed to several persons, to whom they became liable upon the the covenant of seizure and general warranty.

DEFENDANTS' MARY GREVE AND HERMAN GREVE'S CASE.

Mary Greve purchased the same property and received a deed from Levi Greve, July 5, 1855, which was duly recorded on the 14th of the same month. After the lapse of 14 years in February 1869, and later, she commenced actions in the state courts, to recover from Coffin and others, the grantees of the complainants, the property in controversy, and judgments were obtained in her favor, and her title thereto sustained. Coffin immediately after his eviction commenced a suit against Goldsmith's estate upon the covenants in his deed, and succeeded in the state court of final resort, and in that suit Nininger was a witness on behalf of Goldsmith's estate.

The records of all the suits are introduced under stipulations made and filed in this suit, and it appears upon the face of the record in the suit of *Coffin adm's vs. Goldsmith executrix*, that the title of Mary Greve by deed from Levi Greve dated July 5, 1855. and the title of Nathan Schwarzenberg, claimed by virtue of the ratification of the sale and conveyance by Levi Greve, attorney, and upon which the complainants in this suit rely, were directly in issue and necessarily adjudicated, and the judgment was in favor of Mary Greve's title.

The only question in this suit, which when settled determines all the issues, is whether Mary Greve or Nathan Schwarzenberg had the better title by virtue of the the conveyances and the ratification by Levi Greve as above stated.

Gilman, Clough & Lane, for complainants.

J. B. Brisbin and *W. P. Warner*, for defendants.

Nelson, J.—The subject in my opinion is *in rem judicatam*. In the suit upon the covenants of warranty, Coffin having been evicted by Mary Greve, relied upon her title to defeat E. Sarah Goldsmith then executrix, who urged the Schwarzenberg title, which is pressed here.

Goldsmith executrix under the code of Minnesota could set up any equitable defense to defeat Coffin in that action, as she might have done in the ejectment suit against him had she been called upon to defend.

Mary Greve under her answer, can take advantage of the fact of *res judicata* as it appears by the record in the suit of *Coffin adm's vs. Goldsmith, executrix*. John Nininger, the other complainant, being a witness in that suit, must be regarded as having notice, and an opportunity if he desired, to become a party and contest Mary Greve's title.

All the conditions then exist of *res judicata*—the same subject matter in controversy between the same parties, or privies, and a previous determination of the litigation in a court of competent jurisdiction.

I have arrived at this conclusion reluctantly for the "Schwarzenberg title," in my opinion, should have prevailed in the previous litigation.

Decree will be entered dismissing the bill.

——oo——

RECENT DECISIONS.

VERIFICATION OF BANKRUPT SCHEDULES.—A bankrupt may swear to his schedules before a Notary Public.

In re John W. Bailey et al., (U. S. Dist. Ct., Dist. of Mass.,) 15 Nat. Bank. Reg. 48.

DECLARATIONS of an agent as to the cause of a particular accident to which he was a party, are not binding upon his principal and are inadmissible as evidence unless made before, or at the time of the accident, and so connected with it as to be part of the RES GESTA (Fawcett vs. Bigley, 9 P. F. Smith, followed).

Bigley vs. Williams, Sup. Ct. of Pa.

LEVY BEFORE BANKRUPTCY PROCEEDINGS.—When an assignment by a debtor is set aside at the suit of an assignee in bankruptcy, a creditor who has levied on the goods before the commencement of bankruptcy proceedings, and after the execution of the assignment is entitled to priority.

MacDonald vs. Moore, et al., 15 Nat. Bank. Reg., 26.

NEGLIGENCE.—A railroad company having a telegraph office in one its stations, open to the public, is responsible to one of its passengers who is injured in going to such office, in consequence of the defective condition of the structures or platforms, by which it is made accessible.

Classman vs. R. R. Co., N. Y. Sup. Ct., Jan. 1877, (4 W. Dig. 34).

LIABILITY OF TEACHER SUSPENDING SCHOLAR.—Boards of education have authority to adopt and enforce necessary rules and regulations for the government of schools under their control and management, and a rule adopted by such board, providing that if a scholar shall fail to be prepared with a rhetorical exercise at the time appointed, without being excused on account of sickness or other reasonable cause, he or she be immediately expelled. is a reasonable rule; and where the teacher of a school acting under such rule and with the consent of the board, suspended a scholar for failure to prepare such exercise, until he should comply with such rule or furnish a reasonable excuse for non compliance.

HELD, that neither the teacher or Board of Education was liable in damages therefor.

Sewell vs. Bd. of Ed., Sup. Ct. of Ohio, Dec. 1876.

JURISDICTION OF FEDERAL COURTS—AMOUNT IN CONTROVERSY.—In determining the question whether the amount in dispute in an action is sufficient in amount to give a Federal Court jurisdiction, reference will be made to the material allegations of the complaint and not alone to the prayer for judgment; and if from the body of the complaint it appears that plaintiff could not recover an amount exceeding $500 (exclusive of costs,) that court will not assume jurisdiction.

In a case where the amount he may be entitled to recover, can be ascertained only by a trial, a standing in court may be obtained by alleging damages at the requisite sum.

Culver vs. Crawford, U. S. C. C., Dist. of Ark., Nov. Tr., 1876, (4 Cent. L. Jr., 198.)

SLANDER.—Words charging clergyman, with drunkeness, and spoken of and concerning him in his office, or calling, are actionable, PER SE (McMillan vs. Birch, 1 Binney 176. Chaddock vs. Briggs, 13 Mass. 251,) and in such action where punitive damages may be allowed, evidence of defendants pecuniary ability is admissible. And where the evidence tended to show that the defendant uttered the slanderous words in a wanton and reckless manner and without reasonable cause to beleive the charge true, that the fact that he did believe the same true, would not relieve him from liability for exemplary damages.

Hayner vs. Cowden, Sup. Ct. Commission of Ohio, (Am. Law Reg., vol. 16, p. 106).

PETITION IN BANKRUPTCY.—In involuntary proceedings in bankruptcy against a separate partner, the creditors of the firm must be counted in constituting a quorum of petitioning creditors, under bankrupt act, as amended by act of June 22, 1874. The two hundred and fifty dollar qualification relates only to numbers and not to amounts; one-fourth or more of the petitioning creditors holding provable debts of over two hundred and fifty dollars, are sufficient if they hold one-third of the aggregate of the provable debts, and must be counted to the exclusion of those holding debts of smaller amount. If one-fourth or more of the creditors of this class have failed to sign the petition or having signed it do not hold one-third in amount of the debts provable, then one-fourth or more of the creditors holding debts, large or small, and holding in the aggregate one-third of the provable debts, must be counted.

In re Loyd, U. S. Dist. Ct. W. Dist. of Pa., (29 Pitts. Leg. Jr., 113).

LATEST PUBLICATIONS.

Burrill on Assignments.—A treatise on the Law and Practice of Voluntary Assignments for the Benefit of Creditors. Adapted to the laws of various States; with an Appendix of Forms; by Alexander M. Burrill. 3d edition, revised, annotated and largely rewritten by James L. Bishop, of the New York Bar. 8vo., 800 pp., Sheep 6 50

Institutes of Common and Statute Law. By John B. Minor, L. L. D., Professor of Common and Statute Law in the University of Virginia. 2d Ed. 2 vols. 8vo., 672, 1098 pp., Sheep, 17 00

Story's Equity Jurispudence.—Twelth Ed. By Joseph Story, 2 vols. sheep, 15 00

The Laws and Practice of Bankruptcy.—By Orlando F. Bump. New edition to January 1877. 8 vo. 1040 pp., law sheep - - - - - 7 50

The Law of Mortgages of Real and Personal Property in the State of New York.—With an appendix of Forms. By Abner C. Thomas, 690 pp., law sheep, - - - - - - 6 00

Practice Pleading and Evidence in the Courts of California, in Civil Suits and Proceedings.—By E. F. Buttemer Harston. 8 vo 713 pp., sheep, 6 50

Hents Forms and Use of Blanks—By J. C. Bates. Second Ed. 8 vo 499 pp., sheep, - - - - - 6 50

Life and Accident Insurance Reports.—Cases decided in the courts of America, England, Scotland and Canada, down to Setember 1876, with notes and references. Vol. V. By Melville M. Bigelow, of the Boston Bar. 8 vo. law sheep, - - - - - - 6 50

Civil Malpractice.—A treatise on Surgical Jurisprudence, with chapters on Skill in Diagnosis and Treatment, Prognosis in Fractures, and on Negligence. By Milo A. McClelland, M. D. 8 vo. Cloth $3.50, sheep, - 4 50

Bishop's Commentaries on Criminal Law.—By J. P. Bishop. 6th Ed. 2 vols., 8vo. - - - - - 12 00

Shaw's Index to Minn. Session Laws, 1849–1875. Full Sheep, - - 4 00

THE SYLLABI.

VOL. 1. SATURDAY, MARCH 31, 1877. No. 24.

PUBLISHED WEEKLY,

By JOHN B. WEST & CO.,

No. 1 Wabasha St., - ST. PAUL, MINN.

Terms 3.00 per annum in Advance.

HOMER C. ELLER, Editor.

IN Tennesee under a provision in their constitution that "all property shall be taxed according to its value, that value to be ascertained in such manner as the legislature shall direct, so that the taxes shall be equal and uniform throughout the state." It was recently held that a law imposing a tax on dogs *per capita* and not *ad valorem* was unconstitutional.

———

THE subject of organized strikes among railroad employees, the effect of which is to interfere with the proper operation of the roads and the interests of the public is begining to attract the attention of the legislative bodies of the different states. The Michigan legislature has passed and the Governor approved an act punishing by imprisonment in the county jail for three months, or in the state prison for one year, any person who shall impede or obstruct the regular business of any railroad in the state. If two or more persons conspire for such purpose the imprisonment may be extended for two years, and in Massachusetts the railroad commissioners of that state have been led by the circumstances attending a recent strike of railroad Engineers to recommend legislature making combinations leading to such results penal offenses———. The second trial of the Frenchman LaPage for the outrage and murder of Josie Langmaid, in New Hampshire has resulted in a verdict of murder in the first degree and a sentenee that he be hanged on March 15, 1878.

———

In the case of *Munn and Scott vs. the People of Illinois*, the Supreme Court of the United States pass upon the power of the legislature of a State to regulate elevators and warehouses belonging to private individuals, and to fix the maxium of charges that may be imposed for the storage of grain in such elevators, or warehouses. Following and applyiug the rule laid down by Lord Hale in his treatise, *De Portinbus Maris*, and by Lord Ellenburough in *Aldiutt vs. Inglis* 12 East 527 that wherever private property, or a business carried on by private individuals, assumes such a character as to be "affected with a public interest" it ceases to be *juris privati* only, and is subject to regulation by the sovereign power, the court hold, that these elevators standing as they do at he "gateways of commerce, "through which from the necessities of business, must pass all grain transported, subject to such toll as may be imposed, certainly come within that class of property or occupations that are clothed with a public interest. And that the establishing by the legislature of a certain rule of charges for the use of such elevators, was entirely proper and in no manner repugnant to Art. 14 Constitution of the United States. That while the owner of the property might be entitled to a reasonable compensation for its use, yet the question as to what would be a reasonable compensation for such use, is only to be determined by a judicial proceeding, in those cases where the legislature has not acted. That the power to regulate, implied the power to fix a maximum of charges to be imposed, and the fixing of such rate by the legislature is conclusive on question of its being reasonable The court also hold that the regulation of such warehouses by the State, is not repugnant to Sec. 8 or 9, Constitution of the United States.

The principles discussed in this case are by the same Court applied to railroads, in the cases of *C. B. & Q. R. R. Co. vs. Cutts. Peck vs. C. & N. W. R. R. Co. C. M. & St. P. R. R. Co. vs. Ackley. Winona & St. P. R. Co. vs. Blake et al., Coleman vs. McIlrath, Rever.*

In all of which the right of the legislature to regulate and control, is affirmed.

Supreme Court, State of Minnesota.

The Winona & St. Peter Railroad Company, *Respondent*, *vs.* The St. Paul & Sioux City Railroad Company, *Appellant*, } Feb'y 12, '77.

When the cause of action as stated in the complaint relates to property, and property rights belonging to a corporation as the absolute owner vested with the legal title, such corporation is the real party in interest to prosecute the action. It is no defense to such an action that another party has become the owner of the sole beneficial interest in the right, property and immunities, of the corporation, and an averment of that character in the answer may properly be stricken out on motion as immaterial and irrelevant.

Appeal from an order of the District Court, county of Blue Earth, striking out portion of amended answer.

Wilson & Taylor, att'ys for respondent.

E. C. Palmer, att'y for appellant.

Cornell, J.—The portion of the amended answer stricken out by the order appealed from, of which appellant complains, is as follows: "That in the year 1867 the Chicago & Northwestern Railway Company, a corporation organized and acting, under and by virtue of the laws of Illinois, became the owner and seized and possessed of the sole beneficial interest in the rights, property and immunities of said plaintiff, and has ever since that time controlled and operated the same, for its sole use and benefit. That said portion of said line, extending from the west side of said range 31, to the western terminus, was constructed and equipped by said Chicago & Northwestern Railway Company, through its own officers and agents, with its own means, and in the mode and manner by it deemed best, and that since said year 1867, the corporate name of said plaintiff has been used by said railway company in the premises but colorably and with no other purpose than to subserve its own interests. That said plaintiff has no real interest in the premises and has not had since said year 1867, or in the event of this suit, as these defendants are informed and verily believe to be true."

Conceding as correct, the position assumed by appellant, that it had the right to answer "*de novo*" the amended complaint as fully, and to the same extent as though it had been the original complaint in the action, still the order must be sustained, inasmuch as the matter stricken out was wholly immaterial and irrelevant to the cause of action, if any, stated in the amended complaint.

The cause of action, as alleged, accrued to the corporation plaintiff, as the lawful owner in whom was vested the right to locate, construct and operate, the line of road in question, together with the legal title to all such other rights and franchises pertaining thereto, as were conferred upon the company to aid in the construction of its road. Among these rights was that of acquiring title to the lands granted to aid in constructing such road upon compliance with the conditions of the act of congress making the grant, and the act of legislature transferring it to the company. The object of the present action is the enforcement of this property right, the legal ownership of which thus belongs, as is alleged in the complaint, to the plaintiff. The real party in interest, therefore within the meaning of the statute, (sec. 26, ch. 66, General Statutes,) is the plaintiff, in whose corporate name alone the action can be maintained and prosecuted.

It is no defense that other parties have beneficial interest merely in the subject matter of the suit.

The stockholders of a corporation have such an interest, but it would hardly be claimed that they were proper parties to an action brought solely to enforce legal rights belonging to the corporation, or to redress a wrong committed against it; and this in effect is the gist of the matter stricken out by the order in question.

If the Chicago & Northwestern Railway Company, has acquired all the stock of the Winona & St. Peter Railroad Company and thus become the sole stockholders of the latter Company as perhaps it legally might, it would as is alleged "have become the owner of the sole beneficial interest in the rights, property and immunities of the Winona corporation," and the road of the latter would undoubtedly be controlled and operated for the sole use and benefit of the former," but these facts would not confer upon said Northwestern Company, any legal title to the corporate property nor in any way affect the legal status or rights of the corporation plaintiff. The averment, "that said plaintiff has no real interest in the premises, and has not had since said year 1867, or in the event of this suit," was manifestly intended by the pleader as a mere conclusion of law from the preceding facts therein stated, and must be so regarded, especially in view of the admitted facts contained in the written stipulation of the parties. On the return of the order to show cause, defendant appeared and was fully heard upon the merits of the motion. His preliminary objection at the hearing raised a mere question of practice under the rules of that court and its decision thereon presents no error for review by this court.

Order affirmed.

DANIEL G. SHILLOCK, *Appellant*, vs. JOSEPHINE B. GILBERT, *Respondent*, } March 20, '77

An important question in this case is whether a certain sealed instrument is the deed of Joseph M. Campbell, who at the time the deed was made, was the owner of certain land described therein, and a minor. To make the instrument his deed it must have been signed and sealed BY him or FOR him. The signature opposite the seal was "Joseph Campbell" and it was written by Antoine Joseph Campbell the natural father of Joseph M. Campbell. Joseph M. Campbell wrote his name under the attestation clause in the place for the signature of a witness. There is nothing in the case showing, or tending to show, that the signature "Joseph Campbell" written opposite the seal, was put there as the signature of Joseph M. Campbell, or that he either expressly or impliedly requested it to be put there as his signature for him, or that he adopted it, or recognized it, as his signature or as written for him, nor that he acknowledged the instrument to be his deed. Neither is there anything in the case showing, or tending to show that Joseph M. Campbell supposed or had any reason to suppose that any of the parties to the business believed or imagined, that the signature, "Joseph Campbell" was the signature of Joseph M. Campbell or written for him. HELD, that the instrument is not the deed of Joseph M. Campbell.

HELD, further that Joseph M. Campbell is not estopped to claim that the instrument is not his deed, or that it conveyed the land by his receipt of the whole or a part of the purchase money; since no person was induced to believe anything that was not true by any acts, representations or silence upon his part.

HELD, further, that the instrument not being the deed of Joseph M. Campbell no question of disaffirmance arises in this case nor any question as to the obligation of Joseph M. Campbell to refund any money received by him from the defendant or any one for her.

HELD, further, that as defendant had no title to the lands to which this action relates and that as from the facts in the case she must be charged with notice of her want of title, her payment of taxes upon the same was entirely gratuitous, and she is not entitled in law to insist that she shall be re-imbursed by the defendant.

Appeal from judgment of the District Court, county of McLeod.

M. O. Little and Davis, O'Brien & Wilson, att'ys for appellant.

A. P, Fitch and H. J. Peck, att'ys for respondent.

BERRY, J.—It is found by the court below that Joseph M. Campbell was the owner of certain land (being the same hereinafter referred to,) under a patent running from the United States to him by the name of Joseph M. Campbell and that at the time of the conveyance hereinafter mentioned to defendants, said Joseph M. Campbell was a minor. The court further finds as follows, viz: "I find that on or about the 25th day of July, A. D. 1872, a deed of conveyance to the defendant in this action of all the land hereinbefore described, in the usual form and with the usual covenants of warranty, (and which is the same land that is, in this action, in controversy,) was made in the office of Francis X. Brosseau in the city of St. Paul. That on the day last aforesaid the said Joseph M. Campbell and the said Brosseau and Antoine Joseph Campbell, (who was and is the natural father of said Joseph M. Campbell) were each and all present in said office of said Brosseau, and that said Brosseau acting as a broker and for his own benefit negotiated a sale of said land to the defendant, in this action with said Antoine Joseph Campbell, father as aforesaid; that said Joseph M. Campbell fully understood the said transaction and fully consented thereto and *fully intended* to convey the said land by means of the acts hereinafter stated, so far as he lawfully could do so, and that thereupon said Brosseau produced and lay before the said father and son, the aforesaid deed of conveyance to said defendant; that thereupon said A. J. Campbell and Joseph M. Campbell signed the said deed in the manner following, to-wit: Said Antoine Joseph Campbell wrote the words "Joseph Campbell" opposite the printed seal on said deed and said Joseph M. Campbell wrote his own proper name, viz: Joseph M. Campbell, at the left of, and two lines lower down than the word so written by his father, and in the place upon said deed where the first witness to said deed should have signed; so that said signing and execution of said deed appears in the following form, to-wit:

"Signed, Sealed and delivered in the Presence of

JOSEPH CAMPBELL. [seal.]

"JOSEPH M. CAMPBELL,"

"ALBERT SCHEFFER."

That immediately after the signing of said deed as aforesaid by the said Joseph M.

and A. J. Campbell, the said Brosseau, the said Joseph M. Campbell and the said A. J. Campbell, left the office of said Brosseau and repaired together in company to the bank in said city of St. Paul, known as "Dawson's Bank," said Brosseau carrying with him said deed. That after entering said bank said parties found therein among others Albert Scheffer, who was an officer in said bank and also a notary public duly appointed and qualified to take acknowledgments of deeds and other writings.

That said deed was by said Brosseau handed to said Scheffer with a request that said Scheffer should sign the same as a witness, and to take and certify the acknowledgment thereof, and that said Scheffer did then and there sign said deed as a witness thereto and immediately beneath the name of Joseph M. Campbell so signed as aforesaid and in the proper place in said deed, said Scheffer signed the certificate of acknowledgment in the presence of each of these persons, viz: Brosseau, A. J. and J. M. Campbell. That said A. J. Campbell was introduced to Mr. Scheffer but whether said Joseph M. Campbell was so introduced to, or made acquainted with Mr. Scheffer, or whether any acknowledgment of said deed was in fact made in words, or in any manner other than by the aforesaid acts of said parties, does not appear by any evidence offered upon said trial. That immediately upon the acknowledgment of said deed as aforesaid, the same was handed to said Brosseau, and that said Brosseau, thereupon presented to said bank an ordinary bank check drawn upon said bank by one G. K. Gilbert (who then was, and still is, the husband of the defendant Josephine Gilbert, in this action,) and which said check was then and there so drawn for the sum of six hundred dollars and was then and there paid in full to said Brosseau by said bank, and the same was by said bank charged to and deducted from the monies deposited in said bank, to the credit of said G. K. Gilbert, and that immediately upon the receipt of said sum of $600.00 by said Brosseau, and before leaving said bank, the said Brosseau paid over to said Joseph M. Campbell, the sum of five hundred dollars of the money so received from said bank, upon said check, and retained the balance thereof for purposes not disclosed by any evidence offered on said trial. I find that the sum of five hundred dollars so paid by said Brosseau to said Campbell, was the full amount and consideration agreed upon by the said parties in said Brosseau's office for the said conveyance of the 240 acres of land, and for 160 acres of other lands, conveyed and deeded at the same time and in the same manner, to some one else whose name is not disclosed by the evidence on said trial." As a conclusion of law from these findings of fact the court finds, "That the deed executed and delivered to the defendant and bearing date of July 25th, 1872, was sufficiently executed and acknowledged to make it, the deed of the infant. Joseph M. Campbell." We think this conclusion of law cannot be sustained. To make the instrument in question the deed of Joseph M. Campbell it must have been signed and sealed *by* him, or *for* him. It was not signed and sealed *by* him. He not only did not write his name opposite the seal but he wrote it in another place, viz: Under the attestation clause, the place for the signature of a witness. His signature in that place cannot on any reasonable ground be taken to be anything but the signature of a witness. It cannot be twisted into a signing of the deed. Neither was the deed signed for him. The signature opposite the seal was written by Antoine Joseph Campbell, the natural father of Joseph M. Campbell, the true patentee. That signature was the name of the person who wrote it, though not his full name. The fact that Joseph M. Campbell was able to write his name and that he did write it as a witness upon this very paper, and that it was entirely unneccessary for any other person to write it for him, is significant upon the question whether the signature "Joseph Campbell" was made for him or intended to be. It is a fact hard to be explained upon any other hypothesis than the hypothesis that neither Joseph M. Campbell nor any of the other parties to the business, supposed that he was executing the instrument or having it executed as his deed. The statement in the findingof the court that Joseph M. Campbell fully understood the transaction between his father and Brosseau, and fully consented thereto and "fully intended to convey the said land by means of the acts hereinafter stated so far as he lawfully could do so," falls far short of showing that he intended to execute the instrument or to have it executed as his deed. It is entirely consistent with an intention on his part, in ignorant good faith, to have his father execute the instrument as his own deed. But independent of these considerations there is nothing in the findings of fact or in the evidence upon which they are based, which shows, or tends to show, that the deed was signed and sealed *for* Joseph M. Campbell or that he acknowledged it to be his deed.

The signature prefixed to the seal, was as we have already observed, the name of the person who wrote it. There is nothing in the case showing, or tending to show, that it was put there as the signature of Joseph M. Campbell, or that he expressly or impliedly requested it to be put there as his signature or for him, or that he adopted or recognized it, as his signature or as written for him. There is not even a shred of testimony showing, or tending to show, that he supposed, or had any reason to suppose, that any of the parties to the business believed or imagined that the signature "Joseph Campbell" was the signature of Joseph M. Campbell, or written for him. The instrument therefore is not the deed of Joseph M. Campbell. It is however urged that even if it is not his deed, he is estopped by his receipt of the purchase money to deny that is, or that it conveyed the land. There is no foot-hold for an estoppel for the reason that the facts, as to the title of the land and as to the execution of the instrument, were at the time fully understood by all the parties, since although defendant was not present Brosseau must upon the finding be taken to have been her agent, even if he was not the agent of both parties. No person was induced to believe anything that was not true by any acts, representations or silence upon the part of Joseph M. Campbell. *Pence vs. Arbuckle, MSS. Oct.* 1875. The instrument through which the defendant claims not being the deed of Joseph M. Campbell, and therefore not conveying any title from him, it follows that no question of disaffirmance is presented by the case, and as no question of disaffirmance is presented, it further follows as respects the plaintiff's right to maintain this action, no question arises in this case as to the obligation of Joseph M, Campbell to restore any money received by him from the defendant or any one for her; It further follows that as the defendant had no title to the lands to which this action relates, and that as from the facts in the case, she must be charged with notice of her want of title, her payment of taxes upon the same was entirely gratuitous and that she is not in law entitled to insist that she shall be reimbursed by the defendant.

The judgment is reversed, and the case remanded for judgment in accordance with the foregoing opinion.

THE ST. PAUL, STILLWATER & TAYLORS FALLS RAILROAD COMPANY, *Respondent*, *vs.* DANIEL M. ROBBINS, *Appellant*, } M'ch 24,'77.

A subscription for stock of a corporation in the following words and figures, to-wit: "We the undersigned do hereby subscribe to the preferred capital stock of the St. Paul, Stillwater & Taylor's Falls Railroad Company, and promise to pay for the number of shares set opposite our respective names. These subscriptions not to be binding until sixty-five thousand dollars of said stock is subscribed for.

"Date October, 1872.	Name of Subscriber, Daniel M. Robbins.	No. of shares 20.	Par Value, $2000."

Taken in the stock subscription book of the company authorized by it to be opened to receive such subscriptions, and the issuance of such preferred stock having been duly authorized by it, constitutes (the $65,000 having been subscribed for,) a valid contract on the part of the company to issue the stock, and on the part of the subscribers, to receive and pay for the stock.

The promises of the respective parties to such a contract are concurrent and dependent, and neither can require the other to perform, without performing or offering to perform on his part. A complaint in an action by the company upon such a subscription, which does not aver that the company has issued, or offered to issue, the stock to the defendant, is insufficient.

Appeal from an order of the District Court, county of Ramsey, overruling demurrer to plaintiff's amended complaint.

A. B. Stickney and L. R. Cornman, att'ys for respondent.

Lamprey & James, att'ys for appellant.

GILFILLAN, C. J.—Appeal from an order overruling a demurrer to the amended complaint. The action is to recover the amount of a subscription to the plaintiffs capital stock, which subscription is alleged to have been made in the regular stock subscription book of the plaintiff in the words and figures following: "We the undersigned do hereby subscribe to the capital stock of the St. Paul, Stillwater & Taylor's Falls Railroad Company, and promise to pay for the number of shares set opposite our respective names. These subscriptions not to be binding until sixty-five thousand dollars of said stock, is subscribed for.

"Date October, 1872.	Name of Subscriber—Daniel M. Robbins.	No. of shares 20.	Par value $2000"

The shares were for $100 each.

The amended complaint alleges that the plaintiff being fully authorized and empowered to issue the preferred capital stock mentioned and set forth in said agreement and for which the defendant subscribed as aforesaid, did, by an order and resolution duly made and adopted by its Board of Directors at a meeting thereof duly convened and held on the 21st of August, 1872, duly authorize and direct the issuance of the preferred capital stock aforesaid, and also did direct that the books of plaintiff should be opened to receive subscriptions for the same. And that pursuant to such authority and direction made as aforesaid, the defendant subscribed for said stock as aforesaid. The amount of $70,500 was subscribed. The amended complaint does not allege any other act done by the plaintiff. Either that any call or assessment upon the subscriptions was made, or any demand for payment, or that any stock certificates were issued; or even that plaintiff is ready and willing to issue them upon being paid the amount of the subscriptions. The subscription of defendant constituted a valid contract on the part of the company to issue the stock to the defendant, and on his part to pay for it. An implied promise to issue the stock, arising from the circumstances under which the subscription was taken, is the consideration for the defendant's promise. The question is: Was there a breach on the part of defendant?

It appears from the complaint, that at the time of this subscription, the company was fully organized, so that it does not stand upon precisely the same footing as a subscription made prior to, and for the purpose of effecting the organization. Such a subscription gives to the subscriber an interest in the corporation, and the right to take part in organizing it; and this interest and right are a sufficient consideration to support the promise. But the snbscription in this case does not appear to have been to the original stock on the contrary, it appears that after the company was fully organized, its Board of Directors authorized and directed the issuance of what, in the amended complaint, is called "preferred capital stock," and also directed that the company's books should be opened to receive subscriptions for the same. The mere subscription to this stock while it constitutes a valid contract on the part of the company to issue the stock to defendant upon his paying for it, and on his part to receive and pay for it, does not give him an interest in the company, nor vest in him the title to the stock. It can be sustained as a contract only on the implied promise of the company to issue the stock to him. No time is appointed, in the writing subscribed, for the payment of the money or the issuance of the stock, except that the subscription should not be valid until sixty-five thousand dollars of the stock, should be subscribed for. We regard the two promises, as concurrent and dependent, and that neither party could require the other to perform without performing or offering to perform the promise on his part. As plaintiff has neither issued the stock, nor offered to issue it, the action is prematurely brought.

The order appealed from is reversed.

JOHN P. KELLY, *Appellant*, *vs.* WM. H. DILL, *et al.*, *Respondent*. — March 22, 1877.

To constitute a homestead, the residence or dwelling of the party claiming it must be, or must have been, situated on the land claimed.

The owner cannot by making the land his homestead, defeat the lien of an attachment previously levied.

Appeal from an order of the District Court, county of Winona, sustaining a demurrer to plaintiffs complaint.

The complaint in this case case set forth among other things that on the 29th of October, 1874, one Gilmore was the owner of certain real estate which he had purchased before that date, for the purpose of a homestead. That on that day in a suit against said Gilmore, an attachment was levied upon said land, and afterwards and on the 2nd day of January, 1875, a judgment was entered and docketed against said Gilmore in said suit, and on the same day an execution was issued therein and afterwards levied upon the land so attached, which land was duly sold at execution sale on the 20th of March, following.

After the attachment and before judgment was entered, Gilmore moved on to the land and thereafter continued to occupy the same as a homestead. The premises before that time having been in possession of a tenant who refused to surrender possession. The plaintiff is a mortgagee subsequent to the attachment, and bring this action to remove the cloud created by the attachment and execution sale.

Wilson & Taylor, attorneys for appellant.

O. B. Gould, attorney for respondent.

GILFILLAN, C. J.—This Court decided in

Kresin vs. Man. 15 *Minn.* 116, that to constitute a homestead the residence or dwelling of the party claiming it, must be, or must have been, situated on the land claimed. In this case Gilmore's residence or dwelling had at the time of levying the attachment, never been situated on the land. He had merely intended to make the land his homestead, and had purchased it for that purpose. It was therefore not his homestead, when the attachment was levied.

The only question is, can the owner defeat the lien of an attachment previously levied, by moving upon the land and making it his homestead.

To sustain the affirmative the appellant relies on Sec. 12, Art. 1, of the Constitution; Ch. 68, of the General Statutes, and Ch. 58, Laws of 1868. Section 12, Art. 1, of the Constitution, provides that "a reasonable amount of property shall be exempt from seizure or sale for the payment of any debt or liability. The amount of such exemption shall be determined by law."

This does not determine the amount nor character of the property to be exempted nor how it shall be ascertained or designated. No property could be claimed as exempt under it until the Legislature should determine what property, and to what amount, the exemption should extend. When *determined by law*, the exemption comes under the Constitutional protection. Section 1, Ch. 68, General Statutes, provides, "That a homestead, consisting of any quantity of land not exceeding eighty acres, and the dwelling house thereon, and its appurtenances, to be selected by the owner thereof, and not included in any incorporated town, city or village; or instead thereof at the option of the owner, a quantity of land not exceeding in amount, one lot being within an incorporated town, city or village, and the dwelling house thereon, with its appurtenances, owned and occupied by any resident of this State, shall not be subject to attachment, levy or sale upon execution or any other process issuing out of any court within this state." The act of 1860 as amended by the act of 1868, merely enables the owner to remove from his homestead without losing the benefit of his exemption. By this section of the general statutes, the Legislature pursuant to the constitutional provision, points out one particular kind of property and the amount of it, that is to be exempt from seizure or sale.

This kind is a homestead, consisting of land not exceeding the prescribed amount with the dwelling house thereon, owned and occupied by the debtor. There is no exemption until it is such homestead and is so occupied. Until that time it stands as any other property, and may be seized for the debts of the owner.

The proposition that property may be seized, attached or levied upon to answer the debts of the owners, includes the further proposition that such seizure, attachment or levy, may be made effectual by a sale, or any subsequent acts necessary for that purpose. The liability to seizure implies the liability to sale. The right to sell is fixed by the seizure, such right is from the time the lien attaches by the seizure a vested right and property.

In this respect there is no difference between a lien secured by a levy of an attachment, and one secured by the docketing of a judgment, or the levy of an execution, except that it may be defeated by dissolution of the attachment or failure to obtain judgment.

There is no reason to suppose from the language, either of the constitution, or of the statute, that it was intended to give to the debtor the power, by his own acts, to deprive others of rights previously obtained in his property. They could be deprived of such rights only by due process of law.

Tuttle vs. Howe, 14 *Minn.* 145,

Judgment affirmed.

———oo———

Recent Decisions.

Indorsement, not a Secured Claim &c.—An indorsement does not render a claim secured within the meaning of the bankrupt law. The claim of a creditor who has issued an attachment within four months prior to the filing of the petition is to be estimated in computing the proportion who must join in an involuntary petition. In computing the amount that must join in an involuntary petition, claims that are under $250, as well as those over that amount must be counted. An indorsee who accepts payment from the indorser while the proceedings are pending cannot join in the petition although the claim was proved but not filed before the payment. If a secured creditor joins in an involuntary petition without referring to his security he thereby waives it, and his claim should be counted. On all claims bearing interest, interest may be allowed to the time of the filing of the petition. If a creditor holds security the excess of the debt over the security, should be counted in computing the number who must join in an involuntary petition.

(Dist. Ct. E. D. Wis.,) In re Briach, et al., 15 Nat. Bank. R. 15.

Latest Publications.

The Notarys' and Commissioners' Hand-Book.—For Notaries Public and Commissioners of Deeds in the state of New York, 8vo 56 pp., hf. bound. $1 00

Reports, Supreme Court of Ohio.—Vol. 26. By E. L. DeWitt, 8vo 739 pp., ... $2 50

Reports, Supreme Court Commission of Ohio.—Vol. 27. By E. L. DeWitt. 8vo 726 pp., sheep. - $2 50

Burrill on Assignments.—A treatise on the Law and Practice of Voluntary Assignments for the Benefit of Creditors. Adapted to the laws of various States; with an Appendix of Forms; by Alexander M. Burrill. 3d edition, revised, annotated and largely rewritten by James L. Bishop, of the New York Bar. 8vo., 800 pp., Sheep 6 50

Institutes of Common and Statute Law. By John B. Minor, L. L. D., Professor of Common and Statute Law in the University of Virginia. 2d Ed. 2 vols. 8vo., 672, 1098 pp., Sheep, 15 00

Story's Equity Jurispudence.—Twelth Ed. By Joseph Story, 2 vols. sheep, 15 00

The Laws and Practice of Bankruptcy.—By Orlando F. Bump. New edition to January 1877. 8 vo. 1040 pp., law sheep - - - - - 7 50

The Law of Mortgages of Real and Personal Property in the State of New York.—With an appendix of Forms. By Abner C. Thomas, 690 pp., law sheep, - - - - - - - 6 00

Practice Pleading and Evidence in the Courts of California, in Civil Suits and Proceedings.—By E. F. Buttemer Harston. 8 vo 713 pp., sheep, 6 50

Hents Forms and Use of Blanks—By J. C. Bates. Second Ed. 8 vo 499 pp., sheep, - - - - - 6 50

Life and Accident Insurance Reports.—Cases decided in the courts of America, England, Scotland and Canada, down to Setember 1876, with notes and references. Vol. V. By Melville M. Bigelow, of the Boston Bar. 8 vo. law sheep, - - - - - - 6 50

THE SYLLABI.

VOL. 1. SATURDAY, APRIL 7, 1877. No. 25.

PUBLISHED WEEKLY,

By JOHN B. WEST & CO.,

No. 1 Wabasha St., - ST. PAUL, MINN

Terms 3.00 per annum in Advance.

HOMER C. ELLER, Editor.

TABLE OF CONTENTS.

THE April Term of the Supreme Court of Minn., opened on Tuesday April 3d, with a calendar of about seventy cases.

IT was recently held by the Ontario, Canada, Court of Appeals, in the case of *McLeon* v. *Dun, et al.*, that the defendants, who conduct a Merchantile Agency, could not be held liable for losses sustained through *bona fide* reports made by them in such business.——Geo. S. Boutwell, Ex-Secretary of the Treasury, has been appointed and confirmed as commissioner to prepare and publish a new volume of the Revised Statutes of the United States.——The legislature of Kansas recently passed a resolution recommending the appointment of Judge Dillon as an Associate Justice of the Supreme Court of the United States whenever a vacancy occurs.——Ex-Secretary Cameron, answering the complaint for breach of promise, filed by Widow Oliver, denies the promise.——The graduating class for 1877, Law Dep't Michigan University numbers 121.

IN the case of *Roberts' Administrator* v. *Cocke*, recently decided by the Supreme Court of Appeals of Virginia, and reported 1 Va. L. J. 168, the validity of an act passed by the Legislature of Virginia in 1873 (Code 1873, chap. 173, § 14,) was involved and passed upon. The act in question empowers courts and juries, in all suits for the recovery of money founded on contracts, express or implied, or other liabilities which were entered into, or existed prior to April 10, 1865, to remit the interest accruing upon the debt therein between the date mentioned and April 17, 1861, and authorizes the court also to modify all decrees or judgments already entered by striking out the amount of such interest. The period named was that during which the war of the rebellion was pending. The court held the statute to be in conflict with the provision of the Federal Constitution forbidding the impairing of the obligation of a contract by State legislation. The court held that a law which lessens the duty of one under a contract, or abridges a right of the other, whether such law acts directly upon the contract or only indirectly through the remedy, impairs the obligation and is void. See *Bronson* v. *Kinzie*, 1 How. 311; *McCracken* v. *Hayward*, 2 id. 608; *VonHoffman* v. *City of Quincy*, 4 Wall. 535; *Walker* v. *Whitehead*, 16 id. 314; *The Homestead Cases*, 22 Gratt. 266. Also *Stephenson* v. *Osborne*, 41 Miss. 119, where it was held that if a law increased the exemption of property, if it went so far as to render the enforcement of an existing contract nugatory and impracticable, it was within the operation of the constitutional provision. How far the statute may be considered as affecting only the remedy, is considered in the case of *Morton* v. *Valentine*, 15 La. Ann. 153, where it is said that "statutes pertaining to the remedy are merely such as relate to the course and form of the proceedings, but do not affect the substance of a judgment when pronounced." See also *Watson* v. *N. Y. C. R. R. Co.*, 47 N. Y. 157.—*Al. Law Jr.*

Supreme Court, State of Minnesota.

D. Sinclair & Co., *Appellants*, *vs.* The Board of County Commissioners of Winona County, Nathan B. Ufford, Auditor, &c., and R. F. Norton, *Respondents*, } M'ch. 20,'77.

This action is brought to restrain the publication, and payment for the publication, of a delinquent tax list in the "Novelty Press," which has been designated by the Board of County Commissioners of Winona county, as the newspaper in which such publication is to be made, under ch. 2, Laws of 1874, as amended by chaps 6 and 8, Laws of 1875, but which the the plaintiffs allege is not a newspaper within the meaning of the statute, and therefore not such as the commissioners have any authority to designate for the purposes aforesaid

The plaintiffs are owners of real and personal property in said county, and taxpayers therein.

They allege, and it is to be taken as true in this case; that the taxes in question, will be imperilled, and the county lose, or be in danger of losing them, if the publication is made in the unauthorized manner proposed, to-wit: In said "Novelty Press." And further that payment for such publication will be a misapplication of county funds.

Held, that upon this state of facts, an injunction is the proper remedy, and that the plaintiffs are proper parties to maintain an action for the same.

Appeal from a judgment of the District Court, county of Winona, dismissing the cause, on the ground that the complaint did not state facts sufficient to constitute a cause of action, and for want of jurisdiction.

C. H. Berry, att'y for appellants.

Lloyd Barber and A. H. Snow, att'y for respondents.

Berry, J.—It is alleged in the complaint, that as directed by ch. 2, Laws 1874, amend- by ch. 6 and 8, Laws 1875, the defendant, the County Auditor of Winona county, prior to May 4th, 1875, prepared a list of lands, delinquent for taxes assessed before 1873, for the purpose of filing the same in the office of the Clerk of the District Court, on the 1st Monday of August 1875, as he intends to do: that professing to act under the statute above cited, the defendant the Board of County Commissioners of said county, have designated the "Novelty Press," which they style a newspaper, as the newspaper in which the Auditor shall publish the copy of such delinquent list, and the accompanying notice required to be furnished by the clerk for that purpose; that it is the intention of the Commissioners and Auditor, to publish the copy and notice in said Novelty Press, and that it also the intention of the Commissioners pay for such publication out of the County Treasury. The complaint then proceeds to allege that the said Novelty Press is not a "newspaper" within the meaning of the statutes, and therefore not such as the County Commissioners have any authority to *designate* for the purpose aforesaid, or to cause the publication before mentioned to be made in. As relief, the complaint prays that the Auditor may be enjoined from publishing said notice or list in said Novelty Press, and that the Board of County Commissioners may be enjoined from paying for any such publication, for, or on behalf of the county.

The case coming on for hearing in the court below, the defendants moved to dismiss, upon the grounds that "the complaint does not state a cause of action, and that the court has no jurisdiction of the matter." The motion having been granted the case comes here upon appeal from the judgment of dismissal.

The effect of the motion to dismiss being to admit that the Novelty Press is not a newspaper within the meaning of the statute, and that therefore the publication of the list therein is entirely unauthorized, the case presents two questions:

1st.—Is an injunction a proper remedy?

2d.—Are the plaintiffs the proper parties to an action for such remedy?

It is claimed, that as the collection of the delinquent taxes, (some fifteen thousand dollars,) depends upon the legality and regularity of the proceeding, for their collection, they will be imperilled, and the county lose, or be in danger of losing them, if the publication is made in the authorized manner proposed. It is further claimed that to pay for the unauthorized publication, out of the county funds, will be a misapplication of the same.

Upon the allegations of the complaint these claims would appear to be well founded. That there is some remedy in a case of this kind, is not questioned. Is there an adequate remedy at law? The defendants contend that there is by *certiorari*. But as respects the designation of the Novelty Press by the Commissioners, a *certiorari* would bring up only the record of the proceedings by the Board of County Commissioners, *Cooley on Taxation*, 535.

It is not to be presumed that such record would show anything whatever as to the question, whether the Novelty Press was, or was not, a newspaper within the meaning of the statutes, and upon the answer to this question would depend the authority to pay for the publication out of county funds. In addition, it is to be observed that the action of the Board in designating a newspaper, as well as in doing the other things objected to, is ministerial, not judicial. This is so, because the duty of the Board in the premises is clearly defined by statute, and they exercise no general discretion in performing it. *People ex rel. Livingston vs. Taylor*, 1 *Abb. Pr., Rep. N. S.*, 200, *People vs. Pease*, 27 *N. Y.* 45 *People ex rel. Dickinson vs. The Board, &c.*, 43 *Barb.*, 232. *State ex rel. Adamson*, 41 *Mo.* 21. *Certiorari* does not lie to review ministerial proceedings. *Pearsall vs. Com'rs, North Hamstead*, 17 *Wend.* 15 *People ex rel. Dickinson vs. The Board, &c., Supra. Crarys Practice*, 154.

There is then no remedy by *certiorari* in this case. No other suggestion of a remedy at law is made which requires particular consideration and we can conceive of no remedy which is completely adequate to the exigencies of the case, save the injunction of a court of equity.

This brings us to the other question viz: Are the plaintiffs the proper parties to an action for an injunction?

It is to be observed at the outset that it is not the object of this action to restrain or interfere with the collection of taxes. It is true that the designation of a proper newspaper, in which the delinquent list shall be published, and proper publication, are parts of the machinery provided for the collection of taxes. But in the case at bar the designation and publication are upon the allegations of the complaint to be taken to be wholly unauthorized and void, so that instead of contributing to enforce or aid the collection of taxes, they will operate to the contrary. As alleged in the complaint they will *imperil* the taxes so that the county will *lose* or be in danger *losing* the same.

With reference to this fact and the further consideration that the Board intend to pay for the unauthorized publication, out of the County Treasury-this is to be regarded as an action, the purpose of which, is to prevent the squandering and misappropriation of county funds.

This case is therefore distinguished from *Scribner vs. Allen*, 12 *Minn.*, 148, *and Libbey vs. Town of West St. Paul*, 14 *Minn.*, 249. It is a case in which the jurisdiction of equity may be sustained on the ground that the injury, which will result from the unlawful action of the Board and Auditor, to-wit: the squandering and misappropriation of county funds, will be irreparable.

The effect upon the taxpayer is to increase his burden of taxation, at least indirectly.

Upon the question whether an individual taxpayer, may in his own name, and on his own behalf maintain a suit in equity to restrain unlawful municipal action, which leads, directly or indirectly, to taxation, the adjudications disagree. But in accordance with the decided preponderance of authority, we are of opinion, that a taxpayer as specially damaged by the increase of the burden of taxation upon his property, has a special interest distinct from that of the general public, in the subject of a suit brought to restrain unlawful municipal action, from which such increase will result.

In a case therefore (like this at bar,) in which irreparable injury will result from unlawful municipal action, an individual taxpayer whose burden of taxation will be thereby increased, may in his own name, and in his own behalf, maintain a suit for an injunction by which such unlawful action may be restrained. *Cooley on Taxation*, 548. *Dillon Mun. Corp.*, § § 731—736.

It follows that the plaintiffs who allege themselves to be owners of real and personal property in the county of Winona, and taxpayers therein, are entitled to maintain this action.

The judgment appealed from is accordingly reversed.

ELIZA A. DUTCHER, ADMINISTRATRIX OF THE ESTATE OF GILBERT DUTCHER, DECEASED, *Respondent*,
vs.
GEORGE CULVER, *et al.*, IN THE MATTER OF THE APPEAL OF R. J. MARVIN, ADMINISTRATOR, "*de bonis non, &c.*," *Appellants*, } M'ch 21,'77

Appeal to the District Court from an order of the Probate Court, does not stay the operation of such order, while the appeal is pending.

Whether it would be competent for the District or Probate Court to direct a stay of proceedings upon an order of the latter appealed from QUAERE.

Appeal from an order of the District Court, county of Ramsey, denying the application of R. J. Marvin, administrator, "*de bonis non*" &c., to be substituted as plaintiff in the above entitled action.

W. P. Clough and T. R. Huddleston, att'ys for appellants.

Harvey Officer and H. J. Horn, att'ys for respondent.

BERRY, J.—The above entitled action was originally brought in the District Court of Ramsey County, by the plaintiff as administratrix of the estate of Gilbert Dutcher, deceased. Afier the commencement of of this action, and on June 14th, 1876, the Probate Court of Ramsey county, entered an order removing plaintiff from administration. On June 26th. following, the plaintiff appealed to the District Court, from the order of removal giving the statutory recognizance in the penal sum of two hundred and fifty dollars.

While the appeal was pending in the District Court, the Probate Court on August 15th, 1876, entered an order appointing R. J. Marvin, administrator, *de bonis non*. On August 17th, plaintiff appealed to the District Court from this order, giving a recognizance as before. On Aug. 18th, Marvin qualified, and letters of administration were issued to him. On August 23rd, while both appeals were pending and undetermined, Marvin applied to the District Court to be substituted in this action as plaintiff in his capacity as administrator, in the place of Eliza A. Dutcher. Upon a hearing, the District Court being of opinion that by the appeals all proceedings in respect to the removal of the plaintiff, and the appointment of Marvin, were superseded, and that therefore Marvin was not entitled to act as administrator, the application to substitute was denied. From the order of denial Marvin appeals to this court.

The question presented is, whether an appeal to a District Court, from an order, of the Probate court, stays the operation of such order while the appeal is pending?

The statute provides that "an appeal may be taken to the District Court from a judgment, or order in a Probate Court, * * * upon questions of fact or law, or both, by the service of a notice on an adverse party, stating the appeal from the order or judgment, or some specified part thereof, and by filing a copy of the said notice in the office of the Judge of Probate, together with a recognizance entered into by the party appealing, with one or more sureties to be approved by the Judge of Probate, conditioned that the party will prosecute his appeal with due diligence to a final determination, and pay all costs adjudged against him in the District Court."

Gen. St., Ch. 49. *section* 14 *and* 16. The determination of the question before us depends upon the scope and meaning of the word "appeal" as here employed. Our statute, no where in terms, defines it. Save so far as its meaning is controlled or influenced by statute there can be no doubt that it is properly defined, as a proceeding, by which a case is taken from an inferior to a superior tribunal, the determination of the former thereby vacated or suspended, and the case brought before the latter to be tried and determined *de novo*. *Powell on Appellate Proceedings, chap. IX, passim.* Is this, its ordinary definition, so controlled or influenced by statute in this state, that a determination of a Probate Court is not vacated or suspended by an appeal therefrom to a District Court? As showing that it is used in its ordinary sense, the plaintiff's counsel cites *sec.* 5, *ch.* 51, *Gen. St.*, which reads as follows: "When there is a delay in granting letters testamentary or of administration, occasioned by an appeal from the allowance or disallowance of a will, or from any other cause, the Judge of Probate may appoint an administrator to act in collecting, and taking charge of the estate of the deceased, until the question on the allowance of the will, or such other question as occasions the delay is terminated, and an executor or administrator is thereupon appointed; and no appeal shall be allowed from the appointment of such special administrator."

The plaintiff's counsel contend, that the language of this section is irreconcilable with the idea, that an appeal does not operate to vacate or suspend, the determination appealed from. "If, 'they ask,' the appeal did not suspend the action of the Probate Court, why should there be any delay in appointing an administrator? Where was the need of the special administrator, during the appeal, if the court go on and appoint the *general* administrator notwithstanding the appeal? Why should it be necessary to forbid an appeal from the appointment of a special administrator, if the appeal would not have prevented him from proceeding?" We think that these questions can be fairly answered without an admission of the counsels position.

It is not necessary to attribute the delay in appointing the administrator, to a suspension of the action of the Probate Court, by an appeal.

There is no reason, why a Judge of Probate may not delay an appointment, in exercising a sound discretion upon the circumstances of a particular case. For instance in the case of a will, contested upon the ground that it is forged or invalid. On some other accounts very grave practical reasons may exist why (notwithstanding his allowance of the will,) a Judge of Probate should hesitate to commission the person named as executor or an administrator with the will annexed, until the appeal from his allowance is determined. The case may involve large interests, it may be one, as to which the Judge entertains great doubt, notwithstanding his determination; a case involving a great deal of feeling on the part of opposing parties, and a case in which as respects the speedy and unembarassed settlement of an estate, the qnestion as to whether one person or another, should administer, is of considerable practical importance. Like considerations are applicable to the granting of letters of administration, upon intestate estate.

Instances of delay in granting letters, "from any other cause" than appeal from the allowance or disallowance of a will, may be found, in cases in which the delay is occasioned by the illness of the Judge or some other person, whose presence or testimony cannot well be dispensed with. The second question put by counsel is answered by calling attention to the fact that the delay mentioned in the statute is a delay in *granting* letters, that is to say in *appointing* a general administrator, or an executor. In that case the propriety of appointing a special administrator, is apparent. In respect to the third question, it is not at all necessary to suppose that the prohibition of an appeal from the appointment of a special administrator, rests upon the idea that if the appeal were not prohibited, he could not have proceeded to act. A special administrator, being appointed provisionally, and to serve a tempoporary purpose, there is manifest good sense and practical wisdom in providing that he shall not be harassed by appeals, upon the same principle upon which it is prescribed *sec.* 7, *ch.* 51, *Gen. St.*, that he shall not be liable to an action, by any creditor, or to be called upon in any other way, to pay the debts against the deceased. For these reasons, although *sec.* 5, *ch.* 51, *Gen'l St.* has some tendency to support the plaintiff's theory, as to the effect of an appeal, we are of opinion that it is by no means conclusive in her favor, nor irreconcilable with the idea, that an appeal dces not operate to vacate or suspend, the operation of the determination appealed from. As there appears to be no other provision, of the statute, specially regulating Probate proceedings, from which any argument is or can be drawn, as to the meaning of the word "appeal" as used in *sec.* 14, *ch.* 49, *Gen. Stat*, we now turn to other portions of the statutes, relating to appellate proceedings, for the purpose of ascertaining (if we may,) in what sense appeal is generally used in our legislation. Turning first to *Title XI*, *ch.* 65, *Gen. St.* we find that in all cases of appeals from the civil judgments of Justices of the Peace, the appellant is compelled to give bond, with one or more sureties, in a sum sufficient to secure the judgment appealed from, and costs, conditioned that he shall prosecute his appeal with effect, and abide the order of the court thereon. The bond having been approved, all further proceeding on the judgment before the justice, are suspended. So in proceedings under the Forcible Entry and Detainer act, *ch.* 84, *Gen. St.*, an appellant is required to give a bond, with two or more sureties, conditioned to pay all costs of the appeal, and abide the order of the Court therein, and pay all rent and other damages justly accruing to the complainant during the pending of the appeal, and upon the taking of the appeal all further proceeding in the case in the court appealed from, are stayed. Appeals in civil actions from the District Courts, to the Supreme Court, are regulated by *ch.* 86, *Gen. St.* Under the provisions of *section* 9, an appeal may be taken, by executing a bond for costs and charges, which may be awarded against the appellant. But by *section* 10, to make such appeal when taken from an order effectual to stay proceedings thereon, and save rights affected thereby, it is requisite that the appellant, or some one for him, execute a bond, with sureties, conditioned to pay the costs of the appeal, and the damages sustained by the respondent in consequence thereof, and abide, and satisfy the judgment or order which the appellate court may give. By *section* 11, a like bond is required, in order to stay the execution of a judgment from which an appeal is taken. Analogous provisions for security where a stay is desired are found in *sections* 12, 13 *and* 14. By *section* 19 it is enacted that in cases not specified in *sections* 11, 12, 13 *and* 14, the perfecting of an appeal by giving the bond mentioned in *section* 9, stays proceedings in the court below, upon the judgment appealed from. These are the principal provisions of our statutes upcn the subject of appeals, which have any important bearing upon the question under consideration. In civil actions, so far as the places of the appeal in chancery, and of the writ of error, are filled at all, they are under our system filled by a statutory appeal. So far as they are covered at all then, our appeal covers the case of the former appeal in chancery, which operated to supersede the determination appealed from, and the writ of error in proceedings at law, which had no such operation. This double character appears to be in some measure, expressly preserved by our statute. Appeals are provided for, both with, and without, a stay of the proceedings below; but unless otherwise expressly provided, the rule is, that in order to a stay of proceedings, indemnity against the consequence of the stay, must be secured by a bond, the sufficiency of which is to be passed upon by the court, or some of its officers.

From all these considerations, it appears to us by a reasonable construction to follow, that where the statute provides, that a party may *appeal* no inference can be drawn from the term *appeal* alone, as to its effect upon the proceedings below; and that in determining what that effect, is, we therefore may properly look at the general policy of the law of appeals, as furnishing a valuable analogy, (if not exactly *in pari materia,*) and to the practical consequences, of giving to the appeal, the effect to stay proceedings below or the contrary effect. Appiying this view to the case, we are of opinion that the appeal from the order of the Probate Court, does not vacate, or suspend the operation of the order. To permit it so to vacate, or suspend it, would be contrary to the general policy and spirit of our law, upon the subject of appellate proceedings. To such appeal the statute does not make it necessary for the appellant to indemnify against the injurious consequences of taking it. It requires only a recognizance, conditional for the diligent prosecution of the appeal, and the payment of costs. The considerations of security which in ordinary civil actions, render it proper and necessary, that an appellant should indemnify against the consequences of a stay of proceedings, upon that from which he appeals, apply with equal force to the orders and judgments of the Probate Court. As an illustration take the case supposed by the counsel for Marvin. An administrator of a large estate and his sureties become insolvent. Upon the application of creditors, or others interested in the estate, the administrator is directed by the Probate Court to execute a new bond, with responsible sureties. Failing to do so the court makes an order removing him from administration. From this order, which until reversed is presumably just and necessary, he appeals. If the appeal operates to vacate or suspend the order of removal, the unavoidable result may be the irretrievable waste and ruin of the estate. Illustrations of a similar tendency might be multiplied to an indefinite extent.

Both then upon the analogies of our law, and with reference to the consequences of disregarding them, we are of opinion, that an appeal from an order of the Probate Court, does not operate to vacate or suspend the operation of the order appealed from. Whether it would be competent for the Probate or District Court, in the exercise of a sound discretion, to direct a stay of proceedings upon an order appealed from, it is not now necessary for us to inquire.

Order reversed.

———:o:———

District Court, First Judicial Dist.

State of Minnesota, County of Dakota.

The City of Hastings,
against,
Jacob Tompson and Jos. Reed,

Crosby, J.—This a criminal action for the violation of the fire ordinance of the city of Hastings.

The warrant charges that the defendants on the 7th day of December, 1876, at the city of Hastings, in the county and state aforesaid, committed the offense of violating the Fire ordinance of said city, entitled "An ordinance relating to Fire limits," approved March 1st, 1871, and amended April 17th, 1871, as follows, viz: "Said defendants having prior to 7th day ot December, 1876, unlawfully caused to be erected within the fire limits of said City of Hastings to-wit: On Lot 5, Block 12, in said city of Hastings according to the recorded plat thereof, on file in the offiee of the Register of Deeds, in and for said county, a certain building, not fire proof, but the walls thereof composed of wood, and then, and since being the owners thereof, and being duly notified on the 7th day of December, A. D. 1876, and since the erection of said building, by John White, Esq., Fire Warden of said city, to refrain from further violation of said ordinance in such case made and provided, did on said 7th day of Dec., 1876, at the place aforesaid, omit to refrain from the violation of, and omit to conform to the provi. sions of said ordinance, contrary to the ordinance in such case made and provided, and against the peace and dignity of the State of Min-nesota."

The ordinance of the city relating to fire limits, prescribes the limits. what shall not be deemed a fire proof building, and provides that "It shall not be lawful for any person or persons to erect or place any building within the fire limits except such as are by the ordinance deemed fire proof.

It further provides, "If the fire Wardens are of the opinion that the ordinance has been or is being violated, that it shall be their duty to notify the person or persons violating it, to refrain therefrom, and to conform to its provisons, and if they do not, to make complaint before the police justice and cause such person or persons to be arrested &c." It further provides that upon the conviction of any person offending against the provisions of the ordinance, he shall be fined, and that "each and every day said person or persons fail to comply with the terms of said notice shall be deemed a separate offense."

The defendant moves to dismiss the action upon the grounds that the warrant does not state facts sufficient to constitute an offense against the ordinance, and that the provisions of the ordinance are not set forth with sufficient particularity.

The charter of the city of Hastings contains the following clause with reference to the ordinances passed by the City Council. "And such ordinances * * are hereby declared *to be* and have the force of *law.*"

The ordinances of the city, then. are private laws, and I am of opinion that it is sufficient to plead them, in a criminal action for their violation. in the same manner as private statutes are required to be pleaded in indictments.

Judge Dillon in his work on Municipal Corporations, says: "The liberal rules of pleading and practice, which characterize modern judicial proceedings extend to, and doubtless would be held to embrace, suits and prosecutions to enforce the by-laws or ordinances of Municipal Corporations."

In *State vs. Reckards*. 21 *Minn.*, 47, in speaking of the pleading of an ordinance Berry, J. uses the following language: "It may be added that there is certainly no reason why any greater strictness should be required in cases of this kind, than in cases of indictment for crimes of the highest grade." In pleading a private statute in an indictment, or right derived therefrom. it is sufficient to refer to the statute by its title, and the date of its passage, and the court thereupon shall take judicial notice thereof. *Gen'l Stat: Chapter* 108, *Sec.* 13.

In pleading an offense against a city ordinance, which is declared to be a law by the charter of the city, it is sufficient to refer to the ordinance by its title, and the day of its passage, and to state the acts constituting its violation. It is not necessary to set out the provisions of the ordinance. The warrant in this action states that the defendants, after being notified to refrain from the further violation of the ordinance, and to conform to its provisions, "did omit to refrain from the violation of, and omit to conform to the provisions of said ordinance." It states no act of the defendants constituting their violation of the ordinance, or their omission to conform to its provisions. The building had been erected prior to the notice being given by the fire warden. They are not proceeded against for its erection. They are not charged in the warrant of maintaining the building after its unlawful erection, without being made fire proof, nor are they charged with the omission to make it fire proof after its erection.

The part of the warrant that charges the offense, state a conclusion, without stating any facts upon which that conclusion is based.

The warrant is insufficient and the motion to dismiss the action must be granted. It is therefore ordered that this action be, and the same is hereby dismissed.

——oo——

Recent Decisions.

Usury.—Plaintiff presented commercial paper to defendant, a state bank, for discount, and thereupon indorsed and transferred the paper to the bank which thereupon credited the plaintiff on its books, and on plaintiff's pass book with the respective amounts for which the paper was drawn or made, less the discount which in each case exceeded the rate of seven per cent. per annum.

Held. a payment of usury under statute of 1870, (chap. 163,) which rendered the bank liable to the penalty therein provided.

Nash vs. Man.& Trad Bank, Ct. of Appeal, N. Y. Feb'y 13, 1877.

NEGOTIABLE PAPER.—Certificates of deposit are negotiable when expressed in negotiable words; and their transfer is governed by the same rules which control other promissory notes. To make a bill of exchange or promissory note (or certificate of deposit) negotiable, the promise must be to pay in money. And unless the instrument on its face affords every element to fix its value, the paper is only a special contract and not negotiable. Hence, a promise to pay in "bank stock" or in "current funds" will render the instrument un-negotiable.

Johnson vs. Henderson, Sup. Ct. of N. C. Jan'y Term, 1877.

SLANDER.—Where words are actionable PER SE throughout the country generally, the complaint is sufficient without alleging that the slanderous words were spoken in the presence and hearing of a third person (7 Ind. 347, 11 Ib. 156.) But where they have a provincial meaning, the complaint must show that the words have an actionable local meaning in the particular place where spoken.

Emmerson vs. Marvel, Sup. Ct. of Ind., Nov. Tr., 1876.

ATTORNEY—LIABILITY—An attorney, or collection agency employed to collect a claim and putting it into the hands of another, is liable in the absence of an express stipulation to the contrary on receipt of it, for misconduct of such other. The statute of limitations ordinarily begins to run from the time of the attorney's collection of the money; but where plaintiff has made repeated inquiries of the defendant and been informed that the claim is uncollectible, the statute only runs from the discovery of the fraud.

Morgan vs. Tenner, Sup. Ct. of Pa., Jan'y 1877.

USURY.—The plea of usury as a defense is a personal privilege that the debtor alone can avail himself of.

Pritchett vs. Rollins, Sup. Ct. of Kansas, Jan'y 1877.

LATEST PUBLICATIONS.

The Notarys' and Commissioners' Hand-Book.—For Notaries Public and Commissioners of Deeds in the State of New York. 8vo 56 pp., hf. bound. - - - - - $1 00

Reports, Supreme Court of Ohio.—Vol. 26. By E. L. DeWitt, 8vo 739 pp., - - - - - - - $2 50

Reports, Supreme Court Commission of Ohio.—Vol. 27. By E. L. DeWitt. 8vo 726 pp., sheep. - $2 50

Institutes of Common and Statute Law. By John B. Minor, L. L. D., Professor of Common and Statute Law in the Uuiversity of Virginia. 2d Ed. 2 vols. 8vo., 672, 1098 pp., Sheep, 15 00

THE SYLLABI.

VOL. 1. SATURDAY, APRIL 14, 1877. No. 26.

PUBLISHED WEEKLY,
By JOHN B. WEST & CO.,
No. 1 Wabasha St., - ST. PAUL, MINN.
Terms 3.00 per annum in Advance.

HOMER C. ELLER, Editor.

TABLE OF CONTENTS.

IT is now six months since the publishers of "THE SYLLABI" commenced the experiment of its publication. Experience has shown them that the name assumed, while entirely in accordance with their original plan, does not properly represent the character of the publication as it realy is, or as they desire to make it, and that its columns do not afford sufficient space for all the matter theydesire the paper should contain. This being so they have for sometime had in view an enlargement of its columns as well as a change of name, and the present is deemed the best time for carrying that intention into effect; This will be done by closing THE SYLLABI with this number, and commencing the publication of the new paper to be called "THE NORTHWESTERN REPORTER" where the old one ends. Subscribers will of course lose nothing as the REPORTER will be promptly forwarded in lieu of THE SYLLABI and the general character of that paper continued. It is the design that the REPORTER shall in addition to matters of general interest to members of the bar, contain full and accurate reports of all the decisions rendered by the Supreme Court of the State and the United States Circuit and District Courts, for this district, within a very short period after their rendition as well as the important decisions, especially on matters of practice, of the District Courts. It will also contain the decisions, either in the shape of abstracts or full reports, of the Supreme Court of Wisconsin. The best endeavors will be made not to only to make the paper of interest to the members of the bar of the state, but an absolute necessity.

THE Legislation of last winter providing that after April 1st, no mortgages should be foreclosed by advertisement, makes it necessary that attorneys should particularly familiarize themselves with the course of procedure in foreclosure by action. To enable them readily to do so, S. L. Pierce, Esq., has prepared a valuable little compendium of the law governing such proceeding, which is published in *brochure* by Messrs. Ramaley & Cunningham, of this city, at the low price of one dollar. It is not an elaborate treatise, but presents in a concise manner the various statutory provisions in regard to the subject, followed by a general statement of the law (supported by authorities,) in reference to parties, defenses, proceedings in court, sales, redemptions, remedy by strict foreclosure, &c., to which is also added a collection of precedents for use in the various proceedings; It is brief, and no doubt will prove useful.

IN the legislation providing for the establishment of a Municipal Court in the city of St. Paul it was enacted that the Justices of Peace, then existing in the city should hold their office only until the expiration of the two years for which they were elected, and not until their successors should be elected and qualified; the intent being to abolish the office of Justice of the Peace in said city. This act also provided that all appeals from the existing Justices should be taken to the Municipal instead of the District Court. Subsequent legislation provided for two Justices for said city to be elected at the coming election; but no special provision was made in regard to appeals from them. This being the case it would seem that such appeals should be taken to the District Court. The question was raised in the recent case of *De-Cou & Co.* v. *Gates*, before Simons, J., upon an appeal taken to the District Court. The appeal was dismissed however, upon the ground that the Justice from who it was taken was one of the existing Justices referred to in the Municipal Court act, the court strongly intimating however, that had he not been of that class, the motion to dismiss would have been denied.

Supreme Court, State of Minnesota.

John Karst, *Respondent*, *vs.* The St. Paul, Stillwater & Taylor's Falls R. R. Company, *Appellant*, } M'ch 20,'77.

This is an action for damages for injury occasioned to plaintiff's premises, by an unauthorized excavation by defendant of a public street in front thereof. Held, that if defendant claims that plaintiff is not entitled to damages for the full amount of the diminution of value suffered by his property 'in consequence of his excavation, AS IT IS, because that excavation can be re-filled at an expense less than the amount of SUCH diminution of value, it is for defendant to establish this claim; and in order to establish the same, it must necessarily be made to appear that the plaintiff has the right to re-fill.

Appeal from 'an order of the District Court, county of Washington, denying defendant's motion for a new trial.

James N. Castle, att'y for appellant.

A. B. Stickney and L. R. Cornman, att'ys for respondent.

Berry, J.—Plaintiff was owner of a piece of land in Stillwater, with the dwelling house thereon. Defendant having been authorized by the city to excavate a public street, running in front of plaintiff's premises, so as to bring it to the established grade, exceeded its authority and excavated the same so as to bring it to a grade 3 23-100 feet below the established grade. The plaintiff claimed that in cosequence of the unauthorized excavation, his premises were rendered inaccessible and greatly damaged. The only question submitted to the jury was as to the amount of damages, which the plaintiff was entitled to receive by reason of unauthorized excavation of 3 23-100 feet. With reference to the doctrine that the owner of land abutting upon a public street is presumably owner of the street to its centre, this court when this action was here before at April Term, 1875, laid down the rule that "for unlawful excavation and removal of his soil a party is entitled to recover not the cost of refilling, but the amount of diminution of the value of his property by the excavation and removal."

In accordance with this rule of damages, the case was given to the jury by the court below, with the further instruction that this was not a case for exemplary damages. The plaintiff had a verdict for $768, and there was testimony in the case reasonably tending to show a diminution in the value of his property to that amount by reason of the excavation. There was uncontradicted testimony in the case, going to show that the excavation (so far as it was made without authority) could have been refilled, and the plaintiff's premises placed in the same condition, as if the unauthorized excavation had not been made, for less than $90. The defendant therefore insists that the verdict was excessive and not justified by the evidence.

The defendant argues that while it is true that the rule of damages for the unlawful excavation and removal of ones soil is not the cost of re-filling, it is equally true that damages in any such case to an amount *exceeding* the cost of restoring the property to its former condition together with the loss, (which it insists was at most merely nominal in this case,) resulting from the excavation and removal during a sufficient length of time to afford reasonable opportunity to effect such restoration, must be something more than the *compensatory* damages to which alone the plaintiff was entitled upon the facts of the case, and the instructions of the court in reference to exemplary damages.

If the plaintiff had the *right* to fill the unauthorized excavation and restore the street to the condition in which it was, before such excavation was made we are by no means prepared at this time to say, that the defendant's position, and reasoning would not be correct. But if it is claimed that the plaintiff is not entitled to recover damages to the full amount of the diminution of value suffered by his property in consequence of the excavation *as it is*, because that excavation can be re-filled at an expense less than the amount of *such* diminution of value, it is for the defendant to establish this claim; and in order to establish it, it must necessarily be made to appear that the plaintiff had the right to re-fill. This fact does not appear in this case, for although the plaintiff owns the strip of land in which the excavation was made it is a public street. Now for the purposes of this case, it may be granted that if the excavation had created an obstruction in the street, or had in any way rendered it impassable, it would be competent, for the plaintiff to remove the obstruction, to put the street in a condition to be used by the public. See *Hunt* v. *Rich*, 38 Me. 195. But if notwithstanding the excavation, the street is unobstructed and in good condition for public travel, it could not be competent for the plaintiff, certainly not without leave from the city authorities, to fill the excavation, if the effect of such action on his part would be to obstruct the street and render the same impassable. For aught that appears in this case, such would have been the effect of the filling of the unauthorized excavation by the plaintiff. It does not then appear that the plaintiff had the right to re-fill, neither does it appear that the city authorities would allow him to do it.

Upon this state of facts we are of opinion that the verdict was justified by the evidence.

Order denying new trial affirmed.

THE STATE OF MINNESOTA, *ex rel.* HENRY WARFIELD, Petitioner and Relator, *Appellant*, *vs.* JOHN C. BECHT, Sheriff of Ramsey County, *Respondent*, } M'ch 20, '77.

Upon proceedings supplementary to execution under the provisions of title XXIV, ch. 66, Gen'l Statutes, the relator against whom the money judgment upon which the execution issued had been recovered, was ordered by the District Court, in which the proceedings were pending, to deliver up certain property to a receiver. Although duly notified of the order the relator after due demand wholly failed and neglected to comply with it. Thereupon he was arrested upon a warrant duly issued and brought into court and upon a hearing it was adjudged that he was guilty of contempt in disobeying the order and it was thereupon further ordered and adjudged that a fine of $25, be imposed upon him, and that he be committed to the common jail of Ramsey county for the term of one month or until he be discharged by due process of law. In pursuance of this order and adjudication, a warrant of commitment was issued and the relator comitted thereunder. The commitment was made under the provisions of section 307, ch. 66, Gen'l St., which enacts, that if any person disobey an order of a Judge in proceedings supplementary to an execution he may be punished as for a contempt, and of ch. 87, Gen'l St., which makes disobedience of any lawful judgment, order, or process of a court, a contempt of its authority, and provides for a regular course of proceedings in accordance with which a person charged with contempt may be brought before the court, the charge investigated, and the person charged, punished, if found guilty.

HELD that the commitment and the statutes, under which it was had, are not obnoxious to section 12, of Art. I, of the constitution of this state, which declares that "no person shall be imprisoned for debt in this state, &c," nor to section 7, of the same article which declares that no person shall be deprived of liberty without "due process of law," nor be held to answer for a criminal offense unless upon the action of a Grand Jury, nor to section 6, of the same article which provides that in all criminal prosecutions, the accused shall enjoy the right to a jury trial, nor to section 4, of the same article which provides that the "right of trial by jury shall remain inviolate, and shall extend to all cases at law &c.

HELD, further, that the general adjudication of a District Court having jurisdiction of the case before it, and of the parties, in the absence of a proper showing to the contrary, is to be taken as involving and including an adjudication upon whatever minor facts are necessary to authorize it.

Habeas Corpus to the defendant John C. Becht, sheriff of Ramsey county,

Davis, O'Brien & Wilson, att'ys for relator.

James N. Granger, for respondent.

BERRY, J.—It is shown by the return to the writ of *habeas corpus* that the relator is held in custody by virtue of a warrant of commitment issued by a Judge of the District Court to the respondent, who is sheriff of Ramsey county. It further appears that upon certain proceedings supplementary to execution under title XXIV, ch. 66, Gen'l St., the relator (against whom the money judgment upon which the execution issued, had been recovered) had been ordered by the District Court, in which such proceedings were pending, to deliver up certain property to a receiver, and although duly notified of such order, the relator had, after due demand wholly failed and neglected to comply with it. That thereupon he had been arrested upon a warrant duly issued and had been brought into court, and upon a hearing, it had been adjudged that he was guilty of contempt in disobeying the order aforesaid. It was thereupon further ordered and adjudged that a fine of $25 be imposed upon him and that he be commited to the common jail of Ramsey county, for the term of one month, or until he be discharged by due process of law. The warrant of commitment under which the relator is held as before mentioned, was issued, and the relator committed thereunder, in pursuance of this order and adjudication. The proceedings which resulted in the commitment were had under the provisions of section 307, ch. 66, Gen'l St., and ch. 87, Gen'l St. Section 307 enacts that if any person disobey an order of a Judge in proceedings supplementary to an execution he may be punished as for a contempt. Sec. 1, ch. 87, makes disobedience of any lawful judgment, order or process of a court, a contempt of its authority; and subsequent sections of the same chapter provide for a regular course of proceedings in accordance with which, a person charged with contempt, may be brought before the court, the charge investigated and determined; and the person charged, punished, if found guilty. It is contended on behalf of the relator that the commitment in this case, and the statutes under which it was had, are obnoxious to certain provisions of our Bill of Rights.

The provisions referred to are found in sections 4. 6. 7 and 12 of the first article of our state constitution. Section 12 which is principally relied on, declares that "No person shall be imprisoned for debt in this state, &c." In the case at bar the imprisonment is for contempt in refusing to obey an order of the court. It is true that the order relates to the debt evidenced by the judgment against the relator, but this in no way alters the fact that the imprisonment is for the contempt, not for the debt. And the contempt does not consist in the relator's neglect or refusal to pay the debt, but in his disobedience of the order directing him to hand over certain property to the receiver. The fact that the property in question is to be handed over for the purpose of being applied to the payment of the judgment is in no way important.

The commitment is nevertheless in no proper sense, imprisonment for debt. Sec. 7 of the Bill of Rights declares that no person shall be deprived of his liberty without "due process of law." By due process of law is to be understood "Law in its regular course of administration through Courts of Justice." 2 Kents Com. 13. *Baker* v. *Kelly*, 11 Minn., 480. *Rowan* v. *State*, 30 Wis. 129. *Sedgwick on Const. Law*, 2d Ed., 474 and note. *Cooley on Const'l Law*. 351.

The commitment in this case was by due process of law within this definition. It was made in the regular course of administration, through a court of justice, of a general law. a law which in the often quoted language of Mr. Webster in the Dartmouth College case; "hears before it condemns, which proceeds upon inquiry and renders judgment only after trial."

Sec. 6 of the Bill of Rights provides that in all criminal prosecutions the accused shall enjoy the right to a jury trial, and section 7 that no person shall be held to answer for a criminal offense unless upon the action of a grand jury &c.

These constitutional provisions have no application to a case of this kind. There was no *criminal prosecution* here, nor was the relator held to answer for a *criminal offense* in the meaning of the constitution. If the relator is punishable criminally for his misconduct at all, it is not under the provisions of law under which the commitment was made, but under section 15 of the chapter upon contempts. (Ch. 87, Gen'l St.) Sec. 4 of the Bill of Rights which provides that "the right of trial by jury shall remain inviolate and shall extend to all cases at law &c," is also applicable to this case. That has reference to cases between parties and not to a proceeding by a court to punish for contempt. Trial by jury in such proceedings would not only be a thing without precedent, but intrinsically inappropriate. It would seem to be a necessity that a court should have in its own hands the power to punish contempts of its authority.

This disposes of the relator's position as respects the matter of unconstitutionality.

It was objected to the warrant of commitment, and the judgment upon which it was founded, that it did not affirmativly and explicitly appear from them that the property which the relator was ordered to deliver to the receiver was not exempt from execution.

The proceedings in the case having been had in a court of General Jurisdiction, the jurisdiction of which over the person of the relator and of the case before it appear, the general presumption in favor of the correctness of the judgments of such courts applies in this instance. In the absence of a proper showing to the contrary the general adjudication is to be taken as involving and including an adjudication upon what minor facts are necessary to authorize it.

It is not required that the adjudication of all such minor facts shall be recited. *People* v. *Nevins*, 1 Hill 154. *Seaman* v. *Duryea* 11 N. Y. 330. 1 *Crary's Pr.* 206. The same remarks are applicable to one or two other points made by the relator to which it is unnecessary more particularly to advert.

The writ of *habeas corpus* is discharged and the relator remanded.

ELIZA A. DUTCHER, ADM'X OF THE ESTATE OF GILBERT DUTCHER, DECEASED, *Appellant*, *vs.* GEORGE CULVER, *et al.*, *Respondents*, } M'ch 22, '77.

A landlords common law right of distress for rent in arrear as modified by 2 William and Mary ch. 5, allowing the property distrained upon to be sold, exists in this state. A landlord to whom prior to taking a distress the property subsequently distrained upon, has, with other property been assigned in trust for creditors does not by accepting such trust waive his right of distress.

Tenants in common should distrain severally, but if they join in distraining, their joinder is an irregularity covered by 11 Geo. I ch. 19, by which it is provided "that for any unlawful act done (in the taking of a distress) the whole shall not be unlawful or the parties trespassers AB INITIO but the party grieved shall only have an action for the the real damage sustained, and not even that if tender of amends is made before action brought." For the purpose of a distress, rent is sufficiently fixed and certain which is capable of being reduced to a certainty by computation.

An order that a receiver shall be appointed to take charge of certain goods, does not place such goods in CUSTODIA LEGIS.

Appeal from an order of the District Court, county of Ramsey, overruling plaintiff's demurrer to defendants' answer.

Horn & Billson and Harvey Officer, att'ys for appellant.

R. B. Galusha and Davis, O'Brien & Wilson, att'ys for respondents.

BERRY, J.—The main question presented by this case is whether the common law right of a landlord to distrain for rent in arrear, exists in this state. Section 12 of organic act of the Territory of Minnesota, (passed March 3d, 1849.) provides that "the laws in force in the Territory of Wisconsin. at the date of the admission of the State of Wisconsin, (May 29th, 1848,) shall continue to be valid and operative therein," (*i. e.* in the Territory of Minnesota,) "so far as the same be not incompatible with the provisions of this act, subject nevertheless to be altered, modified or repealed by the Governor and the Legislative assembly." The constitution of this state (adopted in 1857,) in section 2, of the schedule declares that "All laws now in force in the Territory of Minnesota, not repugnant to this constitution shall remain in force until they expire, by their own limitation or be altered or repealed by the legislature."

If at the date of the admission of the State of Wisconsin the common law right of distress for rent was in force in the Territory of Wisconsin, it is in force here if it is not incompatible with the provisions of our organic act, nor repugnant to the constitution of this state, and if it has not been altered or repealed by our Territorial or State Legislature. That it was in force in the Territory of Wisconsin at the date mentioned, is authoritatively settled so far as the State of Wisconsin is concerned by the case of *Coburn* v. *Harvey*, 18 Wis., 156. The decision in that case is of course not binding or conclusive in this state; but the conclusion arrived at, as well as the resoning by which it is supported, are entirely satisfactory to us. We therefore accept the decision, not only as an authoritative statement of the law of Wisconsin because pronounced by the highest tribunal of that state, but as in itself, and independent of the matter of authority, establishing the fact that at the date of the admission of the State of Wisconsin, the common law right of a landlord to distrain for rent in arrear, was in existence in the Territory of Wisconsin. See also *State* v. *Pulle*. 12 Minn., 165. *Blackman* v. *Wheaton*. 13 Minn., 326. It is not claimed (and we see no ground upon which it could be claimed,) that the right of distress in question is incompatible with our organic act.

It is claimed however that by section 1, ch. 137 of the Revised Statutes of the Territory of Minnesota, the Wisconsin statute of 1839 referred to in the opinion of the court in *Coburn* v. *Harvey* was repealed. If this be admitted, it does not follow that the right of distress was thereby taken away. This law of 1839 as the Supreme Court of Wisconsin say, "recognized the existence of this right," and "assumed it as already existing." The repeal of this law, (a statute regulating the action of replevin where the property had been taken for a distress.) did not take away the right of distress. since the statute did not create the right, but merely testified to its existence by recognizing it and assuming it to exist. That it was not in fact the intention of the Revised Statutes, either in section 1, ch. 137, or elsewhere to take the right away is fairly inferrable, from sec. 39, ch. 70, Revised St.. which prescribes the place of trial of an action "for the recovery of personal property distrained for any cause." If, as is claimed by the plaintiffs' connsel, no other right of distress existed, or was understood to exist here, except the right to distrain beasts *damage feasant* the general words "distrained for any cause" would hardly have been used. In their natural and ordinary meaning, they recognize more than one species of. distress and so far as we are aware, the only kinds of distress to which they would have reference are the landlords right of distress and the right to distrain beasts, *damage feasant*, both of these may fairly be presumed to have been contemplated by the statute.

Upon this question of repeal sec'ts 31, 32,

33, ch. 49, Rev. St., are also of some value.

Sect. 31 enacts that every person in possession of land out of which rent is due shall be liable for the proportionate amount of rent due, from the land in his possession although it be only a part of what was originally demised. Sect. 32 enacts, that such rent may be recovered in a civil action. Sect. 33, provides that "Nothing contained in the preceding sections shall deprive landlords of any legal remedy for the recovery of their rent, whether secured to them by their leases or provided by law:"

This section though it is not conclusive, has some tendency to show that it was the intention of the Revised Statutes to preserve whatever legal remedies for the recovery of rent were possessed by landlords and among others the remedy by distress which as we have before endeavored to show was "provided by law."

What we have thus said, with reference to the Revised Statutes, is equally applicable to the general statutes in which section 39, ch. 70, Rev. Statutes, appears as section 38, ch. 66 and sections 31, 32, 33, ch. 49, Rev. St., as sections 18, 19, 20, ch. 75.

Our references to these provisions of the Revised and General Statutes, and our comments upon them, are also a sufficient answer to the position taken by the plaintiffs' counsel that "the theory of our code is inconsistent with, and repugnant to," the remedy of distress.

The plaintiffs' counsel argue that the remedy by distress is repugnant to the constitution of this state.

They claim that it violates section 8, art. I, which declares that every person is entitled to a certain remedy in the laws for all injuries or wrongs which he may receive to his property, because to entitle a person whose property is distrained for rent to replevy he must give security, which he may not be able to give. As suggested by the defendant's counsel this claim begs the whole question by assuming that the right of distress, which, if it existed at all is a legal right, is a wrong or injury to property. If exercised in a proper case it is no more a wrong than the right of a chattel mortgagee to take possession of property mortgaged upon the mortgagors default. If the distress is not made in a proper case, if it is wrongful, the owner of the property distrained, has his remedy by action, in the nature of trespass, trover, or on the case, as circumstances may require. *Taylors' Landlord and Tenaant* ch. XV. He need not resort to replevin, to obtain a remedy. If he does, it is upon the same terms, upon which he can resort to it in any other case, namely by giving security. So far as replevin is a remedy for a wrong or injury to property the same objections will apply to the requirements of security in any other case, as for instance a case of replevin for beasts distrained *damage feasant* as in that of a distress for rent. Several other answers to plaintiffs' claims under this head are suggested by defendant's counsel but we need not consider them.

The othor grounds upon which plaintiffs' counsel claim that the right of distress is incompatible with our constitution are not very much insisted upon, and it seems to us that no argument is needed to show them to be untenable. Upon this branch of the case then, our conclusion is, that as at the date of the admission of the State of Wisconsin, into the Union, the landlords' common law right of distress for rent in arrear was in force in the Territory of Wisconsin, and as such right of distress is not incompatible with the provisions of our organic act nor repugnant to the constitution of this state, and has not been altered or repealed by our Territorial or State Legislature, it is in force in this state.

With reference to the statute 2 *William & Mary* ch. 5, which gave the right to sell a distress (in that respect changing the common law,) we agree with the Supreme Court of Wisconsin in *Coburn* v. *Harvey, supra.* It is there held upon grounds to which we see no objection, that the common law of a state which had no political existence before the Revolution, is the common law as modified and amended by English Statutes passed prior to our revolution.

This definition of course has no reference to sueh portions of the common law as are inapplicable to a given state, or to any changes or repeals which may have been affected by legislation in such state. As the statute of William & Mary was passed long before the revolution it was held to be part of the common law of distress in Wisconsin and for the same reason it is to be held to be part of the common law of Minnesota.

This disposes of the main question in the case and brings us to consider the plaintiffs objections to the manner in which the distress was made,

The lease under which the rent distrained for accrued was made by George Culver, John Farrington and William J. Cullen, owners of the leased property.

Culver and Farrington are defendants in this action. The other defendants except Mullens are the heirs at law of Cullen who has deceased, and are owners of his interest in the demised premises. All of the defendants, except Mullens, joined in the distress, and by their warrant authorized and empowered Mullins as their bailiff *for them and each of them*, to distrain &c.

By the terms of the lease the rent was payable one-half to Cullen and the other half in equal portions to Culver and Farrington. The warrant specified the whole amount of rent due and the proportion of the same due to each of the distrainers. It appeared also that Culver was holding the property distrained as assignee under an assignment, the validity of which is called in question by the plaintiff. It is claimed by the plaintiff that Culver by accepting the trust conferred upon him by the assignment waived his right of distress the two being incompatible. In our opinion the supposed incompatability does not exist. It is true that there is to some extent a conflict of interest between Culver as assignee, and Culver as landlord. Nevertheless there is no reason why he cannot exercise his right of distress and with all due regard to the rights of creditors interested in the assignment. His double position is certainly somewhat delicate but we see no reason why he may not hold it and exercise all its rights, being responsible for an misconduct or neglect of duty. It is further claimed that the distrainers being tenants in common could not make a joint distress. The rule certainly is that such tenants should distrain severally. *Taylor Landlord and Tenant* § 569. We are however of opinion that the joinder may properly be regarded as an *irregularity* in the manner of procedure. As such it is covered by the statute 11 Geo. II, ch. 19, by which as Blackstone says (2 Com. 15,) it is provided "That for any unlawful act done (in the taking of a distress) the whole shall not be unlawful or the parties trespassers *ab initio*; but the party grieved shall only have an actlon for the real damage sustained and not even that, if tender of amends is made before any action is brought."

See also *Taylors' Landlord and Tenant*, § § 613. 614—736, 737.

It is further objected by plaintiffs that there was no right of distress in this instance because the rent was not fixed or certain.

By the terms of the lease the rent is to be not a precisely named sum of money, but ten per cent of the gross receipts, and earnings of the leased property, to be estimated upon a full account made up at the end of each month. Upon the maxim, *Id certum est., &c.*, this provision of the lease sufficiently fixes and ascertains the rent; for it is capable of being reduced to a certainty by computation. *Smith* v. *Fyler*, 2 Hill 648. *Taylors Landlord and Tenant*, § § 561, 562. Besides the allegations in the answer that the gross receipts and earnings were properly stated and ascertained, and that the amount specified in the warrant is due, are admitted by the demurrer. The plaintiffs last point is that the property distrained upon, was *in custodia legis*, because, before the distraint, the District Court had made an order that a receiver be appointed to take charge of this, with other property. What would have been the case if a receiver had been *appointed* we need not inquire, a mere order that one *shall be* appointed certainly does not have the effect claimed.

The order overruling the demurrer to defendants' answer is affirmed.

It is to be observed in connection with the foregoing decision, that the right of distress for rent, is expressly abolished by act of Legislature "approved" March 3d, 1877.—[Ed.]

——o||o——

RECENT DECISIONS.

CONTEMPT—A mere refusal on the part of a witness, in proceedings supplemental to execution, to answer a question, unless the court shall decide that it is proper he should answer it, is not contempt.

Faley vs. Rathbone, N. Y. Sup. Ct., 1st Dept. Jan'y 26, '77.

NEGLIGENCE.—An employer is bound to give persons of tender years whom he employs, due caution, explanation and instruction when he puts him to work in a dangerous and hazardous place, and the mere fact that such employee, could have seen that the place was dangerous and hazardous by exercising his faculty of sight, is not sufficient of itself to hold him accountable for contributory negligence; but that is a question for the jury to determine from all the facts.

Hartman vs. Gust, Sup. Ct. Ind. Nov. Tr. 1876.

DESERTION.—Desertion as a ground for divorce consists in the cessation of co-habitation coupled with a determination not to renew it. The intent being the decisive characteristic, and a mere temporary separation caused by the husband's inability to provide for his family by reason of which the wife is compelled to support herself or rely temporarily on the aid of friends, and the parties are thereby forced apart, though desiring to resume co-habitation when circumstances will permit, does not constitute desertion.

Bennett vs. Bennett, Sup. Ct. of Com. September, 1876.

Latest Publications.

The Notarys' and Commissioners' Hand-Book.—For Notaries Public and Commissioners of Deeds in the State of New York. 8vo 56 pp., hf. bound. - - - - - $1 00

Reports, Supreme Court of Ohio.—Vol. 26. By E. L. DeWitt, 8vo 739 pp., - - - - - - - $2 50

Reports, Supreme Court Commission of Ohio.—Vol. 27. By E. L. DeWitt. 8vo 726 pp., sheep. - $2 50

Institutes of Common and Statute Law. By John B. Minor, L. L. D., Professor of Common and Statute Law in the Uuiversity of Virginia. 2d Ed. 2 vols. 8vo., 672, 1098 pp., Sheep, 15 00

Story's Equity Jurispudence.—Twelth Ed. By Joseph Story, 2 vols. sheep, 15 00

The Laws and Practice of Bankruptcy.—By Orlando F. Bump. New edition to January 1877. 8 vo. 1040 pp., law sheep - - - - - 7 50

The Law of Mortgages of Real and Personal Property in the State of New York.—With an appendix of Forms. By Abner C. Thomas, 690 pp., law sheep, - - - - - - - 6 00

Practice Pleading and Evidence in the Courts of California, in Civil Suits and Proceedings.—By E. F. Buttemer Harston. 8 vo 713 pp., sheep, 6 50

Hents Forms and Use of Blanks—By J. C. Bates. Second Ed. 8 vo 499 pp., sheep, - - - - - 6 50

Life and Accident Insurance Reports.—Cases decided in the courts of America, England, Scotland and Canada, down to Setember 1876, with notes and references. Vol. V. By Melville M. Bigelow, of the Boston Bar. 8 vo. law sheep, - - - - - - 6 50

Civil Malpractice.—A treatise on Surgical Jurisprudence, with chapters on Skill in Diagnosis and Treatment, Prognosis in Fractures, and on Negligence. By Milo A. McClelland, M. D. 8 vo. Cloth $3.50, sheep, - 4 50

Shaw's Index to Minn. Session Laws, 1849–1875. Full Sheep, - - - 4 00